towards the end of my days
THEOLOGICAL & SPIRITUAL REFLECTIONS

BISHOP GEOFFREY ROBINSON

CO-ORDINATING EDITOR
SEAMUS O'GRADY BSC (HONS), MED, MA (THEOLOGICAL STUDIES)

Published in Australia by
Garratt Publishing
32 Glenvale Crescent
Mulgrave, VIC 3170
www.garrattpublishing.com.au

Copyright in this work remains the property of the contributing authors.

Copyright © Geoffrey Robinson 2022

All rights reserved. Except as provided by the Australian copyright law, no part of this book may be reproduced in any way without permission in writing from the publisher.

Typesetting by Mike Kuszla
Co-ordinating Editor, Seamus O'Grady
Edited by Greg Hill
Cover image iStock

Scripture quotations are drawn from the New Revised Standard Version of the Bible, copyright © 1989 by the Division of Christian Education of the National Council of the Churches of Christ in the USA.
Used by permission.
All rights reserved.

ISBN 9781922484192 (paperback)
ISBN 9781922484338 (ebook)

Cataloguing in Publication information for this title is available from the National Library of Australia.
www.nla.gov.au

The authors and publisher gratefully acknowledge the permission granted to reproduce the copyright material in this book. Every effort has been made to trace copyright holders and to obtain their permission for the use of copyright material.

The publisher apologises for any errors or omissions in the above list and would be grateful if notified of any corrections that should be incorporated in future reprints or editions of this book.

With the heart of an engaging poet and the courage of a great bishop, *Toward the End of My Days* by Bishop Geoffrey Robinson (this) is an inspiring witness – when the chips were down – to a deep and abiding faith that can inspire and lend hope to us all.

– Thomas Groome
Professor of Theology & Religious Education at Boston College

In this posthumous collection of essays on theology and spirituality, the late Bishop Geoffrey Robinson is revealed not only as a multi-talented scholar but also as a sympathetic pastor with a genuine concern for Catholics struggling with contemporary issues that challenge their faith. In a spirit of encouragement he shares with clarity, insight and ecumenical sensitivity his thoughts about a wide range of subjects, many of which have bedevilled the Church in the decades following Vatican II. By way of conclusion he presents a list of pertinent questions that will assist the reader to further 'process' the wide-ranging content of this very readable book and provide parish discussion groups with topics for their meetings.

– Dr Brian Grenier is Christian Brother
Author, former college principal, book reviewer & in-service presenter

Bishop Geoff's last book is a wonderful gift to all the faithful. It is serious reading for all of us who yearn as church to find a new heart. While I might pause over some sections and question others, *Towards the End of my Days* offers me reflections that I will return to for insight, inspiration, encouragement and courage. We've been enlivened by his refreshing and relentless candour in earlier writing. These last reflections breathe life and common sense into faith, theology and church. There is a determined insistence beneath the moderate language. There is stern advice within the measured tones. If one can have fierce modesty, then the book, *Towards the End of my Days* has it in abundance.

– Anne Benjamin
Honorary Professor ACU, co-author *Leadership in a Synodal Church*,
co-editor *Not Forgotten, Australian Catholic Educators 1820-2020*,
former Executive Director Catholic Education Parramatta

Acknowledgements

I would like to recognise the following people for their contribution to the publication of this book:

Colleen O'Shanassy, Jack O'Grady, Geoffrey Joy, Natalie McNamara, Francis Sullivan, Kelvin Canavan fms, Julian McDonald cfc, Brian Grenier cfc, Rodger Austin, Brian Croke, Tony Ishak, Fr Joseph Camilleri, Dante Aspite, Richard Allcock, Karen Tayleur and Greg Hill.

– **Seamus O'Grady, 5 October 2021**

Vale Bishop Geoffrey Robinson

Bishop Geoffrey Robinson died on 29 December 2020 aged 83. In this subdued time of Christmas and New Year celebrations, the sombre news of his passing seems quite apposite. He was a talented, sensitive man who cherished his priestly vocation.

Despite his academic achievements and scholarly output, he was humble, often understated and reluctant to occupy the limelight. As an internationally regarded canonist and trailblazer for the just treatment of victims of clerical sexual abuse, he regularly found himself at the frontier of church/state relations a place populated by power brokers and vested interests. His quiet, polite demeanour and formidable intellect usually paved the way for a collegial approach to problem-solving. It was this strength of character along with a capacity to negotiate the multitude of stakeholders that comprise the Catholic Church, that led the bishops and religious leaders to turn to Robinson to lead a new approach in the handling of child sexual abuse.

Public revelations of the scandal were more commonplace by the 1980s and the bishops and religious leaders seemed clueless, even incompetent, in handling the moral and legal aspects of the abuse cases. Criminal accusations were dealt with behind closed doors, victims were disbelieved almost by default, allegations were fiercely defended and Church authorities instinctively took the side of perpetrators lest the image of the Church be put at risk. When settlements were made, they were usually paltry and the details were kept secret. In short, the Church authorities were driven by risk management, not moral leadership. The interests of the institution, both reputational and financial, were paramount and the aversion to involving the police was universal.

Robinson's appointment in the early 1990s to chair a committee to review and recommend on the handling of sex abuse matters, was the turning point for the Church. It was a shrewd appointment. For too long the rubrics of canon law had been ignored by the bishops. So too their ethical obligations to victims. Robinson was exquisitely qualified to not only rectify but to reform the situation. He spearheaded a far-reaching and effective change to the protocols for complaints handling and the violations of professional standards. This was all the more impressive for the fact that very entrenched and powerful interest groups wanted nothing to do with a more transparent and accountable approach. He was adamant that the needs of the victim, not the interests of the institution, should shape a pastoral as opposed to a legalistic protocol. He actively engaged with victims, something which up to that point was alien to Church policymaking.

He consulted widely with Church bodies, civil authorities and community stakeholders. This broke new ground for a Church more comfortable with its separatist stance. In 1997 the new national policy, Towards Healing, was adopted across the country by dioceses and religious orders. It was lauded for its capacity to craft restorative measures for victims according to their circumstances. It introduced the requirement that victims receive a formal apology and a reparation package. It encouraged the reporting of suspected perpetrators to the police. In addition, it called for compliance with professional standards in Church workplaces and for safety guidelines and measures wherever children were involved with Church agencies. The protocol was expanded to include any vulnerable person involved in Church activities. Robinson had effectively overseen a paradigm shift that placed the victim as the priority and insisted on a contemporary best practice approach to child safety. The fact that only the Archdiocese of Melbourne did not take up the protocol was a testament to his leadership and credibility. Towards Healing was a world first in the handling of sex abuse cases and was replicated in other Western countries.

Robinson was a serious man, introspective and considered. He gave the impression that the labours of life wore a heavy toll on his spirit. Yet his experience with the sex abuse scandal changed him. In an odd way, it liberated him. He was a prophet. A reluctant and shy one at that, but never timid to speak his mind. He was every bit a bishop of the Second Vatican Council. The notion that somehow the Church should act as a bulwark against modernity was alien to his thinking and vocation. After his days in episcopal office, he used his expansive intellect and writing skills to explore avenues through which the Church could more effectively engage with modern Australian life. He was particularly perturbed by the growing disinterest of Catholics with their Church and the schism between its teachings on sexuality and the lived experience of ordinary Catholics.

He was convinced that the Church needed a Third Vatican Council. The abuse scandal had laid bare the corruption and complicity within the Church's culture. It had revealed the fragility of the institution's integrity. Moreover, the abuse revelations only further fuelled the growing discontent amongst Catholics as the Church struggled to keep pace with advances in the social and biological sciences. Unless an open and honest dialogue was undertaken, Robinson feared the relevancy of the Church in the West was at severe risk.

His writings ranged from the abuse of power and authority in the Church to matters of sexuality, gender and marriage. He strove to find a pathway for Catholics who felt at odds with their Church through no fault of their own. His instinct was pastoral and his imagination was creative and refreshing. He was not always popular with the reactionary elements within the Church, nor with bishops who bristled at his suggestions for reform. His persistence was a testament to his deep commitment to the Gospel and to the naming of inconvenient truths. That he gave time to study, reflect, write, pray and publish speaks of a desire to make a difference and to effect change for those who were the subject of discriminatory and naïve attitudes. It seemed that his time with victims of sexual abuse awakened in him a sensitivity to the plight of anyone struggling to be heard and respected. He was one that did listen. And he has been respected widely for his openness and honesty.

In his final years he was once again embroiled in the sex abuse scandal. This time as an expert witness for the Royal Commission. His expertise and experience were invaluable as the Commission came to terms with the history of the Church's response to the crisis. His testimony was frank and compelling. As it happens it now stands as his last commentary on what has been the most destructive influence on the credibility of the Church he so faithfully served.

His was a voice that echoed the spirit of the Gospel – a siren for truth and justice. His legacy will sit comfortably with the style of missionary Church Pope Francis proclaims. He was a loyal and obedient servant, a courageous and dedicated disciple.

– Francis Sullivan, 5 January 2021
**as CEO of the Truth, Justice and Healing Council
guided the Australian Catholic Church's engagement with the
Royal Commission into Institutional Responses to Child Sexual Abuse**

CONTENTS

FOREWORD FROM DR MARY MCALEESE ii
PREFACE FROM SEAMUS O'GRADY vii
CHAPTER 1 – THE LOVE FROM WHICH WE CAME 1
CHAPTER 2 – WHERE WAS GOD AT AUSCHWITZ? 18
CHAPTER 3 – THE SINGER AND HIS SONG 29
CHAPTER 4 – THE STORY OF A JOURNEY 40
CHAPTER 5 – GOD, ONE AND THREE 64
CHAPTER 6 – FULLY DIVINE AND FULLY HUMAN 75
CHAPTER 7 – THE BEATITUDES 83
CHAPTER 8 – FAITH WORKING THROUGH LOVE 87
CHAPTER 9 – THE DIVINE IN HUMAN HANDS 88
CHAPTER 10 – THE BATTLE FOR THE IMAGINATION 108
CHAPTER 11 – UNITY IN THE EUCHARIST 114
CHAPTER 12 – LIFE TO THE FULL 119
CHAPTER 13 – THAT THEY MAY ALL BE ONE 130
CHAPTER 14 – THE RIGHT TO BE WRONG 143
CHAPTER 15 – STRUCTURAL CHANGE IN THE CHURCH 165
CHAPTER 16 – THE SEEKING OF GOODNESS 184
CHAPTER 17 – THE SMELL OF THE SHEEP 251
CHAPTER 18 – OBLIGATORY SANCTITY 263
CHAPTER 19 – SEXUAL MORALITY 270
CHAPTER 20 – A UNION OF EQUALS 292
CHAPTER 21 – EXCLUDING THE FEMININE 323
CHAPTER 22 – ABORTION IS NOT A SIMPLE QUESTION 331
CHAPTER 23 – EUTHANASIA IS NOT A SIMPLE QUESTION 341
CHAPTER 24 – THE PLACE OF MARY IN THE CHRISTIAN WORLD 346
CHAPTER 25 – THE SECOND VATICAN COUNCIL 355
CHAPTER 26 – RELATIONSHIP WITH THE RELIGION OF ISLAM 385
APPENDIX – THE STRUCTURE OF A COUNCIL 393
QUESTIONS & REFLECTIONS 403

FOREWORD

In these simply written yet profound end-of-life theological and spiritual reflections, the late Bishop Geoffrey Robinson leaves the members of his troubled Church with a powerfully argued, accessible and thoughtful agenda for a credible debate on Catholic Church reform. Regrettably, not a single one of his ideas is likely to get past the 2023 Synod on Synodality censors which is a pity at one level for it is a ready-made hugely insightful schema for discussion of everything that is relevant to the contemporary Church. On the other hand, the fact that such a schema would frighten the Curial horses is not terminal for the Curia has no copyright on the words *synod* or *synodality*. The fact is that the People of God have already long since embarked on the Church's most significant synodal journey, and it is their own – informal betimes, spontaneous betimes, increasingly organised and progressively growing in confidence. Bishop Geoffrey can take real credit for the fact of the synodal journey of the People of God.

The kaleidoscope of issues that are being debated on that journey are all dealt with here in Bishop Geoffrey's legacy document, with no dissembling, no hesitation. The tone is forthright but humbly conversational, as if the bishop and his readers are walking together on the synodal Camino – chatting over coffee, lunch and dinner – for this is a gentle if urgent invitation to dialogue, not a stern command to magisterial obedience. The sheer breadth of Bishop Geoffrey's scholarship and experience is matched by a towering intellect and analytical skills that can synthesise the profoundest of subjects into unpretentious conclusions, for which he claims no infallibility and exercises no canonical superiority. His patience with human frailty is commendable. His impatience with magisterial absurdity is refreshing and entirely understandable

I first met Bishop Geoffrey Robinson at the Rosemary Goldie lecture in Sydney in 2014. Though he did not then know it, he had been a source of real spiritual strength to me since the publication seven years earlier of his powerful critique of the role of clericalism and patriarchy in the contemporary Church, *Confronting Power and Sex in the Catholic Church*. Coming from the Irish Church, where bishops normatively stay safely within the episcopal bunker where internal critique of the Church is definitely not normative, the courage and conviction of this rare episcopal honesty intrigued and reassured me. I was grateful to him for making himself so vulnerable, for his was a lonely road. There is little tolerance of clerical dissent or internal criticism at governance level in the Church. More than that, he as an eminent canon lawyer knew he was likely inviting censure.

The sheer lucidity and forthrightness of his views have always been underpinned by his formidable biblical scholarship and training as a canon lawyer and that is evident again in these reflections. By the time I met him I was a qualified canon lawyer and in the throes of doctoral studies on an unloved, neglected area of canon law, the rights and obligations of child members of the Catholic Church.

It is hard to credit given the scandalous revelations about the systemic culture of physical and sexual abuse of children throughout the Catholic Church that – with the exception of Bishop Geoffrey and the then former Archbishop of Dublin, Diarmuid Martin – no bishop has ever bothered to ask me what my research and subsequent book on the subject has to say. Bishop Geoffrey asked with real interest, with probing questions and with delight. Sometimes meeting one's heroes can be a journey into disappointment, but not on that memorable day in Sydney.

Here was a humble priest with a brain full of wonder and empathy and feeling and curiosity that had not been pulped by an intellectually impoverished clerical formation and canonical obligations of obedience to the magisterium that conduced to silence and even cowardice. He was courageously prepared to train its guns on that no-go area, the dysfunctional, patriarchal inner workings and structures of the Catholic Church, not in order to further damage the Church but to limit the damage, to heal it and to liberate the divine grace long dammed up by ignorance, and a smug narrow-mindedness that must surely still make Jesus weep.

Here was a man who made Christ credible among an episcopacy almost hell-bent on consigning Him to an irrelevance that has become the tragic zeitgeist of the Western world. Bishop Geoffrey's thoroughgoing view of God made him first a child of God, a brother to all God's human family regardless of their view of God – and yet with humility he freely admits here that his views and vision are inchoate, imperfect, dimmed by just being human and incapable of anything as expansive as defining faith, or God, or timeless doctrines, or forever teachings.

Geoffrey's illness and death seemed at first to silence that rare and welcome voice, but with this new book that fine voice and fine mind speaks from the grave: strong and confident, perceptive and prophetic, timely and providential. Maybe, just maybe, Bishop Geoffrey's wise and urgent words – distilled from a lifetime of searching and seeing the sacred with an open heart and curious mind – may yet redeem a disoriented Church futilely chasing the long-gone ghost of early Church synods past, and lately embarked on a rash, chaotic so-called synodal journey into even greater bewilderment. Are we listening? We should be, for there is more insight, more guidance, more clarity, in Geoffrey's brief last words than in all the acres of impenetrable verbiage to which an increasingly uninspired, bored and disinterested People of God have been subjected from the Curial central command and control. Christ is visible, audible, credible in Bishop Geoffrey's beautiful, poetic *vade mecum* for the journey in faith ahead of us.

Yet he warns us over and over that we should be careful about assuming we have got our heads around the infinite, that God is our possession. The gravitational pull of man-made certainties is always threatening but that way lies a loss of growth, a paralysis that keeps grace out. Here in this one, marvellous excerpt, is Geoffrey's recipe for the kind of dynamic spiritual growth that excites and energises a life, gives it momentum, and lights it up from the inside – not with a self-righteous faith but with a burning love of God and neighbour.

> "To promote growth, we must move from a god religious authorities believe they can possess, package and dispense to others to a god of infinite surprise
>
> We grow in moral and spiritual stature when we constantly ask and live the question:
> 'What is the most loving thing I can do here and now?'
> It is persons, not religions, that God loves. No individuals may claim to be pleasing to God solely on the basis of the particular religion they belong to.
> War, terrorism, violence, oppression, hatred or despising others, in the name of religious beliefs, is an abomination to God and a cursing of God's name.
>
> There are no writings in any religion that were written or dictated or inspired by God in such a manner as to stand above the limitations of human agency and the inadequacy of human words. God has revealed important truths to us, but God has not revealed to us detailed answers concerning all we must believe nor detailed orders concerning all we must do, neither through sacred writings, nor through any human being speaking in God's name. It is God's gift that, both individually and together, we must constantly search for truth and goodness in uncertainty, for this is how we grow."

The Robinson roadmap to spiritual maturity is only part of the story, for to understand why one should even bother to embark on such a journey – especially now when a cloud of pervasive and righteous cynicism hangs over the major global institutional infrastructure that promotes faith in Christ – it is necessary to go back right to the beginning of us and confront as he does the difficult questions about the point or pointlessness of Creation. If there is a God then why did they bother to create us? Why subject us to suffering, disease, death? Bishop Geoffrey does not shy away from the awkward questions, the unresolved paradoxes of hatred, greed, genocide, famine, violence, sexism, racism, sectarianism, homophobia and all the rest that make people wonder, where is God in all this? Is there a God at all? Is God responsible for the chaos?

And it is in reflecting on those questions that the ill, dying Bishop Geoffrey, with one foot in this world and one in the next, gives us his best guess, his best assurance with an opening chapter that is stunningly stark in its image of the relationship between God and creation and humanity:

> "Science tells me that the world began with a big bang; faith tells me that this big bang was an explosion of God's love ... The final goal of God's plan is that the human race should continue to grow in its physical, intellectual, emotional social, artistic, moral and spiritual life until it in some manner returns the world to the love from which it came. If this process takes more billions of years, then so be it, for God can wait."

Bishop Geoffrey allows that God watches and waits but also equips us with the tools to solve the problems that torment us and our journey back to his love starts with taking responsibility into our own hands for bringing solutions to *"a world of randomness and uncertainty"* for *"God is delighted when the human race makes progress without needing any intervention from God"*.

In other words, confronted by suffering, confronted by grave moral dilemmas such as abortion, euthanasia, militarism or migration, our response should not be to ask why God has allowed this but much more importantly to ask: "How shall I respond?" It is in answering that we find our feet as followers of Christ, cast adrift from the doctrinaire and the legalistic, the ritualistic and the perfunctory, from a narcissistic denominationalism that conduces to sectarianism. Now we are in an unmoored boat, out in the deep where faith and fear allow us to feel what the late Catholic feminist theologian Ann Louise Gilligan has called "the surprise of life": God with us, God beside us, God all around us, embracing us kindly, not in a vice-like grip, but in the gentle surprise of love offered and ever-available.

No matter how alone we feel, no matter how unloved by others, Bishop Geoffrey is sure of one thing: that we can come to know that this God loves each of us unconditionally; carries us when we do not even notice; is our faithful, enduring companion, wherever we are in our life's journey and whether we believe in God or not. It is that one belief that allows us to cope with wakening each day to "uncertainty and groping through the dark". It is that conviction which should open our hearts to our common brotherhood and sisterhood, taking us beyond diffidence or fear of "the other" to a heartfelt gratitude for the abundance of God-ordained diversity from which comes the creativity of poetry, music, science, art, technology, imagination

– the very tools of problem-solving, or as Geoffrey would have it – returning ourselves to God's love and the very purpose of our creation.

As the Catholic Church embarks upon a universal synodal journey that the hierarchy is already fearful of, already attempting to control, already micro-managing into disappointing dullness, we would all benefit from a reading of Bishop Geoffrey's fearless last words, his inspired gift of a bold vade mecum, a navigational instrument designed to stop us from, as he says, arguing over doctrines, which are ill-fitting ideologies that can only be made to fit the facts "by violence" and keep us "going round and round in circles and lead nowhere". A synod with that agenda would be worth the effort, worthy even of Christ.

– Dr Mary McAleese, President of Ireland 1997–2014
Professor of Children, Law & Religion
University of Glasgow

PREFACE

There were people both within and outside the Catholic Church who admired and respected Bishop Geoffrey Robinson. Many of these were his friends, and I was privileged to be one of them. I first encountered Geoff (as he preferred to be called) when I was interviewed for a significant role in the Catholic Education Office Sydney. He rang to tell me that I was unsuccessful – a task he had to do for many aspirants and which he told me recently was the most difficult part of his role as Chairman of the Sydney Archdiocesan Catholic Schools Board. Fortunately, some years later he rang me with good news that I had been appointed to another position, as the Director of Religious Education and Curriculum for the system of primary and secondary Catholic schools in the Archdiocese of Sydney. Following that appointment in 1996 through many meetings, gatherings, professional learning and social events – but particularly in the Masses he celebrated for teachers – I came to realise that this was no ordinary man (or priest, for that matter).

People said that Geoff was a man of few words, reticent in social settings, but ever courteous and grateful. He particularly enjoyed a simple restaurant meal with my co-directors in Catholic Education. My wife, Colleen, and I were privileged to host him, along with close friends, in our home on a number of occasions. Here we enjoyed some delightful conversations. I came to count him as a friend, and felt honoured to be counted as one of his. Thus I also felt immensely affected by his passing.

A fortnight before he died, Bishop Geoffrey Robinson sent Colleen and I a beautiful letter:

> I look back in gratitude to all the people who have made my life a time of warmth and wonder. You were a significant part of that process and I thank you for all you have been for me. I have been truly fortunate in my family and my friends, and I thank God daily for this.
>
> I hope to go to God soon and I will do my best to carry your memory and your presence with me.
>
> May your life be filled with inspiration. May you continue to grow in your physical, intellectual, emotional, social, artistic, moral, and spiritual being, for this is what we are all called to do.
>
> (Handwritten) *Thank you for the wonderful enjoyment you always brought to life and for the profound seriousness that lay beneath it.*
>
> God bless
>
> Geoff

Much has been written about Geoff's courage in standing up for victims of abuse. He was chosen by the Australian Bishops in the 90s to be the spokesperson for the sexual abuse of minors by clergy and religious. In 1993 Geoff was chair of the Bishops' Committee (now designated) Professional Standards. By 1996 it was largely Geoff's leadership that gave us Towards Healing – pastoral protocols on how to receive complaints of abuse by Church personnel.

Next step was Integrity in Ministry, a code of conduct setting standards of behaviour for those involved in the ministerial life of the Catholic Church. Geoff outlined further steps in the process of the Church facing up to this issue, an issue which has done irreparable damage not only to victims and survivors, but also to secondary victims: their families, the parish, the school communities, and other people as well as to the credibility of the Church at large.

Geoff began by personally listening to victims; hearing their stories, witnessing the pain and damage done to them. Through that, he began to understand something of the complexity of factors which lead to abuse. He also realised the need to get into the mentality of those responsible for abusing. Geoff urged his brother bishops to listen to victims and to deal decisively with complaints of abuse. He saw the need to go further, trying to understand the weaknesses and failures in the Church's systems that enable such a betrayal of trust and power. All this was years before the Royal Commission of 2014. At the time, some thought Geoff was going too far. Subsequent events have shown that we all owe Geoff a tremendous debt of gratitude. Didn't Jesus say, "The truth will set you free"?

I believe history will show Geoff Robinson to be one of the very significant leaders of the Catholic Church in our country – a real champion. His focus was on the pastoral side, reaching out both to victims and perpetrators with compassion and mercy. He was a light in the darkness, ahead of his time – prophetic. As with all prophets, he suffered for his honest appraisal of our situation.

In many ways, the wheel has come full circle. For while the Vatican was initially alarmed at Geoff's proactive stance and he was even taken to task by the Nuncio at the time, we now have Pope Francis setting up the Vatican's Commission for the Protection of Minors. The Pope's spokesman, Fr Hans Zollner, endorses the very insights Geoff had taken, back at the end of the 20th and beginning of the 21st-century. A prophet is not welcome in his own country.

As Bishop Power wrote, Geoff "was a faithful son of the Church wanting the Church to be its best self while knowing it was *ecclesia semper reformanda* – the Church continually in need of reform. Bishop Geoff's courageous book, *Confronting Power and Sex in the Catholic Church - Reclaiming the Spirit of Jesus* came from his deep-held desires for the Church to be true to its mission of bringing

PREFACE

Christ to the world and from his own great honesty and courage in naming the challenges facing the Church today.

In August 2020, a group of Geoff's former colleagues in Catholic education – Br Kelvin Canavan (Executive Director of the Catholic Education Office, Sydney 1987-2008), Miss Natalie McNamara (Director of Human Resources, CEO Sydney, 1992-2010), Mr Seamus O'Grady (Director of Religious Education and Curriculum, CEO Sydney, 1997-2012), and Dr Brian Croke (Executive Director of the NSW Catholic Education Commission, 1992-2016) – gathered in the presbytery of Enfield parish to discuss Bishop Geoff's contribution to the Church and society, in particular his stellar contribution to Catholic education. We had been chosen for this privilege by Geoff at the request of parishioner Tony Ishak of World Media International PL. Tony, was keen to create a video recording for use at the forthcoming parish celebrations to mark Geoff's 60 years as a priest.

Time and again in this gathering, tributes flowed about his integrity, scholarship, loyalty to a Church that largely rejected him, compassion, honesty, and love for his fellow human beings worldwide.

Particularly noted was his ability as chairman to ensure all sides of an issue were considered, and his concern for all parties – whether the decision went for or against them. His gentle wisdom was a huge gift in a period when Catholic education faced major issues particularly with respect to governmental policy around funding of Catholic schools.

On 13 December 2020, the Parish of St Joseph's Church Enfield honoured their special bishop and friend with a celebratory Mass and luncheon. Geoff, battling the final stages of cancer and wheelchair-bound, delivered his moving homily, "The Song that Jesus Sang". An overflowing congregation responded to Geoff with extraordinary affection and affirmation. Twice during the celebration they gave him an extended standing ovation. It was to be Geoff's final public Mass.

A memorial plaque was unveiled in the church which reads:

> St Joseph's parishioners are grateful and blessed to have had Bishop Geoff in residence since October 1988. We are very honoured to call him our Bishop. He is our Preacher, Counsellor, Teacher, Listener, Friend and Faith journey companion. This community is blessed to have been brought closer to Christ by his ministry. He has shown us that he is a true disciple of our loving God and Saviour, Jesus Christ.

A few days later, on 15 December, I visited Geoff in his modest flat. We shared some great conversation over a cup of tea. A nurse visited and dressed his bandaged legs. He asked me to stay and chat while this was happening (if I wasn't too squeamish). I realised then that he had not long to live. We joked about the Netflix show, *The Crown*. I knew that the lunch we had planned when he was feeling better was not going to happen.

Towards the end of those two hours, I queried whether he had done any more writing. To my surprise he said yes, he had written a book. I asked what he intended to do with this book. He asked me to critique it. I said, "surely you have others better qualified than I to do such a task". He smiled and said, "They would regard it as heresy!" He walked me slowly into his study where he showed me some 26 separate chapters of a book entitled, *Towards the End of My Days*. He had disaggregated the chapters because he was worried about losing the whole book should he press the wrong key! We managed to send all the chapters to my email address and I promised to get back to him. Over the following days I read through this beautiful work.

The following Friday I rang him (he was actually visiting his birthplace in Richmond, NSW) and asked what he wanted done with the questions at the end of some of the chapters. He said, "check that they make sense" and asked whether he should alter the text in the light of my responses. I said there wasn't much that I could disagree with! The following Tuesday I dropped by to deliver a copy of a book that a colleague and I had recently published. He gratefully received it and we agreed that his book must be published. He was clearly not looking well and left it in my hands… two days later he was admitted to Concord Hospital where he died on 29 December, 2020. Geoff had 'returned to the Father'.

Geoff had given me permission to show the book to a few colleagues and friends, all of whom were enthusiastically emphatic that the book should be published. Accordingly, I contacted the executors of Geoff's will and was given the go ahead by their solicitors in early April 2021. Garratt Publishing had handled Geoff's previous books and it was logical to approach them for this one. Karen Tayleur and her team were keen to proceed as soon as possible and I am indebted to them for taking up this challenge. Worth noting that Geoff directed the royalties from his previous books to a struggling diocese in PNG. This will continue with royalties from *Towards the End of My Days*.

This wonderful book – bequeathed to us as his final testament – is the culmination of his scholarship, reflection and experience. Loyal to his Church to the end, Geoff was determined to leave no stone unturned in exploring every aspect of a Catholicity faithful to its founder Jesus Christ. In so doing he has made 'being a Catholic' a grown up, contemporary, intelligent, and nuanced response to a humanity in need of love and justice.

To act justly, love tenderly and walk humbly with your God (Micah 6,8) is the precise epitaph for Geoffrey Robinson RIP.

– **Co-ordinating Editor, Seamus O'Grady**
BSc(Hons), MEd, MA (Theological Studies)
Balmain East, NSW
19 April 2021

CHAPTER 1
THE LOVE FROM WHICH WE CAME

A GOD OF INFINITE PATIENCE

SCIENCE TELLS me that the world began
with a big bang;
faith tells me
that this big bang
was an explosion of God's love.

If I do not have proof
that this religious claim is true,
no-one else has proof
that it is not true.

Unimaginable amounts of energy
swirled in the cosmos
until, over immense periods of time,
more solid objects began to form,
and stars, planets and galaxies came into being.

This world had its great beauty and majesty,
but there was no thinking and feeling being there
who could respond to the love that had created it.

TOWARDS THE END OF MY DAYS

More billions of years passed,
until on the planet we inhabit
the first primitive life forms came into being,
then crawled out of the sea
and began to colonise the land.

An extraordinary and beautiful variety
of plants and animals developed.
But there was still no being
who could respond to God's love.

More aeons of time went by,
until a few animals
began to stand upright on two feet
and develop their conscious lives.

Human beings slowly evolved
who could think and feel
and, at long, long last,
respond to God's love.

From the explosion of love in the big bang
to the first conscious response to this love
had taken the scarcely imaginable time of
13,800,000,000 years.

Over all that immense time God
had waited,
and waited,
and waited,
not interfering, but,
with infinite patience,
allowing things to develop at their own pace.

God waited all this time
for the level of growth we have achieved
and, if necessary,
will wait further billions of years
for the full working out of the divine plan.

THE LOVE FROM WHICH WE CAME

The final goal of God's plan
is that the human race
should continue to grow
in its physical, intellectual, emotional
social, artistic,
moral and spiritual life
until it in some manner returns the world
to the love from which it came.

If this process takes more billions of years,
then so be it,
for God can wait.

HUMAN MISUNDERSTANDINGS OF GOD

THERE IS only one God,
but an endless variety
of human misunderstandings of God.

Unable to grasp the infinite God,
we constantly create
a lesser god in our minds
and worship that god.

Human ideas of God will always
be infinitely inadequate,
but some can at least assist
rather than hinder our growth.

To promote growth, we must move:

from a god about whom we use many words
to a stunned awareness of an "otherness"
beyond the reach of either words or images;

from a god who is contained within a book
or the teachings of a human authority
to a god who cannot be contained by any created thing;

from a god religious authorities believe they can
possess, package and dispense to others
to a god of infinite surprise;

from limited human ideas,
e.g. an elderly white male ruler,
to a god who is above all limitations,
e.g. a god who is neither male nor female;

from a god who should always agree with our ideas
to a god who constantly challenges our ignorance;

from a god greatly concerned with glory and majesty
to a god not concerned with self at all,
but caring passionately about what we do
to each other, to ourselves, and to the community;

THE LOVE FROM WHICH WE CAME

from a god whose glory is to be found
in our obedience
to a god whose glory is to be found
in our growth;

from an angry god,
not to a god of soft love,
but **to** a god who, out of love, wants our growth
and, like a good parent or teacher,
is not afraid to challenge us to grow;

from a religion in which
beliefs, moral rules, worship
and membership of a religious community
hold first place
to a religion in which
a love relationship with God and neighbour
holds first place.

from a commercial relationship with a god
whose rewards can be earned
by doing right things
to a love relationship with a god who is pure gift;

from a relationship in which we are firmly in charge
and determine exactly what part
of God shall be allowed in our lives
to a love relationship of total giving;

from a god who demands
that we bridge the gap between us
to a god who always takes the first step
and comes to us.

WORKING WITH GOD

ALL PEOPLE are called by God
to the development
of their full potential
– physical, intellectual, psychological
social, artistic, moral and spiritual –
so that we may use to the full
all the gifts God has given us
to help both ourselves
and the whole world to grow.

We grow in moral and spiritual stature
when we constantly
ask and live the question,
"What is the most loving thing
I can do here and now?"

The communal path we walk
on this spiritual journey,
Jewish or Christian or Muslim or other,
is important,
for no one can find all answers alone.
But so is our continuing individual search,
for each must take personal responsibility.

A way to God is authentic
if it eventually leads us
to find God in the very depths of our own being.

It is persons, not religions, that God loves.
No individuals may claim
to be pleasing to God
solely on the basis
of the particular religion they belong to.

A good Jew is more pleasing to God
than a bad Christian;
a good Christian than a bad Muslim;
a good Muslim than a bad atheist;
a good atheist than a bad Jew.

THE LOVE FROM WHICH WE CAME

Holding true beliefs is less important
than sincerely seeking true beliefs.
Seeking only beliefs that suit oneself
can never be sincere.

Any coercion to join a particular religion,
or imposing of penalties for changing religion,
is hateful to God.

Suicide can never be martyrdom.

War, terrorism, violence,
oppression, hatred or despising others,
in the name of religious beliefs,
is an abomination to God
and a cursing of God's name.

THE SEARCH FOR RIGHT BELIEFS

WRITINGS CONSIDERED sacred arose because
their authors believed they had experienced
the presence of the divine in their lives
and sought to reflect it to others.

While strongly influenced
by this perceived contact with the divine,
they remained human authors
writing in human words.

There are no writings in any religion
that were written or dictated or inspired by God
in such a manner as to stand above
the limitations of human agency
and the inadequacy of human words.

God has revealed important truths to us,
but God has not revealed to us
detailed answers concerning all we must believe
nor detailed orders concerning all we must do,
neither through sacred writings,
nor through any human being
speaking in God's name.

It is God's gift that,
both individually and together,
we must constantly search
for truth and goodness
in uncertainty,
for this is how we grow.

There are two sources of our knowledge of God:
• sacred writings inspired by an experience of God,
• the world around and within us created by God.

There is one tool given to us
to understand the two sources
– discernment –
which includes reason, feelings, spiritual insight,

and a respect for the development
of understanding over time.

In this study, faith, reason and feelings
can and must work together in mutual respect.

To apply sacred writings to our own times
we must seek to understand
the human story that gave them birth,
discern as best we can
the presence and voice of God in that story,
and then bring this discernment into dialogue
with the knowledge of the divine we can gain
from the world around and within us.

There is no subject on which
we have been spared the hard work
of using all our powers of discernment
to discover God's truth.

We must also humbly acknowledge that
faith can often do no more
than help us to live
with the mysteries and paradoxes of life
in an ambiguous world.

Faith does not claim to have an answer
to every conceivable question.
It can offer us,
"enough light for those who want to believe
and enough shadow for those who do not."[1]

Whether we have religious faith or not will depend
above all on two factors:
- our own personal story, and
- whether we **want** to believe.

---

1   Blaise Pascal (1623-62).

THE SEARCH FOR RIGHT ACTIONS

PEOPLE GROW in moral stature when,
at one and the same time they
- constantly seek God's truth rather than create their own,
- and take personal responsibility for their decisions.

It is possible to increase in our understanding
of what God's goodness asks of us,
but this involves a serious and never-ending search,
both for individuals
and for the whole human race.

We should spend our whole life in this search,
while also constantly making decisions and acting
on the basis of the best understanding of that goodness
that we are capable of at the present moment.

The relationship between our conscience and God's goodness
should be a constant, humble and loving dialogue.

We may discern six levels of moral living:

6) Superiority and Vengeance.
    The pointless and endless cycle of revenge

5) Justice without Mercy.
    Getting even: an eye for an eye, a tooth for a tooth

4) The Usefulness of Others to Ourselves

3) Respect for Human Dignity.
    Respect for Life and Physical Integrity
    Respect for the Relationships that Give Life Meaning
    Respect for Material Possessions
    Respect for Good Name

2) Love as You Love Yourself.

1) Love as God Loves Us.

THE LOVE FROM WHICH WE CAME

There is no one who cannot fall back
to the lowest level in a single moment,
but there is also no one
who is not capable
of rising to the highest level.

A person who strives to live at the higher levels,
but has some incorrect beliefs,
will always be closer to God
than a person who has correct beliefs,
but does not strive
to live at the higher levels of moral living.

THE SPIRITUAL AND THE UNSPIRITUAL

WITHIN EVERY human heart
there are both longings and fears.
They occupy every waking moment of our day,
and fill our nightly dreams.

The deepest and most constant longing
is always
the longing for love.

Indeed, all our longings
are nothing more than
different expressions of this
one longing for love.

Many expressions of longing are immediate
(I'd love an ice cream, a glass of wine, a good meal).
But we are always aware of deeper longings.

We long for a life-work
that will inspire us
and give meaning to our lives.

We long for a soulmate, a life-partner,
who will share our journey,
support and inspire us.

We long with all our hearts
for the safety, growth and happiness
of our children.

We long for family and friends around us.

We long for a world
not bound by constant greed
and the striving to be the greatest.

We long for a world without war,
where no family will be forced to join
the millions of refugees
trudging through the ice and snow

THE LOVE FROM WHICH WE CAME

towards an uncertain future;
where no child will be washed up on a beach
like a piece of garbage.

We long for a world willing to sacrifice
to overcome global warming,
so that we may not leave a barren world
to our children.

We long to do all in our collective power
to ensure that we never again have to see
the enormous eyes and distended stomachs
of thousands of children dying of hunger.

We long for many things in the depths of our hearts.
We are frustrated by our own limitations,
and we long to soar beyond the stars.

Somewhere in the very depth of our being
we long for a love without limits,
a love so deep that we cannot find
words for it,
and do not even know what it is
that we are searching for.

We know only that
we will never be fully satisfied
until we find it.

TOWARDS THE END OF MY DAYS

Advertising spends vast sums
seeking to concentrate our minds
on superficial longings
for things that can be bought with money.
It strives hard to get us to buy
things we do not need.
But those who
seek to meet only
their more immediate longings
are unspiritual people.

Those who genuinely seek to respond
to their deeper longings
are spiritual people.

The deeper we descend,
and the harder we work
to fulfil our deepest longings
the more spiritual we will be.

THE CIRCLE OF LOVE

WE USE the simple word "love"
for the most noble feelings in human life,
such as parents at the bedside
of a desperately sick child.

But we also use the same word
for quite selfish feelings,
such as love of self
or love of money.
The ancient Greeks expressed it better
by using three different words.

Eros means love as ***desire***.
It expresses the unquiet aspect of love,
the creative fire within,
the restlessness and loneliness,
the wildness and ache
at the centre of our being.[2]
All love starts as this desire.

Philia is the deep ***affection***
we feel for those important to us.
We want them to be
a constant part of our life,
and we want all that is good for them.
We want these two things so much
that strong feelings spontaneously arise in us.

Agape is the ***action***
that goes out to others
without looking for anything for ourselves.
It is the love we feel for people far away
who are suffering or in need.
It can be known only from the actions it prompts.

There is a beautiful circle of love,
for all true love begins as desire,

---

[2] Ronald Rolheiser, *Seeking Spirituality*, Hodder and Stoughton, London, 1998, p.4.

TOWARDS THE END OF MY DAYS

leads to affection,
then rises to self-giving actions.

A couple desire a baby *(eros)*,
are overwhelmed by feelings of love
when they first hold their baby in their arms *(philia)*,
but that very night quickly discover
that love involves immense self-giving *(agape)*.

The circle must then be completed,
for the self-giving actions
must be constantly renewed
by the desire and the affection.

Love of God must also be a circle.
It must begin with the desire *(eros)*
that God be an important part of my life,
and lead to the desire
for all that God wishes for this world.
This will lead to an affection *(philia)*
for the God
who inspired the desire.
And this in turn will lead
to a giving of self *(agape)*
to bring about all that God desires for this world.

We grow through this process
when the giving of self constantly leads us back
to the desire and affection that inspired it.

For many thousands of years
people have followed the ways of violence,
coercion, force and domination,
but every day brings further proof
that these ways have not created a better world.

Is it not time
to try working with God
by entering into the circle of love?

ESSENTIAL ELEMENTS OF PRAYER

MY GOD,
I adore you in your infinite greatness.
I thank you for your constant, loving care.
I need your help at every moment of my day.
Forgive the failings of my weakness.
Do not let me drift away from you.
Help me always to love you more.

CHAPTER 2
WHERE WAS GOD AT AUSCHWITZ?

THE SUFFERING of some people is so terrible
that in its presence
believers in God can be reduced to silence, confusion,
and feelings of helpless impotence.

Many victims have every right
to rage at the unfairness of their suffering.

Yes, those who smoke, or eat or drink too much,
are at greater risk of cancer, a stroke or a heart attack.

But there is so much
undeserved suffering in the world,
and the jarring contradiction
between this and a God of love
is so radical
that suffering must continue
to cry out and irritate our thought.

WHERE WAS GOD AT AUSCHWITZ?

There is not, and cannot be,
any positive meaning
in the unjust and terrible suffering
that destroys persons.
We must refuse absolutely
to justify, ignore, spiritualise or glorify it.
Instead, we need to cry out,
protest, lament and shout indignation.

If we believe in God,
it must be a god who welcomes this rage,
and sees it as a positive first response on our part,
a necessary and proper affirmation of self,
a denial that all suffering is based on justice.

A false piety has disapproved of this rage,
but the Bible is full of it
e.g. Job and the Psalms,
and Jesus himself cried out
from the cross
that God had abandoned him.

We should never say
that God does not cause suffering,
but only allows it,
for a god who created a world containing cancer
is responsible for the suffering of cancer;
a god who could prevent
a tsunami or earthquake or cot death,
and does not do so,
is responsible for the suffering caused.

We should never resort to platitudes:
"Suffering is a punishment for sin",
"In the end good will triumph",
"God has good reasons for all that happens",
"Suffering is sent as a test to strengthen us",
"It is God's will".
Such statements may make the speaker feel better,
but they do nothing for the person suffering.

TOWARDS THE END OF MY DAYS

Those who do not feel
a glaring contradiction between
a god of love and human suffering,
and those who reject God altogether,
have in common that
they have both ceased to search.

And yet evil and suffering are a reality so deep
that certainty is not possible.
The only persons
who can claim to be on the right path
are those who are constantly searching.

A god whom human beings
could understand or explain
is not God.
A true relationship with any real god
involves a never-ending search,
and the constant search for truth
is always more important
than the few shreds of truth we might possess.

If it is not possible to give "answers"
to questions concerning evil and suffering,
it is at least possible to find food for thought.

FOOD FOR THOUGHT

IN EVEN the lowest forms of life
there is a constant struggle
towards something higher and better,
an insistent thrusting upwards and forwards.

All living things feel this urge
to grow to become
all they are capable of being.
The urge is so powerful
that grass can push through concrete.

~

All parents want their children to grow
in their physical, intellectual emotional, social,
artistic, moral and spiritual lives.
All their energy goes to this end,
and they celebrate each stage of growth.

As the children grow,
their journey will lead them
down many paths
and through many struggles.

It will become clear
that they are meant to do their growing
in and through
a world of randomness and uncertainty,
and that this is an important element
in their growth.

It will become equally clear
that they should strive to bring to this world
all the order and certainty they can,
and seek to overcome
all the suffering they can.

While they will grow through
the tasks that they set themselves,
much of their most important growing

will come from their response
to the things that happen to them from outside,
that they do not want or welcome,
that take them down to the depths of their being.

I do not believe that God says,
"Let's give this one a bit of cancer,
that one a bout of pneumonia,
that other one a car accident."
I believe that the cancer happens
because the person smokes
or must live in an unhealthy environment,
the pneumonia because of a weakness in the chest,
the accident because of the carelessness of another driver.

God allowed the world to develop
by itself for 13.8 billion years.
When human beings evolved from the apes,
God gave the world to them
and allowed them
to learn gradually to control its destiny
without constant divine intervention.

I believe that God wants to see
cancer banished from this world,
but wants us to be the ones
to banish it.
God wants us to discover
how to control cyclones and earthquakes,
how to organise universal healthcare,
how to educate all children,
how to base government
on the good of all.

Parents are delighted
when their baby takes its first step unaided,
and God is delighted
when the human race makes progress
without needing any intervention from God.

~

WHERE WAS GOD AT AUSCHWITZ?

All the people I most esteem
suffered greatly from factors from outside,
as they struggled to be true to themselves,
and grew to become
people I can admire and imitate.
I know of no exceptions to this.
Think of people like
Theresa of Avila,
Mahatma Gandhi,
Marie Curie
Dietrich Bonhoeffer,
Nelson Mandela,
Mother Teresa,
Oscar Romero,
Martin Luther King Jr,
and many others.

~

There is no statement that will "explain" human life,
and it is only by living it at its depths,
and opening ourselves
to the full pain and tragedy of the world
that we grow to a deeper understanding.

The nearest we can come to a statement
of "the meaning of life"
is that it consists
in growth towards perfect love.

~

There are powerful desires within each of us,
some more superficial, some more profound.
It is only when we put aside the more superficial,
and seek to respond to the most profound desires
in the very depths of our being
that we come to a deeper understanding
and a more perfect love.
There are no shortcuts to this understanding.

~

TOWARDS THE END OF MY DAYS

There is an illness (congenital analgesia)
in which the nerves do not transmit
sensations to the brain,
and persons with this condition
feel no physical pain.

This might seem like an ideal world
until we remember
that they also feel no physical pleasure,
and receive no warnings
of problems arising in the body.

We must think very carefully
before we decide
that a world without any suffering
would be desirable.

~

Free will,
the freedom to choose between right and wrong,
is our greatest possession,
at the very heart of our humanity
and of our ability to grow.

Unless we had the freedom to choose
what is wrong and harmful,
we could not choose
what is good and helpful.

The only way the harmful effects of wrong choices
could be prevented
would be by the taking away of freewill itself
and our consequent ability to grow.

God has total respect for human freewill,
even to the point of allowing human beings
to make the most terrible and harmful choices.

~

If God constantly intervened
to remedy the harmful effects of our choices,

would that make us better persons?
Or would we quickly become even more careless,
demanding that God do more and more for us?

If God intervened to cure every human illness,
would scientists bother looking for a cure for cancer?
Would we bother building hospitals
and seeing that better health care
reaches all peoples?

If we want God to work only some miracles
for the very worst cases
and solve only some problems,
where could we ever draw the line?
Would it not be inevitable
that we would demand that
God solve all problems?

~

God refuses point blank
to be put into a situation
where human beings could
create any problem (e.g. global warming)
and then demand that God cure the problem.
That is not a way in which
human beings will ever grow.

~

When suffering comes into a person's life,
this does not mean that God is punishing that person,
nor that God has specially chosen
this particular suffering for this individual.

It means only that God created a world
in which random suffering occurs,
and that God will not coerce human free will.

It is pure chance, not God's specific choice,
if a rock falls and one person is killed,
while another a metre away is unharmed.

~

TOWARDS THE END OF MY DAYS

The meaning that suffering has,
comes from our response.
The more important question is not
"Why has God allowed this?"
but "How shall I respond?"

~

From our perspective this is the only life we know,
but from God's perspective there is eternal life,
our individual return to divine love.

It is my profound belief that
those who have suffered unjustly in this life
will be the very first
to be given an eternal life of happiness.

Eternal life may never be used as an excuse
for not doing everything we possibly can
to overcome the suffering in this world,
but it is an overwhelming fact
that should change the very way we see this world.

~

For a Christian the only response God has ever given
to the problems created by the existence of suffering
has been, not to take suffering away,
but in Jesus to share it with us.

Jesus died, not because of some divine will,
nor to fulfil a saying in Scripture,
nor to placate an angry god,
but because he had to be true to himself
in the face of human demands
that he conform to lesser ideas.

Though he possessed power,
he had to show
the superiority of the ways of love.

~

WHERE WAS GOD AT AUSCHWITZ?

Where was God at Auschwitz?
God will never take away human freewill,
even when it chooses
to do the most terrible things,
for to take away freewill
would be to destroy growth.

I believe that God was present at Auschwitz
in the minds and hearts of those suffering,
crying out to the world through them
at the inhumanity of all such actions.

~

The Roman Empire
advanced civilisation in many ways,
and yet large numbers flocked to blood sports,
where gladiators killed each other,
and others were torn to pieces by wild beasts
while the crowd cheered.

When Tamerlane led his forces across the map,
slaughtering millions of people,
the world took it for granted
as a seemingly unchangeable fact of life.

In our own day, on the contrary,
when Adolf Hitler started a war
that led to the deaths of 55 million people,
the world said that this was a terrible wrong,
and rose up in condemnation.

In the slow development of moral sense
this was at least progress.
We have moved forward,
but we have a very long way to go.

~

I realise that
every single statement just made
leads to as many questions as answers,
but so does the total denial of God.

TOWARDS THE END OF MY DAYS

We seem to be caught between
a god who created a world of suffering
and a world without meaning.

Our deepest convictions need to be
that we must never cease to search,
and that living this world's pain
and working to diminish it
are more important than
any intellectual thinking about it.

We are meant to return the world
to the love from which it came,
and this will never happen
in a world in which
there are no problems
or God solves every problem for us.

~

I do not expect or even want
anyone who reads this chapter to say,
"Good, this explains everything."
I hope they will say,
"I still feel profoundly dissatisfied,
and I know that my answer
must not be one
I have read in a book,
but one I have lived and experienced."

Perhaps the final question is this:
When I look at everything around me,
with all its hopes and disappointments,
its joys and sorrows,
its pleasures and pains,
do I wish I had never been born?
Or am I glad that I was born?

CHAPTER 3
THE SINGER AND HIS SONG

JESUS THE TEACHER

HE NEVER taught a lesson in a classroom.
He had no books to work with,
no blackboards, maps or charts.
He used no subject outlines,
kept no records, gave no grades.

He spoke of planting crops, catching fish,
baking bread and cleaning the house,
drawing his lessons from the familiar.
He told simple stories that could be endlessly applied.

His students were the poor, the lame,
the deaf, the blind, the outcast,
and his method was the same
for all who came to hear and learn:
he opened eyes with faith,
he opened ears with simple truth,
he opened hearts with a love born of forgiveness.

TOWARDS THE END OF MY DAYS

He delighted in seeing his students gradually grow
towards all they were capable of being.

His first teaching was always that of personal example,
as he lived the lessons he taught to others.

A gentle man, a humble man,
he asked and won no honours,
no gold awards of tribute to his expertise or wisdom.

And yet, this quiet teacher from the hills of Galilee
has fed the needs,
fulfilled the hopes
and changed the lives of millions.
For what he taught brought heaven to earth
and God's heart to all.

THE SONG

IN EVERYTHING he did
and in everything he said,
Jesus Christ sang a song.

Sometimes, when he cured a sick person,
he sang softly and gently,
a song full of love.

Sometimes, when he told one of his beautiful stories,
he sang a haunting melody,
the kind of melody that,
once heard, is never forgotten,
the sort of melody you hum throughout the day
without even knowing that you are doing it.

Sometimes, when he defended the rights of the poor,
his voice grew strong and powerful,
until finally, from the cross,
he sang so powerfully
that his voice filled the universe.

The disciples who heard him thought
that this was the most beautiful song
they had ever heard.
And after he had returned to his Father,
they began to sing it to others.

They didn't sing as well as Jesus had
– they forgot some of the words,
their voices lacked force and went flat –
but they sang to the best of their ability,
and, despite their weakness,
the people who heard them
thought in their turn
that this was the most beautiful song
they had ever heard.

~

TOWARDS THE END OF MY DAYS

The song gradually spread out
from Jerusalem to other lands.
Parents sang it to their children
and it began to be passed down
through the generations
and through the centuries.

Sometimes, in the lives of the great saints,
the song was sung with exquisite beauty.

But at other times and by other people
it was sung badly,
for the song was so beautiful
that there was power in possessing it,
and people used the power of the song
to march to war
and to oppress and dominate others.

So the song was argued about, fought over,
treated as a possession, distorted,
and covered by many layers of human additions.

And yet, despite all that was done to it,
it was still capable of captivating people
whenever its sheer simplicity
and aching beauty
were allowed to pierce through.

~

One of the last places the song reached
was a land that would later be called Australia.
At first the song was sung there very badly indeed,
for the beauty of the song was drowned
by the sound of the lash on the backs of the convicts,
and the cries of fear of the Aboriginal people.

But the song was always greater than the singers
and, in small wooden homes and churches,
it began to spread throughout a vast and dry land.

Whole communities accepted it
and began to sing it in their own way.

THE SINGER AND HIS SONG

People of many languages came
and adapted the song to their own yearnings.

At last the song came down to me,
sung softly, gently and lovingly by my parents.
Like so many millions of people before me,
I, too, was captivated by the song,
and I wanted to sing and dance it
with my whole being.

~

The song must not stop with our generation,
and we in our turn must hand on its beauty
to those who come after us.

And, as we do so,
we should always remember that this song
has two special characteristics.

The first is that, while we too sing it badly,
nevertheless, as long as
we sing to the best of our ability,
others will hear not just our weak voice,
but behind and through us
they will hear a stronger and a surer voice,
the voice of Jesus himself.

The second is that we will always sing it better
when we can learn to sing it together
– not one voice here, another there,
singing different words to different melodies –
but all singing together as one.

For then at last the whole world will truly know
that this is still the most beautiful song
the world has ever known.

FAITH IN A PERSON AND A SONG

MY RELIGIOUS faith is first and foremost
faith in the person and the song of Jesus Christ.
From that song flows a series of truths that I believe,
moral rules that I seek to follow,
a worship that I willingly give,
and a religious community to which I belong.

But the response to the person and the song comes first.

Without a love relationship
with the person at the heart of the song,
the truths would be lifeless,
the norms of living burdensome tasks,
the worship empty,
and the community a soulless institution.

With the relationship, the truths come alive,
the norms of living are
the most natural things in the world,
the worship is life-giving,
and the community is a source of strength and support.

Most of the problems within all religions arise
when the simple truth is forgotten
that religion makes sense
only as a love relationship
with a person and a song.

Jesus called this love relationship
the kingdom
or kingly rule of God,
for he wanted to see all his followers
welcoming God to rule with love in their hearts.

If this is not present,
religion will never satisfy
the longing for love
that drew us to it in the first place.

THE SINGER AND HIS SONG

If it is not a love relationship,
it will probably be a commercial relationship
in which we do certain things
and then expect God to give certain rewards.
But this will never satisfy
our deepest longings.

It is in the person and song
that I most powerfully feel
that God is constantly saying to me,
"I love you",
and that it could never be enough to answer,
"I believe all the truths you have revealed"
or "I will obey all of your commands"
or "I will go to church every Sunday"
or "I will be a member of the church community".

The only genuine answer is a response of love to love,
and that means a response of my whole person –
my mind, my heart, my feelings and my very core.

Truths, norms of living, worship and community
all have their legitimate and important place,
but religious faith must never be reduced
to intellectual assent to truths,
external compliance with norms of living,
physical attendance at public worship
or nominal membership of an institution.

Presenting faith as a series of propositions
and moral rules
to be learned by heart
can never be a substitute for
the passing on of a living faith
in a person and a song.

At every moment of every day
God is saying to me through this song,
"I love you.
There are no conditions.
I love you exactly as you are,
with all your faults and weaknesses.

TOWARDS THE END OF MY DAYS

I do not demand that you
change into a better person
before I will begin to love you."

This is the foundation of my religious faith,
and that faith is born
when I can begin to answer,
however timidly,
"I love you too."

Only then has the kingly rule of God
come into my life.
Only then does religion
begin to make sense.

THE SEARCH FOR MEANING

THERE ARE questions that all people ask themselves:
Who am I? Where do I come from?
What is the purpose and meaning
of my existence on this earth?
We ask these questions because they reflect
one of the most profound drives within human life,
the search for meaning.

When people become bored with their marriage,
or their job, or their lot in life,
they can begin to feel that their life lacks meaning,
that it is going nowhere.
And there are few things that can so eat away
at a person's sense of dignity and self-worth
as a lack of meaning.

There is only one source of meaning in the world: love.
Love is the deepest longing of the human heart
and it comes from the centre of our being.
It is constant and it is insatiable.
All other longings within us
are simply expressions
of this one fundamental longing.

Our sense of meaning in life comes from
the sum total of all the loves of our life,
the many people, objects and activities that we love.
The more love we have, the more meaning we will have
and we can never have too much love or meaning.

We know that we always long
for a deeper and fuller love and meaning.
We feel that we are prisoners within our bodies
and we long to fly beyond the stars.
We long for the infinite
and for perfect love and meaning.
So God is part of our meaning-making.
Without God we feel
that there will always be something missing.

TOWARDS THE END OF MY DAYS

From the story of the passion,
death and resurrection of Jesus
we learn the all-important lesson
that the best way to satisfy
our infinite longing for love and meaning
is not by searching for love
or even receiving love
but by giving our love to others.
Jesus teaches us that,
in giving love extravagantly,
in giving love without thought of return,
we receive an abundance of love.

We should always be grateful
for all the love we already have in our lives.
We should thank the people who love us,
and be grateful to God
for flowers and music,
sunsets and snow-capped mountains,
and all the many things that bring us love.

But we are also invited
to imitate Jesus Christ,
and fill this world with a sense of meaning
by loving as he loved,
without thought of return.

A CLOUD OF UNKNOWING

RELIGION IS not something that we think,
it is something that we do and live.
It is not acceptance of a series of beliefs,
it is essentially a program for action.
We must engage with religion
and allow it to change us,
or it will come to have no meaning.

We need a religion that asserts less
and is more open to silence and unknowing.
We need a religion that allows for
uncertainty and groping through the dark.

Its purpose is to create societies
that honour the stranger, the refugee,
the poor and the oppressed.

CHAPTER 4
THE STORY OF A JOURNEY

The Bible contains abundant treasures of religious wisdom of great grandeur and beauty.

> He has told you, O mortal, what is good;
> and what does the Lord require of you
> but to do justice, and to love kindness,
> and to walk humbly with your God?[3]
>
> Is not this the fast that I choose:
> to loose the bonds of injustice,
> to undo the thongs of the yoke,
> to let the oppressed go free,
> and to break every yoke?
> Is it not to share your bread with the hungry,
> and bring the homeless poor into your house?[4]

The divine wisdom that is reflected in the Bible is, however, inextricably mixed with the human wisdom (and lack of wisdom) of the many different human authors of the Bible, and it is a most difficult task to separate the two.

---

3   Micah 6:8.
4   Isaiah 58:6-7.

Alongside the stories of good people, the Bible contains stories of bad people as well – Ahab and Jezebel, for example.[5] Together with sublime religious thought, it contains many insights that are at best partial and much that is far from sublime. A poem that begins as a profound spiritual longing,

> By the rivers of Babylon-
> there we sat down and there we wept
> when we remembered Zion,

ends as a bloodthirsty call for revenge:

> Happy shall they be who take your little ones
> and dash them against the rock.[6]

It contains examples of good deeds we are meant to imitate, bad deeds we are meant to avoid, and mixed deeds where we must distinguish the good from the bad. It contains profound sayings that are reflections of divine wisdom:

> Cease to do evil, learn to do good;
> seek justice, rescue the oppressed,
> defend the orphan, plead for the widow[7]

and sayings that reflect no more than the most blatant worldly wisdom:

> When you sit down to eat with a ruler,
> observe carefully what is before you,
> and put a knife to your throat if you have a big appetite[8]

that is, this ruler may be able to do many good things for you, so impress him with your moderation and self-control.

It contains abundant amounts of both racism and sexism. It takes for granted the existence of slavery and makes little comment on it.

The Bible must always be approached with intelligence and prudence.

The Story of a Journey

God could have chosen a group of people who lived at an oasis in the desert, a people separated from all the movement of the times by the desert that

---

5   1 Kings 16:29-22:40.
6   Psalm 137.
7   Isaiah 1:16–18
8   Proverbs 23:1-2.

surrounded them. Under the influence of divine inspiration, this group of people could have contemplated the grandeur of the heavens, plumbed the depths of human nature and written a book of sublime spiritual poetry. Instead, God chose a very different method of conveying a message.

In ancient times the two great centres of civilisation in the Western world were two long river valleys: the Nile valley in Egypt and the valley of the two rivers of the Tigris and the Euphrates in modern day Iraq. Traffic between these two civilisations could not pass directly across the forbidding desert that separated them, so it followed what was known as the Fertile Crescent, up along the line of the Tigris-Euphrates and then down the Mediterranean Coast through Israel to Egypt and the Nile valley. Thus, Israel stood on the main road of ancient times. Jerusalem sits on top of hills just fifty kilometres from the coast and the desert starts immediately outside the city, so all traffic passed through the narrow corridor between the sea and the desert.

It was the place where the three continents of Europe, Africa and Asia met, and it could not escape the wars that raged between any two of these continents. It was open to all the strategies, alliances, politics, culture, business and ferment of the times. It was open to all the religious influences that were involved in this ferment. There was always a mixed population and there was continual intermarriage. There were always too many interests competing for too few resources. The narrow corridor of Israel was one of the most turbulent places on the face of the earth.

If God wanted a book that contained only pure divine wisdom, unmixed with any human ideas, God might have chosen the tribe at the oasis. But if God wanted a book containing a mixture of the divine and the human, and the story of a god who spoke to people, less by divine oracles from heaven, and more in and through the turbulence of the world around them, then Israel was the perfect place.

The Bible is the *STORY* of a people's long and painful journey through a world of turmoil towards a deeper understanding and a higher morality.

It does not present to us only the perfect end-product but also contains the beginning and the middle of the journey, the false paths as well as the true ones. To separate the false and true paths and to see the many steps of the long journey takes much thought and meditation. We would wander far astray if we saw the Bible as only pure divine wisdom, unmixed with any human ideas.

In reading it, it becomes obvious that, rather than directly reveal divine answers to all questions, God wanted human beings themselves to struggle slowly and painfully towards a higher understanding. God's intention in all of this was that human beings should grow towards all they are capable of being, just as this is the desire of all human parents for their children. And it is only through this struggle that they will grow.

In other chapters of this book I have suggested six stages to the moral journey:
- Revenge
- Getting Even
- Self-Interest
- Respect for Dignity and Rights (the Ten Commandments)
- Loving as I Love Myself
- Loving as God Loves

As we read the Bible and come across many different events, we see evidence of these stages, and we also see a very gradual progress from the first towards the sixth level. The progress is never neat and there are steps backwards as well as forwards, but the story of the journey is there.

As an example, one small part of the journey is represented by the Book of Proverbs. Many of the proverbs contained there are not particularly religious, and some of them reflect pure worldly wisdom. They do not come out of Israel's religious tradition, but were written by sages of many nations and many religions. They have been collected and put into the Bible, not because every detail of every proverb expresses perfect divine wisdom, but because they are collectively an essential part of the **story of a journey**.

Talking in Pictures

An Aboriginal leader in Australia, who in his youth had been thoroughly trained in European thought patterns, tells the story against himself of when he was once addressing an Aboriginal community and one of the elders sat on the ground beside him. After a while the elder became agitated and started constantly interrupting him with the advice, "Talk in pictures, talk in pictures."[9] This is the way of many peoples, and it was the way of Jesus. Much Christian preaching on Sundays would vastly improve if preachers paid heed to this advice rather than speaking in abstract ideas.

Scholars of the Bible believe that the people who fled from Egypt were utterly convinced that they had experienced a genuine action and presence of their god in their escape and in their coming into the land of Israel. They believe that the people of Israel then told the story of this escape, not literally, but in vivid, imaginative, powerful and highly effective stories. What we find in the Bible, therefore, is neither a literal account of exactly what happened nor pure fantasy, for the authors told of a real and divinely assisted escape from slavery, but they did so by 'talking in pictures'. The ancient Hebrews, like many other peoples, told their factual history through pictorial stories, and many

---

9   Patrick Dodson told this story about himself in a newspaper article. I regret that I cannot give the reference.

Christian problems began only when people began to reverse this process and take the stories as factual history.

Most of us have gone through three stages in our understanding of the stories contained in the Bible.

The first stage occurred when we heard the story as children and probably believed it literally. Thus, I once actually believed that a prophet named Jonah was swallowed whole by a large fish and spewed up onto the shore three days later. Children have a good understanding of the word 'story', and I would hope that in the future children will not be told anything that must later be contradicted.

The second stage occurred when we came to understand that the stories were not to be taken literally. Our increasing knowledge of science led us to understand that the first chapter of Genesis is not intended to be scientific, for example that one cannot speak of 'days' before there was even a sun. For many people this stage is experienced as liberation: "I no longer have to believe all that nonsense I was told. I'm free." As a result, many never reach the third stage.

The third stage occurred when we realised that the writers of these stories would have been quite disconcerted to think that anyone would take their stories as literal accounts of exactly what happened. They were always nothing more and nothing less than stories designed to tell important truths.

Thus I have come to understand that the person named Jonah in the book bearing his name was not a real flesh-and-blood person but a symbol, a personification, of the whole Jewish people of the time, and the book is a powerful message about the obligation of this people to hand on to other nations the message of God's love that had been given to them. In the story, Jonah was told to go to the hated Assyrians and tell them of God's love for them. But he (that is, they, the people of Israel) believed in a god in whom justice came before love, so he was (they were) convinced that the Assyrians should be punished, not loved. Jonah took ship and headed in the opposite direction in order to avoid God's command. The storm, the fish and the later visit to Nineveh are a story, with deliberately comic elements (for example, cattle repenting), about God bringing the people of Israel back to their obligation to reach out to other nations, even the most hated.

The inspired message of the book was that God loved all people and that the people of Israel were meant to share with others the gifts that God had given to them. The whale was nothing more than 'talking in pictures', a story designed to convey this inspired message.

Because of the way in which the Western mind has been trained to think, there is the danger that many people will have great difficulty in moving to this third stage of understanding, where story and symbol reign. They will conclude that, because many Bible stories are not 'true', that is, accurate literal accounts of what happened, they are, therefore, "untrue" and can be ignored. We must always try to move to the third stage of seeing the stories as being designed to tell important truths, and ask why the story is contained in the Bible, and what the people who put that story there might have been trying to say to us.

This leads us to the question of literary forms in the Bible.

Literary Forms

To understand any piece of writing, one must have some idea of its literary form, for if one reads poetry thinking that it is prose, if one reads a novel thinking that it is a history book, a great deal of misunderstanding will occur.

The Bible is a collection of books written by many people in many circumstances over a period of more than a thousand years, and each book bears the stamp of the distinctive personality of its human author. One finds the same variety of writing in the Bible as one finds by perusing a thousand years of the literature of any culture. Prose, poetry, myth, legend, allegory, parable, prophecy, wisdom literature and apocalyptic writing are all to be found there.

There is also historical writing, but there is a greater variety of types of historical writing than we would be familiar with today. Together with factual reporting, there are, for example, stylised court records and tales of tribal heroes passed down through storytelling, poetry, dance and song.

As a general comment, one can say that the writers were always concerned with the religious meaning of the events and, in order to bring out and emphasise this meaning, they sometimes dealt with the factual details of the events in a way that the modern mind can find disconcerting. The writers, however, were not modern Western writers, but Semitic people of an earlier age. For them, stories, allegories and parables were a natural way of thinking and writing. The dry and prosaic telling of facts did not come easily to them and, more importantly, was in their eyes a poor means of bringing out the significance and meaning of the facts.

The best way to explain this is by giving an example of a modern symbolic story. An example of this from some years ago is a folk song with these words:

> On a wagon bound for market
> There's a calf with a mournful eye.
> High above him there's a swallow
> Winging swiftly through the sky.
>
> "Stop complaining", said the farmer,
> "Who told you a calf to be?
> Why don't you have wings to fly with
> Like the swallow so proud and free?

> Calves are easily bound and slaughtered,
> Never knowing the reason why.
> But whoever treasures freedom
> Like the swallow must learn to fly."

Viewed as literal history, the story is false, untrue, pure nonsense, in the sense that no calf has ever grown wings and flown through the air. However, this is a Jewish folksong and it was written as an allegory or symbolic story of modern Israel. The calf is a symbol of the six million Jews bound and led to slaughter under Hitler; the swallow is a symbol of the independent State of Israel, fiercely proud and free. It is a true story in the sense that millions of Jews were killed in Nazi Europe and the survivors fought for the State of Israel to ensure that they would be "proud and free". In the telling of the story, however, there is also an interpretation of the events. If one asked Hezbollah or ISIS to tell the same story, they would no doubt give a very different interpretation of the same events.

Furthermore, for the teller of the story the most important consideration is the meaning or message of the events – 'Don't ever be led to slaughter again! Fight, stand up for yourselves, be free!' It can also be seen that the story is told from a faith perspective, for it is told by a person who believes passionately in the Jewish cause.

In this type of story, where the meaning or message is all-important, there must be some truth behind the events related or the message does not exist, but the details of the events have become subservient to the meaning or message.

It can be seen from this that even today we have historical writing that breaks away from the prosaic recounting of events, but we are not nearly as familiar with it as the writers of the Bible were.

The Gradual Understanding of God

In the popular mind one of the deepest convictions about the Bible can be that in the First Testament there is a constant story of a totally unlovable god of horrendous anger, a petty and even spiteful god.

In any religion everything, without exception, depends on the kind of god that is worshipped. There is no factor more important than this in determining what kind of religion it is and how people will live their lives within it. So the perception of an angry god is one of the greatest negatives of the Bible, and it must be admitted that there are places in the First Testament where this perception is not without a seeming basis. We must seek to assess this perception, once again by seeing the Bible as **the story of a journey**.

One of the first great religious insights of the people of Israel was that the god who was revealed to them in their slavery in Egypt was a god who "hears the cry of the poor", a god passionate about justice, a god who saw the misery and injustice of their slavery and determined to do something about it. In its very beginnings, therefore, the religion of Israel was based on a god of justice and all else developed from this. The idea of a god of love was also present, but it developed more slowly. The god of justice and the god of love were not always brought into harmony and, as a consequence, the god of love was sometimes pushed aside by the false idea of a god who could be vengeful in the pursuit of justice.

Indeed, there were times when the Israelites falsely interpreted their god as ordering them to follow a quite perverted sense of justice, for example by exterminating all the peoples of the land as they moved into it. At a purely pragmatic level, it may have made sense to exterminate the inhabitants of the land if they intended to take that land for themselves, but to turn it into a divine command is nothing less than blaming God for what they themselves had decided to do. It is a cautionary tale about how easy it is for human beings to convince themselves of what they want to believe, no matter how horrendous, and then blame God for it. It is not divine revelation, but part of the story of a journey as human beings slowly sought to understand.

Even in the First Testament there is abundant evidence of a people who left this level of morality behind. For example, the book of Jonah says that Jonah became angry when God spoke of mercy rather than justice towards the people of Nineveh, but God contradicted him and said that the prophet's task was precisely that of preaching a God of infinite love for all people (Jon 4:9-11).

In the Second Testament there is overwhelming evidence of a god of love, a god willing to sacrifice self in order to help human beings.

> You have heard that it was said, "You shall love your neighbour and hate your enemy." But I say to you, Love your enemies and pray for those who persecute you, so that you may be children of your Father in heaven; for he makes his sun to rise on the evil and on the good, and sends rain on the righteous and the unrighteous. For if you love those who love you, what reward do you have? Do not even the tax collectors do the same? (Mt 5:43-46)

> For the son of man came not to be served but to serve, and to give his life as a ransom for many. (Mk 10:45)

If the Bible is taken as a whole, the evidence points strongly to **the story of a journey** in regard to their understanding of the nature of God as well, a long and gradual progression from more primitive human ideas of God towards the more exalted idea of God we find in the latter books of the First Testament and on the lips of Jesus.

Inspiration

Christians have always believed that the Bible is inspired. In many cases this was taken just as literally as were the Bible stories and it was thought that the human writers were no more than hands holding a pen, while God moved the hand and wrote the words. The massive and quite overwhelming evidence of human imperfection in the Bible means that this theory must be decisively abandoned.

In the first place, inspiration must mean that there was a genuine presence and action of God in the origins of the people of Israel, and that the many decisions by many individuals to tell the Bible story were *inspired* by, that is, were a response to, this divine presence and action.

In a similar way, a young man might fall in love and be "inspired" to write a love poem. The resulting poem may be quite awful, but the inspiration is still genuine, for the love is genuine and the desire to express that love in poetic words is genuine. In the same way, inspiration in the Bible is genuine even when the resulting book contains many defects. In the Bible the first action came from God and human beings were *inspired* by this action to tell the story of God's action.

In the second place, inspiration must mean that human beings worked with God, sought to open their minds and hearts to God, in some manner experienced God, and then sought to express as best they could that part of **the story of the journey** that they had within themselves.

In the light of all that is contained in the Bible, we must conclude that among the many human authors there were degrees of working with God, degrees of opening the mind and heart to God, degrees of experiencing God, degrees of understanding God's message, degrees of the ability to put religious thoughts into words, degrees of the ability to tell stories and paint word pictures, and hence degrees to which the human authors could allow God's inspiration to be expressed. I suggest that this is the only explanation that fits the mixed nature of the material we find there.

Even if we admit these degrees of inspiration of the different authors, we may still claim that the whole Bible is inspired, for it seems evident that God did not want a perfect book of unalloyed divine wisdom, but **the story of a journey** towards a deeper understanding and a higher morality. In that story there was room for the primitive as well as the sublime, and for every stage between them. While the words came from human authors, with all their limitations, the Bible as a whole is exactly the book God wanted: not a book of pure divine wisdom, but the rich, vivid, graphic and very mixed **story of a journey**. Understood in this sense, we may continue to affirm that the entire Bible is inspired**,** that it is, in its entirety, a response to God's action and is exactly the kind of book God wanted. Thus we may still claim that God speaks to us in some manner through every page of the Bible.

Can we determine more exactly how God may have inspired the writers of the books of scripture? Precisely because this question concerns the mystery of the work of the Holy Spirit, it is obvious that no clear and exact answers can be given, though I believe that we are closer to the truth if we see inspiration as a process rather than as a sudden flash of light. Let me take the example of the gospels.

When the early disciples first set eyes on Jesus, their choice to respond to him was a free one, but it was also their response to the presence of the Holy Spirit in their hearts. As they painfully struggled to understand Jesus over the following months, the Holy Spirit never deserted them, even on the many occasions when they failed. As they went out after the Resurrection to tell others of all they had seen and heard, the Holy Spirit accompanied them.

As they strove to remember the actions and words of Jesus and present them in a way their hearers could understand, the Holy Spirit worked with them. As whole communities began to ponder the deeds and words of Jesus and to pray to him, the Holy Spirit sought to lead them gradually to a deeper understanding.

As a disciple named Mark increased in knowledge and love of Jesus, the Holy Spirit helped to inspire him to want to put the story into writing. As he painstakingly gathered all the material he could, checked the various traditions against each other, thought long and hard about the deeper meanings that people were beginning to perceive and gradually began to see the outlines of his gospel, the Holy Spirit was with him constantly. As he laboriously wrote and rewrote each scene until it finally reflected the understanding he had come to, as he gradually developed his powerful themes through his arrangement of passages, as he constantly revised and thought and prayed, the Holy Spirit was continually at his side.

As he came to the end of his writing, did he feel a sense of great satisfaction? Or was he like many authors in allowing his manuscript to be published only after he had been continually revising it for so long, and only then when someone finally prised it out of his fingers because otherwise it would never be published? I do not know the answer, though from his literary style I suspect the latter, for he tried his hardest to be faithful to the Spirit, and he knew that it would never be possible to give the perfect presentation of the very essence of the person of Jesus.

As his gospel was read and pondered in the Christian communities, the Holy Spirit worked within the hearts of their members, with some responding and some, for a variety of reasons, not responding. As the entire Christian community gradually came to realise and accept that Mark's was one of the four gospels that were, in their entirety, authentic and inspired expressions of the meaning of Jesus Christ, the Holy Spirit continued to work. As men and women down through the centuries have struggled to live according to these gospels, and have pondered, prayed, spoken and written, the Holy Spirit has been with them to the extent that each would allow.

Throughout this long process countless human errors have been made. No doubt there were errors of recall and errors of emphasis in the telling of the story to others by different disciples. There would have been false understandings of deeper meanings by individuals and even by whole communities. Within Mark's Gospel itself he once gets a basic fact wrong by citing Abiathar when he should have cited Ahimelech (2:26). In the early centuries there were many false allegories seen by different persons, while the divisions that rent Christianity at different times are convincing proof of errors of understanding. The multitude of different images of the person of Jesus that exist today demonstrate clearly that we are no better than our ancestors.

In the midst of all these errors we have only two guarantees. The first is the guarantee from the entire Christian community that the first disciples, the early communities and the writers of each of the four gospels worked so closely with the Holy Spirit that in these four gospels we have authentic expressions of the meaning of Jesus Christ. The second is the guarantee from Jesus himself and from the entire Christian community that the Holy Spirit is present in the assembly, the congregation, the community, and the church that Jesus founded.

The Essential Truth

What is the essential truth about the Bible that we must believe if we are to call ourselves Christians? It is not whether history is told factually or through stories, and it is not whether every word was directly inspired by God. It is something more fundamental than either of these considerations. One writer has expressed it well:

> For Christians, the status of the Bible as sacred scripture means that it is the most important collection of writings we know. These are the primary writings that define who we are in relation to God and who we are as a community and as individuals. This is the book that has shaped us and will continue to shape us.[10]

The Bible is "the constitution of the Christian world",[11] "the ground of the world in which Christians live"[12], "the primary collection of ancient documents with which Christians are to be in continuing dialogue". This continuing conversation is definitive and constitutive of Christian

---

10   Marcus J Borg, *Reading the Bible Again for the First Time*, Harper, San Francisco, 2001, p. 29.
11   ibid., p. 30.
12   ibid., p. 30.

identity. If the dialogue ceases or becomes faint, then we cease to be Christian and become something else.[13]

To be Christian means to live within the world created by the Bible. We are to listen to it well and let its central stories shape our vision of God, our identity, and our sense of what faithfulness to God means. It is to shape our imagination, that part of our psyches in which our foundational images of reality and life reside. We are to be a community shaped by scripture.[14]

It is the story of a people's journey towards God, and it is through the Bible that we make ourselves a part of that story.

The Faith Dimension

The gospel writers had either met Jesus personally or had come to know him through others. They had found out all they could concerning him, thought about him and listened to others speaking of him. All of this made up their personal experience of Jesus, and they reacted to this experience with that response of their whole person that we call religious faith. They then wrote their gospels out of this religious faith, and I doubt that it even once occurred to them to leave out the faith dimension and present only the plain, unvarnished facts, for the spiritual significance of the facts was for them an essential part of the facts themselves. Whether we approach their gospels from the perspective of faith or of reason, it surely makes sense to say that, if we wish to understand their gospels, we must seek to understand their faith perspective.

There is a close analogy between faith and human love. When a man and woman fall in love, human reason can seek to analyse that love, but cannot fully understand or explain it. Despite this, it would be foolish to conclude that the love does not exist or that only those aspects of it that can be understood and explained are real or worth consideration. Love is not a purely rational response, but a response of the whole person, and it is based on faith in another person rather than a purely rational assessment of that person.

The response of religious faith to God's revelation has much in common with this, for it, too, is not a purely rational assessment, but a response of the whole person. It exists just as surely as love exists and, like love, faith cannot be dismissed solely because it cannot be fully understood or explained. Love can be foolish or sensible, and religious faith can be foolish or sensible, but both undeniably exist. If we are to study love letters, we must start from the reality

---

13 ibid., p. 30.
14 ibid., p. 31.

of that love, or we will never understand the letters, and if we are to study documents based on religious faith, we must start from the reality of that faith.

This is the basis of the great contribution of the early centuries of Christianity to the interpretation of the scriptures, for the great early writers of the Church insisted again and again that the scriptures must be read "in the Spirit", that is to say, by looking there for spiritual understanding. If we look solely at the facts, we are seeing only part of the scriptures. The questions I need to ask myself as I read are not only "What happened? What are the facts?" but also, "Does the spiritual understanding of life and death and human existence contained in this book convince me? Is it coherent, profound and satisfying? Does it take me into a world beyond the limitations of my human experience? Does it give purpose, meaning and direction to my life?" In the words of St Gregory, "with one and the same word it tells a story and unveils a mystery", and unless we are trying to see the mystery as well as the story, we will never understand.

The writers of the early centuries were lost in wonder at the extraordinary depths of the scriptures, and the greatest of them freely confessed that, at the end of a long lifetime of work, study and prayer, they had barely scratched the surface of the mystery.

We must always remember that in the scriptures we are dealing not only with facts, but also with faith-based interpretation, meaning and message. We therefore encounter poetry, painting and parable, art, allusion and allegory, symbol, sign and song. Such things are not capable of laboratory tests or mathematical certainties. Poetry must be approached as poetry, symbolism as symbolism, parable as parable, and to attempt to put any of these things under a microscope in a laboratory is a misguided exercise. It can be added that it will always require the collective wisdom of many people to bring to light the riches that are there.

This explains both the greatness and the weakness of the scriptures. Their greatness comes from the fact that, being the type of literature they are, they always contain depths greater than we have realised. Their weakness comes from the fact that this type of literature lays itself wide open to the danger of people reading their own ideas into it.

The Tradition

In every religion, alongside the sacred writings, there is also a tradition that must be attended to. The sacred writings belong to their own time and reflect the values and customs of that time. With the passage of time, some of those values and customs will no longer be accepted and the tradition will declare that they do not concern the essence of the religion, and thus the tradition will leave them behind.

Jesus himself was a major contributor to the tradition concerning the First Testament. For example, the Gospel of Mark says, "Thus he declared all foods clean" (7:19). So the Christian tradition left behind the many laws of the First Testament concerning clean and unclean foods. There were many statements condemning "abominations" that were left behind by the tradition, for example eating seafood that did not have fins and scales (Lev 11:12). In a similar way, the penalties for sexual violations have been greatly modified by the tradition, for example, "If a man commits adultery with the wife of his neighbour, both the adulterer and the adulteress shall be put to death" (Lev 20:10).

Even in the Second or Christian testament this tradition has applied, as when the Church left behind the requirement of Paul that women should always have their heads covered in church (1 Cor 11:2-16).

The scriptures are held to be "the word of the Lord", but a number of their words belong only to their own time and reflect the values of that time. While it must be used carefully, the tradition becomes a necessary corrective. Where it is absent, religion inevitably falls into a form of fundamentalism.

The Language

Much of the First Testament was written in Hebrew, while some of the later books of that Testament and the whole of the Second Testament were written in Greek. It was not the Greek spoken in Greece today and it is not the Classical Greek of the great Greek writers such as Homer some centuries before Jesus. It is a particular form of Greek spoken at the time of Jesus and known as the *koine* (or "common" Greek), in which words had changed and developed in their meanings since the time of Classical Greek. To know what a writer meant, it is necessary to see exactly what meaning a word had in the world of the first century. This is done by comparison between the various parts of the Second Testament, and by comparing these with all the other literature of the time.

Translations

Since the vast majority of people will read the scriptures only in a translation, it is necessary to look at what translations do to the text. It has been said that every translation is a lie – a polite lie, to be sure, a well-meaning lie, but still a lie. This is a dramatic way of saying that no translation can hope to present exactly the thoughts and shades of meaning expressed in the original language.

Language expresses culture and is conditioned by culture, so that a translation attempts to take thoughts, words and meanings out of one culturally conditioned world and place them in an entirely different one. When to this difference in culture we must add a two- to three-thousand-year gap in time between the writer and the reader, the difficulties are immense, for the writers of the scriptures lived in a world and a culture that we can only dimly imagine, and they had no idea that a world like ours would ever exist. One is reminded of the saying, "The past is a foreign country. They do things differently there."[15]

Every translation must strike a balance between accuracy and readability: the more exactly it keeps to the original text, the less fluent and readable will be the translation; the more fluent the translation, the greater will be the problems of accuracy. Different translations of the scriptures have struck different balances between these two elements, but most modern translations are very concerned with fluency and readability, with many sacrifices of accuracy in the process. Some of the most popular are based on the idea of "dynamic equivalence", that is, rather than simply translate the words, they attempt to take the basic thought behind the words and express it in fluent modern idiom. This approach is a legitimate one in the effort to communicate to the people of today the meaning of the scriptures in a language they can easily and readily understand, but it carries with it its own dangers.

The writers of the scriptures were not twentieth century English-speakers; they did not think in the way such a person would, and they did not express themselves in the same way. Even when we put aside their lack of knowledge of English, they would be quite lost in the London or New York of today. The very fluency of the translation can then place barriers between ourselves and the real writers, for it is no longer Isaiah or Matthew that we are reading, but a modernised Isaiah, or a Matthew who has never existed.

If we do not intend to translate the words, but rather the thought behind the words, it is essential that we have understood exactly, fully and in detail the thought that is being expressed. If we have failed to see some part of the meaning, some nuance, some connection with other phrases, then we are not merely translating, we are also interpreting the text. We are in danger of presenting scriptures according to ourselves rather than according to one of the actual authors.

In every translation, no matter how literal it may be, there is always interpretation. It is not possible to avoid it, for it is inherent in every attempt to transpose thoughts from one time and culture to another. There are, however, degrees of interpretation, and today's insistence on fluency and readability means that the degree of interpretation in many modern translations poses real dangers to our understanding of what the authors actually wrote. All readers must decide whether they will be content with the modernised and interpreted version available in a fluent modern translation, or whether they will wish to make the effort to meet the real Isaiah, Jeremiah, Mark and Matthew, those strange-sounding foreigners who wrote their books in their own unique way.

The King James' Version

The most famous English translation is the Authorised or King James version

---

15 The famous first line of: L P Hartley, *The Go-Between*, Hamish Hamilton, London, 1953.

of the Bible, produced in 1611. Though it is now four hundred years old, whenever one hears a quotation in English from any part of the Bible, it is still more likely to be from this translation than from any other. Since the printing press had by then been invented, it could be and was made available to people in a way that had not been possible before, and for four centuries countless millions of people have grown up on it and been formed and sustained by it.

Viewed simply as a translation, its greatness lies in the beauty and majesty of the language used, and it will stand forever as a masterpiece of English prose. The great, majestic phrases roll off the tongue, giving a sense of immense satisfaction to all who appreciate a fine use of language, whether they share the religious beliefs expressed or not. So beautiful was the language that it seemed that here at last the human race had a vehicle worthy of God. The very greatness and success of the Authorised Version, however, highlight the difficulties and dangers of any translation.

The Greek texts on which the translation of the Second Testament was based were poor ones, for they were late texts, with the accumulation of many centuries of copyists' errors in them. The errors were faithfully translated into the same majestic English so that the translation was in constant need of revision.

Furthermore, the style of writing of the different books of the Bible varies greatly, for it is a thousand years of literature from many different individuals and schools. In the King James Version all of these differences of time, language, personality and style have been swamped by the tidal wave of majestic English, and a formidable barrier of magnificent English sound has been erected between us and the real writers with all their personal traits.

The major difficulty with this translation is even more serious and consists in the fact that for many people the Greek text became irrelevant, for they began to think that in this marvellous translation they had the direct Word of God. They of course accepted that that Word had been revealed when the scriptures were first written but felt that it was only now being revealed in all its brilliance in this superb vehicle. As a result, they felt no need to look any further, for the inspiration of the scriptures was, for them, transferred to the translation. It alone was truly worthy of God, it alone reflected God's true grandeur, holiness, wonder and majesty, and the poor, rough Greek texts could not possibly compare with it. It is a small wonder that people who seek the certainties of a literal interpretation of every word of the Bible are drawn to the King James Version as to a magnet. They can reject the kind of scholarship which speaks of Greek texts, copyists' errors, the cultural world of the first century and the inherent inaccuracy of all translations.

However, the King James Version is not the direct Word of God, but merely a human translation of it into another culture, and nothing can take the place of the personal effort needed to come close to those foreigners with their strange sounding language who actually wrote the different books of the scriptures.

Scripture Studies

There is a science of scripture studies and a person can pour a lifetime of work into this science without exhausting the field. There are ten areas in particular that need study: history, social history, the text, the language, the traditions, the editing, the faith dimension, the literary forms, the relationship between the gospels and the community, and inspiration. I have already looked at some of these but must now mention a few of the more technical.

History

Successive invasions of Israel by Assyrians, Babylonians, Greeks and Romans all leave their traces in the scriptures. The Greek culture left by Alexander is most important, while the Roman occupation of the country is essential to any understanding of the gospels. The consequent presence of groups such as the Pharisees, the Sadducees, the Essenes, the Herodians and the Zealots are relevant to the story. The better people understand this history, the better they will understand the scriptures.

Social History

The people of the Bible are between two and four thousand years distant from ourselves and it would obviously be false to assume that they thought in the same way we do, had exactly the same way of doing things and shared the same values and priorities as we do. Their laws, their customs and their ways of thinking and acting were vastly different from our own and we need to understand them if we wish to understand the scriptures more fully. For example, in interpreting the parable of the people called to work in the vineyard at different hours of the day, we must not judge the story from a framework of modern industrial relations. The parable of the wicked vinedressers who killed the owner's son demands knowledge of the means of acquiring and retaining property in the ancient world. The parable of the wicked steward must be seen against the background of the powers of a steward in the Israel of the time. The word "divorce" as used in the gospels presupposes a very different world to that in which modern divorce practice takes place. The list could go on, for there are few passages that do not demand some knowledge of the social customs of the time.

The Original Text

There were, of course, no printing presses at the time the scriptures were written, and all copies of a manuscript had to be laboriously written out by hand. Copies were made from the original manuscript; these copies were carried to other communities and copies were made from these copies. This created an obvious problem: Whenever a handwritten copy is made of a document, there is always the danger of mistakes being made, and these mistakes accumulate, so that if copyist B makes a mistake in copying document A and copyist C has only document B available, then C will contain all the mistakes of B, plus any new ones made in preparing C. In studying a book of the Bible, therefore, the first step is to try to determine the original text. Scholars do this by comparing the various ancient copies of it that have been discovered. The subject is complex, but in general terms, the older the copy, the more valuable it is; the larger the number of independent copies that have a certain text, the more probable that text is; and certain copies have emerged as consistently more reliable than others.

The Traditions

By the beginning of the twentieth century archaeological research had begun to bring to light buried treasures of knowledge concerning ancient civilisations and a wealth of information concerning their languages, laws and customs. In assessing recent studies of the scriptures it must always be remembered that scholars of the last century have had available to them a vast amount of information that was not available to scholars of earlier centuries.

Armed with this growing body of information, a group of scholars known as the Form Critics began to make a minutely detailed study of each passage of Scripture in an effort to discover the origin of each word and phrase. It is certain that Jesus repeated the same ideas many times in different ways in different contexts to different groups, so that those who were with him all the time received an abundance of material and witnessed the actions of Jesus in a wide variety of contexts. There was, of course, no-one to record his actions on a videotape or his words on a tape-recorder, no-one to take down his words in shorthand, so his listeners relied on their memories. After he had left them, they went out into various parts of the world to spread the message they had received.

If the same thing is said to twelve different people, they will inevitably hear it in twelve slightly different ways, for each will adapt what is said to his or her own understanding and experience. When twelve people are present for several years of the life of another person, each will remember certain events with greater clarity, for they will have a special memory for events in which they were personally involved and for events which somehow spoke to their own needs, for example a fisherman will remember a miraculous catch of fish, while a tax collector will remember the acceptance of a poor person as being equal to a rich person. If the twelve then go in different directions, they will encounter different needs and values among their different listeners and will adapt their telling of the story to their audience. In the process, the details of the events will inevitably start to become subservient to the meaning of the events.

All of this happened in the proclaiming of the words and deeds of Jesus, for all the evidence shows that, between different communities, there were differences in the recall of events and words, differences in their understanding of the meaning and differences in emphasis. Each community then discussed what it had heard, thought about it, meditated and prayed. Whole communities spent many years in this process and gradually came to realise some of the deeper meanings of the words and actions of Jesus. Out of this work, often called "the traditions", came much of the gospels, for the writer of each gospel used this collective work or tradition of his own community. What we have in the gospels, therefore, is not simply one individual's objective eyewitness account of what was said and done, but a whole community's deeper understanding of the meaning of what had been said and done.

It was this layer of the community traditions behind the scriptures that the Form Critics discovered. Needless to say, there are many opinions among them, and one must choose with caution. If their work is taken collectively, however, we owe them a great debt, for they have deepened our understanding of the scriptures. Commentators are no longer faced with the daunting and, indeed, impossible task of explaining away the differences between the four gospels. Instead, a new and rich level of understanding has been reached.

The Editing

Despite the contribution they made, there were limitations to the work of the Form Critics, for they considered each passage only in itself, and did not give enough attention to the relationship between one passage and the other passages surrounding it. Many of them also seemed to assume that the writer of each gospel did little more than place side by side the various passages as they came from the community, with nothing more than a connecting phrase or word. In this they overestimated the community and underestimated the writer.

For these reasons, a new school of study has emerged, that of the Redaction Critics who have studied the redaction or editing of the community's material. Writers of this school have been concerned with why a particular passage has been placed exactly where it is, its relationship with the passages that go before it and come after it, the themes that are being developed through this arrangement of passages, the ways in which each passage has been crafted in order to fit in with this development of themes and, not least, the overall structure or story of the entire book. Redaction criticism is very recent, and it must be admitted that the work is nowhere near completion, for we are still in the middle of the long and painful process by which the findings of one person are assessed by others, with some being rejected and others subjected to further scrutiny, and definitive works are still a long way off.

The Anti-Intellectual Stream

Modern studies of the scriptures can be said to date back to the second half of the eighteenth century when, under the influence of the rationalism of the period, some writers began to look at the scriptures in a hard and unsentimental way. Their writings contained much that was an attack on cherished beliefs. For example, there were writers who attempted to explain the miracles of Jesus as natural phenomena misunderstood by credulous individuals. For such writers, Jesus walking on the water was the disciples' misunderstanding of Jesus walking along a sandbar in the mist. The various miracles of raising people from the dead were misunderstandings of events where people were aroused from a coma, and so on. These writings caused a strong reaction among believers.

It must be added that, if the rationalists rightly attacked a number of the assumptions of believers, they themselves were also guilty of assumptions, and one of these was that the people of the time of Jesus were far more primitive than they were and could not have had the same powers of observation and reason. Believers were right to reject such assumptions.

The reaction against these criticisms had some bad effects for our understanding of the gospels, for all studies of the gospels were tarred with the brush of the rejected theories and were themselves rejected by many. This was a pity, for the writers of that time raised some serious and legitimate questions. They realised that the gospels were not simply "lives of Jesus", and they began to study the problem of the notable differences between the four gospels. We owe a debt to the people who began to grapple with these questions. It is never right to reject everything written by everyone because of some things written by some.

Carried to its extreme, the rejection became a rejection of the very idea of the study of the gospels: "One does not study the gospels, one reads them and believes." For the adherents of this anti-intellectual stream, any form of scientific enquiry into history, literary forms or texts was rejected. In their view, work which had produced evil results such as the rejected theories on miracles had to be evil in itself. Such were the shock waves from the rejected theories that this anti-intellectual stream of thought has existed ever since that time, and in today's world it has been strengthened. For some, study of scripture is evil and can produce only evil fruits. To restore religious faith, it is said, we must put aside all this study, return to the words of the gospels and believe.

It must be admitted that study of the gospels does contain its own dangers, for the motives of writers have varied all the way from sincere enquiry to contempt, scorn and pride. In a field as subtle and intangible as religious faith, scholars can lose touch with the needs and fears of ordinary people and can say things that disturb without enlightening.

While granting all of this, one cannot accept the anti-intellectual attitude, for the gospels are specific documents written in a definite time and place, with a history and content of their own and, as such, it is just as legitimate to study them as it is to study anything else on earth. It is an obvious truth that faith goes beyond reason and is frequently unintelligible to the person who does not share it, but this does not mean that we should not use our intelligence when considering such things as the documents that express our faith. Study must be cautious and must always be subject to review, but if study leads to genuine enlightenment, it helps our faith and gives a true joy in discovering greater depths of religious truth.

The anti-intellectual approach to study of the Bible has today come to be identified with what is usually referred to as fundamentalism. Fundamentalism is based on a series of assumptions that cannot be proven, and yet can be articles of faith to their adherents, unquestionable and beyond discussion.

There are many degrees of biblical fundamentalism. Its followers may believe some, or in extreme cases even all, of the following assumptions:

- The authors of the various books of the Bible were merely hands holding a pen, with God guiding the hand and writing the words.
- Every word is inspired and true. There is no distinction between truths of religion, truths of history and truths of science. All are correct.
- God inspired the choice of a Hebrew or Greek text from the many manuscripts available.
- God inspired the translators, so that the translated text is God's direct Word to us in our own language.
- In inspiring the translation, God crossed all boundaries of time and culture, so that God now speaks immediately to our culture without any need to understand the times and cultures in which the Bible was written.
- God also inspires each reader to understand the Bible perfectly, without any need for study.
- Somewhere in the Bible can be found the direct, immediate answer to any modern problem, even if that problem did not exist at the time the Bible was written.
- The meaning of a phrase from the Bible is not dependent on its context. Each phrase has a life of its own and can be inserted into any context.
- There are no contradictions between any parts of the Bible at any level. All seeming contradictions can be explained.
- The gospels are "lives of Jesus" in the modern sense of that phrase. They simply give the factual details of the life of Jesus exactly as they happened and in the order in which they happened – differences and contradictions between the gospels can be explained.

In a rapidly changing and uncertain world, where religious truths are openly challenged, there is a tendency to place clear and certain lines around one's beliefs and to reject everything that seems to threaten them. People look to religion for certainties and they need those certainties to be simple and easily available to them, and fundamentalism can appear to offer such certainties. At the level of the spiritual and psychological needs of people, I hope that I have an understanding of and a concern for their position. I hope that I know what it is like to feel challenged by many modern ideas and to feel the need for the certainty of religious truth in my life. I hope that I have a concern for the genuine fears of so many people, for I, too, was trained in a manner which, if not nearly as extreme as that I have just presented, was definitely a form of fundamentalism.

My own search for truth, however, has shown me that fundamentalism offers a false hope, for God's revelation came in the way that God chose, and we cannot build our own world of certainties on a series of assumptions that come from our own minds without basis in or in opposition to what the whole Christian world has been able to discover. If we attempt to do so, we will become disillusioned or we will retreat further and further into a world of our own creating, for fundamentalism is ultimately a security blanket.

God is not our property, and we have no right to demand that God's revelation be in a form instantly intelligible to and usable by the people of a place, time and culture far removed from those of the writers.

The insistence on literal, factual accuracy means that there is little room for symbolism, though much of the riches of the Bible are contained in its wide and varied use of symbolic meanings.

There is a profound flaw in fundamentalism. The divinity of Jesus was real and complete, his humanity was real and complete. For the fundamentalist, the scriptures are the word of God with no human element influencing them, but to deny the human contribution to that word leads to its radical distortion, just as much as Jesus is distorted by denying the fullness of his human nature, for this is a denial of the full reality of the incarnation. In the scriptures the Word of God has become flesh in human words.

One important part of the humanity of the scriptures is that God's revelation is the first step in a loving dialogue that might lead to our response of faith as we gradually come to realise the truth and attraction of the God who is revealed. Yet for the fundamentalist the scriptures consist solely of divine imperatives or directives that demand no dialogue, no human searching, no journey of faith – only obedience. This explains why it is so difficult to establish constructive dialogue with fundamentalists, for how can one have a conversation with people who speak only in divine imperatives? The tragedy is that, in resolving their own need for security, the god that fundamentalists present to others is a distorted and unattractive god. Fortunately, it is not the God who is revealed in the wonderful blend of human and the divine that is contained in the scriptures. In the final analysis fundamentalism is actually a form of unbelief, for it is a demand for an absolute certainty that is simply not possible in this fallible and human world.

God has revealed true riches to us. Is it really so unreasonable that God should ask for an effort on our part if we are to come to these riches? The certainties are there, but God has paid us the compliment of bringing them to us through human agents and in a human form.

The Gospels and the Community

The four gospels we possess today are not the only documents that claim to be accounts of the words and deeds of Jesus. From the second century we have a large literature of "gospels". Some must be dismissed as unconvincing attempts to prove a point of view or as fanciful inventions, but others must be taken more seriously. Why, then, do we now have four gospels and not one or twenty? The answer to this question lies within community.

The four gospels came from four communities and relied on their collective memory and interpretation of meaning. These gospels were then read in the communities at their public meetings. In varying degrees, the other "gospels" were also circulated among the communities and some were read aloud at public gatherings. The collective wisdom of the entire Christian community then came to the conclusion that four gospels alone were, in their entirety, authentic expressions of the life and meaning of Jesus Christ. The process was a long and gradual one. Though most major communities had agreed on the point by the end of the second century, it was only around the year 400 that four and only four gospels were universally accepted.

For fundamentalism, the gospels created the Christian Church, but it is more true that the Church created the gospels. Put clearly, Jesus created the Church and God inspired the gospels from within the Church. The gospels exist within the community: the community gave rise to the gospels, the community determined which ones were authentic and it is the community alone which can give an authentic interpretation of their meaning.

The leaders of the Christian community have the role of waiting, being circumspect and fostering study and prayer. That even after two thousand years we still have so far to go testifies both to the greatness of the scriptures' and to the human race's tendency to hear only what it wants to hear, to read its own ideas into the gospels, to fail to cross cultural boundaries and to be satisfied with the world it creates for itself.

Reading the Bible

There is no basis on which to claim that the Bible is a book of divine answers to every possible question, that every word is part of these divine answers, and that our only task is to read the Bible and obey.

The contents of the Bible strongly indicate that, while God did reveal powerful truths, God refused point-blank to do people's work for them. God wanted people to grow and it is only a free response that brings growth, so God did everything possible to encourage free response. Obedience on its own does not bring growth, so God did not give the people of Israel specific orders on all possible subjects, God did not give them answers to all questions. Instead, they had to struggle through turmoil in order to understand what they should do. They frequently had to make their decisions in the midst of uncertainty and in the absence of any divine revelation. There is much divine wisdom in the Bible, but there is nothing there that excuses us from the hard work of separating that divine wisdom from all the faulty and misleading human ideas that the Bible also contains. God wants our growth rather than simply our obedience, and the way to grow is to be found in struggle, challenge, free decision and responsibility. At the heart of the story of a journey found in the Bible is the freedom to grow.

In our reading of the Bible, is there a danger that divine wisdom can be made subject to human wisdom? Yes, this can certainly happen but, if we look at the history of the last two thousand years, there is an equal danger that weak human wisdom can be mistaken for divine wisdom. It is wrong to seek to manufacture certainties for ourselves where God chose not to provide certainties. Instead of seeking to manufacture certainties, we must question if God wished us to live in uncertainty. We must find a balance between the need to study and assess all the elements that make up the Bible and the need to approach a divine mystery with humility and reverence.

CHAPTER 5
GOD, ONE AND THREE

WITHIN EVERY human being
there are both profound longings and profound fears.
The longings have led
to ideas of a God of love, mercy and compassion;
the fears have led
to ideas of a demanding God,
for whom justice comes before mercy.

Both our longings and our fears are always with us,
and are so powerful
that many people from many religions
either believe in two gods,
or worship an inconsistent god
who is sometimes kind
and sometimes threatening.

~

When God spoke to the people of Israel in the Exodus,
the words used were a powerful denial
of this idea of two gods:
"The Lord our God is one."

GOD, ONE AND THREE

The god of our longings and the god of our fears,
the god of justice and the god of mercy,
are one and the same.
There is only one God.

Our primary task in this regard
is to do all in our power
to combine justice and mercy
in a coherent and satisfying way
in our understanding of the one God

~

Jesus never used the word "Trinity".
He simply began to speak of his Father
by using the familiar word "Abba",
meaning "dad" or even "daddy",
and inviting his disciples to do the same.

The Trinity is an attempt
to see God though the eyes of Jesus,
and to see the relationship between them
as that of a loving son
and a loving father.
Everything about the Trinity starts from this.

~

When God reached out to the world
in the person of Jesus Christ,
this experience set up
such a powerful encounter with the Holy
that it seemed to require a new language,
and the language offered to us by Jesus
was that of the Trinity.

This language was not an attempt
to describe, far less define,
the very essence of God,
but a desire to see God with fresh eyes
in the light of the coming of Jesus into the world.

TOWARDS THE END OF MY DAYS

Just as the God of the First Testament
is a denial of two gods,
the Trinity is a denial of the opposite extreme
of God as a solitary and elderly individual
sitting on a throne,
and distanced from human life far away.

It insists that God has a rich inner life
and is in constant activity.
At its most basic it simply says,
"God is love".

~

If the idea of Trinity
denies the idea of a solitary individual,
it has its own dangers,
for "Trinity" can all too easily reflect
ideas of loving and angry gods.
In pastoral work I have certainly heard
some Christian people
speak of God the Father with fear
and God the Son with love.

~

Too many human words have been used
for the unknowable mystery of God,
and our relationship with God
has suffered greatly from this.

The obvious problem is that,
because the infinite God
must remain a mystery to us,
we have neither the **imagination** to think
nor the **words** to speak about God.

In trying to explain to amateurs
Einstein's General Theory of Relativity
a number of scientists have used the same analogy.
They tell us to think of a taut mattress.
If we roll a tennis ball along it,
it will move in a straight line.

But if we place a heavy metal ball on the mattress
and then roll the tennis ball,
it will move sideways and downwards
towards the heavy ball.[16]
They then say that the General Theory of Relativity
is "like" this.

Other scientists will promptly respond and say
that this does not begin to explain the theory,
it is nothing "like" it.
They may, however, be forced to add
that they don't have a better analogy.

One of religion's most difficult problems is that,
when speaking of God,
analogy is the only language we have,
and yet absolutely nothing else in our entire universe
is remotely "like" God.

So the scientist's problems
in speaking about the General Theory of Relativity
are as nothing compared to the problems
of the religious person in speaking about God.

~

And yet, though our images and words
will always be totally inadequate,
we have a strongly felt need
to both think and speak about God.

Jesus himself did this,
though even he could not turn
inadequate human words
into adequate ones.

He chose the words Father and Son,
even though he and God are not father and son
as our limited human minds understand these terms
the Father does not pre-exist the Son,

---

16 I have borrowed this from Bill Bryson, *A Short History of Nearly Everything*, a Black Swan Book, 2004, p. 166.

there was no "mother" to give birth to the Son,
not all fathers are kind and loving,
the term "mother" is at least as good as the term "father".

What Jesus appeared to be saying
was that his personal experience of God
was that of a son towards a loving father,
a limited and imperfect analogy.

He then felt the need to add the term "Spirit",
and we may argue forever
about what the term adds
to those of Father and Son.

It certainly indicates
that Jesus experienced God
in a deeply interior and spiritual manner.

Jesus had to use these inadequate terms
because limited human words and images
were all that was available
in speaking about an infinite God.

~

The Creed itself creates difficulties
when it begins with the words,
"I believe in God the Father almighty",
seemingly identifying God with the Father
and thus creating difficulties when the Son and the Spirit
are suddenly introduced without further explanation.

Surely the Creed could contain a clear statement
that there is only one God
before there is any mention of the Trinity.

It could begin with the words:
"Hear, O Israel:
The Lord our God, the Lord is one.
You shall love the Lord your God
with all your heart,
and with all your soul,
and with all your mind,

and with all your strength.
And you shall love your neighbour as yourself."[17]

~

A major mistake made by some writers was to think that,
rather than analogies,
the terms "Father, Son and Spirit"
give us new and intelligible information about God,
enabling us to understand God better.

Some took this up and began
to parse and analyse the idea of Trinity.
But in doing this they lost touch
with the story of Jesus,
where all Trinitarian meaning
must have its foundation.

To speak of God as a Trinity
is not to give us information about God,
but to acclaim the God who shared our story,
and through this story led us to a greater appreciation
of the mystery of God.

In so doing,
it speaks of a divine life structured in love,
and this love always reaches out towards the world.

In the words of St Gregory of Palamas,
"God is mystery,
surpassing all reality and all knowledge,
and yet God is at the core of our being,
closer to us than our own heart."[18]

~

The most far-reaching mistake
was to use the word "persons"
in speaking of the Trinity.

---

[17] Mark 12:29-31; cf. Deuteronomy 6:4-5, Leviticus 19:18.
[18] Quoted from Kallistos Ware in *The Oxford History of Christianity*, Oxford University Press, 1990, p. 157.

One of the words used was the Greek word *prosopon*,
which means a public persona,
like a mayor donning his robes of office
or an actor playing a part on a stage.

But Father, Son and Spirit
are not three public personae
that the one God plays
in different circumstances;
they are not three face masks
that the one God puts on at different times.

~

The word "persons" has another and obvious difficulty,
for its ordinary meaning in human language
is that of individual human beings
with their own centre of consciousness
and their own free will.

Once people apply this ordinary meaning to God,
they inevitably end up believing in three gods,
and then try to convince themselves that,
despite this, they believe in only one God.

St. Augustine admitted that the most we can say
about the word "person" as applied to God
is that it is the best of a totally inadequate lot.
Others would deny even this,
saying it is not the best of a bad lot,
for it leads too easily to false ideas of three gods.

St. Anselm of Canterbury
tried to come to terms with the problem
by speaking of "three something-or-others",
"three I-know-not-whats"
(tres nescio quid).
He recognised that, whatever word we use,
it cannot be taken literally,
but must be seen as poetic, allusive and inadequate.[19]

---

19 And this explains why I have felt the need to use a more poetic and allusive form and language in this chapter.

In the twentieth century the theologian Karl Rahner
suggested that we abandon the word "person"
and speak instead of
"one God in three manners of subsistence".
A critic said that people would not understand,
and Rahner replied that that may well be so,
but at least they would not get the false ideas
they do when the word "person" is used.[20]

~

Some have suggested that we should say,
"I baptise you in the name of God the Creator,
God the Redeemer
and God the Sanctifier",
naming the three members of the Trinity
after their perceived roles.

But this could imply that
the Father does not redeem or sanctify,
the Son does not create or sanctify
and the Spirit does not create or redeem.

At this point we are back to three gods,
each with a specific role
that the other two do not fully share.

We must accept that there is no language
that is not totally inadequate.
We should be aware of this
even when we speak of Father, Son and Spirit,
realising that these three human words
cannot be more adequate than any others.

~

Our human words
on the subject of the Trinity
should be limited
to those that do not attempt
to speak of the reality of the Trinity,

---

[20] For the last three paragraphs, see Elizabeth Johnson, *The Quest for the Living God*, Continuum, New York, 2007.

but only of **our ways of thinking**
about the Trinity.

Many people speak of God up there,
God beside us
and God within us.
If these words are intended
as an explanation of the Trinity,
they fail as badly as any other human words.

But if they are intended as nothing more
than ways in which we human beings think about God,
they reflect a reality
that is shared by many people from many religions.
There are many images in religious literature
that reflect each of the three.

We can speak of God as an eternal rock,
a pillar of fire, a storm, a flood, a raging bushfire,
and these images reflect the idea of God up there,
a God of power and majesty.

We can speak of God as a friend,
a companion, a shepherd, a lover,
and these are images of God beside us.

St. John of the Cross spoke of God as a fire
that turns a piece of wood black and ugly,
but then transforms the wood into itself
and makes it as beautiful as itself,
so that it can now transform
other pieces of wood in the same way.
This is an image of God within us.

Much of the literature about God
speaks in one of these ways:
God above us, God beside us, God within us.

They are all perfectly legitimate,
as long as we never cross a line
and think that together

GOD, ONE AND THREE

they somehow explain the Trinity,
with the Father being God above us,
the Son God beside us
and the Spirit God within us.

They are nothing more
than our weak ways of thinking about the Trinity.

~

The same can be said of the three ideas
of the lover, the beloved and the love itself.
These terms may be helpful,
but only as ways for human beings to think about God,
not as explanations of who God is.

~

It is legitimate to use such images.
Indeed, it is good that in our thinking
we do not limit ourselves to one single image,
but move around among many images,
thinking now of the many facets of love,
now of a God of power and majesty,
now of a God who is close to us and walks beside us,
now of a God dwelling within our own hearts.

We should have an acute awareness
of the inadequacy of all images,
and use many images
to minimise the dangers
of taking any one too literally.

~

There is only one God.
Nothing we say about the Trinity
must ever be allowed to take away from this.
The rest is a matter of
how we attempt to think about God
with our weak human minds.

Silence, wonder and awe

will usually be a better response than words,
for the only language we have is
that of always inadequate
and potentially misleading images.

In all fields of religion
it is always easy to use too many words.
Nowhere is this more true
than when speaking of the Trinity.

CHAPTER 6
FULLY DIVINE AND FULLY HUMAN

It is the belief of the Christian world that Jesus Christ was both fully divine and fully human. It seems to me that, if he was fully human, at least four things must have been true of him.
- He had to be able to suffer physical pain.
- He had to feel all human emotions such as joy, sorrow, anger, hurt, disillusionment, uncertainty, fear.
- He had to experience temptation, such as the temptation to feel pride because of his superior understanding.
- He had to struggle through limitations in his understanding.

If he did not experience these four things, then it is impossible to say that he was fully human. If these four were not true, he would have been a divine being moving over the surface of human living, but not fully involved in it. We would even have to say that he was pretending to be fully human, but in fact was not, for someone who does not experience these four things is not fully human.

This must mean that he freely surrendered certain divine privileges in order to become fully human.

The Church has no difficulty with the idea that he suffered real pain in his passion and death. No Church authority has ever suggested that, when the whip struck his back or the nails pierced his wrists, he felt nothing.

The gospels speak frequently of his emotions, especially the Gospel of Mark. For example: "Moved with pity (or 'indignation'), Jesus stretched out his hand ..." (Mark 1:41). "He looked around at them with anger; he was grieved at their hardness of heart …" (3:5). "He was amazed at their unbelief …" (6:6). "As he went ashore, he saw a great crowd; and he had compassion for them …" (6:34). "Isaiah prophesied rightly about you hypocrites …" (7:6). "I have compassion for the crowd, because they have been with me now for three days and have nothing to eat …" (8:2). "And he sighed deeply in his spirit and said, 'Amen I say to you if a sign will be given …'" (8:12). "He rebuked Peter and said, 'Get behind me, Satan!'" (8:33). "You faithless generation, how much longer must I be among you? How much longer must I put up with you?" (9:19).

And also, "Jesus, looking at him, loved him and said, 'You lack one thing …'" (10:21). "And he entered the temple and began to drive out those who were selling and those who were buying in the temple … 'My house shall be called a house of prayer for all the nations. But you have made it a den of robbers'" (11:17). "But knowing their hypocrisy, he said to them, 'Why are you putting me to the test?'" (12:15). "It is one of the twelve, one who is dipping bread into the bowl with me … It would have been better for that one not to have been born" (14:21). "'I am deeply grieved, even to death; remain here, and keep awake.' And going a little further, he threw himself on the ground and prayed that, if it were possible, the hour might pass from him" (14:34). "My God, my God, why have you forsaken me?" (15:34).

The Letter to the Hebrews says that he was tempted: "Therefore he had to become like his brothers and sisters in every respect, so that he might be a merciful and faithful high priest in the service of God, to make a sacrifice of atonement for the sins of the people. Because he himself was tempted by what he suffered, he is able to help those who are being tempted" (Heb 2:17-18). "We do not have a high priest who is unable to sympathise with our weaknesses, but we have one who in every respect has been tempted as we are, yet without sin" (Heb 4:15).

It is Jesus' fourth statement concerning the limits of his knowledge that seems to have caused difficulties for the Church. Certainly Jesus was a highly intelligent person in all matters and an outstanding genius in the field of religion, but did he still have to struggle to know what was the best thing to do or say? Or did he at all times possess divine knowledge?

To put this in simple terms: imagine that an adventurous person from China at the time of Jesus had travelled far from home in search of new markets and had actually reached Israel and there happened to meet Jesus. Would Jesus have been able to speak with him in fluent Chinese?

Just as a Jesus who died on a cross but felt no pain would not be close to us, so a Jesus with perfect knowledge would seem distant. A Jesus with only human knowledge would be far more closely identified with our struggles, our ignorance and our temptation. Just as his suffering brought him closer to us, so his lack of perfect knowledge would make the incarnation far more real and we could identify more closely with such a Jesus.

The question is a relevant one. If Jesus at all times possessed divine knowledge, then one might argue that anything he said about the Church he was founding was a divine law laid down for all times. If Jesus did not possess divine knowledge, but had to struggle as we do to know what was the best thing to do, then one might argue that the structures that appear to have been given to the Church by Jesus are not divine structures binding for all times, but human structures that can be adapted to the different circumstances that arise.

For example, when Attila the Hun was advancing down through Italy towards Rome, the people did not want a pope who would call a council to conduct a widespread dialogue on the matter; they wanted a pope who would act instantly and decisively, confront Attila in their name and halt his advance. Today, on the contrary, the people want a pope who listens to their needs and hears their voice in determining the faith of the Church. Is the Church at liberty to adapt its structures to the needs of the time?

In a similar vein, Pope John Paul II argued that, because Jesus chose only men as his apostles and ordained only men at the Last Supper, therefore women may never be ordained. This was said to be an infallible teaching, so that the question may not even be discussed. It is clear that the argument was based on the assumption that Jesus possessed divine knowledge and it would lose most of its force if Jesus had only human knowledge.

Or again, there have been many calls for a revisiting of mandatory celibacy for priests because of the shortage of priests and because of questions raised both by revelations of widespread abuse, and the acceptance of married Protestant priests into the Catholic Church. In defending celibacy against these calls, a number of highly placed persons in the Vatican have begun to say that priestly celibacy is not just a law but a theological necessity, and Pope John Paul II appeared to listen to them willingly. To support this argument, they have been increasingly calling on the idea that Jesus, with divine knowledge, chose celibacy.

Should we be concerned by this process of creeping infallibility and the manner in which the question of the knowledge of Jesus is being caught up in the process?

Despite the importance of the question, we have to say that a crystal clear answer does not emerge, neither from the gospels, nor from Church teaching.

a) The Gospels

Though some phrases require understanding, the three gospels of Mark, Matthew and Luke seem to support the idea of the gradual development of the knowledge of Jesus. They speak of Jesus growing in wisdom and stature, of his being genuinely tempted, and they quote him as saying that he did not know the "time of the end". On the other hand, the Gospel of John goes its own way and presents Jesus as at all times possessing divine knowledge. On this point it is important to understand that this one Gospel of John has dominated Church thinking for nearly two thousand years, and it is only in our own day that scholars are gradually seeking to assert the message of the other three gospels.

Over the last two thousand years most Christians have believed in a composite Jesus, that is, they have taken passages from each of the four gospels and put them into one whole in a way that we would now realise is not legitimate. One example is that they have taken the idea of the perfect knowledge of Jesus from the Gospel of John, but they have also included the scene in the garden of Gethsemane when Jesus prayed that he be spared the suffering of the cross. This scene appears in the three gospels of Mark, Matthew and Luke, where it sits easily with the idea of a Jesus who did not have perfect knowledge. But it does not appear in John's Gospel, for the simple reason that the Jesus of that gospel is presented as so perfect and complete that he would not have made this very human prayer. We must accept that there are differences between the four gospels and that we cannot neatly reconcile them.

b) Church Teaching
The Council of Chalcedon
Five comments may be useful.

The first is that the Council of Chalcedon was concerned directly with the fundamental question of whether Jesus was both God and man, and only indirectly and marginally with other questions such as whether he had divine knowledge or only human knowledge.

The second comment comes from Edward Schillebeeckx:

> From the Council of Nicaea onwards one particular Christological model – the Johannine – has been developed as a norm within very narrow limits and one direction; and in fact, only this tradition has made history in the Christian churches. For that reason, the course of Christian history has never done justice to the possibilities inherent in the synoptic model; its peculiar dynamic was checked and halted, and the model relegated to the "forgotten truths" of Christianity.[21]

Chalcedon, and all the councils since then, up to and including the Second Vatican Council, have been based on this Johannine model which clearly presents Jesus as possessing divine knowledge, and it needs to be complemented by the synoptic model.

The third comment comes from Fr David Coffey of the Catholic Institute of Sydney:

> A category mistake frequently made by Catholic as well as Protestant theologians is to treat the dogma of Chalcedon as a hermeneutical

---

21 *Jesus: An experiment in Christology*, New York, Crossroad, 1981, p. 570.

principle, a theology. But it is not. All that ... [this] does is to set the parameters of faith in the God-man; it requires for its complete intelligibility the application of a hermeneutical principle, a theology from without. In one sense it is an end; it was meant to conclude the Christological controversy. But in another sense, it was only a beginning, as it spawned several theologies in competition with each other to carry out the hermeneutical task ....[22]

The fourth comment comes from Declan O'Byrne:

... although the doctrine of Chalcedon remains the classical statement of Christological orthodoxy, it suffers from an imbalance inasmuch as it fails to address the question of the relation between the divine and human natures in Christ. In a similar vein, Joseph Ratzinger pointed out that if one takes Chalcedon as the terminus of Christological reflection, then "dogmatic Christology comes to a stop with a certain parallelism of the two natures in Christ". Note also the view of the International Theological Commission to the effect that the Council of Chalcedon should be read in conjunction with the later Christological councils.[23]

The fifth comment is that the Council of Chalcedon occurred in the period when the more concrete and Semitic world of the Bible was encountering the more abstract world of Greek philosophy. New terms and new ideas came into play and it was always difficult to harmonise them with the words and ideas of the Bible. The scriptures were widely quoted in the debates, but sometimes out of context and in senses the authors never intended. What was said in these early councils obviously had great authority, but there was still a long way to go in the process of bringing together the world of the Bible and the world of speculative theology. Indeed, this task is still far from finished, and there will always be a serious tension between the two, for it can never be legitimate to "canonise" a particular system of philosophy.

As these observations show, we must be circumspect in the conclusions we draw from the statements of the Council of Chalcedon.

---

22 *The Theandric Nature of Christ*, Theological Studies, Sept. 1999, vol.60, p. 418. Coffey finds this theology in the concepts of *enhypostasia* and *communicatio idiomatum*. By *enhypostasia* he means that the human nature of Christ subsists in the hypostasis of the divine Word; and by "subsists" he means that the human nature exists in its own right, but only by (and in that sense in) the existence, in and of itself, of the divine Word. By *communicatio idiomatum* he means an interchange of attributes between the divine and human natures in Christ.

23 Declan O'Byrne, *Spirit Christology and Trinity in the Theology of David Coffey*, Peter Lang, Bern, 2010, p. 88.

c) The Second Vatican Council
The Second Vatican Council insisted on the completeness of the humanity of Jesus.

> (Jesus Christ) worked with human hands, he thought with a human mind. He acted with a human will, and with a human heart he loved.[24]

Pope John Paul II referred to the question of the knowledge that Jesus possessed, and called it the "frontier zone" of the mystery of Christ. He insisted that Jesus eventually came to the clear self-awareness that he was God, but he notably left open the question of whether he possessed perfect and complete knowledge at all times.[25]

d) The Catechism of the Catholic Church
This Catechism states that Jesus possessed, in addition to his acquired human knowledge, three other types of knowledge:
- the intimate and immediate knowledge the Son of God made man has of his Father
- divine penetration into the secret thoughts of human hearts and
- the fullness of understanding of the eternal plans he had come to reveal.

Each of these three deserves a special comment.

e) Intimate and Immediate knowledge of God
There have been saints such as Teresa of Avila who had a mystic understanding of and closeness to God that went far beyond anything that ordinary mortals experience. Nevertheless, however far it was beyond the rest of us, it remained a human understanding and experience of God. Jesus no doubt had this human understanding of and closeness to God to an eminent degree, but one cannot conclude from this that he had a divine understanding.

f) Infused knowledge of human thoughts
The Catechism quotes only one incident from the synoptic gospels to prove "divine penetration into the secret thoughts of human hearts".

---

24 Pastoral Constitution on the Church in the Modern World, *Gaudium et Spes*, no. 22.
25 Apostolic Letter *Novo Millennio Ineunte*, 6 January 2001, no. 24. "In his self-awareness, Jesus has no doubt that: "The Father is in me and I am in the Father" (John 10:38). However valid it may be to maintain that, because of the human condition which made him "grow in wisdom and in stature and in favour with God and man" (Luke 2:52), Jesus' human awareness of his own mystery would also have progressed to its fullest expression in his glorified humanity. There is no doubt that already in his historical existence Jesus was aware of his identity as the Son of God."

> When Jesus saw their faith, he said to the paralytic, "Son, your sins are forgiven." Now some of the scribes were sitting there, questioning in their hearts, "Why does this fellow speak in this way? It is blasphemy! Who can forgive sins, but God alone? At once Jesus perceived in his spirit that they were discussing these questions among themselves ..." (Mk 2:5-8).

I cannot see that we need to consider divine knowledge in order to explain the response of Jesus in this incident. The views of the scribes were well known, and any moderately intelligent observer would have anticipated their response. In addition, there are many occasions when the views of other persons are clearly known to us through facial expressions and body language, and Jesus would have been an acute observer of such language. It seems to me that our starting point, our default position, in any incident in the gospels, should be to ask: can the response of Jesus be explained by ordinary intelligent insight into other people? We should not too easily accept infused knowledge, as the Catechism appears to do.

g) *Understanding of Eternal Plans*

Once again comparing Jesus with the great saints, there were occasions when these saints closeness to God enabled them to follow God's will for them in a manner that was beyond ordinary mortals. I have no problem with the idea that Jesus possessed this ability to a supreme degree. In other words, his unique closeness to God enabled him to follow God's will in all matters, without necessarily calling on divine knowledge.

Even the greatest of the saints had to live by faith, and Mary, the mother of Jesus, is a good example of this. An argument can be put forward that Jesus also had to live by faith rather than by a divine knowledge of what to do.

For two thousand years there have been two strong and opposing understandings in relation to Jesus: to make him too divine, and thereby take away his humanity, or to make him too human, and thereby take away his divinity. For many people he was either fully God or he was fully human, but they find it difficult to accept that he was both. And yet that Jesus was fully divine and fully human at one and the same time is at the centre of Christian belief. We are meant to see God suffering in the garden and God dying on the cross, and we are meant to see a human being, one like us, actually rising from the dead. A Jesus who was God but who, in becoming fully human, gave up the four privileges I spoke of at the beginning of this chapter seems to come nearer to the truth.

John wrote his gospel a number of years after the other three gospels, and it is certainly possible that by then some people were denying or downplaying the divinity of Jesus, so that John felt the need to stress it.

There are three possible conclusions from the evidence. The first is that it is a proven fact that Jesus had only limited knowledge, and I feel that this statement goes further than the evidence warrants. The second is that it is a proven fact that Jesus had complete and perfect knowledge at all times, and this also goes beyond the evidence. The third conclusion is that the biblical evidence is conflicting, and we cannot draw certain conclusions.

I believe that this last is the soundest conclusion, the one that best respects the conflict of the evidence and the humility that we should always have before the divine. We are, after all, speaking of exactly what went on within the mind of Jesus, an individual unlike any other who has ever walked on this earth, a person within whom the divine and the human were bound together in a singular manner. In the absence of crystal clear and consistent evidence, is it not dangerous for any mere human being to claim to have certain knowledge of what went on within the mind of Jesus?

My conclusion is that we cannot say that it is a proven fact that Jesus possessed perfect knowledge and, therefore, it is not a proven fact that Jesus determined for all time all details of his future Church with perfect knowledge and divine authority.

It would follow that the divine origin of many elements in the Church could not be simply assumed but would have to be proven. If their divine origin could not be proven, we would have to conclude that God deliberately left the choices to us and that we are free to decide whether such elements should or should not be part of the Church of the future.

CHAPTER 7
THE BEATITUDES

Blessed are the poor in spirit for theirs is the kingdom of heaven

To be poor in spirit is to be humble in an ultimate sense. Real humility is about knowing your gifts and making them available for use in bringing about the Kingdom of God. It's not about "only the poor will go to heaven". That idea makes all we do and all we are here for in our lives meaningless and worthless. Our lives mean everything to us and everything to God. Because we are alive, God's extraordinary plan for the world to be a place of justice, freedom, acceptance, kindness, love, patience – all the good stuff – is possible here and now. Making yourself and all your gifts available for God and living out or bringing about his plan is not a limiting thing, it is freeing. When you do it you are freed from the limitations of the demands of this world. You are free from the expectations of others, society, fiscal policy, market pressures … Like Ignatius suggests, the ultimate response to being loved unconditionally by God, is to serve as God deserves, and doing God's will is all the reward we need. Poverty of Spirit is about being deeply happy in serving God, in living and loving.

Blessed are the gentle for they shall possess the land

This makes great sense in this age of Global Warming and land degradation. In Jesus' time, if you had land then you were set. You had a supply of wealth and food for generations to come. The Jews were constantly being conquered and their land taken. The popular idea is that if you are strong and violent then no one will take your land. They wouldn't dare. But a violent attitude toward resources doesn't work. You might get rich in the short term, but only at the expense of others further down the track. We know that if you are gentle, respect the delicate balance of nature, respect the rights of others to security, and respect the needs of people to provide for themselves and their children, then the land will remain useful and you will have it as a resource for ever.

Blessed are they that hunger and thirst for justice

You are already blest if you believe that justice is worth fighting for – not for yourself, but for others. Your blessing is that you must already know the extraordinary joy that justice can bring, you must already know the worth or every human being, you must know the deep bond that exists between every person on the face of the earth and in that you must already know in every fibre of your being that in that bond is God. To thirst for justice, to make it your priority, so that it is in your thoughts at every moment – like looking for a drink when you are beyond thirsty – such constancy is a glimpse of what God intends for our world. Justice is paramount. Only in a just world are all people honoured as being created in the image and likeness of God, honoured as being worth dying and rising for.

Blessed are they that suffer gladly for justice' sake

If suffering takes place because we stand up for what is right, if we stand up for others who need support, then we are blest. We are blest because we know what the world could be if justice reigned. We have the dream, the vision, and we feel that the dream or vision is bigger than our own safety, our own comfort. We are standing in the shoes of Jesus, and will walk a mile or two in them, even to Calvary. Wow!

Blessed are they that mourn, for they shall be comforted

In Christ we find comfort from all our troubles because Jesus is the bringer of peace. "Peace be with you" is what Jesus greets his disciples with after the resurrection. We are his disciples. He brings us peace.

Also, we know that sadness, sorrow, suffering and pain is necessary for growth. We suffer change and loss, but we grow through it. Our suffering is like a little death, where we curl up and often find it hard to go on living. We take time out of life because we are consumed by our sadness. But out of the suffering comes a new life. Out of each little death comes resurrection. That is the ultimate comforter. The loss of a person we love either through death or separation is a cause to mourn. It is right to be sad. We miss the person, the idea or the dream of what the future would be **with** that person. We are already **blest** because we have experienced that relationship, that love, that dream. The person lives on in our life because of the changes they brought to us.

Blessed are the clean or pure of heart for they shall see God

We could think of having a clean heart as being without sin and so we would go to heaven after we die and see God, but a better way to understand this beatitude is to think of a clean heart as being a heart without prejudice. A person with a clean heart doesn't have any baggage that they bring to encounters with others. Their emotional slate is 'clean'. They accept people as they are, do not assume nasty things about them, and are always willing to look for the good in people. A person who looks at others this way will see God in every person they meet.

Blessed are you when they revile and harm you, and speak all evil against you untruly for my sake

People only speak badly of others when they are challenged by what they do, when they are jealous of the goodness of others or when they are ashamed of their own attitude or behaviour. This beatitude is a call to be a risk-taker, to go against the flow of what others do or say that might stop you being kind or good or generous. When we hear that someone is saying bad stuff about us – and it is wrong – the temptation is to retaliate and say bad stuff back. Then THEY have the power. We have the power when we do things the way Jesus would, to be kind and tolerant and accepting and helpful, to be on the side of the underdog. This sort of behaviour is often not tolerated in our society. We tend to talk about 'my rights' and litigation is the key to peace … hardly. There is often a contempt for doing things Jesus' way. It can look weak. Jesus wants us to be different, to do things his way and risk having bad stuff said about us. The positive thing here is that if people are saying nasty things about the good stuff you do then at least your actions are being noticed and there is a chance that you will change the world. Fighting escalates violence. Jesus' way negates violence.

Blessed are the merciful for mercy they will find

If you are kind and forgiving, then chances are others will be kind to you and forgive you. It is a call not to expect perfection from people, but to help them to meet expectations. Then someone might help you. Revenge never works – look at Palestine and Israel! The only way to get through or past hurt is to forgive – to talk it over, to try to understand what went wrong in a relationship or in a situation and to FORGIVE. It is the only way to peace.

Blessed are the peacemakers for they will be called God's children

Jesus is the son of God and is the ultimate peacemaker. This is a call for us to be peacemakers, to be more like Christ, to bring peace to our families and friends and our school. People will notice our peace-making efforts and will see Christ-like qualities in us. This behaviour inspires people. But you need to be like a child, not to be proud or to stand over people or to be pushy. You are called to be simple and truthful and accepting and loving – like a little child.

Who can you think of who is a peacemaker in the world?

CHAPTER 8
FAITH WORKING THROUGH LOVE

The most controverted issue at the time of the Reformation was that of justification by faith alone.

On this subject I have not done the study necessary to write a chapter, so I here do no more than present two ideas that might serve as the beginning for the chapter.

The first idea concerns the origin of the teaching. In trying hard to be a good monk, Martin Luther was tormented by what he saw as the impossibility of constant right action before a judgemental God and developed his ideas on justification by faith alone as a response to this. It is a sad fact that if only someone close to the pope had actually taken the trouble to travel to Germany, sit down with Luther and listen sympathetically to his personal story, then the Reformation may have taken a different course. Luther was profoundly right in saying that constant right action before a judgemental god was not what Jesus had had in mind. This idea needs to be developed.

The second idea comes from a phrase in Paul's Letter to the Galatians, a letter often quoted in any conversation about justification by faith alone. The phrase that attracted me is found in 5:6:

> For in Christ Jesus neither circumcision nor uncircumcision counts for anything; the only thing that counts is faith working through love.

Perhaps answers can best be found in this idea of "faith working through love."

CHAPTER 9
THE DIVINE IN HUMAN HANDS

AT THE end of his time on earth
Jesus Christ returned to his Father –
and everything went downhill from there!

In the minds of many,
Jesus made one terrible mistake:
he brought incredible beauty to earth,
but then, inexplicably, he gave it all
into the hands of weak human beings.

Surely, they say, he had to know
how badly his disciples
would fail to understand him.

Surely anyone could have told him
that even his most devoted followers
would never live up
to the ideals he put before them.

They feel that the whole sad history
of the next two thousand years
was already there in that one catastrophic mistake.

~

The Gospel of Mark tells us of
the three intractable problems
that would always bedevil
all religious bodies (Mark 3:7–35).

The first is that people will always crowd in on Jesus
desperately asking that he cure their ills,
make life easier for them,
and get them into heaven,
but stop short of the love relationship with God
that alone makes sense of religion
and answers the longings
that draw people to it in the first place (3:7–12).

The second is that members of any religion
will always extol leaders, saints and martyrs,
but will fail to realise that all leaders
are ordinary human beings
who will constantly fail.
They will always claim divine authority
for purely human statements
and think that their religious body
is far more perfect than it is (3:13–19).

The third is that both members and leaders
will permanently be tempted
to believe only in a god
who always agrees with them.
In a thousand different ways
they will be drawn to put this god
of their own creating
in the place of the real God (3:22–35).
Either God is – or *I* am God.

These three factors have been constantly at work,
and no church can ever be free from them.

~

The only explanation
that can be given for the actions of Jesus
is that God's overwhelming desire
is that we should grow

towards all we are capable of being,
so that we may return the world
to the love from which it came.

And God knows that
the only way that this can happen
is by our taking responsibility
for our own actions
and gradually and painfully
learning and growing.

However messy this process
and however long it takes,
there is no other way.

God waited 13.8 billion years for the world
to reach the stage of development it has,
and God can wait for as long as is needed
for the glacially slow development
of the Christian Church.

The essential requirement for proper growth
is humility –
the recognition that the example of Jesus is far above us,
and that we have to keep learning.

The worst fault is that of pride,
particularly in thinking that human beings
have certain answers
to every question about Jesus,
so that they now possess him,
can wrap him up in a package
and hand him to others.

This inevitably leads
to the creating of their own religion
rather than being faithful to that of Jesus.

THE EMPEROR CONSTANTINE
(October 28, 312)

For the first two centuries of its existence Christianity was a small religion in a large Roman Empire, so it could have no pretensions to grandeur or political influence. There was occasional persecution (for example when the Christians were a convenient scapegoat for Nero after the burning of Rome) but the Church was too minor to arouse large-scale opposition.

It was in the third century that the Christian religion grew significantly, so it was then that persecution also grew. One of the worst of these persecutions broke out at the beginning of the fourth century in 303 under the emperor Diocletian.

Then, a mere nine years later, on October 28, 312, Constantine defeated his rival Maxentius at the battle of the Milvian Bridge just outside Rome and believed that it was the Christian God who had given him the victory and the consequent imperial power.

Constantine rewarded the Church, began to pour wealth into it, and gave great civil power to bishops and priests, so that the Church went from persecution to power, wealth and influence within a very brief period. The popes began to imitate the imperial court. Bishops were placed on an equal footing with Roman senators in rank and prestige, and priests were so favoured that a number of members of the Roman aristocracy joined the priesthood as a way to power and influence.

> FOR EVERY hundred persons who can handle adversity,
> there is only one who can handle prosperity.
>
> Under the adversity of Roman persecution
> the Church was a better church
> than it was under the prosperity provided by Constantine.
>
> The following centuries would show
> that the Church did not handle prosperity well
> and constantly gave in to the temptation of power.

What happened in 312 determined much that would happen over the following seventeen centuries. No doubt the Christians of the time saw it as liberation from the persecution they had been suffering, but it is a pity that they were not able to put up a greater resistance to the temptations of power.

Many individuals over the centuries have lived a far more simple life, closer to the ideal of Jesus. Think of Francis of Assisi or Teresa of Avila, to name only two among a multitude, and there are still many people today who have not lost sight of the ideal. But it remains true that, despite the presence of many admirable individuals, too many popes, bishops and priests succumbed to the attractions of power and influence.

> MATERIAL ASSETS cannot help
> being spiritual liabilities,
> and the greater the material assets,
> the greater the spiritual liabilities.

Often a church will need material assets in order to do its work, for it cannot remain forever in the catacombs. In each parish the people will want a place of worship, and they will want God's house to be beautiful. Priests, nuns and brothers need a place to live. From early times the Church has always been involved with schools, hospitals and assistance to the poor, and has needed buildings in which to carry this out. In most cases where the Church has acquired land, it is possible to give a justification for the purchase and for the buildings that have been constructed on it. In a church with more than a billion members, it is inevitable that there will be a vast array of material assets.

And yet, material assets cannot help being spiritual liabilities. Many priests come to regret the sheer size and number of buildings on parish land and the enormous cost and energy that go into their maintenance rather than into work with people. There always have been, and always will be, scandals when individuals build too lavishly, and when the richness of the church buildings contrasts with the lives of the poor. There will always be some bishops who glory in expensive mitres, rings and vestments, and who believe that the house where they live should reflect this exalted perception of themselves. Though most Church bodies are paying off a debt and have very little ready cash, their sheer amount of property and buildings is huge. This wealth of the Church has long been the source of fierce criticism and has helped to turn away large numbers of people.

How do we assess the extent of this wealth? It would be impossible to sell St Peter's Basilica in Rome, for who could put a price on it and who would buy it? A large part of the Vatican's art treasures are murals that cannot be moved without destroying them, and so cannot be sold.

The only realistic way I can think of to gain some idea of the Church's material wealth is to imagine that all buildings on land owned by the Catholic Church throughout the entire world were demolished, the land was cleared and this land was then put up for sale. I have no means of assessing the amount of money this would bring in, but my guesstimate is that it would amount to a number of trillions of euros or dollars.

What would the gentle teacher of Galilee make of all this? How uneasy and out of place would he feel if he walked through the Vatican Palace today?

Can anyone imagine that this is what he had in mind, or that this is part of the song he sang?

I cannot pretend that I have had no part in all of this, for I was for twenty years a senior figure in the Archdiocese of Sydney. Among other things I was chairman of the Archdiocesan Schools Board during a time of rapid growth flowing from large scale immigration, and I approved of many land acquisitions and new school buildings.

But I repeat again: for a Church, material assets cannot help being spiritual liabilities. Can a Church whose entire responsibility is to sing the song of Jesus afford to carry on its shoulders at all times a spiritual liability of this overwhelming size? Is not the Church like a man who is grossly overweight and must carry that weight with him wherever he goes?

> IT WAS in 312 that the Church
> began to take the fatal steps that would ensure
> that the hierarchy of power
> would be dominant over the hierarchy of holiness,
> that the ruler would be more important than the prophet,
> that the role of mysticism and contemplation
> would have to contend with lawyers and accountants.
>
> That year saw the beginning of a serious change
> in the very song that the Church was singing,
> and it will be a massive task
> to regain the full purity and beauty of the song.

THE "DICTATUS PAPAE" (1075)

Towards the end of the first millennium the last vestiges of the Roman Empire were replaced in Europe by the empire of Christendom.

The clergy were by and large the only educated people, so kings and emperors relied largely on clerics to staff their civil services. Appointment as a bishop inevitably became an important civil as well as ecclesiastical appointment. Church and state became inextricably mixed, and no one knew how to separate them and assign a proper role to each. There was, therefore, continuing conflict between pope and emperor concerning who was supreme. At various times popes insisted on crowning and even choosing the emperor, and at other times emperors insisted on authority over the Church, and especially on the right to name and control bishops.

The matter reached its climax in the confrontation between Pope Gregory VII and Emperor Henry IV in the eleventh century. The emperor had an absolute power, so an absolute pope was opposed to him, for in this epic confrontation there was no room for a pope whose power was in any way restricted by that of the bishops.

It was in this atmosphere of a struggle for control over both church and state that the twenty-seven propositions of a document known as the *Dictatus Papae* appeared (1075). No one knows who wrote them, and they were law rather than doctrine, though it is unclear what legal authority they had. Nevertheless, they came to have a long-lasting importance as an expression of how the medieval papacy saw itself.

The document contained propositions such as the following list of principles.

- The Roman Pontiff alone may wear the imperial insignia (8).
- The pope is the only man whose feet all princes are bound to kiss (9).
- He is the only man whose name is pronounced in all the churches (10).
- His name is unique in the world (11).
- The pope may depose emperors (12).
- He may not be judged by anyone (19.;
- No one may condemn a decision of the Holy See (20).
- The Roman Church has never erred and, as Scripture shows, can never err (22).

The ideas behind these propositions had a powerful influence for several centuries. They led to a Church that included the Inquisition and the burning of heretics and which would eventually trigger the Reformation.

> IT IS quite impossible to imagine
> the words of the *Dictatus Papae*
> on the lips of the gentle and humble teacher of Galilee.

They are a long way from the song he sought to sing:
"Blessed are the poor in spirit.
for theirs is the kingdom of heaven.
Blessed are the meek,
for they will inherit the earth.
Blessed are those who hunger and thirst
for all that is good,
for they will be satisfied."[26]
"Come to me,
all you that are weary,
and are carrying heavy burdens,
and I will give you rest.
Take my yoke upon you,
and learn from me,
for I am gentle and humble in heart,
and you will find rest for your souls.
for my yoke is easy,
and my burden is light."[27]

---

26   Matthew 5:3-5.
27   Matthew 11:28-29.

THE COUNCIL OF TRENT (1545–1563)

The Council of Trent was the Church's response to the Reformation. In the minds of many it was too little too late, but when one studies the history, the most remarkable thing about the Council of Trent is that it was held at all, let alone that it was actually brought to some sort of conclusion. To a modern reader the influence of the secular rulers, particularly the Holy Roman Emperor and the kings of France and Spain, makes for an incredible story. For a long time there was extreme cynicism about the council's ability to achieve anything at all.

Luther had presented a double challenge to the Church. He posed theological questions, especially that of justification by faith alone, and he reflected the widespread popular cry for the reform of the offices of the Church "in head and members". Trent decided to alternate between documents on theological questions and questions of reform from the top down.

Despite the seemingly impossible obstacles it faced, Trent did finally succeed in bringing about a serious reform of bishops and priests. It was far from perfect and it took time to percolate through the Church, but it was a serious reform. In particular, it insisted that bishops and priests should live and work in their diocese or parish, and so could not hold several benefices at the same time.

The situation was quite different, however, when it came to reform of the papacy and the Roman Curia. Since defects in the papacy were without doubt a major cause of the Reformation, any hope of overcoming the divisions within Christianity had to include a serious reform of the papacy. Four successive popes, however, refused to allow the council to discuss the question of reform of the papacy, each insisting that this reform was best done by themselves.

Time and again these four popes promised that they would undertake a reform of the papacy, and each of them in fact made some changes.

> But they faced heavy obstacles: the threat to the financial base on which their court operated; the challenge to a way of life so long-standing and ingrained as to make change unimaginable; the resistance of the cardinals, whose support the popes needed for ongoing business; and, perhaps most important, the ambivalence or even aversion they felt themselves.[28]

As a broad generalisation, it can be said that the popes after Trent were significantly better than the popes in the century before Trent, so some sort of reform had taken place and a number of the more glaring scandals diminished. But a prized and unique opportunity for a thorough reform of the Church "in head and members" was missed. In this, Trent failed in one of its major

---

28 John W O'Malley, *Trent: What Happened at the Council*, Belknap Press of Harvard University Press, Cambridge Massachusetts, 2013, p. 271.

purposes, and the effects of this would last. Too much of the mentality of both Constantine and the *Dictatus Papae* would still remain. In particular, no structural changes affecting the pope were made, so full papal power would remain, and better performance would depend on nothing more than the will of individual popes.

> TRENT DID make progress
> and for a moment there was hope
> that the voice of the teacher of Galilee and his song
> might be heard more clearly,
> but it was not to be,
> and the song of a powerful papacy
> continued to dominate.

THE FIRST VATICAN COUNCIL (1870)

The 18th century saw the beginning of the long process of the birth of the modern world, including the end of the divine right of kings and the rise of democracy. It began with the Enlightenment in France, in which a group of highly intelligent people advocated the abolition of both the monarchy and the Catholic Church that was seen as so closely bound to the monarchy. They sought a new explanation of everything on earth without any need for religion, and placed reason above all else.

This was followed by the French revolution, which did away with the monarchy and sought to do away with the Church. Many priests and nuns were put to death. Napoleon kidnapped the Pope and held him prisoner for two years. There were further revolutions in France in 1830 and 1848. In Italy there was the movement to unite the country and do away with the Papal States. The same century also saw the rise of atheism in Europe through the work of writers such as Voltaire, Feuerbach, Marx, Nietzsche and Freud.

The response of the worldwide Church to all these phenomena was greatly varied, but in the Church within the city of Rome itself it was overwhelmingly defensive and negative. This was a time when democracy and many of the freedoms we enjoy today were being developed, and the Roman church was firmly against these developments, defending both monarchy and the divine right of kings. So, the popes were consistently opposing the creation of the modern world; they were simply not part of the movement to bring it about.

Gregory XVI became pope in 1831, at a time when there was a general uprising in the Papal States against "the rule of priests". He actually used the papal army to suppress these uprisings and called in mercenaries from Austria and France to assist him. He wrote the encyclical, *Mirari vos*, in which he dismissed the idea that changes needed to be made within the Church, "as if she could be subject to defect or uncertainty". He attacked freedom of conscience as "an absurd and erroneous proposition". He lamented that "shameless lovers of liberty even go so far as to advocate the separation of church and state." He denounced both freedom of the press and the election of governments, and he even condemned gas lighting and the recent invention of trains.

In 1848 he was succeeded by Pius IX. At first, he was a rather liberal and very popular pope, but he then changed. In 1864 he published his *Syllabus of Errors*, in which he condemned the idea that it was no longer proper for Catholicism to be the state religion, with all others banned. Later he condemned the idea that people should have full liberty to express their ideas. He also famously condemned the idea that the Pope should reconcile himself and make peace with progress and modern culture.

In Italy, in an immensely popular movement, Garibaldi raised an army, conquered the Papal States, and founded a united Italy. The pope was bitterly resentful and declared himself the "prisoner of the Vatican". He forbade Catholics to hold any public office in the new nation or even to vote in elections. This stand-off was not resolved until 1929. To replace the loss of temporal authority Pius IX called the first Vatican Council, which declared his greater spiritual authority through papal primacy and infallibility.

The holding of national, provincial and diocesan councils, with both clergy and laity present and voting, had been a constant, vital and normal part of Church life from the earliest times right up to 1870. Then, overnight, papal infallibility rendered councils obsolete, for now the pope alone had power and he would rule through encyclicals. In most places councils died out.

The next pope, Leo XIII, published no less than seventy-five encyclicals. He was less strident than Pius IX, but he believed firmly in the divine right of kings and was strongly against democracy. He did, however, write the first of the social encyclicals.

The next pope was Pius X, and he continued in the same vein. He said that "there are two categories of persons in the Church, the pastors and the flock. The duty of the former is to direct the multitude, and the one duty of the multitude is to allow themselves to be led and, like a docile flock, to follow the pastors".[29] He reserved the appointment of bishops to the pope. He condemned "that most pernicious doctrine that would make of the laity a factor of progress in the Church". He began the purge of what he called Modernism, and by that he meant virtually anything that was new or that was in any way against the defensive stand taken by the popes since the French Revolution. He referred especially to advances in the study of Scripture, but the term was so vague that it could refer to almost anything. Even the future John XXIII was investigated on suspicion of Modernism.

The First Vatican Council did many good things, but instead of completing what Trent had failed to do by reforming papal power, it greatly increased papal power and further reduced the power of bishops by making councils and synods irrelevant and replacing them with encyclicals. It seemed to place the pope more above the Church than part of it.

---

29 Pius X, Encyclical *Vehementer Nos*, 3:47,48.

TOWARDS THE END OF MY DAYS

ONCE AGAIN it is hard to see
the gentle teacher of Galilee in this
or hear the song
that he sang so lovingly and humbly.
"I thank you, father,
because you have hidden these things
from the wise and the intelligent
and have revealed them to infants.
Yes, Father,
for such was your gracious will."[30]

---

[30] Luke 10:21.

THE SECOND VATICAN COUNCIL (1962-65)

Pope John XXIII

I was a student in Rome throughout the entire time that John XXIII was pope (1958-1963). I met him two days after his election, when the then Archbishop of Sydney took the Sydney students with him for his visit to the Pope. I remember this new pope as exuberant and constantly moving about, so that his brand new white skull cap kept slipping off his bald head and, as the youngest person present, I had the job of picking it up and handing it back to him.

I remember that first exhilarating month when he left the Vatican more often than the pope before him, Pius XII, had in nineteen years. I remember him visiting the major prison in Rome and, rather than delivering a profound discourse on the morality of prison life, telling the prisoners of an uncle of his who had done time for sheep stealing. He won my imagination and my affection, as he did for millions of other people.

There are three reasons why I consider him one of the greatest popes in all of history. The first is that for him the gospel truly meant what the word itself means, "good news". This good news filled him with joy, and he constantly radiated a true Christian joy to all around him. He decried the "prophets of doom" and he wanted to dialogue with the world rather than condemn it. Ever since that time it has seemed to me that one of the first tasks of any pope or priest is to tell the world with their whole being that the gospel is indeed good news.

The second reason is that, though he carried the office of pope with great dignity and distinction, the greatness of the office was never allowed to obscure his humanity. Pope John XXIII and the boy and man Angelo Roncalli were never two different people. If you want a good priest, even a papal one, first find a good Christian, and if you want a good Christian, first find a good human being. One builds on the other and, without the good human being, there is little hope of building a good priest. The wholeness and goodness of a most likeable human being shone through everything Pope John did. He possessed the "natural virtues" in abundance and the Christian and priestly virtues built on them.

The third reason is that he had the humility to know that he did not have all the answers to the problems facing the Church as it entered the new and difficult world of the 1960s. And so it was with his heart first and his head second that he instinctively turned to the collective wisdom of the whole Church and called a Council.

An integrated and whole human being, whose priesthood and papacy were built on the firm foundation of his humanity, filled to overflowing with the joy of the good news of Jesus Christ and with the humility to turn to the collective wisdom of the whole Church – to me this will always be the model of a good pope. I may now belong to another era, but the inspiration of those years formed my priesthood and my life. I have never wanted to leave it behind, and I will not do so now.

Fidelity to the Past v Bringing Up to Date

The personality of Pope John XXIII was also the basis for the Second Vatican Council. This council was a clash between the forces that had dominated in Rome since the Enlightenment and the forces that had created the modern world. After nearly two hundred years of a largely negative response to events by the Church in Rome, the universal Church would finally begin to come to terms with the Enlightenment, the French Revolution and the modern world.

In doing this it faced a tension between the need to be faithful to its origins and the need to be relevant to the modern world. The solution the council found to this dilemma was in the combination of two words, one Italian and one French. The Italian word was *aggiornamento*, meaning "bringing up to date"; the French word was *ressourcement*, meaning "going back to the sources". The council sought to bring the Church up to date, not by confronting the immediate past head on, but by going back to a far older tradition based on Scripture and the teaching of the ancient Fathers.

It followed a principle that one writer has called "discontinuity for the sake of a greater continuity"[31], that is, in attempting to reconcile opposing views the council often reached back behind a particular formulation of truth to an earlier and greater truth. For example, the council went behind the more static categories of the Church as a perfect society to a more dynamic concept of a "Pilgrim Church" on a journey and involved in history. It went behind one thousand years of teaching that said the bishops' power of governance came from a delegation of papal power, to a teaching that all episcopal power came from ordination. It went behind Gregory VII's virtual rejection of the bishops in his confrontation with the emperor, to a teaching concerning the college of bishops as an equal holder of supreme power within the Church. It went behind the Council of Trent and the whole Counter-Reformation to an appreciation of the independent reception of the great tradition by the separated churches and to open dialogue with them. It went behind the same Council of Trent and Counter-Reformation to a better balance between Scripture and tradition in the life of the Church. It went behind the attitudes and style of Gregory XVI, Pius IX and Pius X in their condemnations of modernity, to a far more open dialogue with the modern world. It sought to go back to a tradition in which papal power was balanced by the power of bishops exercised within synods.

---

31 Ormond Rush, *Still Interpreting Vatican II, Some Hermeneutical Principles*, Paulist Press, New York, 2004.

The Spirit of the Council

There was also a powerful change in the *style* of the council. Until then all councils were legislative bodies, they made laws. Their canons consisted largely of words of threat and intimidation, of surveillance and punishment, words of a superior speaking to an inferior. They consisted of power words, the most powerful and constant being "let him be anathema". The Second Vatican Council preferred a pastoral tone. It used equality words such as people of God, collegiality, co-operation, partnership, dialogue, conversation. It used humility words such as pilgrim and servant. It used words expressing change, such as progress, development and evolution. It used interiority words such as charism, conscience and the call to holiness. In this language is to be found much of "the spirit of the Council", that overriding vision that transcends the particulars of the documents.

In this there was a profound paradigm shift. A church of decrees is resistant to the changes and chances of history, insisting that anything else leads to ethical relativism and doctrinal division. A pastoral paradigm accepts the chances and changes of history, and the risk of relativism is considered necessary in order to counter the far greater risk of irrelevance.

A Human Council

All of this may seem to be sweeping reform. Unfortunately, the documents produced by this council were the result of fierce disputes between opposing sides. On the one side were those who were still strongly influenced by the defensiveness of the nineteenth century, who saw Modernism rampant within the council itself, and who clung to papal infallibility as the only foundation that would save the Church. On the other side were those who embraced the principles of *aggiornamento and ressourcement*, and sought to implement them. For the first group, you could not go back to an older teaching if it meant abandoning or contradicting a more recent one; for the second group, the argument was that, if it had not always been thus, it did not always have to be thus in the future. These forces would clash continually within the council and there would be no neat resolution.

Who Made the Final Decisions?

The other massive practical factor in the workings of the council can be expressed through the question: Who made the ultimate decisions in this council, the pope or the bishops? Under Pope John XXIII it seemed that he trusted the council and would follow whatever it decided, but Pope Paul VI, who took over at the end of the first session, was a cautious man, acutely conscious of his own responsibilities and under great pressure from the more conservative group. He would bend over backwards to ensure that the council did not end in a schism.

People went to him to express their concerns and he made the mistake of letting his agreement with some of them become publicly known, so that more and more people began to see him as an alternative source of authority and went to him more and more often. Eventually the serious question arose: Where is the true seat of this council – on the floor of the council or in the papal apartments? On several important matters he overrode the council and imposed his own will, for example on ecumenism and in his famous Explanatory Note concerning collegiality. He wrote the document setting up the Synod of Bishops and imposed this on the council, so that the only body set up to implement collegiality left the bishops with nothing more than an advisory role towards the pope.

The Drama of the Council

There were many moments of high drama as opposing sides clashed, and even drama between the Council and the pope, as he intervened more and more often. But the major drama of the Council lay elsewhere. Much of the Council developed through a conflict between the theologians of southern Europe (including Rome) and those of northern Europe. A large majority of the bishops from around the world were totally unprepared for this conflict. They were not theologians, they were not familiar with the issues, and in the early days of the council they were quite out of their depth. The real drama of the Council then consisted in this large majority gradually coming to realise that the very future of the Church actually lay in their hands and gradually educating themselves on the issues over the four years of the Council until they were ready to vote. It is extraordinary, and the clearest sign of the presence of the Holy Spirit at this Council, that some ninety percent of these unprepared bishops finally voted with the reformers.

The Greatness of the Council

Among the irreversible fruits of the council are that:
- it saw the Church as a divine mystery and a pilgrim people rather than simply as a hierarchical institution,
- it placed the Bible back beside the sacraments at the centre of Church life, and opened up the Bible to a deeper understanding,
- it put the pope into the context of the college of bishops,
- it greatly promoted the active role of the laity,
- it renewed enthusiasm for Christian unity,
- it sought to resolve ancient tensions between Christians and Jews,

- it made landmark statements on religious liberty and conscience,
- it brought the liturgy to the people,
- it gave us a glimpse of what the Church could be, and for the last sixty years it is this vision that has inspired my life and my priesthood.

Without doubt, the Second Vatican Council was a great event for the Church, and the sound of the song of Jesus was heard many times and in many ways, for example,

> THE JOY and hope,
> the grief and anguish
> of the people of our time,
> especially of those
> who are poor or afflicted in any way,
> are the joy and hope,
> the grief and anguish
> of the followers of Christ as well.
> Nothing that is genuinely human
> fails to find an echo in their hearts.[32]

Despite all its immense positives, however, this council, like Trent and Vatican I before it, failed to achieve the full and genuine reform "of head and members" that the people of God had been crying out for since the time of Gregory VII, and even since the time of Constantine. In particular, papal power, greatly enhanced at Vatican I, remained untouched by Vatican II, collegiality was a beautiful but ineffective idea, the whole concept of the *sensus fidei* could be conveniently forgotten as irrelevant, and everything could go on as before.

Pope John Paul II

Between the years 1965 and 2013 there was a certain clawing back of a number of the innovations made by the Second Vatican Council. The major agents were the cardinals of the Roman Curia, aided in no small way by Pope John Paul II (1978-2004).

By nature, temperament, personal experience and conviction, John Paul II was a powerful pope. It was as though he said to himself, "God has given me this global role at the head of the Church. Very well, I'm going to do nothing less than take hold of the entire world and change it for the better. And if I don't fully succeed, it will not be for want of trying."

To this Herculean task he brought a breathtaking level of intelligence, vision, charisma, energy, dedication and hard work. He became a media megastar and a colossus on the world stage. He travelled many times to each

---

32 *Gaudium et Spes* 1.

continent, spoke on every possible topic and created powerful symbols. For twenty-six years there was such an outpouring of energy that it could make one tired just to look at it.

He also brought to the task a genuine goodness, holiness and desire to help people. Even those who criticised aspects of his papacy felt that they were in the uncomfortable position of criticising a person who was far greater and better than they were.

Despite all of this, the reservations would not go away. While constantly praising the Second Vatican Council, he undermined some of its key teachings, especially collegiality. While vigorously pursuing Christian unity, he moved the governance of the Church further towards a papal absolutism that other Christians will never accept. While powerfully preaching the dignity of every single human being, he pursued a moral line that at times hindered the expression of this dignity, such as in declaring that a married couple could not use a condom even when one of them had contracted AIDS. While constantly lecturing the world on human rights, he did little to ensure human rights within the Church. By his continuing silence on the subject of revelations of sexual abuse within the Church, he failed to give leadership on the greatest moral question facing the Church during his time as pope, and this failure has done immense and lasting damage to the Church. The personal experiences he had undergone in the Polish Church of his youth under Nazi and then Communist regimes tended to be universalised and imposed on the entire Church.

While showing extraordinary global leadership, he tended to overwhelm the more local leadership of the bishops. While pouring out an abundance of ideas on every subject, he did not always encourage others to express their ideas. Through his encyclicals and speeches he showed immense trust in his own thinking and had few qualms about imposing it on the whole Church. While constantly speaking of responsibility, he demanded a level of loyalty that could reduce the responsibility appropriate to adults to the obedience appropriate to children. Through the Roman Curia he kept the bishops on a very short leash, and they were quickly brought back into line if they strayed outside his ideas. He seemed willing to take the entire load of the Church on his own strong shoulders but may well have done better to share that load with others. He did not always understand that true leadership must generate leadership in others, or it will risk undermining its own effectiveness. He encouraged a generation of bishops to follow papal leadership in all things rather than truly think for themselves.

Included in this process was what came to be called "creeping infallibility", in which more and more teaching is not explicitly called infallible, but is referred to as "definitive" or even "irreformable", and is then insisted upon as though it were infallible. There was also "gradual infallibility", whereby a teaching increased in authority the more often it was repeated, the more a pope invested personal energy and prestige in it. These movements undermined the clear principle of the Second Vatican Council that "no doctrine is to be understood as infallibly defined unless this is manifestly demonstrated."[33] Since his time, I have to note the determination to canonise every deceased pope, as though to say, "See, they are not merely infallible, but also saints, so you have to accept every word they say."

The stark differences between the personalities of John XXIII and John Paul II show the dangers of the idea of a monarchical pope. The death of a pope and the election of a new one should not lead to a different Church. Someone who is loyal and orthodox under one pope should not suddenly become dangerous and disloyal under a successor. There must be a church that stands above the personality of any pope.

At the recent Synod meeting (2014) Pope Francis made a strong appeal to the bishops to express their real thoughts without fear or favour, and all bishops present declared that this synod had been like no other before it. Despite this, it is too soon to say whether Pope Francis represents an effective change in these long-standing tendencies to exalt ever higher the position of the pope in relation to the Church. It will only be possible to believe in real change when *structural* changes (changes in the structure and laws of the Church) have been made, making a true juridical reality out of collegiality and the *sensus fidei*.

>   THE SONG of Jesus remains
>   as powerful as it has always been.
>   But there is much work to be done
>   in removing all the human elements
>   that stand in its way.
>   We still await the
>   comprehensive reform of the Church
>   "in head and members".

---

33   *Lumen Gentium*, no. 25; cf. canon 749, #3.

CHAPTER 10
THE BATTLE FOR THE IMAGINATION

In recent years religion in general, and the Catholic Church in particular, have been rapidly losing the all-important battle for the **imagination** of people.

> WHAT SEIZES your imagination
> will affect everything.
> It will decide what will
> get you out of bed in the morning,
> what you do with your evenings,
> how you spend your weekends,
> what you read,
> who you know,
> who breaks your heart,
> and what amazes you with joy.[34]

I am reminded of the words of Wolfhart Pannenberg: "Religions die when their lights fail", when they no longer speak to people, when they no longer fire the imagination, when the weakness of the human beings who make up the Church obscures the beauty of the story of Jesus Christ.

There are many factors contributing to this crisis, with some factors coming from inside the Church and some from outside.

Dictatus Papae appeared (1075).

---

34   Pedro Arrupe S.J.

FACTORS INSIDE THE CHURCH

The Pope is still an absolute monarch. Pope Francis may speak the language of working together with others, but nothing has changed in the laws and structures of the Church; nothing has changed in the theology underlying it. The reform "in head and members", so long awaited, has not taken place. There is nothing to stop a future pope from reverting to a purely monarchical form of government. In practice bishops are still monarchs in their dioceses and in practice priests are still monarchs in their parishes. A monarchical form of government will never inspire the imagination of the people of today.

The revelations of widespread sexual abuse of minors and the abysmally poor response of Church leaders have been overwhelmingly powerful countersigns. Forty years ago, children reporting abuse by a priest would have been the last to be believed; now they are the first. Priests, supposedly the best people among us, seeking sexual gratification by abusing innocent children, is still something that people struggle even to comprehend. The incredible slowness of the Church to respond to such a blatant wrong is then the greatest scandal of all. How could a church with a problem of this depth and magnitude, and which has done so little to overcome it, appeal to anyone?

Many Church leaders still seem to have little idea of the depth of the harm all this has done. Too many of them still seem to want to do the minimum necessary and then get back to "business as usual". They do not realise that the very idea of "usual" has changed forever.

Another factor that most people single out is the teaching of the Church on sexual morality. The encyclical *Humanae Vitae* (1968) was a watershed moment in the history of the Church, for it was the first moment when the Catholic people of the world heard a solemn statement by a pope, paused to measure the pope's words against their own experience in family life, then collectively said a firm "No". We must not underestimate the permanent importance of this moment. It led to the near-universal conviction that popes and bishops can be wrong, especially on sex, so people have to make up their own minds on matters such as premarital sex, contraception, gay sex, divorce, the ordination of women, and anything else dealing with either sex or gender. Catholic people feel that they are left without a credible teaching on these matters.

Catholic teaching on homosexuality is seen as harsh, lacking in understanding or mercy, failing to appreciate what is natural for homosexuals, and as perpetuating one of the worst discriminations the world has known.

In these matters I suggest that there are two issues at stake. Firstly, the teaching of the Church on sexuality seems to rely entirely on authority: "Do this because we say so." This is an argument that Catholic people since *Humanae Vitae* simply will not accept. In all other aspects of their lives Catholics expect people to treat them as intelligent beings and persuade them rather than order them. We insist on the same in the field of religion. Secondly, on the rare occasions when an authority seeks to explain Church teaching in these fields, people are completely unconvinced and even quite mystified by the assertion without proof that God has somehow determined that every act of intercourse must be open to pregnancy and is deserving of eternal punishment if it is not.

There are many deeply spiritual Catholic women who have abandoned the Church because of a profound feeling that there is no place for women there. In all parts of modern life there are questions concerning how far women have come and how far there is for them still to go. But there is an overwhelming conviction that in all of this the Catholic Church is dragging along in the rear, reluctantly making small changes years after the rest of humanity has moved on. The Church is still one of the most male-dominated institutions in the entire world.

What has emerged is a broad impression of a church of rules in every area of life, rules laid down by a deeply tarnished authority and without any serious attempt to explain or persuade. Life in Christ has too often been presented in terms of obeying rules rather than building a personal relationship with Jesus. In this process Jesus can become a somewhat abstract exemplar we are supposed to imitate rather than a living person we engage with and through whom we experience God's infinite love and mercy. The necessity of right behavior can dominate at the expense of a love relationship. The Christian life can be reduced to a form of Stoicism where people are driven by duty rather than drawn by delight.

The hierarchy of holiness is still marginalised by the hierarchy of authority. Mystics and contemplatives are sometimes honoured, but less often listened to.

There is a morality of rules that leads to immaturity rather than growth. There is too little respect for the proper use of conscience as the only way to true growth.

There are too many teachings of the Church, particularly in the fields of sex, gender, marriage and family life, that are not seen as reflecting a God of love, for they are lacking in a basic humanity that is greatly prized by people, such as is demonstrated with the idea that a divorced and remarried Catholic is excluded for life from large and essential parts of Church life. There seems to be a lack of understanding of God's mercy.

There is clericalism, the idea that priests are different from and above other people. This is expressed through archaic titles (Your Holiness, My Lord, Your Grace, Your Eminence, Monsignor) and archaic forms of dress that do not belong in the world of today. It reflects the idea of an authority that can tell people what to do rather than enter into intelligent conversation with them. It opens itself to careerism, the desire to rise higher in the hierarchy. It has contributed significantly to sexual abuse by giving clerics power over minors and making them feel privileged and entitled.

There is the wealth of the Church and the great contrast between this wealth and the simplicity of the life of Jesus.

There is the fact that the Church lectures civil society on the important social justice principle that all people must have a real voice in their own governance, but this principle does not apply anywhere in the Church – not the parish, nor the diocese, nor the universal Church.

There is a Sunday liturgy that still consists of too many thousands of words and intellectual ideas poured over a largely passive congregation. There are too many sermons that do not inspire. The prayers of the Mass are still overwhelmingly about getting into heaven rather than working to change for the better the lives of people in this world. There are still too many aspects of liturgy that were invented in monasteries and then imposed on parishes. For 95 per cent of Catholics, it is only when the Sunday parish Mass appeals to their imagination that the Church is appealing to their imagination, and not nearly enough creative thinking is being devoted to this priceless asset.

There is still too much condemning of words ending in "ism" (relativism, materialism, hedonism, individualism etc., etc.), and not enough appreciation of all that is good in the world. There is too little willingness to enter into dialogue with the world, and there is still too much of a tendency to lecture the world.

There is the fact that faith is still too often presented as intellectual assent to propositions rather than as a personal response of love to God's declaration of love for us. If people believe all the truths set out in the Creed, they are said to "have the faith", even when there is no love in their hearts. There often appears to be an obsession with right doctrine and right behavior rather than a response of love.

There are far too many statements about God, and not enough of the humble recognition that God is beyond our imagination and beyond all human words.

There is still a lack of humility in the Church. One might have thought that sexual abuse would make the Church humble, but there is little evidence of that happening. There is still too much of the church of Constantine and the *Dictatus Papae*.

The Sacrament of Reconciliation is still a dead letter for most Catholics, and it would have to become a positive experience for them before it could be resurrected.

Authorities in the Church can still act with harshness and even ruthlessness in bringing people into line with their own ideas and wishes. There is hard power and soft power. Hard power is the power a policeman has – to give me orders, demand obedience and threaten penalties. Soft power is the power my doctor has – not to give me orders, but to urge me with authority to take actions good for my health. The constant use of hard power over the last two thousand years has harmed the Church, while soft power has helped it.

It takes far more than hard power to reach the imagination of people, and the beautiful song of Jesus becomes lost. If the Church keeps insisting on the old ideas and old formulas, the effects of losing the battle for the imagination will be catastrophic.

If all the many millions of people who have left the Church in recent decades were asked to use one adjective of the Church, I am sure that the word "heavy" would be high on the list. They would see the Church as heavy on authority, but light on persuasion, imagination and inspiration.

It has been said that tradition is not the worship of ashes, but the preservation of the fire that created the ashes. Too often the Church has worshipped ashes, while allowing the fire of the past to die out.

At the same time, the Catholic Church is still the place where I first met Jesus Christ. It is a place where I have met many inspiring people, whose example will remain with me always. There are still inspiring ceremonies that move my heart. I do not seek to harm that Church, but I passionately long to see it renewed in heart and soul, so that it may appeal to the imagination of all who come near it.

FACTORS OUTSIDE THE CHURCH

Apart from these defects within the Church, there are also deeper currents at work in society that are leading people away from all religious belief, for example:

- the immense attraction of science together with claims of a contradiction between science and religion
- claims of an opposition between worship of God and the promotion of human dignity and growth
- the rejection of fundamentalism, leading to a rejection of the Bible as a whole
- the rise in material prosperity in most places in the West, leading to a lessening of a perceived need for God
- the placing of the individual before the community
- the lack (in the words of Nietzsche) of a "taste" for religion in the modern world.

To leave out these factors and concentrate solely on problems within the Church is to present a distorted picture. It is to seize on the external and obvious and leave out the deeper currents beneath the surface.

THE BATTLE FOR THE IMAGINATION

Catholic people are affected by the secular currents all around them in their lives. They do not leave these secular ideas at the church door, but bring them with them right up to the altar.

The problems posed to the Church by the currents in society today must receive more than a negative response, a condemnation of a series of "-isms".

> UNFORTUNATELY, FOR too many people,
> the Church no longer seizes the imagination
> or attracts people to fall in love
> with the singer and his song.
>
> The Church must make choices,
> and the time for doing so is running out.
> If it is not done,
> the loss of the battle for the imagination
> could affect the Church for centuries.

CHAPTER 11
UNITY IN THE EUCHARIST

There is universal agreement that the Eucharist was meant to be something that both symbolised and brought about the unity of the followers of Jesus. And yet it has actually become both a cause and a symbol of disunity. At the time of the Reformation fierce battles were fought over it.

We might make progress if we adopted two principles:
- abandoning the language of the Reformation and seeking a new language to express a common faith, and
- limiting ourselves to a statement of those truths that are essential.

Mark, Matthew, Luke and Paul

The three gospels of Mark, Matthew and Luke and the First Letter of Paul to the Corinthians all give an account of the Last Supper. There are some differences between them, but all four have Jesus taking bread and saying, "This is my body"[35]. Then all four have Jesus taking the cup. Mark and Matthew have him saying, "This is my blood"[36], while Paul and Luke have, "This cup (is) the new covenant in my blood"[37].

If we are to find a statement of essential truths concerning the Eucharist, it seems that we must start with the phrases, "This is my body" and "This is my

---

35   Mark 14:22, Matthew 26:26, Luke 22:19.
36   Mark 14:24, Matthew 26:28.
37   Luke 22:20.

blood". They are the words of Jesus as recorded in three gospels and a letter of Paul and it would be very difficult to justify departing from them.

Chapter Six of John

Before drawing any conclusions, however, we must also include chapter six of the Gospel of John, which contains the great discourse on the "bread of life".

The chapter begins with two miraculous events, the multiplication of the loaves (1–15) and Jesus walking on the water (16–21). John rarely repeats material from the earlier three gospels, and yet he has these two stories and places them precisely here at the beginning of his treatment of the "bread of life". Surely it is significant that these two miracles show a) Jesus feeding a large crowd with a small amount of food, and b) the body of Jesus not subject to the ordinary laws of nature. These stories are a perfect introduction to the idea that the body of Jesus could itself become food for vast crowds of people. In the light of what follows, it seems impossible to ignore these messages contained in the two stories.

The discourse that follows has Jesus at first speaking of himself as the "bread that gives life" and the primary meaning would appear to be that of the message and person of Jesus as spiritual food for people. The objection raised by some of his hearers was that Jesus claimed that this bread had "come down from heaven" (42) and Jesus replied by reasserting his claim and saying that those who eat this bread "will never die" (48–50).

In verse 51 a distinct change comes over the passage, for the gospel tells us that Jesus then said:

> "I am the living bread
> that came down from heaven.
> Whoever eats of this bread
> will live forever;
> and the bread that I will give
> for the life of the world is my flesh."

This was a much more concrete and down-to-earth language, so the objection was equally concrete and down-to-earth:

> "How can he give us his flesh to eat?"

If someone gives a speech and the questions that follow show that the audience has completely misunderstood what the speaker intended, the questions become the opportunity for the speaker to correct this false understanding. That a speaker would not seize this opportunity with both hands and correct a false understanding of an essential and important matter is almost inconceivable.

So this was the perfect opportunity for Jesus to say, "Oh no, of course I don't mean actually eating my flesh. Let me explain the idea more clearly." Instead of this, over a period of five verses Jesus repeated the same message in the same concrete and graphic language. If he believed that the people had misunderstood him, his words did nothing to correct that misunderstanding, but served only to reinforce it strongly.

Furthermore, between v. 53 and v. 54 there is a change of verb. Up to v. 53 Jesus is reported as using the verb *phagein*, meaning "to eat", but in 54–58 he changes to the word *trogein*, a graphic and down-to-earth word having overtones of "to munch, to chew, to gnaw, to masticate". In other words, rather than draw back from his statement, Jesus actually became more graphic.

There was a second objection in v. 60:

> "This teaching is difficult; who can accept it?"
> But Jesus still did nothing to correct a misunderstanding. The crowd then moved from words to actions:
> "Because of this many of his disciples turned back and no longer went about with him."

A crowd was leaving him because of these graphic sayings about eating his flesh, and Jesus still did nothing to mitigate what he had said. He would not retract or explain away a single word. So Jesus asked the twelve, and said,

> "Do you also wish to go away?"

In the light of the significance of the two miracles of the loaves and the walking on water, and in the light of the manner in which the discourse develops, it is hard to avoid the conclusion that here John is strongly reinforcing the "is" of the accounts of the Last Supper in the other three gospels.

Body and Blood

The idea of blood adds a whole new dimension to the scene, for the body already contains blood, such that body and blood are not natural complements of each other, neither in our culture nor in the cultural world of first century Israel. The natural complements are flesh and blood, which together form a body, and John, in Chapter Six of his gospel, uses flesh and blood in this way. In speaking of "body" Jesus was giving us his whole body, his whole person, both flesh and blood, as our spiritual food. In then saying "this is my blood" Jesus was not adding a new physical element that was not present in the body, but was rather adding a new dimension of sacrifice, for blood separated from flesh signifies the body offered in sacrifice. For the Jewish people, blood was the life force of the person, and the shedding of blood was the giving of the life of the body. So the gift that Jesus gave to his followers in this banquet was not just a body, but a body offered in sacrifice.

The Essential Truth

My conclusion from all of this is that, in relation to the Eucharist, the essential truth must contain the word "is" and must reject the words "is not". To say only that the bread reminds us of the actions of Jesus at the Last Supper or that our eating of the bread is a symbol of our receiving the spiritual food that Jesus represents, would certainly seem to come under the heading of "is not" rather than "is". If Jesus had meant no more than this, we might confidently have expected him to correct the misunderstanding of his disciples. After the words of the Last Supper concerning both body and blood have been spoken over the bread, we must in some manner be able to say and mean, "This is the body of Jesus offered in sacrifice".

The question then arises, "In what manner is it the body of Jesus?" My response to this question is to say I understand why people ask this question, but the fact is that we not only do not know, but cannot know, the exact manner in which the bread and wine become the body of Jesus, and we must leave that to God. Surely this is a place for a proper humility rather than a claim of knowledge of divine mysteries.

Furthermore, is the answer to this question essential to our belief concerning the Eucharist? Is it not enough to say that the essential truth is that this 'is' the body of Jesus, and that everything else belongs to the field of the non-essential where freedom must prevail? If this means that there will be some diversity of views, does this matter as long as we agree on 'is' and reject 'is not'?"

If the idea of receiving the flesh of Jesus through our mouths seems offensive to some people, we need to remind ourselves that it is a gift of love, a desire by God to be so united to us that we become one. "What you eat today walks and talks tomorrow" says the old advertisement, and God wants to be so united with us that God becomes part of what walks and talks in us. If the story seems offensive to us, there is the danger that this is because the love it shows is too much for us.

There is one further step we must take and it is best illustrated by a story.

A liberal-minded Catholic priest visited a retreat centre run by a Protestant church. Being liberal, he attended a communion service. He found that the celebrant was a woman, but being liberal, he was easily able to accommodate this. The celebrant used an ordinary loaf of bread for the Eucharist, and again his liberal mind could accept this. After the ceremony, however, he saw that the portion of the loaf not consumed at communion was taken to the kitchen, sliced up and put into the toaster for breakfast, and at that moment even his very liberal Catholic soul rebelled.[38]

His response was visceral before it was intellectual ("She's burning Jesus!"). It seemed to him at this point that the celebrant was saying loudly and clearly, "This is not the body of Jesus".

Even if we leave aside all questions about what the celebrant intended, a further question arises: Are there things that in a united Christian church we should not do because they would be seriously offensive to the sensitivities of others?

I am, of course, aware that many Protestants react in the same visceral manner to the word "transubstantiation". At best this word is an attempt to express a human understanding of a divine mystery in the words of a particular philosophy. There is a long and bitter history of conflict around the word. It seems quite impossible to claim that it expresses an essential truth.

Should we reject both a purely symbolic understanding on the one hand and words such as "transubstantiation" on the other hand? In rejecting these two extremes, can we not leave the rest to God? Is there anything that it is truly *essential* to add to the words, "This is the body of Jesus", provided we genuinely mean "is" rather than "is not"?

---

38 Geoffrey Plant, *Tell Me a Story*, Harper Collins Religious, Melbourne, 2000, p. 83.

CHAPTER 12
LIFE TO THE FULL

KEY WORDS

At the heart of ecumenical discussion today about the Church are three terms used in the New Testament[39], two coming from St Paul, the other used frequently in the gospels by Jesus himself.

Mysterion

The first word is *mysterion*. It is usually translated as "mystery", but this is misleading, for the word "mystery" implies something that is obscure and even unknowable. As St Paul uses the word, however, it is not simply a Greek word whose meaning comes largely from the Greek mystery religions, but rather an inadequate Greek translation of Hebrew concepts with its meaning coming from the Old Testament. Understood in this way, the *mysterion* of which Paul speaks is a vast sacred reality produced by God's power and revealed by God in the very act of bringing it about. It refers to God's eternal plan for the whole world, first revealed in the Old Testament, then in Christ. This eternal plan of God, rather than being unintelligible, can be said to be of "inexhaustible

---

39   In the presentation that follows I acknowledge my debt to Charles Hill, *Mystery of Life, A Theology of Church*, Collins Dove, Melbourne, 1990. I have, however, taken his ideas in my own directions and drawn my own conclusions, and so take responsibility for what I have written.

intelligibility"[40]. Our difficulty with the idea comes less from its unintelligibility and more from its sheer magnitude. To translate the word as "mystery" and thus place the accent on the obscure and unknowable, is to miss the point made by Paul: that in Christ, God has revealed this eternal plan.

Paul sensed the groaning of all creation for fulfilment (Rom 8:1922) and saw this as a reflection of God's eternal plan seeking its fulfilment. To express this concept he used words such as "mysterion", "wisdom", "purpose" and "will" as being almost interchangeable.

> ... this grace was given to me ... to make everyone see what is the plan of the mysterion hidden for ages in God who created all things; so that through the Church the wisdom of God in its rich variety might now be made known to the rulers and authorities in the heavenly places. This was in accordance with the eternal purpose that he has carried out in Christ Jesus our Lord. (Eph 3:811)[41]

Koinonia

This term has been traditionally translated into English by Protestants as "fellowship" and by Catholics as "communion". In other European languages "communion" has been more common and it is the translation now used in ecumenical dialogue.

Koinos means "common", and *koinonia* means a sharing or participation or fellowship in something. It means "to make common to others what is personal to oneself". It is always God who initiates *koinonia* by making common to us in Christ what is personal to God, and we are then invited to share this gift with others. What belonged to God alone and which was then shared with us in Jesus Christ was "life to the full" (Jn 10:10). To speak of the Church as having *koinonia* refers, therefore, to the work of sharing with others God's gift of life to the full.

Koinonia and *mysterion* go together, for God gives us "life to the full" through a sharing in the *mysterion*, the eternal plan. Just as *mysterion* is larger than Church, so is *koinonia*. This is because the whole world, and indeed the whole of creation, is called to share in the "life to the full" that comes from God.

Basileia

In the four gospels the term *mysterion* occurs only once (Mk 4:1 1) and the term *koinonia* does not occur at all. Instead, we find on the lips of Jesus the frequent use of the term *basileia*[42]. It is usually translated as "kingdom", but the

---

40   John O'Grady, *Models of Jesus*, Image Books, Garden City, 1981, p. 22.
41   Cf. Romans 16:2527; 1 Corinthians 2:78; Colossians 1:22-28.
42   Only five times in John, but over a hundred times in the four gospels.

translation is misleading. As in the case of *mysterion*, the meaning of *basileia* must be taken not simply from the Greek but from the Hebrew meanings behind the Greek. On the lips of Jesus, the word *basileia* does not refer to a place but to an activity, not to a kingdom but to a kingly rule, for Jesus did not come to found a kingdom, but to implement a kingly rule based on the values of justice and love.

In Mark's Gospel, Jesus first announces his presence with these words:

"The time is fulfilled, and the kingdom of God has come near." (Mk 1:15)

In Jesus, God's kingly rule was present in a new way and with a greater immediacy, but the fullness of that rule was still to come. The kingly rule had "come near", but it was not fully present because Jesus had not yet died and risen again, and because the kingly rule of which Jesus spoke exists only when it is accepted. Mark develops the idea that acceptance of God's kingly rule has the meaning of acceptance by each individual of the seeming contradiction of the suffering son of man and the glorious son of God, the Messiah and the Suffering Servant. When taken together, these two very different ideas constitute a deep spiritual reality and acceptance of this reality can occur only within the hearts of individuals, so that the kingly rule of God never exists on this earth as some sort of external reality outside the hearts of individuals. It follows that the growth of God's *basileia* cannot simply be identified with the external growth of the Church, both because it is something that exists within human hearts and because the *basileia* of God is broader than the Church and extends to the whole world and the whole of creation.

Connecting the three

In terms of the three words we have been considering, Jesus issued an invitation to share in God's eternal plan *(mysterion)* of life to the full *(koinonia)* through God's kingly rule *(basileia)* within the hearts of human beings.

Baptism is the conscious acceptance of *mysterion/koinonia/basileia*, a conscious will to share in this sacred reality, and the Church is the community of those who have taken this step. The three Greek terms, however, are all broader than the term "church", and there are several conclusions that we must draw.

Firstly, Catholics, Orthodox and Protestants have all equally accepted the sacred realities of *mysterion*, *koinonia* and *basileia*. These terms are now at the centre of all ecumenical dialogue as the common foundation on which Christian unity is to be built[43]. Without minimising the many and serious

---

43   Cf. *Church as Communion: an Agreed Statement by ARCIC II*, Catholic Truth Society, 1991.

differences that still exist, an adequate notion of church must include all those who through the one baptism have accepted these sacred realities. In this sense the one church of Christ already exists and always has existed in a real but not complete *koinonia*. As St Augustine said,

> Whether they like it or not, they are our brothers and sisters, and they will only cease to be our brothers and sisters if they cease to say "Our Father".[44]

Secondly, God's eternal plan, sharing of life and kingly rule are for the whole world and the whole of creation. It follows that the Church is not the goal of its own strivings; this goal is the kingly rule of God in its fullness. The Church exists for the sake of the world and is at the service of the world. As Johannes Metz has put it, God is concerned with the world, not really with the Church as different from the world[45].

A number of Christian writers still seem to reflect a dualism between church and world, sacred and secular. Dietrich Bonhoeffer spoke strongly of the consequences of this dualism.

> *The attack by Christian apologetic upon the adulthood of the world I consider to be in the first place pointless, in the second ignoble and in the third un-Christian*[46] ...
> *The place of religion is taken by the Church... but the world is made to depend upon itself and left to its own devices, and that is all wrong.*[47]

Other writers speak of a "churchianity"[48] that turns in upon itself and does not sufficiently look out to the world. The Church is not primarily an institution or an experience of ritual and worship or a belief system. It is primarily an offer of life to the whole world and the whole cosmos. If it is not this, it is failing in its task.

Thirdly, the images that we find in the parables of Jesus are not directly images of the Church, but images of the kingly rule of God ("The kingly rule of God is like ..."). The parables speak directly, not of the Church, but of God's eternal plan of life to the full through a kingly rule of justice and love within the hearts of human beings, and the Church is only a means to implement this plan. The Church must always remain at the service of this greater reality.

Fourthly, in all three terms the first action lies with God: it is God's eternal plan, God's sharing of life and God's kingly rule. The Church is always

---

44 St Augustine, Commentary on Psalm 32, The Divine Office, Vol. III, Tuesday, Week 14.
45 Johannes Metz, *Theology of the World*, Herder and Herder, New York, 1969, p. 50, note 51.
46 Dietrich Bonhoeffer, *Letters and Papers from Prison*, Fontana, London, 1953, p. 108.
47 ibid., p.95.
48 Ccf. Edmund Flood, *Work and the Gospel*, . The Tablet, May 4 May 1991, pp. 538540.

responding to God's action rather than acting on its own and it must always be contemplating the wonder and inexhaustible intelligibility of God's action. As Paul expressed it,

> To *God who is able to strengthen you ... according to the revelation of the* mysterion *that was kept secret for long ages but is now disclosed ... to the only wise God, through Jesus Christ, be the glory forever. Amen. (Rom 16:2527)*

CONFUSION OF TERMS

The Non-Ordained

The Greek word λαός (*laós*), meaning 'people', expresses a common element shared by all members of the Church. The Latin term *laici* (laypersons) was derived from the term *laós*, but in the process came to refer only to those who were not clerics (*Lumen Gentium* no. 31). *Laós* expresses a positive concept, *laici* expresses a negative concept.

As an analogy, we can say that all people are citizens of their own country. Most are also civilians, but this latter term is both negative and relative: it is negative because it really means "non-military"; it is relative because it has a meaning only in relation to the military. Some rights and obligations flow from being a civilian, but the major rights and duties of any individual flow from being a citizen, and the negative and relative term "civilian" cannot express the whole reality of those who do not belong to the military. In a similar way, the term "laypersons", which is also negative and relative, cannot express the whole reality of those in the Church who are not clerics.

It must always be remembered that the first meaning of the word "laypersons" is "non-clerics". The full effect of the word would become apparent if we went through Vatican documents substituting "non-clerics" every time we found the words "laypersons" or "laity". It would often become evident that the basic perspective of the document was a clerical one, just as we would immediately be aware that a document had a military perspective if it continually referred to the vast majority of the members of a particular society as civilians. In such documents the clergy or the military are the basic point of reference for everything in the document, and everything revolves around them.

There are times when it is legitimate for the military to refer to civilians, or for doctors or lawyers to refer to laypersons (i.e. non-doctors or non-lawyers), and there will be times when it is legitimate for clerics to refer to laypersons (non-clerics), but if the term is used constantly, if it is the normal term, we know that we are meeting a military or medical or legal or clerical outlook on life.

Furthermore, the terms tend to be elitist and discriminatory, denying the essential contribution of, for example, army reservists in relation to the military, nurses in relation to doctors, law clerks in relation to lawyers and religious in relation to clerics. There are also such things as the citizen's concern for the defence of the country, first aid and care of the sick in the home, the concern of people to know the law and obey it in driving a car or filling in a tax form, and the marvellous variety of particular charisms that exist within the Church. In such perspectives, "laypersons" become an amorphous mass, their special talents and possible contributions are not recognised and, inevitably, their full potential will never be realised.

To see this more clearly, take the perspective of another sacrament, that of Marriage[49]. From this perspective we may refer to the married and the unmarried in the Church. Almost all clerics would come under the heading of the unmarried, but would rightly object if this became the dominant perspective and the normal language, for they would say that to class them simply as unmarried does not do justice to their role in the life of the Church and does not allow their full potential to be realised.

In light of the vision of Church given to us by the Second Vatican Council, the sacrament that should determine the dominant perspective must surely be neither Marriage nor Orders, but Baptism. A document working from this Perspective of Baptism would speak of Christians or *Christifideles* (Christ's faithful) throughout, for these are the two positive words that can be used of all members of the Church. In speaking about them, the document would eventually begin to speak about different groups. On the basis of gender it would speak about women and men; on the basis of age it would speak of the old and the young; on the basis of marriage it would speak about the married and the unmarried; on the basis of orders it would speak about clerics and non-clerics; on the basis of religious profession of the evangelical counsels it would speak about religious and those who are not religious, and it would give each group its proper importance, neither denigrating nor underestimating the role and contribution of that group.

The Sacrament of Orders creates three categories of action in the Church: 1) There are actions that require the Sacrament of Orders and are reserved to clerical members of Christ's faithful (the *Christifideles clerici*), such as celebrating Mass; 2) There are actions that are forbidden to clerics and which are performed only by those members of Christ's faithful who are not clerics (the *Christifideles laici*), such as those standing for election to parliament; 3) There are actions that

---

[49] Cf. Teresa Pirola, *Laity A Block to the Mission of the Church*, Australasian Catholic Record, October 1989, p. 425.

are neither reserved nor forbidden to clerics and are performed equally by all members – *Christifideles* or Christ's faithful, whether clerical or lay.

This last category is a rich one, containing much of the work of the Church but, because it is neither specifically referring to the lay or the clerical, there is the danger that it can at times be forgotten. We can speak of clerical roles (things reserved to the clergy) and lay roles (things reserved to the laity) and leave out the rich field that is common to both. Thus, a Church document should never use the term "laypersons" when it is referring to an activity that is common to all members of Christ's faithful and is neither reserved nor forbidden to clerics, such as working cefor peace.[50]

These distinctions underline the difficulty of attempting to define laypersons by means of their "secularity" or involvement "in the world"[51], as though laypersons are in the world but clerics are not. This leads to many anomalies: for example, contemplative nuns would have to be considered as "in the world" because they are not clerics, but a married deacon who works in a factory throughout the week would have to be considered as not "in the world" because he is a cleric. At best this is an unusual and forced understanding of the word "world", and it appears to be a dangerous basis on which to build a theology.

It is not possible to give a positive definition of the essentially negative term "laity". It is the perspective, not the definition that must change.

Assigning the sacred to clerics and the secular to the laity comes too close to identifying the sacred with actions reserved for clerics and the secular with actions forbidden to clerics, while leaving out altogether the actions common to both. While it is often legitimate to speak of sacred and secular things, a complete separation between the two must be avoided. Spiritual and temporal, sacred and secular, church and world, faith and life – all constitute the one reality created by God, and they interpenetrate and complement each other. If Christ's faithful are to integrate their faith into their lives, a dualism between sacred and secular must be avoided, for all Christ's faithful without exception live "in the world", that is, in a world that is both sacred and secular. As Pope Paul V1 said, "The whole Church has an authentic secular dimension."[52] This

---

50   Cf., for example, the Post-Synodal Apostolic Exhortation *Christifideles Laici* of His Holiness John Paul II on the Vocation and Mission of the Lay Faithful in the Church and in the World, December 30, 1988, n. 42: "The lay faithful cannot remain indifferent ... in the face of all that denies and compromises peace ... On the contrary ... the lay faithful ought to take upon themselves the task of being 'peacemakers'." But surely all members of Christ's faithful have this duty equally and there is nothing specifically 'lay' about it.

51   ibid., n. 15.

52   Pope Paul VI, Talk to the Members of Secular Institutes, February 2, 1972, AAS 64 (1972), p. 208.

approach is important if the Church is to fulfil its role of offering life to the full to the whole cosmos.

Religious

It is generally agreed that the document on religious life issued by the Second Vatican Council, while it contains valuable insights, was not the most radical document of that Council. Despite this, the Council had a profound and radical effect on religious life. It did this by what it said about the Church rather than by what it said about religious life.

In *Lumen Gentium* the Council spoke of the universal call to holiness, and in *Gaudium et Spes* it spoke of the involvement of the Church in the world. For religious, these two foundational statements of the Second Vatican Council were an earthquake that destroyed the two pillars on which religious life was then built. Before the Council there was an assumption that all Christians were called to goodness, but that those who sought true holiness should enter a religious order. The universal call to holiness destroyed this pillar. There was a second assumption that those who sought holiness should come apart from the world and devote themselves entirely to the things of God. The call to an involvement in the world destroyed this pillar. It is small wonder that religious entered a period of intense turmoil.

Despite this, it was recognised that religious life was still a valid option and that it had much to contribute to the life of the Church. It is the hope of many that the aftershocks of the earthquake have now begun to die away and that a process of rebuilding can begin. But this rebuilding will involve a rethinking from the ground up and the juridical categories of clerical, lay and religious may well not survive the process. The juridical categories have long had their problems, for congregations such as the Vincentians have common life but no vows, while secular institutes have vows but no common life. Many other, and newer, experiments have been tried in recent years.

It is here that I have found an American theologian, Sandra Schneiders, most helpful[53]. She speaks of a dominant perspective that people can have in their lives. People interested in football or politics or the environment can have this as a dominant perspective from which they see all reality. A journalist can go through life seeing everything in terms of possible headlines, while a businessman can see all reality in terms of possible profits.

Schneiders makes the very basic statement that religious are first and foremost those who are concerned with religion, that is, those whose dominant perspective on life is a religious one.

In this sense, no one would have to join an organisation in order to be

---

53 Sandra M Schneiders IHM, *New Wineskins, Re-Imagining Religious Life Today*, Paulist Press, New York, 1986.

a religious, and married persons could be religious, for there is no necessary conflict between marriage and a dominant religious perspective. Traditional forms of consecrated religious life would become valuable and legitimate forms of living out the dominant religious perspective, but not the only forms. The particular form of commitment a person should adopt would be an individual choice. The essential element would be the desire to live out the dominant religious perspective to the best of one's ability, and the juridical categories would have to be broadened to accommodate a far greater variety of religious life.

It must also be noted that being a religious in the sense used here is no guarantee whatsoever of holiness, for religious fanatics and exponents of "churchianity" also have a dominant religious perspective. There are true religious perspectives and false ones, and either can be a dominant perspective. Those who wished to live a true religious life would have to find a way to distance themselves, not from those sometimes called "lay people", but rather from those with false religious perspectives.

IDEOLOGIES

Dictionaries generally give the word "ideology" a first meaning of "the science of ideas" or "the political or social philosophy of a nation, movement or group", but invariably add a second meaning of "abstract or fanciful theorising", "dealing with ideas rather than facts", or "occupied with ideas of an unpractical nature". I suggest that this second meaning has, in the modern world, become the dominant meaning.

In this section I shall understand the word "ideology" to mean a situation where an individual or a whole society starts with an idea or theory and then seeks to force the facts to fit this idea, rather than starting with the facts and then deriving ideas and theories from the facts.

It is obvious that most prejudices are based on one form or another of ideology, where facts are forced to fit a theory. Even in most relationships between men and women, ideologies are powerfully at work.

Adolf Hitler started from the idea that the Aryan people were superior to all other people such as Jews or Gypsies, so these latter could be exterminated, and the Aryans had entitlements to land that no other people possessed. He avoided giving gold medals to black athletes such as Jesse Owens at the 1936 Berlin Olympics, because the inconvenient fact of their victories did not fit his ideas. Fifty-five million people died before this ideology had run its course.

There were strong elements of ideology also in Communism, for example that everything in any society derives from economic considerations, or that "the Party" was the seat of all wisdom and had to be given unquestioning obedience. Nearly one hundred million died because of these ideologies.

All societies need to be alert to ideologies that arise and seek to deal with them before they cause great harm.

Religious Beliefs and Ideologies

Religion has always been a fertile source of ideologies, for its most basic beliefs come from faith rather than from scientifically proven facts. The most basic belief of all, the very existence of God, is a faith belief rather than a scientifically proven fact. Reason can at best give us indications, not proofs, of whether we should believe in God or not. Whether one then actually believes will usually depend on two factors more than anything else: i) one's own personal life history, and ii) whether one *wants* to believe. It is all too easy for ideologies to enter into this process.

We should note, however, that both religious belief and atheism are equally faith beliefs, for the existence of God can neither be proven nor disproven by scientific enquiry. Atheism is, therefore, equally as open to spawning ideologies, as is shown by the history of Nazism and Communism.

Rather than start with yet another ideology – that all religion is bad and should be abolished – we should respect religion but seek to deal with any and all ideologies that arise within it.

Wahhabist Islam

One of the major difficulties in dealing with extremist Islam today is precisely that it is an ideology more than a religion.

There is no basis for saying that God hates all religions other than Islam, or that it is legitimate to kill members of other religions. These are simply ideas without basis, and the facts are then forced to fit the idea. It is virtually impossible to have a rational conversation with people who hold such ideas. The people who piloted the planes into the World Trade Centre in 2009 acted out of an ideology rather than a fact-based belief.

Christian Fundamentalism

The idea that God wrote every word of the Bible, that every word must be taken literally, and that the Bible contains the answer to every possible question, are again ideas that come before the facts and cannot be reconciled with them. An ideology rather than a faith is at work here and again it is impossible to have a serious conversation with people who hold such ideas.

Catholic Ideologies

In recent years it has been obvious that the two subjects within the Catholic Church that have been most controversial are power and sex. Between them they have led to more arguments and opposition than all other subjects combined.

In both cases it seems to me that we are dealing with an ideology: where the idea has no serious basis, comes before the facts and dictates to the facts.

In relation to sex, the idea is that every single act of sexual intercourse between human beings must, by divine will, be open to the birth of a child, and if it is not, then that intercourse is mortally sinful. It is hard to see this idea as founded in reality. How can we possibly know that this is God's express will? It seems to be a clear example of a situation where the idea comes first, and the facts are then forced to fit it. In many cases the facts do not fit the idea and can be made to do so only by violence. It is no wonder that arguments on this subject seem to go round and round in circles and lead nowhere.

All ideas based on what is seen as the "specific nature" of either men or women are also in grave danger of becoming ideologies.

The same is true in relation to power. Here the idea that comes before the facts is that Jesus Christ gave all authority within the Church to one individual, the Pope. The loss of temporal power in 1870 led almost immediately to a search for spiritual power through the idea of infallibility, even though the arguments for infallibility were weak.

I suggest that the Catholic Church must look at its teachings across the board to see how many other examples there might be of ideologies. The pursuit of God's eternal plan of life to the full through the kingly rule of God within the heart and mind can never be successful if it is based on ideologies, that is, unsupported ideas that ignore facts.

CHAPTER 13
"THAT THEY MAY ALL BE ONE"

There are certain principles that would seem essential if significant progress is to be made towards Christian unity.

1. The Essential Foundation of All Christian Unity Must Be a Profound Humility before God

As the third millennium begins, we must ask of all Christian churches more humility, more modesty in the claims that are made, more recognition of human weakness, more understanding of what human beings have done to a divine message, more awareness of the limitations of all human words, and more recognition of mystery in all things to do with God. We must call for an admission that all Christian churches have been too ready to give definite answers to too many questions (some more than others, true, and yet all have been guilty). We must call for an emphasis on the fact that the constant and sincere search for God is more important than the necessarily imperfect statements about God we may come across.

We must also call for the abandonment of all external signs of a Christian Empire and a return to the humble service shown by Jesus.

If the next two thousand years are to be superior to the last two thousand, they absolutely must begin with a far greater humility. This is the first principle because it is the essential starting point. Without it there will be no progress.

2. Only When All Present Churches Seek to Be United with Jesus Christ Can They Truly Be United with Each Other in the One Christian Church

It is possible for the present churches to come to an intellectual agreement on many matters of belief, and some good progress has been made in this field. It is possible for them to study the Bible together and draw from this common source. It is possible for them all to obey basically the same moral rules. It is possible for them to worship together in ecumenical services. And it is possible for the churches to work together on many practical matters such as assistance to those in need or global warming.

If all our efforts were concentrated on agreements in these areas, however, we would never come to Christian unity, for Christian unity must ultimately be spiritual unity. This means that there must be a conscious effort on the part of each church to be united with Jesus Christ at a profound spiritual level, for only in him do we have any hope of being united with each other.

To some people this may seem nothing more than the pious language that churches all too frequently use, but it is essential. No present church will ever achieve perfect unity with Jesus Christ, but it must be a goal towards which we seriously strive. There will never be Christian unity unless it is first and foremost a spiritual unity in Jesus Christ.

3. True Unity Must Include Unity in the Eucharist

At one end of the spectrum of what might be called Christian unity is the present situation in which all our differences of belief, practice and attitude remain, but we are by and large far more friendly towards one another than in the past and we work together on certain projects. In the past, followers of Jesus have hated and made war on each other, so our current level of unity is not to be despised. But is it enough of a response to the prayer of Jesus at the Last Supper: "That they may all be one"?

At the other end of the spectrum of what might be called *Christian unity* is the unity that involves a high degree of agreement in belief and practice and which is organised around some form of human authority structure, whatever that structure may be.

There is much room between these two poles. True unity worthy of the name must be more than doing things together, but it does not necessarily involve complete agreement on every detail of belief and dogma.

The most important point is surely that true unity must in some manner participate in the organic unity of a body, or a family, in which life is being mutually communicated throughout. In practice this will not happen without unity in the central act of worship of the Christian people, the Eucharist, through which Christian people throughout the world communicate life to each other because they first receive that life from Christ. This level of unity must be the minimum goal of Christian unity.

4. At Some Point in the Future, Full Christian Unity Will Require that All Present Churches Become Part of a New Church that Does Not at Present Exist

There is no practical possibility that one present church will prevail and all other present churches will simply say, "You were right in all things and we were wrong, so we will cease to exist and join you." We must acknowledge that the Church of Jesus Christ is greater than all of us.

For many years there was an Australian Council of Churches to which the Catholic Church did not belong. After some years of the ecumenical movement, the Catholic Church indicated that it would be interested in belonging. Rather than invite the Catholic Church to join the Council as it existed, the Council voted to open a dialogue in which all churches would together found a new body and the old Council would then go out of existence. This sensitivity was greatly appreciated and avoided many problems. The same sensitivity would greatly assist Christian unity as a whole.

All churches need to say: "Christian unity is greater than any of us. Through humility, prayer and dialogue we will together seek to find the shape and structure of the church and then we will all join it."

5. We Must Want Unity and Believe It Is Possible

Within our own particular church there are many familiar things that give each of us much comfort and inspiration. We have learned where to find beautiful things and how to come to terms with elements that are less beautiful. And we do not want to change more within ourselves than we have to. There is a need, therefore, for each of us to convince ourselves of the need for Christian unity. Otherwise, why should we expend all that energy?

The first answer to this question is that, despite the great progress that has been made, it would be foolish to think that all is at peace between the present churches. History has not been forgotten. The hurts and bitter wars of the past are still present in the hearts of many people, there is still prejudice and anger, and there are still strong disagreements over many issues.

The second reason why we should spend energy on uniting all Christian churches as one church is that a divided church will inevitably be marginal and irrelevant to life in the third millennium. All forms of religious belief are under severe pressure, and in these circumstances divisions between Christians are a luxury we simply cannot afford. If Christians cannot agree among themselves, why should others listen to any of us?

The third answer is that Jesus himself desired a profound unity, so that the world might know that he came from God. Full unity is not an option for Christians, it is a binding and pressing duty.

If we are to achieve unity, we must want it. We must want it passionately; we must hunger and thirst for it. We must also be prepared to sacrifice things in our own church that are not essential, no matter how much we cherish them. If we approach unity with anything less than this attitude, we cannot hope to succeed.

We must also believe it is possible, that we can make the impossible happen. We must never be so satisfied with our own church that we see no need to reach out to any other. We must feel the lack of unity acutely.

6. We Must Accept an Imperfect Church

Within each of the Christian churches there is both ugliness and beauty. People who cannot see the ugliness are refusing to see what is before their eyes. People who cannot see the beauty do not really know their churches or live their lives within them. When the Christian churches are ugly, they are very ugly indeed and the world turns away in disgust from the pride, greed, ambition and cruelty that seem to abound. But within them there is also a beauty that can take the breath away, renew faith in human nature, and fill us with joy.

The beauty exists because it is inspired by the example of Jesus Christ; the ugliness exists because the beautiful message of Jesus was given into the hands of weak human beings.

Any church will always be made up of human beings, so Christian unity does not mean that all ugliness will disappear forever. It does not mean creating an ethereal church that is not of this world. It does not mean excommunicating everyone who is not perfect. A church of nothing but beauty will never exist in this world. In the past there have been elitist churches that set very high standards for their members and enforced them rigorously, but it can be argued that such churches were even more prone to hypocrisy than others.

If all the present churches are to become the one Christian church, there must be room within that one church for the weak as well as the strong, for the sinner as well as the saint. There must be room for the thief and the liar, even the murderer, paedophile and hypocrite. Jesus warned us that stone-throwing is a dangerous exercise. Those people who would only consider joining a perfect church will be forever disappointed.

If an intense desire for spiritual unity with Jesus Christ is an essential element of Christian unity, this must be balanced by the necessity for a church that is open to all, where we accept that the ugliness and the beauty will always exist side by side, and where we work hard to overcome the ugliness and enhance the beauty.

7. We Must Look Inwards Only so that We May Better Look Outwards

There is always the grave danger that any talk of Christian unity, and hence of the beliefs, practices or structures of the churches, will turn the attention of Christian people inwards towards their own present churches and their own concerns. Yet the very essence of the Christian faith is that it should be reaching out to the whole world and God's eternal plan (*mysterion*) of life in all its fullness (*koinonia*) through the reign of God (*basileia*) within the hearts of people. The only legitimate reason for looking inwards at ourselves is so that we may better look outwards.

Reform of a church can become an all-consuming topic that takes up the energies of many people, especially of those most involved with that one unified church. It can take up so much energy that there is little energy left to reach out to the world.

It is important that, whenever two or three Christians begin to discuss reform and Christian unity, they make sure they begin and end with some discussion of how they can reach out to the world, listen to the world, learn from the world and help the world. They must not be guilty of turning the Christian world inwards upon itself, for this would be a denial of its own essential being.

8. The Whole Church Must Be Involved in the Search for Christian Unity

At the Council of Ferrara-Florence (1438-1445) many of those present believed that they had resolved all the differences between the Catholic and Orthodox Churches and that full union could take place immediately. When they attempted to put this into practice, however, the leaders discovered that they had left the members of their churches behind and the council was angrily rejected by the people on the streets of Constantinople. This reminds us that the word "church" does not mean only leaders such as popes, bishops or moderators; it means a gathering, an assembly, a people of God. Christian unity cannot be agreed by a few leaders or a few experts in theology. It must involve all members of the churches involved.

This will require that very serious effort be put into keeping people informed of all developments and seeking their agreement to each step that is taken towards unity. It will include the difficult task of making every effort to express complex and subtle religious truths in the simplest possible language.

9. Christian Unity Will Require Serious Study by All Christians

There is a widespread popular movement that considers progress towards Christian unity to be glacially slow and believes that, if fair-minded people sat down together, they could solve all problems in one session and reach immediate unity. We should have at least some sympathy for this position, in so far as the prison of the past, the inability to look at matters with fresh eyes, is probably the greatest obstacle to Christian unity. We must add, however, that a unity that is achieved too easily can just as quickly dissolve again. Unity must be based on profound truth and the search for truth can be arduous and painful.

Every single Christian person must be asked to go beneath the surface of the questions that arise and study them as profoundly as is possible in the different circumstances of each individual. This will, of course, provide different insights for different people, but the questions are serious and they deserve serious answers. We are talking about nothing less than the direction the Christian churches should take in the third millennium, and that is not to be determined by casual or superficial answers. This process will not be easy, and following are some of the reasons why:

- There is a long history behind most religious differences and many people will explore the questions with their own preconceived ideas and will not want to change.
- In today's world there are many factors that militate against a serious study of any question by a whole community. This is made more difficult by community ideas frequently being based on feelings rather than on careful thought.
- There is today a widespread expectation and insistence that even the most profound and complex questions be given an instant and simple answer before a television camera.
- The democracy with which people are familiar counts only the number of votes cast, not the level of thinking behind each vote, with the consequent desire to move to a vote long before the issues are fully understood.
- There is a strong tendency today to launch a personal attack on opponents rather than present the arguments for one's own case clearly.
- It is easier to manipulate public opinion by playing on fears than by presenting rational arguments.

So strong are these factors that many people will say it is impossible to have a serious community discussion on anything as esoteric as religion. Despite these many powerful factors, serious study by the whole community is essential. No matter how many people tell us it is impossible, we must prove them wrong.

If the eighth principle means that religious leaders must make every effort to express thoughts clearly and simply and to include all members of their churches in the discussions, this ninth principle means that the members of the churches, for their part, must be prepared to go well beyond their present comfort zones and seek to understand the issues involved to the very best of their ability.

10. We Must Abandon all Gratuitous Assumptions

To base faith on gratuitous assumptions is to place an absolute barrier in the way of Christian unity, for one cannot seriously demand that others share these assumptions. It is, for example, nothing more than a gratuitous assumption that the Bible contains the immediate and simple answer to every religious and moral question we ask, and that our only task is to find the right page.

11. We Must Go Behind the Language of Division

There are certain words and phrases (for example "transubstantiation") that, because of the long and bitter history behind them, arouse instant and strong feelings. The only possible way forward is to banish entirely the words themselves from all discussions, and to discuss the issue in other words that do not have the same history of use.

This was the agreement between the Pope and the Archbishop of Canterbury when the official dialogue between the Anglican and Roman Catholic Churches was first established, and by and large it has worked very well. This process should be used in all dialogues between individual churches on all subjects.

12. In Condemning a Perceived Error, We Must Be Careful Not to Condemn a Truth it Contains

People do not embrace an error because it is an error, but because they see a truth in it. God alone sees the whole truth, while we see only parts of the truth. Because of our limitations, our personal history and our feelings, we can be led to see truth in something that also contains error. For example, people did not become communists because they believed it to be an error, but because they saw the truth and beauty of the vision of a classless society in which each would contribute according to ability and receive according to need.

Throughout Christian history there have been examples of misunderstandings when one church condemned what it perceived to be an error of another church, while the other saw only the condemnation of a truth that was important to them. An example of this is the question of justification at the time of the Reformation, when Protestants thought that Catholics saw salvation entirely as a matter of their own efforts, with little role for God, while Catholics thought that Protestants were asking God to do our work for us, with no need for any effort on our part.

In seeking Christian unity, we should always do everything in our power to discover and appreciate to the full the truth that other churches see in any statements they make. We must be very careful to avoid seeing condemnation of a truth as being synonymous with pointing out an error.

13. Whenever Strong Feelings Prevent a Resolution of a Controverted Issue, the Two Sides Need to Listen to Each Other's Story

In trying hard to be a good monk, Martin Luther was tormented by what he saw as the impossibility of constant right action before a judgemental God and developed his ideas on justification by faith alone as a response to this. It is a sad fact that, if only someone from Rome had actually taken the trouble to travel to Germany, sit down with Luther and listen sympathetically to his personal story, the Reformation may have taken a different course.

Within the Anglican Communion there is intense conflict over the issue of homosexuality, with the Americans leading the movement for change and the Africans the resistance. In this controversy it has been largely forgotten that it was Western missionaries who brought the Christian faith to Africa and, having attracted converts with the beauty of the story of Jesus, then told those converts that homosexual acts were one of the worst of all sins. The king of Uganda demanded that his male Christian slaves submit to sex with him, but they followed the teaching given to them by the Westerners and died brutal deaths as martyrs rather than submit. Now the same Westerners are telling the Africans that homosexual acts are not sinful and the martyrs died for nothing. If there is ever to be a calm study of the scriptural evidence, both sides need to be extremely sensitive to this story.

I remember a time when a little girl of four stood in front of me and stared at me with the intensity that only a small child can have. Eventually I gave a little wave and said, "hello", and she replied, "When I grow up, you'll be dead." Her mother came over and explained that her own father had recently died, and the girl was coming to terms with the idea that people grow old and die. To her I was very old, so she was simply stating facts. Often things make sense only when we know the story behind them.

Behind all beliefs, whether of an individual or a community, there is a story, and the belief can never be divorced from the story. If we wish to understand a belief, we must know the story that led to that belief.

I can argue with the ideas of others, but I cannot argue with their psychological needs, and often their ideas will have come from their psychological needs and cannot be separated from them.

14. We Must Constantly Seek the Middle Way

Whenever there is a bitter dispute between two groups of people, there is a tendency for each group to be driven to the extreme of its own position and to adopt the rhetoric of that extreme. This happened between the Christian churches at the time of the break between East and West in the eleventh century and at the time of the Reformation in the sixteenth century. There is also the tendency to react against one extreme by going to the opposite extreme. For example, there was always a danger of answering the Protestant "Scripture alone" with a Catholic "pope alone", and now Catholic theologians admit that one of the great fruits of the Second Vatican Council was to bring the Scriptures back to the centre of the Catholic Church. We must constantly seek the middle way.

15. There is No Christian Who Does Not Need to Change

A statement that can be made with total certainty is that, if Christian unity is to be achieved, every single present church will have to change and every single individual within every single church will have to change. The Pope of Rome, the Patriarch of Constantinople and the Archbishop of Canterbury will all have to change in many ways.

Every Christian must say, "The Christian faith is far greater than my understanding. I do not have all the answers, I do not possess the whole truth, I am not fully united with Jesus Christ. The work of Christian unity must take me beyond myself into something higher than I have ever experienced before. I must be open to change in my thinking, my feeling and my way of relating to God and to other people."

Within the Christian churches recent decades have been a time of change and hence of turmoil. Most Christians have perceived that their own church has been changing and, being human, each has wanted it to change in the direction he or she favours. I believe that this explains why there have been such strong factions within the churches in recent years, with such strong feelings on all sides. Perhaps many have forgotten that, just as a god created by human minds will never satisfy us, so a church created by human minds will never satisfy us. We must not want our church to change in the direction we desire; we must want it to change in the direction God desires, and this can take us well beyond our comfort zone.

16. We Should Always Seek the Collective Wisdom of the Whole Community

On many occasions we can go to a meeting with a definite, even fixed position, on a particular topic, only to find that the different perspective of another person causes us to see the matter in a new light and to change our opinion. Within the present churches there is an immense store of collective wisdom on almost every topic. Should we not in all circumstances use this collective wisdom? Should not one of our most urgent tasks be the putting in place of structures and procedures to use this immense collective wisdom as best we can?

17. We Must Learn to Forgive

There is much history behind the present situation of the different churches, and there is much hurt in that history. And yet the past cannot be changed.

There are two levels of forgiveness, that of 'leaving behind or letting be' (ἀφίημι, the word in the gospels translated as 'to forgive') and that of 'giving for' (*per-donar*, 'pardon', the word now used in Western languages). Both of these levels of forgiveness must be asked of the present churches.

The churches must be invited to accept that the past cannot be changed and to be willing to leave it behind, to let it be, to not dwell on the past. They must then be invited to see whether, for the sake of the unity for which Jesus Christ prayed, they can find within themselves something of the greatness of mind and heart of Jesus on the cross, when, instead of seeking to condemn and punish those who had crucified him, he *gave* himself *for* them.

18. We Must Seek Divine Truth by Using to the Full the Wisdom of the Present (Discernment) and the Wisdom of the Past (Tradition) in order to Learn from the Two Sources of our Knowledge of God: the Bible and the World Around and Within Us

There are two *sources* of our knowledge of God: The Bible and the world around and within us. There is one *tool* for understanding and interpreting both of these sources: discernment, a term that includes reason, feelings and spiritual insight into a person and a story. The *tool* of discernment is not, and cannot be, a third *source* of our knowledge of God. Not even a consensus of Christian people or a constant belief over many centuries can turn the tool into a source. The tool can lead to insights into divine truth that have never been put into words before, but the *source* of the insights remains the Bible and/or the world around us.

Over a period of time the insights gained by means of discernment have built up into a body of beliefs, attitudes and customs called "tradition" (with a small "t" and better expressed in the plural as "traditions"). These traditions are not a new *source*, but the *accumulated result of the use of the tool on the sources*. More dynamically, they are the result of the ongoing interpretation of the Bible and the world around and within us and the application of this interpretation to the concrete circumstances of the present. When we seek to resolve a particular question, we may legitimately place this accumulated result alongside the Bible and the world around us, not as a new source, but as a body of knowledge representing the wisdom of the past. It is not on the same level as the two sources, and yet we cannot ignore it without arrogantly dismissing the past.

In studying any particular question, it would seem wise to consider *together* the Bible, the world around and within us, and what we can learn from the wisdom of the past. No decision the Christian church arrives at should ever contradict a genuine truth of the Bible OR a genuine insight into the world around and within us OR a genuine insight of the past.

There is also the Great Tradition, the essential truth concerning Jesus Christ, and any of the particular traditions must always be seen and judged in the light of the handing on from one generation to the next of this Great Tradition.

19. Christian Unity is More Important than Anything Not Essential

Within every present church there are beliefs that are held to be essential to the very identity of that church, for example, that a person named Jesus and called "the Christ" lived and died in Palestine two thousand years ago. Anyone who denied this truth could hardly claim to be a member of the church. No member of that church would dream of sacrificing one of these basic beliefs for the sake of Christian unity. There are some things, however, that can be asked of every church.

There are no laws or customs, no matter how ancient, that are more important than Christian unity. There are no forms of liturgy or prayer or music that are more important than Christian unity. All members of all churches must, therefore, be prepared to sacrifice some or many of these things if such a sacrifice would prove greatly helpful to Christian unity.

Even within the field of belief, all churches can be asked to look again to see if every single part of every single belief is truly essential to the identity of the church.

20. There Is Room for Great Diversity Within the Christian Church

This principle is the other side of the coin of the previous principle. While Christians must be prepared to sacrifice anything that is not essential, there is no need for total uniformity on all matters. Does it matter if people follow different customs and different forms of liturgy, if they like different kinds of music or prayer? A big church should have room for much diversity.

21. The Divine Origin of Any Element in the Church Cannot Be Assumed and Requires Proof

We may ask whether in the past the desire to be right, and to be seen to speak with authority, at times led different churches to a too-facile claim to a divine origin for particular teachings. This should lead to a willingness to look again at many elements, in the light of newer understandings of the Bible and the world around us, in order to see whether the reasons for claiming a divine origin have a foundation that is truly solid.

22. In Essential Matters Unity, in Non-essential Matters Freedom, in All Matters Love

This statement changes the ancient dictum, in that it demands freedom, not only in doubtful matters, but also in all matters, no matter how certain, that are not essential to the identity of the Christian faith. It is based on the equally ancient principles that both laws and statements of belief impose obligations, that obligations should always be kept to a minimum, and that a presumption in favour of freedom should always prevail.

23. All Christian Churches Must be Set Free from the Prison of their Past

It is important that each church look carefully at any ways in which, and any subject on which, it is in fact a prisoner of its past, unable to look calmly and objectively at some aspect of its own self. This is frequently not a matter of how solemnly a particular teaching has been proclaimed, but of how much emotional energy has been invested in the belief. It is probably at least as much a principle of psychology as it is of theology. An example would be the one quoted earlier regarding the question of homosexuality in America and Uganda.

If a church is called to make a new decision between a particular tradition and freedom, the presumption in the voting must always be in favour of freedom.

24. What You Do Is More Important than What You Believe

The essence of the Christian faith does not consist in professing creeds, but in loving God and neighbour. You can believe every word of the Creed, but if you have no love in your heart, you are not a genuine Christian. In the period after the Reformation, wars were fought over beliefs and people were burned at the stake for what they believed or did not believe. And yet Jesus said, "By this shall all people know that you are my disciples, that you love one another," and not, "that you all believe the same Creed". If we seek Christian unity, orthopraxis (correct or proper behaviour rather than belief) must come before orthodoxy.

In both Judaism and Islam, the balance between orthodoxy and orthopraxis is weighted in favour of what you do, while in the Catholic Church it seems to be weighted in favour of what you believe. Christian unity will be better fostered in a world in which orthopraxis is more greatly esteemed.

25. Every Church Has Its Strengths

Every church has its strengths, certain insights into truth that it has grasped better than other churches. As a principle of Christian unity, we should systematically look at each present church and ask, not where it is wrong, but where it is right, what its strengths are, where it has had a deeper insight into God's truth than other churches. We have had centuries of picking faults with other churches. It is time we looked at their strengths. If we did this honestly, the shape of the future unified church might become clearer.

26. Christian Unity Demands a Relationship with All Religions

It will not be possible to achieve unity between the Christian churches unless at the same time there is a reaching out to non-Christian religions. The work of striving for Christian unity of its very nature involves a reaching out to all people.

In the past, each of the major religions has often heard only the worst about the other religions. At times false and quite scandalous stories have been widely believed.

Here, too, I believe that the first step should be a presentation of the strengths and insights into the truth of each religion. This study should aim to show why many millions of good, intelligent and insightful people have willingly joined and remained in each of these religions. This could be of great help in understanding all religious belief, including our own. Among the other religions that must be studied, we must include today's "secular religion" and such phenomena as the New Age movement.

I have spoken largely about attitudes, and yet it is all too easy to give intellectual assent to attitudes while in practice paying no more than lip service to them. For example, it is easy to accept the need for humility, but it is far harder to actually be humble. The principles we accept are meaningless unless we work hard to put them into practice.

CHAPTER 14
THE RIGHT TO BE WRONG

THE CATHOLIC Church is in a prison.
It was not evil people who put it in this prison.
No, it constructed the prison for itself,
locked itself in and threw away the key.
That prison is the prison
of not being able to be wrong.

One of the rights I treasure
most greatly in my life
is my right to be wrong.

I absolutely demand this right
one hundred times a day,
in big things and small things.

I demand the right to say,
"Sorry, I was mistaken."
"Sorry, I did not understand."
"Sorry, I acted without sufficient thought."
"Sorry, I was insensitive."

I could surrender many other rights
and still live a satisfying life,

but I could not survive a single day
without the right to be wrong.

Far too often the Catholic Church has believed
that it had such a level of divine guidance
that it did not need
the right to be wrong.

It can be unable to move forwards,
even when clear evidence emerges
that earlier decisions
were conditioned by their own time
and that the arguments for them
are not as strong
as they were once thought to be.

It has not been able to face the idea that
on important issues
and for centuries of time
it might have been wrong.

I have been re-reading
some statements of earlier centuries
that, for either theological
or psychological reasons,
the Catholic Church
does not believe it can change.

Among them I find some
that interpret the Bible
in too literal or too legal a manner.

I find interpretations of the Bible
that I believe should be revised
in the light of more recent knowledge
of biblical meaning.

I find statements that take a text
of the Bible out of its context
in a manner that is not legitimate.

I find statements that canonise

a particular system of philosophy
in a way that is not possible.

I find statements that are not sufficiently aware
that human words
are inadequate carriers of divine truth.

I find in places a psychological inability
to admit ignorance or error.

~

There is also
the whole mixed history of the Catholic Church
over two thousand years.

I have long had difficulty with the idea
that I must give "submission of mind and will"
to the **words** of a pope, even non-infallible ones,
but **deeds** throughout history
that were far from the mind of Jesus Christ
seem to be brushed aside.

In our own day,
how can we maintain
the infallibility of the pope
in the light of
the most fallible response of popes
to one of the greatest moral crises
the Church has ever faced,
that of the widespread sexual abuse of minors?

If infallibility means a divine assurance
that the Church will not
go astray in important matters,
how has God allowed it to go so far astray
on this matter of sexual abuse?

If infallibility is singularly absent
in a crisis of this magnitude,
what does the word mean?

TOWARDS THE END OF MY DAYS

Surely we cannot separate
words and deeds in this manner.
Surely deeds speak more powerfully than words.

Is it not the entire history of the Church
that we must look at
and ask ourselves whether we are once again
locking ourselves in a prison of the past
if we say that this past
must determine our future?

I strongly believe that
the future health of the Church
depends upon its being set free
from the prison of the past.
Only then can the Church as a whole
have the freedom to grow.

The question must be asked:
Can the Catholic Church
definitively leave behind
the prison of the past
without two changes being made?

Should binding statements be limited strictly
to those truths that are genuinely essential
to the identity of the Church?

Should a later universal Church council
have the power to adapt the teachings
of an earlier universal Church council?

TRUTHS ESSENTIAL TO IDENTITY

There is an ancient saying, that in necessary matters there must be unity, in doubtful matters there must be freedom, and in all matters there must be love.[54]

In the Catholic Church there are necessary matters, that is, truths that are essential to the identity of the Christian Church, for example, "Jesus was a real person who lived on this earth." A person who does not believe that someone called Jesus once lived on this earth can hardly be called a member of the Church. If the Church community did not have even this belief in common, it would not be a community. If the members of the Church could believe whatever they wished to believe, the Church would lose all coherence and identity.

On the other hand, every truth declared necessary creates an obligation, and such obligations should not be multiplied without good cause.

The history of Creeds within the Church shows both sides of this dilemma. On the one hand, they were seen as necessary so that the Church would have a clear identity and would be a true community of people who shared common beliefs and values. On the other hand, bitter battles occurred in their formulation, wars were later fought over them and, rather than a means of building community, they sometimes became a means of excluding people from the Church, persecuting them and even burning them at the stake.

The overriding principle must surely be that freedom should prevail, so the necessary statements should be strictly limited to those truths that are quite essential to the identity of the Church.

In other words, freedom should prevail, not just in doubtful matters, but in all matters that, whether they are doubtful or certain, are not essential to the identity of the Church. One of the problems of the past was that, whenever a truth was considered certain, it was automatically considered to be essential, and this must be queried. The ancient saying I have quoted could be revised to read, "In essential matters unity, in non-essential matters freedom, and in all matters love."

The question then becomes one of finding the balance between the necessity of having clear statements of the beliefs that are essential to the identity of the Church, and the need not to place more obligations on individuals than is absolutely essential. It would take the collective wisdom of the entire Church, working closely with the Spirit, to find this balance. All I can do here is give an example of each of the two types of question that can arise:
a) a belief that is not essential to the identity of the Christian Church;
b) a belief that is essential in its core, but some non-core details are not essential.

---

54 "In necessariis unitas, in dubiis libertas, in omnibus caritas."

A Belief that is Not Essential

On the first of November 1950, Pope Pius XII declared infallibly that, at the end of her life, Mary, the mother of Jesus, was assumed bodily into heaven.[55] One must surely ask whether it was wise and prudent to make an infallible statement on this matter. Does it belong in the category of essential matters on which unity is necessary? The authoritative nature of the papal statement certainly placed it in this category. For a Catholic, a denial of the Assumption became a denial of the Catholic faith, so it became a very real and powerful obligation. If any persons believed everything else in the Catholic faith but denied the truth of the Assumption, they were considered as outside the Catholic Church, no longer part of it.[56]

If Jesus Christ never existed, the Christian faith would cease to exist. But if Mary was not assumed bodily into heaven, the essentials of the Christian faith would appear to remain intact. So, was it wise and prudent to create such a serious obligation concerning it? Should people be perfectly free to believe in the Assumption, but not bound to do so under pain of being excluded from the Church?

There are many statements in the teachings of the Church that come into this category of teachings "not essential to the identity of the Church", and one must ask whether so many obligations should be created concerning them without strict necessity.

An Essential Truth with Non-Essential Details

The Nicene Creed includes the words "he ascended into heaven" and this has always been part of the faith of the Church. The Gospel of Luke (24:51) and the Acts of the Apostles (1:9–11), written by the same author, give a description of this event. There might seem to be nothing more to discuss.

Nevertheless, we must make a distinction. At the end of his time on earth, Jesus returned to his Father. This is an essential part of Christian faith, for, if Jesus did not return to his Father, we would have to query whether he had come from his Father in the first place, and this would place many essential truths in jeopardy. However, did he return to his Father by means of his physical body ascending in a vertical direction from the earth up into the heavens? This is not nearly as certain and is not essential to the Christian faith. If Jesus returned to

---

55 Pope Pius XII, Apostolic Constitution *Munificentissimus Deus*, November 1, 1950, DB, no. 2331-2333.

56 "Therefore, if anyone should freely dare (may God prevent it) to deny or call in doubt that which has been defined by Us, let him know that he has completely defected from divine and Catholic faith." *loc. cit.*, quoted from *The Christian Faith in the Doctrinal Documents of the Catholic Church*, (editors J Neuner and J Dupuis), Collins Liturgical Publications, London, 1983.

his Father by some less spectacular means, the Christian faith would appear to remain intact.

There is only one writer (Luke) who speaks of the body of Jesus being seen to ascend from the earth towards the heavens. Neither Mark nor Matthew nor John speak of this. The writers of the Bible preferred concrete rather than abstract language and their concrete language was often pictorial (they "talked in pictures"). If Luke were alive today, he might be surprised to hear that many modern people took his image so literally.

It would, therefore, seem more prudent to place this question of the exact manner in which Jesus returned to his Father in the category where freedom reigns. People would be free to believe that Jesus ascended bodily from the earth in a vertical direction, but would not be bound to do so, as long as they believed that he returned to his Father.

There are many other statements in the Christian faith where we must distinguish between those parts that express essential religious truths and those parts that do not. Indeed, this is a question we need to ask concerning every religious statement.

Non-Essential Beliefs

If the Church decided to base itself on a system of statements "essential to the identity of the Christian faith", there would still be a need for many statements that commented on non-essential aspects of the Christian faith in order to inform, explain, educate or edify.

Whether one wished it or not, there would in fact be a hierarchy of authority in such statements. For example, the statement of a universal church council would have more authority than the statement of a local bishop or priest. This would, however, refer only to the attitude of mind with which an individual should approach the document. It would not change the fact that, while the statement represented the particular authority's best endeavour to express religious truth, it was not a binding statement of essential beliefs and the individual was free to accept its contents or not.

There are two opposing dangers in this situation. For Church authorities there is always the danger of having so intense a desire to see the entire Church sharing the same beliefs that some binding authority is claimed for every statement made. If the Church gives in to this temptation, it opens the door to multitudinous levels of authority of documents and to the constant desire to upgrade the authority of each level.

The danger for individuals is that of thinking that, apart from the essential beliefs, they are free to believe whatever they wish, to pick and choose the non-essential truths that suit them. However, one of the truly essential beliefs of the Christian faith is surely that in all matters and at all times we must seek God's truth and goodness. We are never free to believe whatever we wish, for we must always be seeking God's truth. This means that I will read the documents of Church authorities with respect and openness, seeking to understand and accept any truths that I find there. The higher the authority, for example a universal council, the greater the respect I will give to its documents. A document may have no authority to coerce my consent, but it can have the authority to demand my respect.

ONE AUTHORITY CHANGING ANOTHER

The second question that must be asked is whether, in order to leave behind the prison of the past, a later universal council should have the power to adapt the teachings of an earlier and equal universal council.

Some Precedents

I am not without company in raising this question. In the fifth century, when Pope Leo the Great developed his theory of papal primacy, his ideas were accepted in the West, but there were serious reservations in the East and in Africa. Writing a few years before Leo, St Augustine from Africa had said,

> The writings of bishops may be refuted both by the perhaps wiser words of anyone more experienced in the matter and by the weightier authority and more scholarly prudence of other bishops, and also by councils, if something in them perhaps has deviated from the truth; even councils held in particular regions or provinces must without quibbling give way to the authority of plenary councils of the whole Christian world; and even the earlier plenary councils are often corrected by later ones, if as a result of practical experience something that was closed is opened, something that was hidden becomes known.[57]

One hundred and fifty years later Pope Pelagius II made a statement that had been drafted by a deacon of his household who, on his death, became Pope Gregory the Great. The document said:

> Dear brethren, do you think that when Peter was reversing his position, one should have replied: We refuse to hear what you are saying since you previously taught the opposite? In the matter [now under discussion] one position was held while truth was being sought, and a different position was adopted after truth had been found. Why should a change of position be thought a crime ...? For what is reprehensible is not changing one's mind, but being fickle in one's views. If the mind

---

57 St Augustine, *De baptismo contra Donatistas*, Book III, chapter 2.

remains unwavering in seeking to know what is right, why should you object when it abandons its ignorance and reformulates its views?[58]

In any other matter the combined authority of Augustine and Gregory the Great would be massive, so why not here?

In the eleventh century, the Eastern half of the Church objected to the introduction of the *filioque* clause into the Creed. This was done on the grounds that the Western half of the Church alone had changed a creed determined by a council of the universal church. In saying this, they accepted that a later universal council could change a creed determined by an earlier universal council.

At the time of the Reformation, the reformers felt the need to go back to the idea of teaching that could be revised and amended in the light of developing knowledge of the sources of our religious knowledge.

Taken together, these are authorities that must be treated with the greatest respect.

The Role of Peter

In the Gospel of Matthew we find the scene in which Simon is formally renamed Peter and Jesus says,

> Blessed are you, Simon, son of Jonah! For flesh and blood has not revealed this to you, but my Father in heaven. And I tell you, you are Peter and on this rock I will build my church, and the gates of Hades will not prevail against it. I will give you the keys of the kingdom of heaven, and whatever you bind on earth will be bound in heaven, and whatever you loose on earth will be loosed in heaven.[59]

These are certainly solemn words about Peter, they come from the gospels and we must pay full attention to them. The words clearly speak of Jesus delegating something of his own authority over the community to Peter. There are, however, three points that must be noted as a balance to these words.

Firstly, it must occasion some surprise that the name Jesus gave to Simon was that of Peter, meaning "the rock", for a rock does not do anything, it simply is. It is solid and firm and makes an excellent foundation, but its role is passive. Needless to say, it is only an image and we must never push images too far. Jesus immediately went on to speak of binding and loosing, and this is a more active role. Nevertheless, Jesus, who could have chosen from a multitude of images,

---

58 Quoted by Robert Markus, emeritus professor of history at Nottingham University, in a review of the book *Papal Sin, Structures of Deceit* by Gary Wills, in *The Tablet*, 2nd September 2000.

59 Peter 16:17-19.

freely chose the powerful and yet passive image of a rock as the image that gave Peter his name, the image that before all others gave him his identity. The statement that Peter was a rock was more basic than the statement that he was the keeper of the keys, for it was the first statement, not the second, that gave him his name.

Secondly, the words of blessing of Peter occur in 16:17–19, but a mere two verses later, in v. 21,

> Jesus began to show his disciples that he must go to Jerusalem and undergo great suffering.

In reply, Peter did not speak in the name of the whole group, but solely in his own name:

> Peter took him aside and began to rebuke him, saying, "God forbid it, Lord! This must never happen to you." (16: 22)

Jesus answered with the strongest words he ever spoke to any human being,

> Get behind me, Satan! You are a stumbling block to me; for you are not intent on the things of God, but on the things of human beings.

These verses seem to go out of their way to reverse the message of the scene that has just concluded. In the earlier scene Peter had been placed in the position of blessing, in front of the eleven and speaking in their name; now he is placed in the position of rejection, behind Jesus, away from the eleven and speaking only in his own name. Earlier he had been called the rock of the Church; now he is called a rock that would trip Jesus on his path, a stumbling block. Then he had been told that it was not flesh and blood that had revealed truth to him, but God in heaven; now he is told that his thoughts do not come from God, but are the unholy thoughts that arise when God is ignored. In fact, Jesus actually told him that he was speaking on behalf of Satan rather than God.

In the First Book of Samuel we are given two stories of the appointment of Saul as king, one favourable (Chapter 8) and the other unfavourable (Chapters 9–10). Together they stress the ambivalence of kings in Israel: a form of government was needed, but the kings would frequently lead the people away from God. Here we are given two stories about Peter side by side, one favourable, the other unfavourable. May we conclude that the message is the same as that concerning kings in the First Testament, that is, that the Church will need leaders but, because those leaders will be human, they will be a mixed blessing and will not infrequently get in the way of God? Does not history tell us that this is indeed exactly what has happened?

Thirdly, this thought that leaders are only human is strengthened by the fact that just two chapters later almost identical words about binding and loosing are spoken by Jesus again, but this time to "the disciples".

> Truly I tell you, whatever you bind on earth will be bound in heaven, and whatever you loose on earth will be loosed in heaven.[60]

Admittedly, these words refer specifically to the question of dealing with a person who has broken unity with the Church, but there are many other ways of saying that the community can deal with such a person, and it is surely significant that the words chosen by Jesus are virtually identical with the words used of Peter in relation to the whole Church. In Matthew the term "the disciples" can refer either to the twelve or to all the followers of Jesus, and the effect in this passage is that both groups share in this authority to bind and loose.[61] Is not the logical conclusion that Peter alone is the rock, but Peter, the twelve and the whole Church all have a share in the authority to bind and loose? If we are to be faithful to the gospels, can we ever exclude the rest of the Church from having the authority to bind and loose?

That a ruler, a single person, had the power to bind and loose was a commonplace in the ancient world. But that a group and even the whole community had a share in the power to bind and loose was a most surprising idea and is typical of the quite radical manner in which Jesus looked at traditional ways of acting. May we not conclude that the followers of Jesus were free to think in new ways and were meant to think in new ways?

The words concerning the renaming of Peter and his being given an authority to bind and loose are powerful, but can they ever be properly understood unless they are balanced with the scene of Peter's failure that takes place immediately afterwards and with the scene in which Jesus, in virtually identical words, spoke also of this power among the disciples?

Successors

Did Jesus intend that Peter and the apostles should have successors, that is, that their roles should continue forever in the Church? As the first part of an answer, we must say that Jesus called the twelve so that they could be the

---

60   Matthew 18:18.
61   The passage begins at Matthew 18:1, "At that time the disciples came to Jesus and asked, 'Who is the greatest in the kingdom of heaven?' He called a child, whom he put among them, and said ..." Matthew 18:18 is part of the following discourse and it is clear that the discourse is directed to all disciples of Jesus. For example, the first words of the discourse are, "Truly I tell you, unless you change and become like children, you will never enter the kingdom of heaven." It cannot be said that these words are directed only to the twelve and not to the rest of the disciples.

eyewitnesses to every single action and word of his life, death and resurrection. When another was chosen to take the place of Judas, he was to be:

> ... one of those men who have accompanied us during all the time that the Lord Jesus went in and out among us, beginning from the baptism of John until the day when he was taken up from us.[62]

Thus, their primary and unique role was that of being eyewitnesses, and it died with them. Needless to say, there would still need to be witnesses after the death of the apostles, and in this sense their role would continue, but the witnesses would no longer be direct eyewitnesses.

Just as the role of witnessing would continue, could there be successors to other parts of the role of Peter and the twelve, for example those binding and loosing? In answer, the early Church appeared to *assume* that there would in fact be successors to Peter and the twelve. The best information we have would say that Peter died under Emperor Nero (64-67 CE), and at least three of the gospels and the Acts of the Apostles were not completed until well after this date. In particular, the Gospel of Matthew was written well after the death of Peter. Why would Matthew stress that Peter and the twelve had a role in binding and loosing if Peter and the twelve were already dead, and that their role had no further relevance at the time he wrote, if it were of no more than historical interest? Why did all four gospels insist that Peter's very name came from his being the rock of the Church if his role as rock had already come to an end and had no relevance for the future?[63]

This argument is strengthened by the fact that there are several instances of

---

62 Acts 1:21.

63 Article 20 of *Lumen Gentium* says that the bishops "have by divine institution taken the place of the apostles as pastors of the Church". However, the limits of what the Council said on this subject must be kept in mind. For example, in commenting on this article, Karl Rahner says, "This transmission (of the apostolic office) is proved (or merely asserted?) very briefly by appealing to the eschatological definitiveness of the gospel. How far this proof is valid, when taken alone is, of course, not decided, and hence it remains a question to be freely debated by both sides in ecumenical discussion ... From the purely historical point of view, it can hardly be denied that in the age of primitive Palestinian and Pauline communities the constitution of the Church still seems to have been somewhat 'fluid'. Thus the question arises as to the exact theological interpretation of the element of divine right in the structure of the Church, a question not further discussed in the text ... (The text) merely says that the Council 'teaches' (*docet*), which is a less forceful expression than those used in earlier drafts." *Commentary on the Documents of Vatican II*, ed. Herbert Vorgrimler, Burns and Oates, London, 1967, Vol.1, pp.190–191. It must be added that the Fathers of the Vatican Council assumed the perfect knowledge of Jesus and what they said must be revisited in the light of the fact that this perfect knowledge cannot simply be assumed.

the leaders appointing others to take over parts of their ministry and complete the work they had begun.[64]

The Second Testament does not present Peter as an absolute ruler over the twelve or over the whole Church. There were occasions when he was made answerable to the Church[65] and there were occasions when others took the role of leadership of the assembly and announced the decision of the group[66].

May we ask whether the singular role that the pope came to play in the Catholic Church comes solely from the gospels, or does it also come from the influence of such things as the conversion of Constantine and the forces that led to the *Dictatus Papae*? Is there now a need to revisit these ideas?

The First Vatican Council

In 1870 the First Vatican Council proclaimed the primacy of jurisdiction and the infallible teaching function of the pope in a document entitled *Pastor Aeternus*.

The decades before this council saw the rise of a movement called Ultramontanism[67], which stressed papal authority as the organisational principle of the Church. The central question it asked may be expressed in the form: Is the pope the centre where everything comes together, or is he the source from which everything flows? Ultramontanism stressed the latter and saw the pope's role in a proactive light. Because of the aftermath of the Enlightenment, the French Revolution and the spirit of liberalism that flowed from these events, the question was discussed more in practical terms as a means of resolving immediate problems rather than in terms of essential principles and permanent teachings. By focusing on the immediate problems, the ultramontane view prevailed and both papal primacy and papal infallibility were solemnly defined at the council.[68]

And yet the two principles of cephality (rule by the head) and synodality (rule by a consensus of the members) have always existed in the Church, and there has always been a tension between them. However useful cephality may have been in resolving immediate practical problems, it would never completely resolve the tension between the two sides, and it would never cause synodality to

---

64 *Lumen Gentium* (quotes "Acts 20:25–27; 2 Timothy 4:6 ff; in conjunction with 1 Timothy 5:22; 2 Timothy 2:2; Titus 1:5.")
65 Acts 11:1-18.
66 Acts 15:6-21.
67 The term literally means "beyond the mountains", that is, the Alps. It originated in the Middle Ages, when it meant things north of the Alps, but in the nineteenth century its meaning was turned around and it meant anything south of the Alps. It came to mean a church centred on the pope.
68 See John O'Malley, *Vatican I, The Council and the Making of the Ultramontane Church*, The Bellknap Press of Harvard University Press, Cambridge, Massachusetts, 2018.

disappear. A century later the Second Vatican Council felt the need to proclaim collegiality as a balance against the cephality of the First Vatican Council, and even that did not resolve the tension. So there are still open questions that need resolving.

"Pastor Aeternus"

The document *Pastor Aeternus* relied heavily on the statement of Jesus to Peter in Matt 16:17–19 – "You are Peter and on this rock …", although without referring to the closely connected failure of Peter in the following verses (21–23) or to the giving of the power to bind and loose to "the disciples" in Matt 18:18.

It also gave great doctrinal and legal weight to two other gospel sayings of Jesus:

> And after his resurrection, Jesus conferred upon Peter alone the jurisdiction of supreme shepherd and ruler over His whole flock in the words: "Feed my lambs … Feed my sheep. (John 21:15,17).[69]

Indeed it was this apostolic doctrine that all the Fathers held, and the holy orthodox Doctors reverenced and followed, fully realising that this See of Saint Peter always remains untainted by any error, according to the divine promise of our Lord and Saviour made to the Prince of His disciples:

> "But I have prayed for you that your faith may not fail; and when you have turned again, strengthen your brethren". (Luke 22:32).[70]

It must surely be queried whether these two gospel sayings can be made to bear so heavy a doctrinal and legal weight, that is whether in and of themselves alone, the two sayings prove that the pope is infallible.

For the rest, the document relies on an appeal to tradition. A major problem with the arguments on this ground is contained in the introduction to the section on infallibility.

> Moreover, this Holy See has always held, the perpetual practice of the Church confirms, and the Ecumenical Councils, **especially those in which the Western and Eastern Churches were united in faith and love**, have declared that the supreme power of teaching is also included in this apostolic primacy …[71]

---

69 Neuner-Dupuis, op. cit., no. 836, p. 233.
70 Neuner Dupuis, op. cit., no. 819, p. 228.
71 Neuner-Dupuis, op. cit., no. 831, p. 232. The emphasis is my own.

One must go so far as to say that it is quite disingenuous to claim that the Eastern Churches ever affirmed papal infallibility. This is simply not true, and the three councils quoted by *Pastor Aeternus* demonstrate this. (The Fourth Council of Constantinople 869–870, the Council of Lyon 1274, and the Council of Florence 1439.)

The Fourth Council of Constantinople (869–870) is controversial to this day because it is claimed to be ecumenical by the West but not by the East. In the time before the council, the pope and the patriarch of Constantinople, Photius, were in dispute over whether the missionary territory of Bulgaria should be subject to Rome or Constantinople. The pope sent bishops to Bulgaria and this so incensed Photius that he called his own council in 867 and actually excommunicated the pope and called on the emperor of the West to depose him. The pope reacted by convoking a new council, Constantinople IV. When the papal legates arrived for this council they presented three papal demands: that Photius be deposed, that no bishop consecrated by Photius be allowed to be part of the council, and that all other bishops be allowed to take their seat only if they signed a profession of faith prepared by the pope.

The First Vatican Council quotes from this profession of faith imposed by the pope, not from any deliberations of the council itself. After Photius was deposed, a new patriarch, Ignatius, was then appointed and he was ordered by the pope not to send missionaries to Bulgaria, but he consecrated ten bishops for that territory soon after the papal legates had left. The pope threatened him over a period of time and eventually sent two legates with power to depose him, but they arrived to find that Ignatius had been dead for a year and his place retaken by none other than Photius himself! In this whole story there is little that is edifying and there was much use of vituperative language on both sides. To call the Fourth Council of Constantinople a council "in which the Western and Eastern Churches were united in faith and love" is hardly accurate.[72]

The second council quoted, the Second Council of Lyons (1274), is equally problematic. *Pastor Aeternus* says that "with the approval of the Second Council of Lyons, the Greeks professed that ..." In fact, however, the quotation that follows comes neither from the council nor from "the Greeks", but from one individual. It is usually called, "The Profession of Faith of Michael Palaeologus." The Byzantine emperor, Michael VIII Palaeologus, had retaken the city of Constantinople after the Fourth Crusade, but faced many enemies. For political rather than religious reasons, he wanted an alliance with the pope and was prepared to make any concession to obtain it. He wrote a letter to the council in which he incorporated a profession of faith written by Pope Clement IV. The letter was not "approved" by the council, nor even discussed, but simply

---

72 For a detailed account of events before, during and after this council, see *Histoire des Conciles Oecumeniques*, Vol. IV, *Constantinople IV*, by Daniel Stiernon, Editions de L'Orante, Paris, 1967.

read out. That it was not the faith of "the Greeks" was quickly shown by the serious troubles the emperor experienced from his own subjects when he tried to enforce the letter. The elderly patriarch Joseph declared that he would prefer death and the ruin of the Greek Church to union with the Latins. Michael VIII was refused Christian burial by his own subjects, and his son Andronikus formally repudiated the letter as soon as he came to power. Once again, talk of "unity in faith and love" is misplaced.[73]

The third council quoted is the Council of Florence (1441–45). At this council a serious attempt was made to reunite the East and the West. At least on this occasion the document quoted in *Pastor Aeternus* was produced by the council itself. More pragmatic considerations, however, were also present, for Constantinople had by this time become a Christian island in a Muslim sea. The emperor, patriarch and people of that city were desperate to have the support of the entire Western world in their battle against the powerful forces of Islam. Historians are divided on the question of how free the members of the Eastern Church were at the time of this council. In the period immediately after the council there were serious divisions among its members and union did not survive the fall of Constantinople to the Turkish forces in 1453, a mere eight years after the council ended.[74]

Furthermore, none of the quotations attributed to the three councils can be said to affirm the infallibility of the bishop of Rome, for they were documents about primacy rather than about infallibility. There is no serious basis for claiming that "the Greeks", the members of the Eastern Churches, would have accepted infallibility if this question had been specifically raised.

One always expects arguments to prove the conclusion that is drawn from them. One might further expect that nowhere would we find more cogent arguments in favour of papal infallibility than in the document which solemnly proclaimed it. The extreme lack of cogency in the arguments given in *Pastor Aeternus* is, therefore, quite startling. It appears obvious that the First Vatican Council, in drawing its conclusions concerning papal infallibility, relied above all on the solemnity of the pronouncement of the council itself.

Reliance on the solemn pronouncement of a council, in the absence of cogent arguments from the sources, seems to assume the truth it proclaims. How can a pope infallibly proclaim papal infallibility unless we assume in advance that the pope is infallible? To answer that it was not the pope who proclaimed this, but a solemn council, seems to do no more than move the question one step sideways, for how can a council infallibly declare the infallibility of the pope unless we assume in advance that the council is infallible?

The First Vatican Council was acting out of a very particular situation that

---

73 See *Histoire des Conciles Oecumeniques*, Vol.VII, *Lyon I et Lyon II*, by Hans Wolter and Henri Holstein, Editions de L'Orante, Paris, 1966.

74 See Joseph Gill, *The Council of Florence*, Cambridge University Press, 1959.

had arisen in Europe in general (the Enlightenment, the French Revolution, liberalism) and Italy in particular (Italian unity and the abolition of the papal states in central Italy) in the nineteenth century, and out of the reaction of Church leaders to these events.

ARGUMENTS AGAINST INFALLIBILITY

In the decades before the First Vatican Council, there were continual discussions and debates concerning the authority of papal statements, with Gallicanism on one side and Ultramontanism on the other. *Pastor Aeternus* attempted to put a stop to this debate by embracing Ultramontanism and rejecting Gallicanism. A century later, however, the encyclical *Humanae Vitae* showed the dangers of the decision to give all power to the pope, and the fierce scandal of sexual abuse showed the catastrophic dangers of relying on the personal opinions and prejudices of the one person of the pope in responding to a major moral crisis. Do we not need to find a more nuanced solution somewhere in the middle? Must any lasting answer be a balance of the two forces of cephality and synodality? Indeed, must synodality go well beyond the bishops and include the whole Church?

Each of the books of the Bible reflects the time and place in which it was written and the personal traits of the writers. In studying any part of the Bible, we must go back to the history of the times, the laws and customs of the age and the literary form in which the book was written. In the same way, it is impossible to conduct a Church council in a vacuum. Any council will reflect the problems and address the issues of its own age. It will do so according to prevailing philosophies, social values and needs. It will use words according to the meanings they have at the time the council is held. It will work from the knowledge of the Bible that people have at that time. With the passage of time problems, issues, philosophies and social values will change, and the meaning of words will change. Knowledge of the Bible and tradition will develop, such that a later generation can clearly see that an earlier generation based itself on quite inadequate understandings of the Bible and the world around it. For these reasons alone, is there not an obvious danger of a church putting itself into a prison if it claims an eternal validity for the statements of a pope or council?

There is both human and divine in the Bible and we are never excused from the serious and difficult work of separating the two. Should we not expect the same confusion and conflict between the human and the divine in the Church today? Both the Bible and Church history are the story of a journey as people struggled towards truth. Is it likely that God would now adopt a quite different plan by giving certain answers to most questions through Church authorities? Both in the Bible and in Church history God placed the emphasis on search and responsibility leading to growth. Is it likely that God would now place the accent on certainty leading to obedience?

Claiming an eternal validity for statements means to claim a level of divine guidance behind each single statement. This cannot be assumed by the Church to be correct – such claims must be proven. Claiming such a level of divine guidance appears to be based on the attitude that God could not allow the Church to be mistaken on matters seen to be important. Surely, we must query whether we really have this level of knowledge of how God operates. Is it not possible that God has permitted Church authorities to err in order to break down its trust in human beings, for wouldn't such a trust always be a temptation for the Church? For example, in relation to the sexual abuse of minors, is it not obvious that God has allowed the Church to make grievous errors, even in a matter of supreme importance that threatens the very credibility of the Church?

At a time when we are coming to realise that Jesus himself may have given up the privilege of perfect knowledge and have had to struggle through his life and mission with only limited knowledge, should we not be looking again at claims which imply that the Church has access to a level of knowledge that it actually may not have had access to?

In discussions between different churches in recent decades it has become evident that there are many people belonging to other Christian churches who would seriously consider the idea of a Peter-figure in a future united Church, but categorically reject the full claims of the Catholic Church on this matter, especially in regard to infallibility. Is it perhaps becoming clear that the Church has a choice between Christian unity and these claims of infallibility? It cannot have both, not now and, with overwhelming probability, not at any time in the future.

The Second Vatican Council

The Second Vatican Council (1962–65) faced a tension between the need to be faithful to its origins and the need to confront the pastoral problems posed by the modern world. The solution the Council found lay in the combination of two words, one Italian and one French. The Italian word was *aggiornamento*, meaning "bringing up to date"; the French word was *ressourcement*, meaning "going back to the sources". The council sought to bring the Church up to date, not by confronting the immediate past head-on, but by going back to a far older tradition based on scripture and the teachings of the ancient Fathers.

It followed a principle that one writer has called "discontinuity for the sake of a greater continuity"[75]. That is, in attempting to reconcile opposing views

---

[75] Ormond Rush, *Still Interpreting Vatican II, Some Hermeneutical Principles*, Paulist Press, New York, 2004.

the council often reached back behind a particular formulation of truth to an earlier and greater truth. (In an earlier chapter I gave examples of this and listed some of the major achievements of the council.)

In doing all of this, the Second Vatican Council modified statements and traditions that had been in place for centuries and which were claimed to be infallible. The Council carried out its "discontinuity for the sake of a greater continuity" despite the fact that, with considerable heat and fury, such action was constantly and adamantly condemned by a number of members of the council.

All of this argues to the surely reasonable principle that a later general council of the Church should have the authority to modify or clarify or adapt the teaching of an earlier general council in the light of developing knowledge and understanding.

This is far from being something new, for it is exactly what happened in the field of Christology over a series of seven councils from Nicaea (325) to Nicaea II (787), as Church understanding was purified and improved.

In the terms used by the Second Vatican Council, I am arguing for *ressourcement*, a going back to earlier sources. I am arguing for *aggiornamento*, a bringing up-to-date in the light of further study of the scriptures. I am arguing for "discontinuity for the sake of a greater continuity." I am arguing for a balance between cephality and synodality. Without all these principles the concept of "development of doctrine" becomes nearly impossible.

In all this I am not arguing for anything more than the Second Vatican Council itself has already done in a number of different fields.

THE CERTAINTY OF FAITH

A provision that a later authority could overturn an earlier authority would not throw all Christian teaching into chaos and would not mean that all certainty was destroyed. No universal council is going to change earlier councils without a very good reason for doing so. The idea that all statements of councils *could* be changed is a long way from the idea that all *will* be changed.

The Nicene Creed would remain basically as it is. There are only a few phrases in that Creed that might be considered in need of change. The *filioque* controversy needs to be resolved. Some might wish to modify the words "he ascended into heaven", in a manner that affirms that Jesus returned to his Father but avoids the literary idea of speaking of this in terms of a body rising vertically from the earth. There will never be a human word that adequately expresses the reality presently covered by the word *consubstantialis*, "of one being with the Father". It could be argued that the opening phrase of the creed identifies the one God with the Father, leaving the position of Son and Spirit ambiguous, and that it would be better to have a clear statement of faith in the one God before making any mention of Father, Son and Spirit. This clear statement of faith in one God before any mention of the Trinity might assist us in our dialogue with both Jews and Muslims.

There are also a few statements that some might consider adding to the creed, for example a statement of faith in the dignity of all people and in the goodness of the world God created and redeemed.[76]

I would also see the Creed as too much a list of propositions to which intellectual consent is required, and would wish to preface it by something that expresses faith as a response of love to a person and a story. The *Shema*, the prayer that a good Jewish person says every morning and evening, does this. Jesus adapted it by combining the first part of the *Shema* (Deuteronomy 6:4-5) with Leviticus 19:18 in this fashion:

> *Hear, O Israel: The Lord our God, the Lord is one. You shall love the Lord your God with all your heart, and with all your soul, and with all your mind, and with all your strength. And you shall love your neighbour as yourself. There is no other commandment greater than these.*[77]

In a world in which we must use weak human words in our attempts to express the divine, this prayer contained in Mark 12:29–31 is as close as we will ever come to a statement in human words of eternal and unchangeable truth. The idea it expresses should be at the beginning of any Christian creed and should guide our reading of the whole creed.

>THE PROMISE of Jesus Christ
>was not that the Church
>will never make mistakes,
>but that it will overcome its mistakes,
>that the truth of Jesus Christ
>will always be present in the Church,
>tarnished and even obscured,
>but always there to be rediscovered.
>
>The promise is that,
>in spite of many errors in detail,
>the Church will be maintained
>in the basic truth of the Song of Jesus,
>and that the ugliness in the Church

---

76 For we as a church believe that all people have an equal God-given dignity and are destined for eternal life with God. We believe that the glory of God is to be found in all human beings living fully. We believe in the wonder and beauty of all creation and in our obligation to preserve it.

77 Mark 12:29–31.

will never completely destroy
its underlying beauty.

"The Church's faith will often be weak,
its love lukewarm,
its hope wavering,
but that on which its faith is based,
its love is rooted
and its hope is built
will always endure."[78]

There is a certainty of faith,
though it is certainty
in something that comes before words.
It is the certainty of faith
in the teacher and his song!

There was a teacher and he sang a song.
The teacher was inspiring,
and his song of love makes my heart sing –
this I believe with certainty.

No other certainty
can be equal to this certainty,
and it is by tortuous paths,
and through many uncertainties,
that we must humbly and hesitantly
seek to return the world
to the love from which it came.

Despite all its faults,
it was within the Catholic Church
that I first heard the Song of Jesus
and learned to love it.
It was within this Church
that I met countless human examples
of goodness and inspiration.

However disillusioned I may have become
with many aspects of it,
I have no desire to leave it

---

[78] Hans Küng, *Infallible?* Collins Fontana Library, 1970, p. 153.

TOWARDS THE END OF MY DAYS

and, standing far off,
condemn its failures from a great height,
as though I were superior to it.

But I do want to see
its continual and radical reform,
so that the Song of Jesus
may shine again in splendour.

CHAPTER 15
STRUCTURAL CHANGE IN THE CHURCH

Pope Francis has insisted that there is a profound need for change in the Church, and his major emphasis has been on the need for change within individuals, a change in heart and mind and a change in attitude. He has above all stressed the constant need for mercy: that the Church must become a merciful church and it must reflect a merciful God, and that it must also become a church for the poor rather than glory in its wealth and power. For the clergy he has strongly and consistently opposed elitism, careerism and any form of lordship over people.

We as the Church can also point to other changes of mind and heart that are essential. In responding to sexual abuse, many authorities in the Church instinctively turned to secrecy, to always presenting a good appearance, and to denying anything that could harm the image of the Church. A profound change of heart and mind in such matters is still urgently needed.

I agree totally that internal change is the most important form of change that must occur. I would add, however, that structural change, changing the procedures and structures of the Church, can help in this change of heart and mind and is needed in order to make such change permanent. Without the structural changes, there is always the danger that future popes will each have their own ideas and priorities and there will be no consistent movement for change. There is no secret about the fact that Pope Francis has met fierce opposition within the Vatican to the changes he has tried to make. He needs the support of many people, and not just moral support. I suggest that it is a matter of using structural change to create the best atmosphere in which the change of heart and mind can occur.

In this chapter I want to propose some basic structural changes. Some of them would involve change in Church doctrine, but most would not.

THE BASIS FOR CHANGE

In its great document on the Church, *Lumen Gentium*, the Second Vatican Council said firstly that the Church is a mystery and a concrete means of God's mysterious presence in the world. It then said that the Church is a vast community of people on a pilgrimage towards God. Only in third place did it say that the Church has a structure, so that it may better co-ordinate the activity of the Church towards its end. I see it as always wrong when people put the structure in first place, at the expense of the mystery and the people.

The Council then made at least a partial move in the direction of change when it spoke of the pope and the college of bishops as co-holders of supreme power in the Church.[79] (N.B. The college of bishops is not the bishops opposing the pope, for the pope is the head of the college of bishops and the college does not exist without the pope.)

The idea of two co-holders of supreme power is obviously of the greatest importance, but it contains the problem that it is inevitable that one or the other will in practice dominate, that one will in fact be supreme and the other will not. In the time since the council, it has been glaringly obvious that, in fact and in practice, the pope has possessed supreme power, while the college of bishops has not.

A solution to this dilemma of one dominating the other would be to maintain that the one holder of supreme power is the college of bishops, with this one power then being exercised *collectively* by the whole college or *individually* by the head of the college, the pope. On this basis it would be possible to draw up a set of wise rules governing the exercise of supreme power, such that both the college and the pope would exercise their proper role and neither would be dominated by the other. This would have to be done with great care, but it does not involve any change in the doctrine of the Church.

However, would it be better to go even further and ask whether all authority in the Church belongs first and foremost to "the Church", that is, the pope, bishops, priests, religious and laity taken together? Would it be in accord with the sources to say that all authority belongs to the *Church*, the entire community, with this authority then being exercised *universally* by the whole Church, *collectively* by the twelve and their successors and *individually* by Peter

---

79 "Together with their head the Supreme Pontiff, and never apart from him, they (the bishops) have supreme and full authority over the universal Church." *Lumen Gentium*, no. 22.

and his successors.[80] If this were accepted, each of the three would possess all the power it required to serve the community of the Church and wise laws could be enacted with the consent of the whole Church to ensure that the three worked in harmony.

In support of this perspective, I would suggest that we look again at the very ancient idea that the diocese of Rome had a primacy in the whole Church, not because this primacy belonged personally to the pope, but because Rome was the supreme place of apostolic witness to Jesus Christ through the martyrdom there of the two great apostles – of Peter, who occupies pride of place in the first half of the Acts of the Apostles, and Paul, who occupies pride of place in the second half. Through them primacy and power belonged to the whole Church acting as one. This primacy was spontaneously recognised by the rest of the Church because of the deaths there of the two apostles. By being in union with the diocese of Rome the early Church felt that it was in union with the supreme apostolic witness to Christ given by these two leaders. The primacy belonged firstly to the place.

This idea could easily be combined with the idea of a successor to Peter continuing to fulfil the role of rock of the Church.

It is only the element of the power of binding and loosing that has caused problems, for this power was in practice separated from the power of the bishops and of the People of God and claimed by the bishop of Rome alone. It is hard to argue that the rest of the Church spontaneously did this and gave such power to the bishop of Rome on a permanent basis. We could solve many of the most profound and bitter difficulties experienced within the Church by one more "discontinuity for the sake of a greater continuity", one more act of *ressourcement*, one more act of going back to earlier sources.

The Second Vatican Council also made the significant change of saying that a bishop's power comes from ordination rather than from a delegation of power by the pope. The change has profound consequences for our understanding of the papacy, for becoming pope involves no new ordination. The only ordinations a pope receives are those as priest and bishop, and there is not the slightest difference between the pope's ordination and that of any other bishop, so the pope is essentially a bishop. The only difference between the pope and any other bishop is the diocese to which the pope is elected, for since the time of the martyrdom of both Peter and Paul in Rome that diocese has been pre-eminent among all the churches. The power the pope exercises is that of a bishop but, because of the pre-eminence of the diocese of Rome, the bishop of that diocese has a special task that no other bishop has, and he has

---

80 Yves Congar speaks of a power given universally to the church, personally to the twelve and singularly to Peter. 'The apostolic college, primacy and Episcopal conferences', *Theology Digest* 34:3, 1987, p. 211. Father David Coffey, formerly of the Catholic Institute of Sydney, suggests that it is better to say "collectively" by the twelve, and I have followed this.

all the authority needed to fulfil the task. That task is to be the rock of unity. A satisfying theology could be built on this foundation.[81]

Indeed, there is no need for the term "pope" itself, and the present holder of that title could fully and accurately describe himself as "Francis, bishop of Rome". Nothing more needs to be said. This simple change could be a symbol of the desire to do away with the theology behind the *Dictatus Papae*.

Let me take this further by raising one small point. Pope Benedict XVI has retired and lives in Rome. He wears the white cassock and skull cap that are exclusive to the one person of the bishop of Rome. But he is no longer bishop of Rome, and it would seem more fitting if he wore the purple skull cap of a bishop to make this point clear. It would also be better if he were referred to, not as "pope-emeritus", but as "bishop-emeritus of Rome".

ELECTING A NEW BISHOP OF ROME

For nearly a thousand years the bishop of Rome has appointed the cardinals who have then elected a new bishop of Rome who has then appointed more cardinals who have then elected one more bishop of Rome who has then … The whole process has been closed and circular. Inevitably bishops of Rome have tended to choose as cardinals people like themselves, people who agree with their ideas and ways of doing things.

Furthermore, for many centuries most bishops of Rome seemed to die in their sixties or seventies, but modern medicine has meant that the normal age of death is now the eighties. The last two have been 78 and 76 when they were elected. I suggest that this is not a good system. It is grossly unfair to the individual to ask anyone to take on a task as massive as this at such an age; it makes it too easy for other forces within the Vatican to frustrate the plans of the pope; and it hardly helps the image of the Church to have a succession of bishops of that diocese in their eighties.

The secrecy of the elections is seriously counterproductive, and there is no longer the need for it that once existed when the bishop of Rome was a temporal power and nations interfered in the election.

Suggested changes:
1. The Church shall determine a specific number of electors of the bishop of Rome – for example 120.
2. The number of electors shall be divided between the different countries of the world, with the exception of five places that shall be given to the members of the Roman Curia, five places to priests of the diocese of Rome, five places to laymen from the diocese of Rome and five places to laywomen[82] of that same diocese.

---

81 J M R Tillard develops this theme well, *op. cit.*, especially at pp. 40–41.
82 Since I elsewhere advocate the idea of ordaining women to the priesthood, I am not seeking

3. The bishops of each country or group of countries shall then elect from their own number the electors for their territory, while the members of the Roman Curia, the priests, and laypersons of Rome shall elect their representatives.
4. In each case those entitled to vote shall elect a second representative to take the place of the first in case of, for example, illness, so that the number of persons actually present at an election would always be the same and all areas of the Church would be represented.
5. The "electors" (those elected) shall be between the ages of 60 and 70 and shall lose their role as electors automatically on their seventieth birthday.
6. Each elector chosen shall hold their position for a term of three years, with the elector being eligible for re-election provided the age limits apply.
7. Those chosen shall be called "electors", with the very word "cardinal" being abolished forever, together with all privileges and titles. The only special dress would be a simple and plain sash given to each elector, specifying only the area or group each represents.
8. Any validly ordained bishop, diocesan or titular, may be chosen as a bishop-elector, with no preference being given to seniority, the size of the diocese or any other consideration. The only criteria shall be whether the candidate is within the required age bracket, is considered to be the most suitable for the role of bishop of Rome, and would have the ability to perceive and assess the qualities of the other electors.
9. During the actual election, the numbers who had voted for the top five candidates shall immediately be made public in St Peter's Square.
10. The ballot papers shall not be burned, but retained for history, and the black and white smoke shall be replaced by a less ambiguous signal, for example a white or red banner on the central loggia.
11. The bishop of Rome thus elected shall also be between the ages of 60 and 70 at the time of the election and shall serve for a period of ten years, automatically ceasing from office on the tenth anniversary of election, unless this conflicts with the celebration of either Christmas or Easter.

---

to discriminate against women here. If there were only five women out of one hundred and twenty members in the conclave now, that number would rise over the years as more women are ordained. It would also be five more than there has ever been in the past, and one must start somewhere. Furthermore, elections can be close and in some cases it could be the single vote of one of the five women that determines the entire election.

THE SYNOD OF BISHOPS

The present synod is no more than an advisory body and is not a full expression of collegiality. It does not make the bishops "co-holders of supreme power within the Church." Since there are no other ordinary expressions of collegiality, this central concept of the Second Vatican Council lacks any concrete expression in the Church and can easily become a dead letter.

I have attended three synods and drawn a few conclusions:
- Synods are not good places for the discussion and resolution of theological matters, for the bishops are not experts in theology. For the discussion and resolution of theological matters, the presence of experts in scripture and theology is essential.
- Having elected their delegates, the rest of the bishops of the world are not involved.
- The appointment of so many members by the Bishop of Rome further emphasises the pope's superiority over the other "co-holders of supreme power".
- It is unsatisfactory that all material is then handed over to the bishop of Rome to write a final document. The end result is a papal document rather than a document of the college of bishops.

Suggested changes:
1. Synods shall be limited to pastoral and practical matters, with theological matters being referred to councils.
2. There will be no formal speeches at the synod. Instead, twelve months before the synod, each member who wishes to shall submit a written statement on the subject of the synod, of no more than 1,000 words. These statements shall be translated into the languages of the synod and published in book form.
3. The purpose of the synod shall then be to draw up, discuss and vote on a list of recommendations on the designated topic.
4. When the recommendations are voted on, the exact numbers for and against shall be recorded.
5. The recommendations, together with the exact voting details, shall then be forwarded to all the bishops of the world.
6. All bishops shall vote on the recommendations and forward their vote by mail to the Papal Nuncio in the area.
7. The exact voting details shall be attached to any publication of the recommendations, so that all may know the strength of the support of the college of bishops on that issue. In this way the work of the synod shall be a truly collegiate act of the entire College of Bishops.
8. It may also be decided that a synod may be held by correspondence through the internet, thus avoiding the expense of bringing so many

people to Rome and housing them there.
9. Rather than add many non-bishops to what is called a synod of bishops, it may be decided that there shall also be synods of other groups, for example a synod of women to discuss the role of women in the Church. It is good that all categories of people in the Church be listened to, but it is not good that a body called "the synod of bishops" become the only vehicle for this.

A fundamental question is whether a synod is a method of expressing the mind of the bishops of the Church or a method of expressing the mind of the entire Church. The structure would be different in the two cases. It seems that the present situation, with selected laypersons added to the bishops, though without a deliberative vote, attempts to be something of both and will always be criticised because it is not really either.

A COUNCIL

The Second Vatican Council spoke of the *sensus fidei* (sense of faith) or *sensus fidelium* (sense of the faithful) – that instinctive sensitivity and power of discernment that the members of the Church collectively possess in matters of faith and morals.[83] The Latin term *sensus fidei*[84] is a useful one because, while it includes rational thinking, it is in itself a sensing, an instinct, an intuition, a head-and-heart discernment of truth.

Sensis fidei is an ancient idea that had fallen into disuse until the Second Vatican Council revived it. The first draft documents at that council followed a traditional pattern by speaking first of the bishop of Rome and then working down through the various levels of the Church until they reached the laity at the bottom. The council changed this, so that its final document speaks first of the mystery of the Church, then of the People of God, and only then of the hierarchy of the Church. In other words, the Church is first a work of God and a means of God's presence, then it is a worldwide community of people, and then, and only then, it is a community with a structure and a hierarchy within it in order to carry out its task. In its essence, the Church is a divine mystery and a pilgrim people, and structure and hierarchy cannot be given the same essential importance.

It was within this context that the council made the statement that "the whole body of the faithful ... cannot err in matters of belief."[85] The disagreements within the council, however, resulted in conflicting ideas being placed side by side and unresolved, so that yes the it is true, the primary message given by the

---

83 *Lumen Gentium*, no. 12.
84 Both the terms *sensus fidei* and *sensus fidelium* are in common use. *Lumen Gentium* speaks of the *sensus fidei*, so that is the term I shall use here.
85 *Lumen Gentium*, no. 12.

council was that the body of the faithful cannot err in matters of belief, but this is the case only if in coming to these beliefs it follows the teaching authority of the bishop of Rome and the other bishops.[86] Despite these ambiguities and conflicts, we must affirm that the council did clearly reintroduce the concept of the *sensus fidei* into Church thinking, and it cannot be made to go away. This is critically significant with the ambiguities of the Second Vatican Council still being with us.

The solution to the conflicts present in the council documents cannot lie in embracing only one side of the conflict. On the one hand, it cannot rest in seeing the *sensus fidei* of the People of God as above or independent from the bishop of Rome and the other bishops. On the other hand, it cannot rest in viewing the *sensus fidei* as primarily being the responsibility of the bishop of Rome and the other bishops to such an extent that it is meaningless. It is a new synthesis that is required – a new understanding of its use.

The essence of this synthesis must surely lie in the idea of dialogue. There must be a dialogue that will enable the *sensus fidei* – the inspired voice of the whole Church – to be heard, and which will enable the bishop of Rome to truly speak in the name of the whole Church.

Highly relevant to this is the fact that all bishops have lost a vast amount of credibility because of the manner in which they have collectively mishandled the entire issue of sexual abuse of minors. This loss has been so great that a council consisting of only bishops would face a serious question of credibility. At this moment in the history of the Church the bishops need the laity as they have never needed them before. In the simplest terms, statements by bishops alone, even in council, would lack credibility, while statements of the whole Church would have much greater credibility. So the council must in some manner include the whole Church.

There is certainly a need for a middle group between the pope on one side and the whole Church on the other side, but the question must be raised as to whether a council representing this middle group should consist solely of bishops or should be a group chosen from the whole Church. And this is much the same question that we are already confronted with.

The process of involving the entire Church would be at least as important as the written outcomes of the council.

The Second Vatican Council spoke of "… the holding of Councils in order to settle conjointly, in a decision rendered balanced and equitable by the advice of many, all questions of major importance."[87] There are certainly questions of major importance facing the Church today, so councils should be normal rather than rare events.

In taking these matters further I have set out a suggested structure for a

---

86 See the entire text of *Lumen Gentium*, nos. 12 & 25.
87 *Lumen Gentium*, n. 22.

council in an appendix at the end of the chapter. Meanwhile a summary of suggested recommendations follows.

Suggested changes:
1. Theological questions should always be resolved by a council rather than by a synod or the bishop of Rome alone.
2. Councils should only be called to discuss carefully selected questions or even only one question.
3. Councils may be conducted through the internet rather than through bringing all the bishops and experts to Rome.
4. Experts in all relevant fields must always have a significant role in a council.
5. The aim of a council always includes enabling the bishop of Rome to speak in the name of the whole Church on a given topic or topics, and proclaim that "This is the faith of the Church on this topic at this moment in its history."

THE ROLE OF THE BISHOP OF ROME

Suggested statements:
1. The supreme authority in the Church may express itself universally through a general council, collectively through the bishops or elected representatives in a synod, or individually through the pope, all in accordance with wise laws developed by the whole Church.
2. The first task of the bishop of Rome is always the more passive task of being the rock of the Church, the firm foundation on which the Church is built, the guardian of the faith of the apostles.
3. Service to the unity of the Church is not simply one aspect of the bishop of Rome's work; it is the whole justification for the special authority given to the office.
4. The bishop of Rome must always be to the Church the representative of a God of love and mercy.
5. Rome is the city of the supreme apostolic witness through the martyrdom of both Peter and Paul, so the role of the bishop of Rome is that of both Peter and Paul.
6. The entire Church must always keep in mind that, barely an instant after Peter had been given the role of being the rock of the Church, he failed and was told to get behind Jesus.
7. The bishop of Rome is at the service of the Church, not the Church at the service of the bishop of Rome. Primacy is at the service of collegiality, not collegiality at the service of primacy.
8. As in most circumstances Peter alone spoke in the name of the twelve apostles, the bishop of Rome alone should normally be the one to speak in the name of the whole believing Church today.

9. Before they can proclaim the faith of the Church, however, bishops of Rome must first enter into dialogue with the Church in order to determine what the faith of the Church on a particular topic is.
10. Encyclicals and other letters to the Church should be a normal part of the way in which bishops of Rome carry out their duties. Their task in these letters, however, is to call the Church back to the faith of the whole Church and to the Great Tradition. It is not their task by their own authority alone to develop doctrine beyond the common faith of the Church and impose these developments on the Church.
11. The bishop of Rome shall be answerable to the Church, as Peter was to the Church of his time. Wise laws of the Church must determine the manner in which this should happen.
12. The role of the bishop of Rome shall not be reduced to that of a figurehead who meekly rubber stamps the decisions of others. It shall rather include the following functions:
    - The local church shall nominate those proposed as new bishops, but it is the bishop of Rome who shall then appoint them, and they shall not be ordained without this appointment. If, the bishop of Rome has difficulties accepting the person nominated, the appointment may be referred back to the local church with a request for dialogue, but the bishop of Rome may not simply overrule the local appointment.
    - The same shall be true for all other major appointments within the Church.
    - The bishop of Rome alone shall have the authority to call a new council or synod of the universal Church, but, in accordance with the laws of the Church, must heed the mind of the Church in so doing.
    - The bishop of Rome shall have the authority to respond to crises in world affairs and to make appropriate statements or take appropriate action. A body representing the whole Church may, however, later approve or disapprove of these actions.
    - The bishop of Rome shall have both the authority and the responsibility to coordinate the Church's response to a moral crisis such as sexual abuse of minors whenever such a crisis arises within the Church.
    - Whenever a serious dispute arises between different groups of bishops, the bishop of Rome shall have the authority to compel the groups of bishops to seek a resolution to their problem and shall determine the procedure to be followed to enable this.
    - The bishop of Rome shall seek to be the sentinel of the Church,

drawing its attention to changing circumstances and powerful new factors in the world to which the Church must respond.
13. There must also be provision made by the entire Church concerning what should happen in the event of:
    - a schism, with more than one claimant to be bishop of Rome
    - a bishop of Rome becoming, through physical or mental illness, incapable of carrying out essential duties
    - a bishop of Rome being prevented from carrying out essential duties by an external force
    - a bishop of Rome falling into formal heresy by denying a truth essential to the identity of the Christian faith
    - a bishop of Rome acting in such a non-Christian manner as to cause serious scandal to the Church
    - a bishop of Rome failing to respond in an adequate manner to a serious moral crisis that has arisen in the Church.

A LEGISLATIVE COUNCIL OF THE CHURCH

Law is a particularly sensitive subject within the Catholic Church. There are three major problems:
- the perception that there are far too many "rules" in the Church
- the perception of a legal morality, that is, of morality as obedience to laws rather than obedience to conscience
- the perception that it is through legislation that the Roman Curia rules the Church, and that people, including many bishops, do not have faith in the Curia.

Suggested changes:
1. There shall be a Legislative Council of the Church, with all new legislation from any source intended to bind the whole Church requiring the approval of this body before it may be presented to the bishop of Rome for promulgation.
2. The major role of the Legislative Council of the Church is to be the voice of the whole Church in this field of legislation.
3. The Legislative Council shall contain a set number of members (such as 120, for example) elected from around the world. Half shall be bishops, clergy and religious, the other half shall be laypeople.
4. The sources of the legislation considered by this body shall be councils, synods, conferences of bishops and the offices of the Roman Curia.
5. To restrict costs, the Legislative Council may carry out as much as possible of its work through the internet.

6. There shall be three conditions governing the Council's work:
   - It must not seek to resolve matters of belief or to canonise one among several legitimate theological opinions, under pain of the invalidity of its decisions;
   - All members must be free to vote before God alone according to their conscience. There must be no requirement to vote according to any form of "party line", under pain of any decisions involving such parties being null and void.
   - The Legislative Council of the Church must make every effort to work by consensus rather than a simple majority, for a majority of 51 per cent in favour and 49 per cent against tells the bishop of Rome only that the Church is divided down the middle and no reasonable law can be imposed.

PRESIDENTS OF REGIONS

In this section I shall propose a system of government for the Latin Church based on that of the Eastern patriarchs. If this were to be adopted, however, there would be a question concerning the use of the name "patriarch", which has strong negative overtones for many women in the West. Pending a better title, I shall here instead speak of the "president".

In the early centuries of the Christian religion there were five patriarchs, one in the West (Rome) and four in the East (Constantinople, Antioch, Alexandria and Jerusalem). Later, as Christianity spread, other Eastern patriarchs were added. Today there are patriarchs in the Orthodox Churches and there are patriarchs within the Catholic Church. Within the Catholic Church the patriarchs are the heads of Eastern communities such as the Copts, Melkites, Maronites, Ukrainians, Siro-Malabar, Syrians, Chaldeans and Armenians. These are parts of the Catholic Church that acknowledge the bishop of Rome as head of the Church, but have always had their own liturgy, language and customs and have enjoyed a measure of self-rule within the Church.

Although these patriarchs are the heads of their community, they can exercise their authority together only with the other bishops of that community. They may carry out certain less important tasks alone, and both the presidency and a certain power of initiative in all matters are in their hands, but in important matters they require the consent of the permanent synod of the patriarchate. Considerable detail concerning the role of a patriarch is already contained in canons 55–150 of the Code of Canons of the Eastern Churches.[88]

Even when taken together, these descendants of the four Eastern patriarchates make up only a small part of the Catholic Church. All of the

---

88 Published by Pope John Paul II, October 18, 1990.

rest of the Church descends from the one Western patriarchate (Rome) and constitutes the so-called Latin Church, in which for many centuries Latin was the official language of the liturgy. In this greater part of the Catholic Church the leader is not only bishop of Rome but also patriarch of the Latin Church.

However, the roles of bishop of Rome and patriarch of the Latin Church are two quite distinct roles and there is no necessity that they both be held by the one person. There is no reason why another person could not be appointed to the office of president of the Latin Church in exactly the same manner as someone is appointed as patriarch of the Copts or Melkites. Just as the original four Eastern patriarchates were expanded and new patriarchates added, so there is no reason why the Latin Church could not be divided into a number of different areas, with each of these areas having its own president. If so desired, there is, indeed, no reason why each country could not have its own president. In all of this, there is no reason why a system of government that is already highly respected within the Catholic Church could not be extended to the whole Church. There could be another "discontinuity for the sake of a greater continuity" and a greater degree of participatory government introduced. The canons of the Eastern code could be adapted to the Latin Church.

In their origins, the patriarchs were the heads of dioceses in major cities, but there is no absolute reason why presidents must have a diocese of their own, let alone a major archdiocese, for there is nothing to be gained by giving two full-time jobs to the one person. However it is managed, they must have the time to attend to matters concerning the whole region. They must also be free to visit Rome at regular intervals together with all other presidents and ensure that the greater autonomy and diversity brought about by this system does not endanger the unity of the Church.

Suggested changes:
1. Serious consideration should be given to the introduction into the Western patriarchate of the system of government already in possession for many centuries in the Eastern patriarchates.
2. The Western patriarchate should be divided into a number of smaller and more manageable entities, or even into individual nations.
3. The canons of the Eastern Code should be adapted to the Western Church.
4. The president should be elected by the bishops of that region and then appointed by the bishop of Rome.
5. The president should be elected for a fixed term rather than for life.
6. At least in larger areas, the person elected should relinquish all other offices and work full-time as president.

THE NATIONAL CHURCH

One of the many problems that arose when revelations of sexual abuse began to appear came from the system of governance within the Catholic Church.

The bishop of Rome is at the head of the universal Church, and the local bishop is at the head of each diocese. In the Latin Church there is no real or effective level of government between the two. There is a Bishops' Conference in every country large enough to have several dioceses, but it has no power to pass laws binding the whole country.

In relation to sexual abuse, whenever one bishop was responding badly, there was no way for the other bishops of that country to compel that bishop to behave in a better manner.

The only way to have a law binding the whole nation has been for the Bishops' Conference, by a two-thirds majority, to request the bishop of Rome to make such a law for the nation.[89] This was a cumbersome process and in practice did not work, especially in a matter where authorities in the Vatican had little knowledge of a subject or of local conditions, as was certainly the case in relation to sexual abuse.

I use this example because it powerfully makes the point that there are occasions when the whole Church of a particular nation *must* speak and act together as one. It is essential to the concept of participatory government that decisions be made at the *appropriate* level, for it is only when decisions are made at the appropriate level that they will be effective. And there are occasions when there is a powerful and urgent need for the Church of a whole nation to act as one, when this is the only appropriate level, and a system of government reflecting this need must be put in place.

Suggested changes:

> There shall be a review of canon 455 of the Code of Canon Law concerning the Episcopal Conference, such that, whenever the national level is the appropriate level, the bishops of a nation can act as one.

I cannot take the matter further than this, for detailed legislation would depend on the decisions made concerning presidents of regions.

THE ROMAN CURIA

A bishop of Rome has so many tasks in so many different fields that it is quite impossible to function without a bureaucracy. The Curia is as essential to the Church as the public service is to any government.

For centuries the Roman Curia has had great power and influence. It has served a monarchical bishop of Rome. It speaks the language of "serving the Church", but in fact it has ruled the Church in the name of the bishop of Rome. It has become an entrenched bureaucracy and recent history has shown just how resistant to change it is.

---

89 See canon 455 of the Code of Canon Law.

Most of the changes needed are changes in heart and mind, and they will not be easy. There are a few changes in structures that may assist.

Suggested changes:
1. The Roman Curia shall equally serve the whole Church, the college of bishops and the bishop of Rome.
2. Those named in charge of congregations, commissions, offices or tribunals shall not be created cardinals or bishops.
3. Synods of bishops or councils may make changes in the rules and procedures governing the Curia in order to make it a better servant of the whole Church, the college of bishops and the bishop of Rome.

THE APPOINTMENT OF BISHOPS

Over the centuries there have been different methods of choosing and appointing bishops. In the case of St Ambrose, the choice took place by public acclamation in the cathedral church (374 A.D.). Usually it was a prince or other secular power who named the bishop. Various Church groups have also had this right at different times, groups such as the chapter of canons in some older dioceses, or the Council of bishops in the Eastern Catholic Churches. With widely differing degrees of success, for some eighteen hundred years the local church had at least some say in the choice of a bishop.

Coinciding with the rise of papal power in the nineteenth century, however, the bishop of Rome more and more reserved the right both to choose and to appoint bishops. Currently, the bishops of a region have a right to submit names and express their views and preferences, but their views can be ignored, for all power belongs to the Papal Nuncio, the Congregation for Bishops, and ultimately the bishop of Rome. Controlling the appointment of bishops is obviously a powerful means of controlling the Church.

The present method has the advantages that unity with the rock of Peter is ensured and a fresh person from outside can be introduced into a diocese when this is greatly needed. It has two serious disadvantages. Firstly, it means that the Vatican alone can control the type of bishop who is chosen, so that all bishops follow the line imposed by the Vatican. Secondly, it means that the local Church has no sense of ownership of the appointment, and this can lead to a lesser commitment both to the bishop appointed and to the work of the Church at the diocesan level.

There is a moment in the ordination ceremony of a bishop when the candidate is presented to the people and they accept by acclamation. This acclamation is always given, for the appointment cannot be changed, so there is little to be gained by refusing to accept the person named. Nevertheless, there are times when the acclamation is less than a heartfelt acceptance of the new bishop.

There is a tension between the needs of the universal and the local Church in relation to the appointment of bishops, and this tension must not be resolved by crushing either side. The two should be kept in balance and the needs on both sides satisfied. The present system fully protects the rights of the bishop of Rome, but it crushes the legitimate desire of the local church to have a voice in the choice of its bishop.

I believe that union with the rock of Peter is so important that the actual appointment should always come from the bishop of Rome, but I believe that three criteria should be observed in choosing the candidate.

The first and overriding criterion is that the method adopted must be the one that is most likely to produce the best candidate for the task. Essential to this is that the candidate should have not only priestly qualities, but also an abundance of human qualities and virtues, including a real ability to relate to people. In Church history there have been too many examples of bishops who were perfect "churchmen" and theologically very safe, but who lacked even basic human qualities. There have been too many men who could only relate through authority.

The second criterion is that the local church should have such a voice in the process that it will feel a sense of ownership of the choice made. The people should not later say, "An outside power placed this person over us; it is up to them to make it work." They should rather say, "We made this choice and it is up to us to make it work."

The third criterion is that the bishops of the region should also have a voice in the process. This should be done in order to ensure that the people of the diocese are not simply looking inwards but are aware of the greater good of the whole Church and are open to the new spirit that a person from outside the diocese might bring.

Neither the Orthodox nor any of the Protestant churches seem to have found the perfect means of choosing their leaders, so we must approach the question carefully.

Given the difficulties involved in choosing the best candidate, groups of people sometimes meet, not to choose a candidate, but to describe the kind of person they want and the qualities their new bishop should possess. This process, however, often produces a description, not of any mere mortal, but of "Jesus Christ on one of his better days". One must query how useful this process is, for in the real world the choice must eventually be made from among a restricted number of very limited human beings.

A popular vote would be pointless unless people knew the candidates, but no one would wish to see candidates putting themselves forward and waging expensive political campaigns asking people to vote for them.

It would seem that a method must be found for choosing a select number of candidates and then providing sufficient detail about them for people to be able to make an informed choice.

There should be room for a questioning of the candidates and a making public of their views. If an informed choice is to be made, then both strengths and weaknesses would have to be mentioned. This has its dangers, especially if heightened emotions were aroused in the process.

Eventually there would be a preferential vote undertaken by the people at Sunday Masses on a given Sunday.

It would most probably be wiser to allow a certain amount of experimentation before fixed forms for electing a bishop were determined.

In these suggestions I believe that I am proposing a discontinuity with the last two hundred years for the sake of a greater continuity with the previous eighteen hundred and, indeed, with the Great Tradition itself.

THE BISHOP IN HIS DIOCESE AND THE PRIEST IN HIS PARISH

It would be inadequate to have a more collegial and participative form of government at the universal level of the Church if the diocesan bishop still had a quasi-monarchical power in the diocese or the parish priest had a quasi-monarchical power in the parish.

At the council of Trent the popes did not reform the papacy, and today bishops could not be relied on to carry out a rigorous reform of bishops in their dioceses or priests be relied on to carry out a rigorous reform of priests in their parishes. Such reforms would also lack credibility. In both cases there must be genuine consultation with the laity, and they must be given a powerful voice.

The beginning of suggested changes:

At the diocesan level:

1. The sections of the Code of Canon law dealing with the diocese shall be revised in such a way as to temper the authority of the diocesan bishop by giving more deliberative power to the priests, religious and lay members of the diocese.
2. The finance committee of the diocese shall have a deliberative vote in the financial administration of the diocese.
3. The existence of a pastoral council in a diocese shall be obligatory, not optional.
4. Whenever two thirds of the members of the pastoral council vote in favour of a resolution, their decision shall be binding on the bishop.
5. The pastoral council shall be convened once a month, unless a majority of the members decide that it is sufficient to meet every three months.
6. If two thirds of the members agree, they may introduce an item to the agenda against the will of the bishop.
7. The members of the pastoral council shall ensure that the whole diocese is kept informed of the deliberations and decisions of the council. On major matters they shall insist on a consultation with the whole diocese.

If two thirds of the members insist on a consultation with the whole diocese, the matter shall automatically be a major matter.

At the parish level:
1. The sections of the Code of Canon law dealing with the parish priest shall be revised in such a way as to temper the authority of the parish priest by giving more deliberative power to other priests in the parish, and to religious and lay members of the parish.
2. The finance committee of the parish shall have a deliberative vote in the financial administration of the parish, but only when two thirds are in favour of an idea.
3. The existence of a parish council in a parish shall be obligatory, not optional.
4. Whenever two thirds of the members of the parish council vote in favour of a resolution, their decision shall be binding on the parish priest.
5. The parish council shall be convened once a month, unless a majority of the members decide that it is sufficient to meet every three months.
6. Two thirds of the members may introduce an item to the agenda against the will of the parish priest.
7. The members of the parish council shall ensure that the whole parish is kept informed of the deliberations and decisions of the council. On major matters they shall insist on a vote by the whole parish. If two thirds of the members insist, the matter shall automatically be a major matter.

DRESS AND TITLES

The dress and titles of cardinals and bishops were developed many centuries ago and reflect the values and mores of those times and places. Today they are seriously anachronistic (belonging to a different period in time) and give out false messages. They are a long way away from what Jesus himself said and did.

Titles still current in many places in the Church (Your Holiness, Your Eminence, Your Grace, My Lord, Monsignor and similar) are such a long way from the practice of Jesus that they should no longer be tolerated. We must go back to the gospels and adopt their language.

The same is true of the forms of dress adopted by many officials. The full red cassock of the cardinal and the full purple cassock of the bishop are surely the first examples. How can one possibly imagine Jesus dressed like that? The cross was made of wood and was an instrument of torture and death, so it is surely contradictory to see expensive or even jewelled crosses worn by bishops. An expensive ring is surely the same contradiction.

Given a choice, the mitre is the very first thing I would abolish (and have done so many years ago in my own life). It screams the message, "I am the tallest person here because I am the most important person here." Surely Jesus would not be seen dead in a mitre, for he never wished to give out such a message.

I have problems with the colour black for priests. It tends to scare children and to be forbidding for adults. It does not project the joy that should be part of being a Christian. Why could a priest not dress in the ordinary attire of laypersons, together with a special tie or other symbols that would identify a priest? Why could something similar not be done for religious sisters and brothers?

Suggested change:
- Serious consideration should be given to all aspects of the dress and titles of all officials in the Church, so that they may better conform to the example of Jesus and the values he stood for.

THE WEALTH OF THE CHURCH

It is time for a serious look at the overall wealth of the Church, the treasures of the Vatican and the existence of treasures of great value in other Church buildings throughout the world, and for decisions concerning the future.

I do not speak as an iconoclast. I do not wish to banish all beauty from church buildings, and I appreciate the desire of Christian people to give to God's house as best they can.

CHAPTER 16
THE SEEKING OF GOODNESS

The greatest minds the world has ever known have struggled with ideas concerning the seeking of goodness, and none of them has ever claimed to have said the last word on the subject. At the same time, every single human being, no matter how limited in intellect, has had to made moral decisions daily. In other words, there are questions that the greatest minds have not been able to solve, and yet the most limited human minds have had to give a practical answer in the here and now and act on it. We must keep this firmly in mind as we begin this chapter.

Graham Greene's novel *A Burnt-Out Case* is rich in the morally ambivalent characters he loved to write about[90]. One of them is a man named Rycker who, after a number of years in the seminary studying to be a priest, left before ordination and eventually drifted to live in a small village in the heart of Africa. In his own words, "At the seminary I always came out well in moral theology."[91] He annoyed the priests at the nearby leper colony with the moral dilemmas he loved to invent and discuss for hours. Despite this, he was not a moral person. Among the mistakes he made were:

- His attitude was negative, so he concentrated on not doing wrong things rather than actually doing something that might help someone.
- He concentrated on the details of his life such as particular actions, but ignored the plot – the whole direction his life was taking.

---

90 William Heinemann, London, 1961.
91 op. cit., p. 46.

- His model of morality was basically legal in that he would obey moral laws laid down by authorities rather than truly taking responsibility for his own actions.
- He was motivated more by fear than by love.
- Because of the kind of morality he practised, a debilitating guilt was never far away from him.
- While avoiding actions that were clearly forbidden, he was a most unloving person towards his wife and the African people who worked for him.
- If asked about goals and means, I would imagine his honest reply would have to have been: "The goal is that of getting into heaven; the means is that of not doing wrong things."

Being called a "moral person" can have overtones of being judgemental, unloving and holier-than-thou. We need to go beneath these ideas.

The Context

The most common understanding of morality is that it is about performing right actions and avoiding wrong ones, and that the emphasis is on individual actions. This approach to morality has two serious difficulties.

The first is that it lacks a context, for it does not address the purpose we hope to achieve by doing right actions, that is, *why* we should want to do good or be good. I shall deal with this question in section A (below).

The second difficulty is that the definition does not face the question of whether performing right actions, in and of itself alone, will make us good. I shall deal with this question in section B.

In its simplest terms, in any human enterprise we first ask two questions: What goal do we wish to achieve and how shall we achieve that goal? The enterprise of living a good life must address the same two questions.

A: WHY BE GOOD?

I shall start the journey by going back to the story of the First Testament.

The first two chapters of the Book of Genesis contain the two stories of creation, Chapter Three deals with the fall, and Chapter Four, verses 1–16, with the story of Cain and Abel. The passage following this (4:17–24) deserves to be as well-known as the ones that come before it. It tells us that, from the time when human beings first inhabited this earth, their natural genius began to assert itself:

> Cain knew his wife, and she conceived and bore Enoch; and he built a city ... Lamech took two wives; the name of the one was Adah, and

the name of the other Zillah. Adah bore Jabal; he was the ancestor of those who live in tents and have livestock. His brother's name was Jubal; he was the ancestor of those who play the lyre and pipe. Zillah bore Tubalcain, who made all kinds of bronze and iron tools. (Gen 4:17–22)

This story tells us that from their earliest days human beings began to live in community, to herd cattle, play music and invent and use tools. But, having said this, the passage is then immediately followed by another which draws a strong contrast between this technical and cultural progress, and the lack of moral ability of people to relate to each other in a manner that would help them to grow as human beings.

> Lamech said to his wives:
> "Adah and Zillah, hear my voice.
> You wives of Lamech, listen to what I say:
> I have killed a man for wounding me,
> a young man for striking me.
> If Cain is avenged sevenfold,
> truly Lamech seventy-sevenfold."[92]

If a whole society were to adopt this criterion of "seventy-sevenfold" vengeance for any wrong done, it would be condemned to endless violence and chaos, and all the technical progress it made would be repeatedly destroyed by the violence.

Genesis then tells the story of a people who gradually began to distance themselves from Lamech and to rise towards a higher morality. They began to see some behaviour as right and other behaviour as wrong. From some source deep within themselves they began to feel a sense of obligation to do what was right and avoid what was wrong. That is, they began to experience a sense of moral responsibility.

They began to feel a call to rise above their own self-interest and to act on behalf of others. In doing this, they sensed that they were acting in accordance with what was deepest within themselves. They felt that, by acting in this way, they were gradually opening themselves to truth, reality and life. They began to understand that, by seeking to act morally, they were becoming more authentically themselves and were growing more fully into all they were capable of being.

Needless to say, there were steps backwards as well as forwards throughout this history. Indeed, in their more sober and humble moments the people realised that they could crash all the way back to the moral level of Lamech

---

92   Gen.4:23–24.

in a single instant. They knew that the moral journey did not destroy the predatory forces within them, but merely enabled them to control those forces better. Despite this, they began to have a clearer idea of where truth, reality and authenticity lay.

Over this long history they understood more and more clearly the very first principle of right conduct, "Do what is right and avoid what is wrong". It is a first principle, so it cannot really be proven. And yet, unless their moral sense has been totally deadened, all people on earth feel within themselves the call to follow this principle. They sense a world of responsibility and accountability that is also a world of challenge, opportunity and growth.

Six Levels of morality

In the moral journey of the people of Israel in the First Testament we may distinguish a number of stages through which they gradually rose. I suggest there are six of these levels.

Level Six

The level of Lamech is surely the most primitive level of relationships between people, and the very starting point of a long journey. As I have already indicated, if a whole society were to adopt this criterion of seventy-sevenfold vengeance for any wrong done, it would be condemned to an endless cycle of violence and chaos, with all its technical and cultural progress repeatedly destroyed. This may be called the level of *superiority and vengeance*, for Lamech sought vengeance because he considered himself superior to all other people. Indeed, in his view, any harm committed against him was seventy-seven times greater than any harm he caused to others, for he was seventy-seven times more important than they were.

One does not have to look hard to see that even today there are individuals, groups and whole nations that can at times fall to this level of morality. Perhaps no group is immune from it. And on an individual level, whenever a serious wrong is done to us it is often our first spontaneous reaction to say or do: "If you hit me, I'll hit you harder."

Level Five

The next level is that of the well-known biblical saying, "An eye for an eye, a tooth for a tooth."[93] This saying is not an order from God concerning the manner in which we should act, but part of the long *journey* of the human race in rising above the moral level of Lamech. Far from being as primitive as it is often thought to be, this law was a conscious attempt to rise above the earlier

---

93   Exodus 21:25, Deuteronomy 19:21.

level, for its force was, *not seventy-seven teeth for one tooth; not even two teeth for one tooth; no more than one tooth for one tooth.* It came from a time long before police forces and prisons, a time when justice tended to be both immediate and physical. Far from requiring vengeance, it sought to restrict it, for it meant that if person A knocked out a tooth of person B, B would then knock out a tooth of A and the violence would stop there. It may be called the level of *justice without mercy.*

In practice, this was still too close to the level of Lamech, and Mahatma Gandhi's comment on it was, "An eye for an eye leaves the whole world blind." It is the morality of "getting even", very common among children in school playgrounds ("he hit me first"), and just as popular with adults, even if they manage to conceal it under more polite words. One is reminded of the chilling phrase attributed to the father of President John F. Kennedy, "Don't get mad; get even." If humanity were to make serious progress, this rule would also have to give way to higher levels of morality. The use of such a phrase to claim divine approval for capital punishment, as though it were God's express will, shows a complete misunderstanding of the development of ideas in the Bible.

Level Four

Throughout human history people have related to other people largely on one of two bases: either the usefulness of others to themselves or the essential dignity of others. Sadly, in all cultures and at all times (including our own) the first has tended to dominate, with people esteeming those who were useful to themselves while pushing to the margins of society those who were seen as "not useful". This is the moral level of *self-interest based on the usefulness of others to oneself.* Needless to say, most of our relationships are reciprocal, that is, we both give and receive, and this is of course desirable. But it leaves the question of how we should relate to both individuals and whole categories of people (for example refugees, the elderly, the Aboriginal people) who may in the eyes of some seem to have little to offer us.[94] This level is reflected in many incidents in the Bible and in statements such as,

> When you sit down to eat with a ruler,
> observe carefully what is before you,
> and put a knife to your throat if you have a big appetite.[95]

That is, if you are invited to eat with a powerful person, the important thing is not the one meal, but your ongoing relationship with this influential person who can do many good things for you, so don't be a glutton, but show that you are a sober and responsible person who is in charge of baser appetites. Even

---

94 For the Christian view on this, see Luke 14:12–14.
95 Proverbs 23:1–2.

though it is in the Bible, there is nothing in the least religious about this advice; it is plain worldly wisdom concerning one's own long-term advantage.

Level Three

The third level is that of the Ten Commandments[96], the level that best reflects the practical influence of the great Covenant between God and the people of Israel. This was the gigantic step upwards of the First Testament, for the Ten Commandments were a serious attempt to base human relationships on the essential dignity of all persons rather than their mere usefulness. It may be called the level of *respect for dignity*. Five consecutive commandments call for respect for one's neighbour's dignity as a human being. In the first four they do this by demanding respect for:

- life and physical integrity (you shall not kill),
- the relationships that make life worth living and give it meaning (you shall not commit adultery),[97]
- material goods (you shall not steal),
- a person's good name (you shall not bear false witness).

There would be little quarrel about life, possessions or good name, but the Ten Commandments insist that we add relationships to this list, for much of our life depends on them. Furthermore, just as "you shall not kill" includes "you shall not wound," so not harming the relationship of marriage through adultery includes not harming any relationships that are important to people in making meaning in their lives, such as relationships with parents or children or siblings or friends.

I suggest that these four commandments are meant to be taken together and seen as four aspects of the one commandment. When seen in this way, they are a powerful affirmation of one's neighbour's dignity and of the rights that flow from this dignity. If one respects any three of the four, but violates the fourth (such as relationships), this is not a 75 per cent success, but a basic failure to respect one's neighbour.

In the fifth of the series the commandments forbid even *desiring* to harm one's neighbour ("You shall not covet your neighbour's house; you shall not covet your neighbour's wife, or male or female slave, or ox, or donkey, or anything that belongs to your neighbour").

As well as being a great step forward, the Ten Commandments are also

---

96 Exodus 20:1–17; Deuteronomy 5:6–21.

97 Within the Catholic Church a whole world of teaching on all aspects of sex is usually given under this commandment. I believe that this is a restrictive understanding, for the sixth commandment does not deal directly with matters of sex, but rather with respect for the relationships that give life meaning.

the essential basis on which any higher level must be built, for it is impossible to truly love another person without having a genuine respect for the dignity of that person. Returning to Graham Greene's novel *A Burnt-Out Case*, (Rycker lived somewhere between the fourth and third levels. He had been taught the theory of the equal dignity of all people, but in practice managed to live most of his life at the level of self-interest. Level two, with all its talk of love, made little impression on him.

Level Two

The third level was based on negative commandments ("You shall not"). That is, "Because you respect your neighbour's dignity, do no harm." The second highest level requires that we not merely do no harm, but also do positive good to our neighbour. If I respect you as my equal, I will at least do you no harm and I will wish to see you given all that belongs to you by right. If to *respect* I add *love*, I will wish for all that is good for you and that is within my power to give you, even when you have no strict right to it. In other words, if I respect you, I will ask, "Do you have a right to this?" If I love you, I will ask only, "Do you need it and do I have it to give?" It is the level of *love built on respect* and of the Golden Rule: "Love your neighbour as you love yourself"[98] or "In all things treat others as you would like them to treat you."[99] The Beatitudes of Jesus start here but then continue into the highest level of morality.

Level One

The highest level is also based on love, but this time on *God's love for us*. It is the level of the actions of Jesus: "I give you a new commandment: love one another ... as I have loved you."[100] It includes the idea of loving even our enemies.[101] Some might think that this level is a mere ideal that human beings could never live up to and that they can ignore in practice. Just occasionally, however, a story appears on our television screens, for example that of a stranger running into a burning house to rescue children. To do this involves far more than loving as one loves oneself; it is a genuine rising up to love as God loves. None of us will ever know whether we are capable of this level of heroism until we are faced with the test, and then we might surprise ourselves. Surely an overwhelming majority of parents rise to this level at many critical moments in their child's life, for there are many moments when they must love their child, not as they love themselves, but more than they love themselves. There are

---

98   Leviticus 19:18.
99   Matthew 7:12.
100 John 13:34.
101 Matthew 5:43.

countless examples of mothers who would go without food themselves in order to feed their starving child.

We may all be capable of falling back to the sixth or lowest level, but there is also no one who is not capable of rising to the highest level.

Frequent examples of all six of these levels of morality are found in the Bible. There were, of course, steps backwards as well as forwards, but in these six levels of morality there is the story of the gradual communal journey of the people of Israel from the lower levels towards the higher levels, and it can become the story of the personal journey of each one of us.

Becoming All We Are Capable of Being

From all of this it follows that the meaning of the word "morality" should go far beyond not doing wrong things, for morality must essentially include *having the purpose* of:

- seeking to rise above our own self-interest and acting on behalf of others,
- seeking to act in accordance with what is deepest within ourselves,
- seeking to open ourselves to truth, reality and life,
- seeking to become more authentically ourselves,
- seeking to grow to become all we are capable of being,
- and seeking to base our lives on love rather than on justice alone.

In this life we are called to become all we are capable of being. If we wish to do this, we must try to live at the higher end of the six levels of morality and, therefore, on the basis of respect and love.

The Response of Love

The story of Jesus tells us that God is constantly saying to each one of us, "I love you" and the only true response on our part is, "I love you too". From this response of love will flow many truths, many principles of right conduct, a genuine worship of God, and membership of a religious community – but the response of love to the person comes first. Without the response of love to the person, the truths will become lifeless, the principles of right conduct will be burdensome tasks, the worship will be empty, and the religious community will be soulless. With the response of love, the truths will come alive, the principles of right conduct will be the most natural things in the world, the worship will be life-giving and the religious community supportive. Right conduct divorced from the response of love will always be inadequate.

It follows from this that morality is *essentially relational*, for it is essentially about the kind of relationship we wish to have with God, and, therefore, with other people. It is about the kind of god we worship – an angry god, a just god or a loving god. Despite all his studies, Rycker had failed to learn this simple truth and was caught in the worship of an angry god, or at best a just god, but certainly not a loving god. He failed to see the fundamental truth that morality is about relationships more than individual actions. Christian morality, therefore, cannot be simply about "not doing wrong things". It must be about deepening our relationship with God.

It follows that it is vitally important that morality and spirituality not be separated, so the saint is the truly moral person and the truly moral person will be a saint. The natural sense we all have within us that we should live morally must be seen as an invitation to holiness. If morality and spirituality are separated, morality will inevitably wither and die.

Commandments and Beatitudes

If a family comes to live next door to me and I do no harm to them, I can hope that they will not become my enemies. But if I want them to be much more than "not enemies", if I want a *relationship* of love and friendship, I must go well beyond "doing no harm".

Our first moral duty is not to harm others and our second is to do what we can to help them. The first duty comes first, for it is foolishness to speak of helping people while we are actually harming them. The concern of the commandments is with this first duty and, because it comes first, we can never do away with them. Jesus never rejected the Ten Commandments: it was wrong to kill, to harm life-giving relationships, to steal legitimate possessions and damage a person's good name, and he proclaimed these truths constantly.

The commandments, however, largely express negative requirements for growth ("You shall not ..."). Even if we observe every negative commandment perfectly, this does not yet say very much about our spiritual state. It says what we have not done but does not say that we have actually done anything positive to assist others. The negative commandments are a necessary foundation, for they ensure that we do not do positive harm to others, but they cannot in themselves build true moral and spiritual growth.

It was for this reason that Jesus, without doing away with the Ten Commandments, added to them the beatitudes.[102] To, "You shall not kill," Jesus added, "Blessed are the peacemakers." Not to kill or harm is the essential foundation, but true spiritual growth is to be found in doing all we can to create peace. To, "You shall not steal," Jesus added, "Blessed are the poor in spirit." Not stealing is the foundation, but true growth is to be found in the active seeking of spiritual values. There is a profound challenge to adopt a true Christian morality in the Beatitude, "Blessed are those who hunger and thirst for all that is right, for they shall be satisfied." That is, blessed are those

---

102 Matthew 5:1–12.

who desire all that is right and just and good, and who desire it with the same degree of intensity as a person dying of hunger desires food or a person dying of thirst desires water.

The Beatitudes are not commandments, so we do not sin if we do not live up to their highest ideals, but it would be a total misunderstanding if anyone were to conclude that they are not, therefore, part of Christian morality. They are ideals rather than laws, but they are what has been called "prescriptive ideals", that is, we do fail if we totally ignore the ideals and make not the slightest attempt to strive towards them.

Any adequate understanding of Christian morality must include these ideals and purposes. If we take them away, morality will lack cogency in our lives, and could become as empty and formalistic as it was in the life of Rycker.

B: TAKING RESPONSIBILITY

As well as determining the goals we are seeking, we must also think about the means by which we will achieve those goals.

Doing Right Things and Taking Responsibility for Them

a) Doing Right Things

Most certainly, doing right things and avoiding wrong ones is an essential part of growing to become all we are capable of being. We do not grow by doing things that harm other people or our own true good, even if we do them in good faith.

> Example 1: In the midst of a powerful history of communal or tribal hatreds, a certain person makes the decision that he should take part in the massacre of his perceived enemies and does so. He may have been doing what at the time he thought was right, but I would have to add that his decision has hurt him. He has become a murderer, and for the rest of his life, whenever he looks in a mirror, that it what he will see. To make serious progress as a human being, he would need to recognise that his decision had been mistaken, and he would need to do all he could to repair the damage he had caused.

> Example 2: Numbers of Aboriginal children from what is called "the stolen generation" were taken from their families and given into the care of institutions (orphanages, schools) or white families, in the belief that this would help their progress within the wider Australian society. Many of the people involved in this, both Government officials and fostering parents, may have acted out of good motives. The results

were, however, disastrous and the whole program involved a level of paternalism and a sense of superiority that caused great harm, not only to the Aboriginal children, but also to those implementing the policy.

b) Taking Responsibility for our Actions

Doing right things is, however, no more than a means to an end and it is not capable, in and of itself alone, of achieving the end. Morality is about growth as moral persons, and for growth more is required than simply performing right actions.

> Example 3: As children grow, it is important that they learn right habits, but it is also important that they gradually learn to take responsibility for their own actions. If they learn wrong habits from their parents, or if they rebel against their parents and adopt wrong habits themselves, they will encounter problems. But if they do not learn to take responsibility for their own actions, obedience to parents will gradually become an obstacle rather than a help to their true growth as persons. A forty-year-old who cannot take responsibility, but must in all things still follow parents, is not an ideal for anyone. If this is true in all aspects of life, it is true also of moral life.

> Example 4: Years ago much marriage counselling was directive, that is, a couple presented their problem and the counsellor responded by indicating the best way to resolve the problem. All too often, however, the couple went away not fully convinced the solution would work, or even not wanting it to work. They may have tried the solution, but in only a half-hearted way and, when it consequently did not work, blamed the counsellor. Then most counselling became non-directive. That is, the counsellor undertook the harder task of helping the couple to find their own solution to the problem, a solution they were both convinced of and committed to. Even if the solution the couple decided on was not the one the counsellor thought ideal, nevertheless, as long as it was sound and represented good progress, it was the best solution in the circumstances because the couple took responsibility for it.

> Example 5: There are persons who, because of fear or laziness, do not want to take personal responsibility for moral choices. They want either the Bible, or Church authority, or a charismatic leader, or popular opinion, or a peer group, to take the responsibility for them, so that all that will be left to them is to follow this authority. These persons have not truly taken personal responsibility for their decisions and will not

> grow as they should. Mere obedience, to either religious authority or popular opinion is not enough.
>
> Example 6: Many moral decisions are easy, so it is easy to take responsibility for them. The more difficult the matter we are dealing with, the more difficult it will be to make the decision. On the other hand, the more difficult the issue, the more we will grow through the process of taking true responsibility for our actions.

This need for personal responsibility is fully in agreement with Catholic teaching.

> By free will one shapes one's own life. Human freedom is a force for growth and maturity in truth and goodness.[103]
>
> Freedom makes us responsible for our acts to the extent that they are voluntary.[104]
>
> The right to the exercise of freedom, especially in moral and religious matters, is an inalienable requirement of the dignity of the human person.[105]

Conscience enables one to assume responsibility for the acts performed.[106]

Thus it is important that we take personal responsibility for our decisions and it is also important that we get them right. We will not grow unless we take personal responsibility for our actions. But, even if we do take personal responsibility, we will still not grow if our decisions harm other people or our own true good. For growth, both of these elements are essential. Any adequate understanding of the meaning of the word "morality" must, therefore, contain both elements.

While both elements are admitted within the Catholic Church, there has been a long history of insistence on doing right things and far less emphasis on taking personal responsibility. On the contrary, the insistence has often been on the idea that the Church would tell us what was the right thing to do and we should simply obey the Church. This substitution of obedience to the Church for the taking of personal responsibility has not helped people to grow. Of course we should listen respectfully to the Church, but it is a means of taking personal responsibility rather than a substitute for it.

103
104 ibid., no. 1734.
105 ibid., no. 1738.
106 ibid., no. 1781.

The Essential Presence of Love

This Section B deals with how we might achieve the goals set out in Section A, and I have insisted that to do that we must essentially add love to justice.

It is only the combination of love and justice that can produce truly moral persons. No matter how just people are, they will never be truly moral persons unless their lives and actions are filled with love. A moral person will always be striving to live at the higher end of the six levels I spoke about earlier, where love is added to justice.

It follows that our relationship with God must be a love relationship if it is to satisfy us and bring us to goodness. In practice, if our relationship with God is not a love relationship, it will inevitably be a commercial relationship in which we say, "Lord, I will accept all the truths you have revealed, I will seek to obey all your moral rules, I will go to Mass every Sunday, and I will be a full member of the Church, and you in return will give me eternal life." The problem with this attitude is that it will never answer the longing for love that brought us to God in the first place.

Religion makes sense only as a love relationship. Anything less than this will not bring real satisfaction and will. But it will cause much frustration and disappointment. Anything less than a love relationship will never win the battle for the imagination of people.

There are profound fears in the idea of a love relationship with God, for I do not know what such a relationship might ask of me. I am afraid that it will inevitably draw me to enter more deeply into myself, and to rise closer to becoming all that I am capable of being. These are profound thoughts and they cause profound fears.

It would be easy to hold back from such a commitment and seek to be in control of my religious life through a commercial relationship. I could then accept God but make sure I kept God at a safe distance. I could even use the formal prayers of religion as a way of being polite to God and saying all the right things, but without actually having to say and mean anything as frightening as "I love you".

And yet the holding back, the less than total commitment, would inevitably harm my personal relationship with God, the obligations of belief would immediately begin to become burdensome and the relationship would no longer speak to the needs that brought me to it in the first place. If I seek to base my whole moral life on a commercial relationship with God rather than a love relationship, I will never achieve either happiness or goodness.

Living Fully

Nearly nineteen hundred years ago an early Christian saint, Saint Irenaeus, wrote words that are still strong today: *Gloria Dei vivens homo* – the glory of God is a living human being. The glory of God is not to be found in millions of people bowing down in fear before God, but in human beings who grow to become all they are capable of being. I prefer to put it in the plural in this form: *Gloria Dei omnes homines plene viventes* – The glory of God is all human beings living fully.

I suggest that there are seven fields in which we all develop over time: the physical, the intellectual, the emotional, the social, the artistic, the moral and the spiritual. To live fully is to achieve the maximum possible balanced development we are capable of in all seven.

The first five speak for themselves, and I shall speak of moral development in the next section. That leaves spiritual development. I find that the most intelligible way to speak of the spiritual development is by saying that people are developing spiritually if they are seriously seeking to recognise and respond to the deepest desires within themselves. Conversely they are not spiritual if they are responding only to the more superficial desires within them. The deeper the desires a person responds to, the more spiritual they are. Growing in all seven of these ways is part of our growth to be a moral person.

C: FORMING OUR MORAL IDENTITY

Moral Choices

Many times each day we make choices between right and wrong. Most of these choices are minor, though major choices can also present themselves. Through these choices we take responsibility for each of our actions. Then, through the sum total of all of these choices, big and small, we gradually and imperceptibly begin to take personal responsibility for the moral direction of our entire lives and to determine our moral identity. Over a long period of time we gradually determine whether we are basically just or unjust persons, kind or unkind, truthful or untruthful, honest or dishonest, loving or selfish. We determine at which of the six levels of morality we habitually act.

Virtues and Vices

Most of the actions we perform each day are the result of moral choices we made long ago and of the *habits* that were formed as a result of those choices, so that we do not think about the morality of the action each time we perform it. There are, of course, right habits and wrong habits. Rights habits are called virtues and wrong habits are called vices. A person possessing the virtue of justice will, from long practice, instinctively react justly in most new situations. A person possessing the vice of injustice will, from equally long practice, instinctively seek an advantage over others without caring whether they might be hurting someone. A truly moral person is one who has worked so hard and long at forming good habits (virtues) that things such as justice, love, compassion, truth, honesty and integrity are a natural part of that person's instinctive reaction to any new situation that presents itself.

The hardest moral struggle occurs when we have deliberately chosen something wrong in the past and must now fight against the wrong habits that have been formed, such as habitually telling lies, spreading gossip, and generally being dishonest.

Experienced policemen would say that for almost anyone a first murder is an overwhelming experience, but that if the same person goes on to commit further murders, even murder can be easy, and become, a habit or a vice. In any particular field, whether it be murder or stealing or anything else, the first sin is the hardest one to commit; after that the sin becomes easier to commit and the habit becomes more and more entrenched.

There are times when we must struggle against habits even when the habit has involved no deliberate wrongdoing on our part. This happens whenever in our upbringing our elders or the community around us transmitted to us habits of thinking and acting that we later came to realise were morally wrong. Unjust attitudes that we may have innocently inherited can relate to the attitudes of:

- men towards women
- 'white' people towards people of a different 'colour'
- Christians towards Jews and Muslims
- people born in a country towards immigrant peoples
- people of richer countries towards those of poorer countries
- people of today towards people of the past (through a sense of pride and superiority)
- people of today towards people of the future (through destruction of the environment).

At times we can be forced to reassess our most simple actions. For example, we long ago accepted that it is morally right to eat with a knife and fork and we have done this all our lives without a single further thought about its morality. But what about all the disposable utensils (and packaging) that are thrown away each day? Can the thought of all this waste of limited resources cause us to think again?

The Basic Choice (the "Fundamental Option")

Through many choices between right and wrong we gradually and imperceptibly form our moral identity. In this process we can then find that in our inmost core we have made a choice, not just between right and wrong, but also between goodness and badness.

Note: For the sake of clarity I prefer to use the terms "good" and "bad" of persons and the terms "right" and "wrong" of thoughts and actions. As I shall use the terms, persons are good or bad (that is, this is the choice they have made in their innermost core), thoughts and actions are right or wrong (that is, a person's particular thoughts and actions can be right or wrong).

Much of Catholic morality comes originally from the Latin language and there the word *malum* means both "wrong" and "bad", while the word *bonum* means both "right" and "good". Thus, the distinction between good and bad on the one hand and right and wrong on the other has no real history behind it. This should be kept in mind in reading any books of Catholic morality.

Furthermore, the word *malum* is all too frequently translated into English as "evil" and this word is too easily applied to many actions. In most cases all the Latin text meant to say was that a certain action is wrong, and it is misleading to translate it as "bad", let alone as "evil". "Evil" is a powerful English word and it should not be used lightly. In particular, the Latin phrase *intrinsice malum* should not be translated as "intrinsically evil", but as "in itself wrong".

The choice between goodness and badness is not simply one more choice, even if at a deeper level than the other choices. It is rather *a self-awareness of who we have come to be at this point in our lives and a choice of who we want to be in the future.* We ought to spend time making goodness conscious and explicit in our lives but, because it is more a self-awareness than a simple choice, it will never be possible to analyse it completely.

Of course, no human being is ever entirely good or entirely bad. A good person can do wrong things and a bad person can do right and even loving things. A good person can have certain vices and a bad person can have certain virtues. A bad person can become a good one and a good person can become a bad one. The basic choice between goodness and badness is always in process, never fully determined once and for all. In a famous sentence, St Augustine once prayed, "Lord, make me pure, but not yet." Did this make him good, bad or on the way?

At the same time, there is an intimate connection between the person one is and the actions one performs. We attain goodness by doing right things and taking responsibility for them, but we will do right things only if we are seeking goodness. First comes the desire for goodness, then the choice of right actions as an expression of this desire. The right actions then reinforce the desire for goodness, turning it into a more powerful and constant striving. This in turn produces more right actions, and so the process continues. The essential starting point is the desire for goodness, for without this the process cannot even begin.

In any moral dilemma we can ask one of two questions: "What is the right thing to do here?" or "Where is goodness to be found here?" The two questions are one and the same question, but the second form of the question, seeking where goodness is to be found, is the more important form, for it better expresses the nature of morality as a *relationship* between ourselves, other people and God, and it better presents the individual action as a desire for the fundamental option of goodness. Also, as we shall see, we can often be in doubt concerning the right thing to do, and the seeking of goodness can sometimes be a surer guide.

Mortal Sin

Within this context, a word should be added on the ideas of mortal sin and hell, for false ideas on these subjects can cripple our understanding of morality.

The word "mortal" means "death-dealing", so I suggest that a mortal sin must be something that is truly death-dealing. To have this effect, it must in some manner touch the inmost core of a person's being, it must be something so fundamental that it changes the moral identity of a person and makes a good person a bad person. The action must in some manner involve the denial of a relationship with God or at least the exclusion of the influence of God over one's actions ("You don't exist or, if you do, I reject you as a guide for my thinking and acting"). Even a single action can turn a formerly good person into a bad one, and we have all heard of examples of such things as murder, rape, sexual abuse of minors or ethnic cleansing that would fit into this category. The change from good to bad can also happen more gradually:

> Example 7: A lawyer faithfully observes the rules of his profession for twenty years. Then one day he sees an investment that will almost certainly bring a rapid profit. Feeling very guilty, he takes a modest amount of money from trust funds he manages for clients and invests it. It brings a rapid profit and he instantly repays the money, feeling very relieved. But he also can't help thinking that, if he had only taken a larger amount of money, he would have made a greater profit. He has committed the first sin, and a second and third will be easier and the amounts will be larger until, somewhere along this road, he has ceased to be a good person and become a bad one.

I suggest that a sin that is not death-dealing, that does not change someone from a good person to a bad person, should not be given the name "mortal".

On this point I find the teaching of the Catholic Church ambiguous. The encyclical *Veritatis Splendor* says that "mortal sin is sin whose object is grave matter" and it specifically adds that:

> care will have to be taken not to reduce mortal sin to an act of "fundamental option". For mortal sin exists also when a person knowingly and willingly, for whatever reason, chooses something gravely disordered. (no. 70).

This appears to say that the free and willing decision to choose grave matter is a mortal sin, even when it does not affect the fundamental option (a choice for or against God). The encyclical, however, goes on to say, "In fact, such a choice already includes contempt for the divine law, a rejection of God's love for humanity and the whole of creation."

This statement, on the other hand, appears to come very close to saying that every free choice of grave matter does affect the fundamental option. Surely this, however, depends on what we understand by "grave matter".

I suggest that the ambiguity occurs because there have been too many cases in Catholic morality of the currency of mortal sin being devalued. For example, it is quite misleading and harmful to moral life to speak of mortal sin in relation to things such as a person missing Sunday Mass or having a "bad thought" about something sexual, or a priest forgetting to say night prayer from the breviary. It is ludicrous to say that such actions necessarily involve "contempt for the divine law, a rejection of God's love for humanity and the whole of creation." It is wrong and harmful to present the moral life as walking through a minefield of mortal sins which are likely to explode at any minute. It is vitally important that this type of thinking be left behind, for this devaluing of the currency of mortal sin has caused innumerable problems and misunderstandings in Catholic morality. It seems that these misunderstandings may all have come from the attempt to coerce people to do things they might otherwise not have wished to do (going to Mass every Sunday, not desiring sex outside of marriage, praying the entire Divine Office each day, for example), and it has caused immense harm in the moral understanding of Catholic people.

I suggest that we are on far safer ground, and have a much better basis on which to build the whole of morality, if we restrict our understanding of mortal sin to those things that truly change a person from a good person to a bad person.

These ideas should not lead us to the opposite extreme of believing that mortal sin is something remote that could never happen to us. We are all capable of a death-dealing sin. We all know that, unless we refuse to allow it to happen, we are capable of great hatred and of the actions that can flow from it. We can all crash back to the level of Lamech at any moment. It can also be said that mortal sin lies at the end of a path, and in order to avoid it, it is better not to take the first step along that path.

We must also be careful not to fall into the mentality of Greene's Rycker and think that, as long as we do not commit a mortal or death-dealing action, everything is in its place. Any attempt to say that a particular action is "only" a venial sin is to fall straight into the mentality of Rycker. We must remember that the only sure way to avoid a death-dealing relationship is to have a life-giving or loving relationship.

There is a corollary to all that has just been said, namely, that to be forgiven of mortal sin requires a profound conversion, for the change in a person must be as life-giving as the sin was death-dealing.

Perhaps the whole matter can be summed up by saying that, at the end of our lives, God is not likely to ask us only whether we have truly repented since we last committed what was considered to be a mortal sin. God is more likely to say to us: "Welcome, please come in. We have all the time in the world, so take your time and tell me your whole story, both the good and the bad. You have had 20/40/60/80 years of life. What have you done with that time? In what ways is the world a better place because you have lived in it? In what ways are the lives of other people better for having known you? What sort of person have you made of yourself? At this supreme moment of your life, tell me, 'Who are you?'"

We will know that we are in the presence of a loving God, so we will not be afraid and will speak freely. However, we will also know that we cannot deceive God or ourselves, so we will speak with total honesty.

Heaven and Hell

Moral monsters have existed in every century, and it is easy to think of several famous ones in recent times. The lives of some have been so shocking that it appears that badness can exist in the innermost core of a person and people can die in this badness. So does hell exist? On the other hand, could a God of infinite love really create a state of eternal torment? I start by saying that I do not believe in a god who enjoys the sufferings of human beings or sees their sufferings as in any way good in itself.

In answering this questions of whether hell exists and if it does, was it made by God, we must be careful of the language that is used. In the Gospel of Mark Jesus is reported as saying, "If your hand causes you to stumble, cut it off. It is better for you to enter life maimed than to have two hands and go to hell, to the unquenchable fire."[107]

It does not make sense to say that the first half of this sentence must not be taken literally ("cut it off"), but the second half must be taken literally ("unquenchable fire"). The language of the whole sentence must be seen as figurative and we must accept our profound ignorance on the subject of what hell might be like. We must firmly put aside all ideas of burning lakes of sulphur, devils, and pitchforks et cetera, for these cannot be anything more than figurative language invented by human beings. All we can really say is that heaven is the presence of God and hell is the absence of God.

I believe that God has an absolute respect for human free will, so I believe that those who firmly and explicitly do not want God's presence after their

---

107 Mark 9:43.

death will not have this presence imposed on them. If hell is understood in this sense as the free choice of God's absence, I believe we must admit that something or other that could be called "hell" exists. Committing a truly mortal sin, in the sense in which I have understood that term, could therefore also be such a choice for hell.

What happens to such people, however, is quite beyond our knowledge. My personal belief is that there could never be a time, in this world or any other, when God would cease to love all human beings or to long for their growth towards goodness. In saying this, I would seem to be in good company:

> For I am convinced that neither death, nor life, nor angels, nor rulers, nor things present, nor things to come, nor powers, nor height, nor depth, nor anything else in all creation, will be able to separate us from the love of God in Christ Jesus our Lord.[108]

Much preaching on hell over the centuries has been overzealous, seriously devaluing the currency of mortal sin, in an attempt to induce fear in people and coerce them to make the decisions the preacher thought they should make. Jesus did not do this, but he frequently presented moral dilemmas in the starkest possible terms. One moral decision on a trivial matter may not seem to be of great import, but it is the sum total of *all* our decisions that creates our very moral identity in our inmost core, and I believe Jesus would insist in strong and even exaggerated language that this is all-important.

D: MAKING MORAL DECISIONS

Conscience

When we must face a serious moral decision, it is important that we leave behind all the noise of the world around us and enter more deeply within ourselves. There we need to listen, to study, to think and to feel. We will listen most carefully to those sources for which we have the greatest respect. They might be:
- a great religious leader such as Jesus Christ
- sacred writings
- a religious community to which we belong
- the writings of a great moral philosopher
- a person whose life of service to others we greatly admire

---

108 Romans 8:38–39.

- someone who has lived successfully through the very problem we are now facing, or
- a friend we trust.

How much value we give to each source will depend on ourselves. The amount of time and energy we spend on a question will depend on many factors:
- the time available before action is required
- the greater or lesser importance of the question
- the availability of persons to consult or material to study
- the extent to which the decision will involve personal action and
- the effect the action will have on others.

This time of serious study and thinking is not yet, however, the moment of conscience. To find that moment we must enter into a room deep within ourselves where we are completely alone with God. We may bring into this room all the study and thinking we have done and which is now in our mind and heart, but we may not bring anyone or anything else. To be a true moment of conscience we must be entirely alone with God, staring into the eyes of God who sees the very depths of our being.

What happens next will depend on the kind of god we believe we are alone with. If we believe it is an angry god, we will probably not think for ourselves; we will probably wish only to obey and get out of the room as quickly as we can. This attitude will not lead to a decision that produces true moral growth, for we will not truly be taking personal responsibility for our decision.

If it is the opposite extreme of an over-indulgent god, a god of soft love, we will probably seek the easiest way out, the softest option, the answer that asks no effort or sacrifice on our part. This will also not help our growth.

If we have worked to find the middle way between these two extremes, we will be alone with a god who, like good parents or teachers, loves us unconditionally, but who also wants to see us grow and so is not afraid to challenge us.

Alone with this God of love and challenge, we shall first seek self-knowledge, for we will know that it is all too easy to convince ourselves of the rightness of whatever it is that we want to do. We shall always seek humility, for we can be dealing with subtle and profound matters. We shall then think about the decision we must make in a dialogue with God. We shall try to be aware of what God might be challenging us to, and the uppermost thought in our mind should be, "How do I best find true goodness in this situation?"

After thinking the matter though carefully along these lines, we will calmly make a decision because we know that God wants us to make decisions and to take responsibility for them. We may be mistaken, and we may later have to change our thinking and even make amends for harm we have caused. Despite this and provided we have made our decision as carefully as we can in all the circumstances of our lives, it is a true decision of conscience. The Second Vatican Council tells us that our very dignity lies in following such decisions of our conscience.

> Deep within their conscience men and women discover a law which they have not laid upon themselves, but which they must obey. Its voice, ever calling them to love, and to do what is right and avoid what is wrong, tells them inwardly at the right moment: do this, shun that. For people have within their hearts a law inscribed by God. Their dignity lies in observing this law, and by it they will be judged. Conscience is the individual's most secret core and sanctuary. There each person is alone with God, whose voice echoes in his or her depths.[109]

Our very dignity lies there, for it is only through such decisions that we can grow to become all we are capable of being.

This is a serious idea of conscience, but the moral life is serious, for my moral identity, who I am, is serious.

Reason, Intuition, Emotion, Imagination

In a decision of conscience, we do our best to make an enlightened and thoughtful judgement before God alone, but the work of conscience is both complex and subtle. There is no such thing as a decision of pure reason, for decisions of conscience engage the whole person and involve an interplay of reason, intuition, emotion, imagination and spiritual discernment.[110]

a) Reason

Reason is important, for it is a major tool in:
- defining the problem to be resolved
- gathering and evaluating relevant information
- seeing all the relevant circumstances
- keeping in dialogue with the sources of moral authority such as the scriptures and the Church community
- investigating how other informed individuals have resolved similar difficulties
- proposing and evaluating solutions, and

---

109 Second Vatican Council, *Gaudium et Spes*, Pastoral Constitution on the Church in the Modern World, no. 16.

110 For this section I owe a debt to L. Hogan, *Confronting the Truth, Conscience and the Catholic Tradition*, Darton, Longman and Todd, London, 2001, pp. 135–164.

- keeping in mind the larger context of which the particular decision may be only a part.

Reason also has its limitations. It has been said that all people carry two large packs on their back, one containing their cultural baggage, the other their personal psychological baggage. It is quite impossible for an individual to leave these two packs behind when coming to a judgement of conscience. Indeed, the cultural and psychological forces at work within us make many of our moral choices predictable or even certain, for they will strongly influence what we find morally right and wrong. If we look back through history, it has often taken a quite extraordinary individual to see that some long-accepted convention in his/her own culture has been morally wrong. Think, for instance, of some of the wonderfully intelligent and good people in Greek and Roman culture who simply took slavery for granted and never thought to question it.

b) Intuition

If, by constant practice, someone has acquired the virtue of respecting others and being sensitive to their needs, and has spent many years trying hard to seek true goodness and to respond to God's challenges, that person may sometimes know intuitively what is the right or wrong thing to do, even though the mind cannot give a full and clear explanation of the reasons. In other words, I would often trust the refined and trained instinct for good of the saint, before the purely intellectual learning of a scholar. Though I freely admit that, if I can have both, this would be even better!

Intuition must always be investigated and placed together with all other factors, otherwise it might merely confirm prejudices or reflect various forces in our unconscious. However, we base significant parts of our lives on intuition, so it cannot be ignored.

c) Emotions

If we care about an important moral decision we must make, and the effects it will have, both on other people and on ourselves, the making of the decision can involve emotional anxiety. Any process of reasoning must then take place in the midst of the emotions aroused.

Also, if I feel no anger or sadness in the face of injustice and violence, or if I have no feelings for other people, I am unlikely to be able to respond appropriately in situations of moral choice.

Furthermore, much of what we do springs from forces in our unconscious mind, and these forces can be quite crucial in the moral evaluations that we make. No amount of rational thinking will uncover them, and it is the emotions that are our only key to an understanding and evaluation of these forces.

Above all, the very desire for goodness, which is the heart of the moral endeavour, lies in the will rather than the intellect. If there is no emotion whatsoever attached to this desire, the will alone is unlikely to carry us very far.

It follows that any intelligent person will take full account of emotions in the process of moral discernment. Indeed, the person who tries to ignore emotions is more likely to be at their mercy than the person who is aware of them. Needless to say, there must be a careful interplay between reason and emotions, so that the emotions will genuinely help rather than hinder the process.

d) Imagination

In facing moral dilemmas people frequently imagine the different scenarios that would result from various options that might be followed. By this method they can gain some critical distance from the problem and see possibilities that might otherwise not be obvious. They can see the problem through the eyes of others, especially of those who will be affected by the decision. Imagination can also help them to go beyond the limits of their own culture and personal history and enter into new realms that present fresh moral possibilities.

e) Spiritual Discernment

Christians believe that within their conscience there is another source of moral evaluation, the Holy Spirit as internal teacher. It is the concept expressed in the quotation from the Second Vatican Council I have already given.

> Conscience is the individual's most secret core and sanctuary. There each person is alone with God, whose voice echoes in his or her depths.

This idea has been part of the tradition of moral understanding from the beginning. In its simplest terms, for a Christian person prayer is an indispensable part of the process of forming one's conscience. Through prayer we do not demand miraculous enlightenment. We rather ensure that our decision will be made within the context of our relationship with God, it will be part of our seeking God and part of our seeking goodness in the core of our being. As I have already indicated, these are often the best questions to be asking in order to find the most fruitful moral decision. How God may wish to be present in this process it entirely up to God.

Original, Social and Personal Failure

At the same time, we must be aware of the limitations imposed on us by the world around and within us.

The story of the *original* Fall in Genesis tells us that we are born into a world containing many limitations. It is part of our heritage and will inevitably form part of our future, for our knowledge and understanding are always partial and incomplete, our desires are often conflicting, and our emotions can overwhelm our reason. The story of the Fall articulates the fundamental truth that limitations of many sorts are embedded in our nature, and our desire to do good is lived out in a context of frailty.

We then live in a *social* environment that bears many marks of social and institutional failure. This social and cultural context of the community we live in exerts a powerful influence on our thinking and feeling, so it can often obscure values and hinder our moral development. It can give priority to non-essentials and desensitise us to particular injustices.

At a *personal* level, all our decisions are affected by our feelings, our prejudices, our vices, our desires and longings, our needs and the pressures that are brought to bear on us. It is all too easy to convince ourselves of the rightness of what it is that we want to do, so we can start with what we want to do and then easily justify it. The truths with which we have to deal can often be profound, complex and delicate. They can demand a knowledge, a sensitivity and an experience that few individuals possess. The proud mind will all too easily claim special insights, while the scrupulous mind will be unable to move at all. The balance required for a clear, open, informed and faithful conscience is one of the longest and hardest tasks that human beings face.

And yet, despite these limitations, conscience must make decisions, for we cannot stand still forever, and we know that God wants us to make decisions so that we may grow. There will rarely be an absolute certainty about the rightness of our decisions, and we must act on the truth as we know it, for this is the best we can do. In the final instance, what is asked of us is not that we get everything right, but that we pursue goodness with all our strength.

The Instant Decision

Sometimes the process of conscience I have spoken of is not possible, for a quite major moral decision can suddenly confront us and the circumstances demand an instant decision. There are two things to say about this situation.

The first is that the more time we have spent in working with a God of love and challenge, in understanding ourselves and the forces at work within us, in studying moral matters, in cultivating virtues and right habits in our lives, and in responding to God's challenges, the better prepared we will be for this situation where we have to make an instant decision.

The second is that, no matter how hard we have worked at these things, we may still make a mistake in this situation. In this case, we need to review the decision after the event, accept our own limitations and God's loving understanding of our limitations, try to understand why we made the wrong decision, and then take whatever action is necessary to repair any damage we have caused. Once again, God does not demand that we always get things right, but that we constantly pursue goodness.

E: THE SOURCES OF MORAL REASONING

If the work of conscience is so difficult, where should we look to find enlightenment and assistance? What are the sources where we might most reliably find the guidance that we seek?

There are two sources of our knowledge of God: The Bible and the world around and within us. They must also be the two sources of our moral reasoning.

The Bible

Morality is essentially relational, that is, it must express our relationship with God. In order to be truly moral, therefore, we should be in constant dialogue with God and hence with the writings or scriptures contained in the Bible.

> For Christians, the status of the Bible as sacred scripture means that it is the most important collection of writings we know. These are the primary writings that define who we are in relation to God and who we are as a community and as individuals. This is the book that has shaped us and will continue to shape us.[111]

The Bible is, "the constitution of the Christian world",[112] "the ground of the world in which Christians live"[113], "the primary collection of ancient documents with which Christians are to be in continuing dialogue. This continuing conversation is definitive and constitutive of Christian identity. If the dialogue ceases or becomes faint, then we cease to be Christian and become something else."[114].

> To be Christian means to live within the world created by the Bible. We are to listen to it well and let its central stories shape our vision of God, our identity, and our sense of what faithfulness to God means. It is to shape our imagination, that part of our psyches in which our foundational images of reality and life reside. We are to be a community shaped by scripture.[115]

In forming our concepts of right and wrong, and hence of what leads to goodness or badness within our very core, this constant dialogue with the scriptures is an

---

111 Marcus J Borg, *Reading the Bible Again for the First Time*, Harper San Francisco, 2001, p. 29. Though I quote Borg with approval here, it does not follow that I agree with all his ideas on all matters.
112 ibid., p. 30.
113 ibid., p. 30.
114 ibid., p. 30.
115 ibid., p. 31.

essential element for a religious person. To abandon the scriptures would be to abandon who and what we are.

Seeking Moral Principles in the Scriptures

At the same time, it must be said that to draw true moral principles of right conduct out of the scriptures takes much hard work.

The First Testament not only presents us with finished ideas and final conclusions: it also tells us the *story of a journey*, the long story of the struggle of the people of Israel towards a higher understanding. It contains both primitive and sublime ideas and tells us of the journey from the first to the second. The tribal chief Lamech, who demanded seventy-sevenfold vengeance for any harm done to him, is a good example of the primitive ideas. To take any of these primitive ideas and apply them literally today would guarantee a false and harmful morality.

On the other hand we have much to learn from the highest levels of morality that were reached in the spiritual journey of the people of Israel, for example:

> You shall not oppress a resident alien,
> You know the heart of an alien,
> for you were aliens in the land of Egypt.[116]

> This is what the Lord asks of you, O mortal,
> to act justly,
> to love tenderly,
> and to walk humbly with your God.[117]

It follows that in the First Testament there is:
- imperfection of understanding
- variety of understanding
- gradual development of understanding.

To understand a passage, it must be read in the light of:
- the whole of scripture
- its place in the gradual development of ideas
- what the prophets and sages say about the idea it contains
- what Jesus says about the idea.

A system of morality based on the idea that every word in the Bible comes directly from God cannot be accepted. It would lead us into many strange and even abhorrent moral ideas. For example, what would we make of the judge

---

116 Exodus 23:9.
117 Micah 6:8.

Jephthah offering his daughter in sacrifice to God because of a vow he had made?[118] We must apply this same principle to the Second Testament as well. An example of this is that the statement of Paul concerning sexual morality is not necessarily the end of all discussion, for questions of sexual morality must be seen in the light of the radical statements of Jesus in abolishing the purity and property laws, and the difficulties experienced by the early Church, including Paul, in responding to this radicalism.

Furthermore, the scriptures cannot give direct answers to questions that the people of the times were not even asking, such as questions concerning nuclear war or the latest ethical concerns in medical science.

The contents of the Bible strongly indicate that, while God did reveal powerful truths, God refused point-blank to do people's work for them. God wanted people to grow and it is only a free response that brings growth, so God did everything possible to encourage free response. Obedience on its own does not bring growth, so God did not give the people of Israel specific orders on all possible subjects, God did not give them answers to all questions. Instead, they had to struggle through the surrounding turmoil in order to understand what they should do. They frequently had to make their moral decisions in the midst of uncertainty and in the absence of any divine revelation.

We must abandon the idea that to every moral problem there is a neat answer contained somewhere in the Bible, and that our only task is to find the right page. The Bible can greatly help us, but we must accept that God meant for us to struggle and to take responsibility in uncertainty, for this is how we grow. There is much divine wisdom in the Bible, but there is nothing there that excuses us from the hard work of separating that divine wisdom from all the faulty and misleading human ideas that the Bible also contains.

A Morality of Relationships

In looking for moral guidance in the scriptures, it is also essential to call to mind once again that morality is not solely about not doing wrong things. If we read the scriptures with the mind of a Rycker (as in Greene's *A Burnt-Out Case*, quoted earlier), looking only for wrong things not to do and the absolute minimum we must do in order to do right things, we will be disappointed, for the scriptures do not give many answers to such questions. If, on the contrary, we read the scriptures looking for how best to respond to God's declaration of love for us, how best to build our relationship with both God and all the people we meet, how best to become all we are capable of being, and how best to fill our lives with the love that is essential to morality, we will find more rewarding answers.

We must remember, however, that just as the First Testament contains primitive ideas of morality, so too it contains primitive ideas of God, that is,

---

118 Judges 11:29–39.

ideas projected by human minds onto God. They include very human ideas of power, domination, anger and revenge.

Once again, what we must work with is *the story of a journey*. We must realise that it was only gradually that a more elevated idea of God was formed. The idea of a God of love is already contained in many places in the First Testament[119], but it was only in some of the later books that there emerged the idea of a God of perfect love for all peoples[120]. This idea then came to its full flowering in Jesus.

The Morality of Jesus

For a Christian, a constant dialogue with the scriptures means above all a dialogue with Jesus Christ. Our constant reference to the manner in which he spoke and acted will be central to the wider dialogue with the whole of the scriptures.

In the four gospels there is abundant evidence of a remarkable and distinctive mind at work in all areas, including that of morality. Jesus made a decisive break from the morality based on law that is evident in the First Testament. At the very time when the rabbis were seeking to spell out the details of what observance of the law meant, Jesus was moving in the opposite direction. For example, by a few simple phrases he abolished the purity ethic and the property ethic, and this should have told his followers that they were to look at matters such as family, sex and the role of women in society in a completely new light. Unfortunately, they found his radicalism on these topics too much for them.

The term "ethic" usually refers to a guiding principle by which we might judge the morality of many actions. In doing this, it refers to the viewpoint from which we look at particular matters, the basic question we ask. For example, a justice ethic will look at actions from the viewpoint of justice and ask, "Is this action just or unjust?", while a love ethic will ask, "Is it a loving action?" The two ethics can come to different answers concerning the same action, for a justice ethic can say that the action is not unjust, while the love ethic can say that, though not strictly unjust, it is not a loving thing to do. Jesus constantly spoke out of an ethic that sought in all circumstances to combine justice and love.

The best example of this is perhaps the parable of the prodigal son[121]. The younger son had no strict right to demand his inheritance while his father was still alive, but the father saw his dissatisfaction and gave in to his wish. Once he had received the full portion he asked for, he had already received his full inheritance and so had no right to any further claims on the property in the

---

119 See Deuteronomy 4:37, 7:8, 10:15; Isaiah 49:14–16; Jeremiah 31:3; Psalms 145:8–9.
120 Cf. Jonah 4:1–11.
121 Luke 15:11–32.

future. Famine came and he was reduced to feeding unclean pigs, so he decided to return home. His motives were hardly pure, for the text shows that he was thinking of himself and his own needs rather than the harm he had done to his father, but at least his pride had gone. The father saw him from afar and his only feeling was of love for a lost son. The son began his prepared speech, but the father cut him short and gave him a robe and a ring, the signs of his status as son, and ordered the servants to put sandals on his feet, a clear sign that they were to treat him as a son of the house. The fatted calf was a sign of how welcome he was.

The elder son heard the sounds of rejoicing and was angry. The father came out to him and to his complaints replied, "Son, you are always with me and all I have is yours." These words were literally true, for the entire remaining estate would go to the elder son, and not one square centimetre could or would go to the prodigal, for he had already received his entire inheritance. He would, therefore, have to work for his living, but the father would always love him, allowing him to live in the house and be treated as a son. In doing this, however, the father would always respect justice and not seek to give to the younger son what now belonged to the elder by strict right, for the younger had already been given his full inheritance. If an extra portion of the land was to be given to the younger son, it would have to be given by the older son, not the father. It was his own rights the father did not insist on, for these could never be as important to him as his love for his younger son. He would love both of his sons equally, but justice demanded that he love them in the circumstances that each had created for himself.[122]

Quite deliberately the parable is left as an unfinished story. The younger son had returned home largely out of self-interest. Did he remain that way, ready to depart again as soon as he had got some money together? Jesus does not tell us, and the choices belonged to the son. The elder son's first reaction had been that of resentment because he felt his own hard and consistent work had not been appreciated. Did he change and welcome his brother home, re-establishing their relationship? Jesus does not tell us, and the choices belonged to the son. The one person of whom we can be absolutely certain is the father, for we know that he had an unconditional love for both of his sons.

Jesus was not the first rabbi to put together Deuteronomy 6:4 ("you shall love the Lord Your God with all your heart and soul and mind and strength") and Leviticus 19:18 ("you shall love your neighbour as yourself"). But he took the idea further than any rabbi before him in replacing law with moral principles and hence substituting an ethic of justice and love for a law ethic. He did this through the commandment of love[123], through the demanding implications of

---

[122] For the source of these comments on the parable, see Duncan Derrett, *Law in the New Testament*, Darton, Longman and Todd, London, 1970, pp. 100–125.

[123] Mark 12:28–34, Matthew 22:34–40, Luke 10:25–28.

this commandment found in their most concentrated form in the Sermon on the Mount, and through the concept of discipleship which included the moral duty to imitate Jesus, even Jesus dying on a cross.[124]

The ethic of justice and love proclaimed by Jesus is a profoundly different approach to moral matters. It explains why most Christian writers today insist again and again that morality is about *relationships*, our relationships with God and with other people. The constant questions asked by this ethic are, firstly, "What does justice demand of me here so that I may at the very least do no harm?", and secondly, "While always being just, what is the most loving thing I can do in this situation?", and, "How can I best deepen my relationship with God and with people through my action here?"

This ethic does not give us immediate answers to all questions and there is still a need to think deeply about moral matters. I shall comment further on this in later sections. For now, it is sufficient to be aware that the attitude of Jesus towards the morality he found around him was radical and revolutionary.

The World Around Us

There is a natural moral law, that is, a moral law to be found from observation of the world around and within us. It is not, however, like a law passed by a parliament. To understand it, it is best to think of it as a law like the law of gravity. The law of gravity does not tell us that we should or should not do certain things. It simply tells us what will happen if we do. It does not tell us not to jump off a cliff. It simply tells us that, if we do, we will fall to the bottom. In falling, we will not break the law of gravity; it will function perfectly, and it is we who will be broken.

The natural moral law works in a similar way. Rather than issue orders, it states facts. It tells us that, if we commit murder we become murderers. If we have a sexual relationship with our neighbour's husband or wife we become adulterers. If we steal things we become thieves. If we tell lies we become liars. We may for a time convince ourselves that there is no such thing as sin, but in performing such actions we will know in our heart of hearts that, as well as harming others, we have harmed our own moral good and our own moral identity as persons.

I noted earlier that throughout human history there have been two bases on which people have related to other people: their usefulness to oneself or their essential dignity. There have been ten thousand excuses offered for acting according to usefulness, but it is impossible to justify it as a principle of right conduct, let alone as a principle of Christian morality. The major reason for this is that usefulness is a poor basis on which to build good relationships with other

---

124 See Adrian Hastings in the article "Morality" in *The Oxford Companion to Christian Thought*, edited by A. Hastings, A. Mason and H. Piper, Oxford University Press, 2000, p. 449.

people. On the contrary, it frequently means, "Because there is no advantage for me, I do not want a relationship with you. Indeed, I would probably be happier if you would quietly disappear altogether." This attitude runs too great a danger of being a denial of the dignity of the other.

The principle of right conduct must surely be to build our relationships with other people on the basis of their essential dignity as human beings. On this basis we can state a series of facts concerning who human beings are in themselves, in their relations with other people and in their relations with God.

The facts become moral laws because we should treat people as who and what they are. For example, I should treat a child as a child and make all the allowances that should be made for a child's lack of knowledge and experience. It would be morally wrong to treat a child as an adult and make the demands that I would make of an adult, such as that the child work for many hours each day. Because we should treat people as who and what they are, the facts about them become the basis of moral laws.

In large part these moral laws can be expressed as a series of fundamental rights that all people have, and contrary laws of a government are a violation of these rights.

> Example 8: Most people agree that the apartheid laws of former governments of South Africa violated basic human rights, that is, they violated basic facts concerning the dignity of non-white people. Most Australians would agree that the rights of aboriginal people were simply ignored in the first coming of the white people to this continent. In neither case did human laws make immoral actions moral. Similarly, if I were to encourage a fourteen-year-old to smoke a first cigarette, I would not be breaking any law, but I would surely be acting immorally, for I would know that smoking is both addictive and harmful, and so would not be respecting the dignity of the young person.

In so far as these moral laws are statements of fact, they can no more be broken than the law of gravity, though this will not always be obvious to everyone. All people know that if they walk off a cliff, they will be broken, but many do not see that. They do not see that if they deny the dignity of another person, they will themselves be hurt in their moral being.

There are many difficulties and dangers in forming principles of right conduct on the basis of our observation of the world around and within us. Despite this, the dignity of the human person should always be a powerful source of moral decisions. I shall return to this question.

The Teaching Authority of the Church

The teaching authority of the Church is a more controversial basis of moral reasoning, for it is not a source, but a use of the tool of discernment in considering the true sources of the Bible and the world around us. I shall devote the next two sections to it, beginning with a brief history of the question.

F: SOME HISTORICAL COMMENTS

The history of Christian morality fills many volumes, so what follows will be the briefest possible summary.

St Paul

Paul was highly innovative on the subject of conscience and gave the Christian religion an excellent start on this topic. For Paul, conscience is a personal evaluation either of God's truth or of the demands of the gospel.

Both in Romans 14:13–23 and in I Corinthians 8–10 he discusses the question of eating meat offered to idols and distinguishes between the good, bad, weak and erroneous conscience. He was the first Christian writer to say that the force of conscience is such that one is obliged to follow it even when mistaken.

Augustine and Aquinas

On the authority of conscience, the dominant view for centuries was that of Augustine (354–430). Using an example of his time, he argued that, just as a lower official cannot pass a law that contradicts the law of the Roman Emperor, so conscience cannot tell us to do something that contradicts God's law, and it is the Church which is the appointed interpreter of divine law.[125] He concluded that, if our conscience and Church teaching are in conflict, we must obey Church teaching.

Against this, Thomas Aquinas (1225–1274) was truly radical in saying that conscience must always be followed, even when it is mistaken, provided only that the mistake is an honest one.[126] He argued that we must always be seeking God's truth and goodness, and must certainly listen to the Church in doing this, but that we must then constantly make decisions based on our present imperfect understanding of that truth and goodness. He promoted a balance of objective morality filtered through personal experience and understanding, and he saw conscience as a collaboration between the objective and subjective

---

125 *Sermo sexta De Verbis Domini*, cap. 8, quoted in *Confronting the Truth*, Linda Hogan, Dartman, Longman and Todd, London, 2001, p. 81.
126 *Commentary on the Sentences*, in Hogan, op. cit., p. 81.

elements of morality, so that the relationship between divine law and conscience is always a dialogue. He concluded that if, after serious and honest study of a matter, including the teaching of the Church on the subject, our conscience and Church teaching are in conflict, we must obey our conscience.

Case Studies

After the Reformation there arose a tradition of "casuistry", so named because it consisted of case studies of individual moral problems. These discussions helped people because they deliberately considered difficult cases and so recognised the complexity of moral decisions and the fact that we frequently cannot have certainty in moral matters. Indeed, it can often seem that the arguments on both sides are about equal. What are we to do in such circumstances? The greatest of the moral theologians of that time, St Alphonsus Liguori, gave security and much peace of mind to people with his principle that an opinion for freedom can be followed if it is equally as probable as the opinion for obligation.[127] This became the common opinion.

Casuistry gave a practical certainty to people in facing many difficult dilemmas, but it had its dangers. Alphonsus was a genuine saint, so the seeking of goodness was always central to his life, and it was on this condition that his principle was valid. Sadly, some people used casuistry to reduce moral discernment to an arithmetic calculation of probability and for them it could lead away from the search for goodness. Casuistry, perfectly legitimate in itself, came to be seen as a bad word.

The Second Vatican Council

To moral theologians the Second Vatican Council could be seen as a disappointment, for it contains many ambiguities and even contradictions on the subject of morality. At times it appears to say that people should follow their consciences, at other times it appears to say that they should simply follow the teaching authority of the Church.

I have already quoted the passage from *Dignitatis Humanae* in which the Council speaks of conscience as the most secret core and sanctuary of a person where the voice of God is heard. Compare that with the following quotation on the subject of contraception:

> Married people should realise that in their behaviour they may not simply follow their own fantasy but must be ruled by conscience – and conscience ought to be conformed to the law of God in the light of the

---

127 This is a very brief summary of a long process. There were lengthy debates between rigorism, tutiorism ("always follow the safer opinion"), laxism and probabilism before the opinion of Alphonsus (known as "equiprobabilism") gained a good measure of acceptance.

teaching authority of the Church, which is the authentic interpreter of divine law.[128]

Despite these serious ambiguities, the Council called for a renewal of moral theology and indicated some trends that would need to be part of this renewal. The need for renewal was expressed in the document on the Formation of Priests.

> Special care should be taken to improve and perfect moral theology, bringing it into closer contact with the mystery of Christ and the history of salvation. Its scientific exposition, more profoundly nourished by the teaching of Holy Scripture, should exhibit the divine vocation of people in Christ and their obligation in love to bring forth fruit for the life of the world.[129]

In seeking to give direction to this renewal, the following trends appear to be present in the documents of the Council taken as a whole

- Morality is essentially about our relationships with God, other people and our own deeper selves, so all morality is essentially relational.
- The Scriptures should have a far greater importance in the entire field of moral theology.
- That moral theology must be brought "into closer contact with ... the history of salvation" argues for the relevance, not only of what is immutable in human nature and outside of history, but also of the ways in which people change and develop in different times and cultures.
- The need to do right things and the need to take responsibility for our actions are both essential to morality.[130]
- The goal of morality is moral growth, and doing right things is essential, but in itself insufficient to achieve this goal.
- Morality and spirituality need to be reunited.
- Justice and love need to be reunited.
- The necessary work of analysis of human actions must be complemented by the work of synthesis, so that each action is seen as part of the individual's lifelong search for goodness and total growth as a person.

---

128 *Gaudium et Spes*, no. 50.
129 Decree on the Formation of Priests, *Optatam Totius*, October 28, 1965, no.16.
130 "Man's dignity therefore requires him to act out of conscious and free choice, as moved and drawn in a personal way from within, and not by blind impulses in himself or by mere external constraint. Man gains such dignity when ... he presses forward towards his goal by freely choosing what is good ..." (*Gaudium et Spes*, no. 17.)

- The desire for goodness is central to all discussion of morality.
- Laws exist for the sake of persons, not persons for the sake of laws, so morality should be based on the growth of persons rather than on obedience to law.[131]
- Moral theology is always and inevitably imperfect, and there must always be a sense of mystery and reverence in all moral discussion.

The documents of the Second Vatican Council contain many compromises, as differing views sought to assert themselves. Its statements relating to moral theology could not escape these compromises. Despite this, it can be said that there are distinct trends in the work of the Council. If those who wish to run with the new do not claim the support of the Council for everything they would wish to say, those who wish to cling to the old may not ignore these trends as though they did not exist. In an event such as the Council, it is not always possible to spell out all the implications of a trend. If distinct trends exist, they are not yet "received doctrine", but we must work with them and carefully seek to see where they lead. It is a synthesis of the old and the new that is now required.

The Time Since the Council

The Catechism of the Catholic Church gives a fairly straightforward presentation of conscience. It says that:

> [Human beings have] the right to act in conscience and in freedom so as personally to make moral decisions.[132]

In speaking of the formation of conscience it says:

> In the formation of conscience the Word of God is the light for our path; we must assimilate it in faith and prayer and put it into practice. We must also examine our conscience before the Lord's Cross. We are assisted by the gifts of the Holy Spirit, aided by the witness or advice of others and guided by the authoritative teaching of the Church."[133]

It is a pity that this statement says that the Holy Spirit merely "assists" while authoritative teaching "guides". This could have been better expressed.

The ambivalence that we saw within the Second Vatican Council continues

---

131 See *Gaudium et Spes*, nos. 12–15. See also no. 26: "At the same time, there is a growing awareness of the sublime dignity of the human person, who stands above all things and whose rights and duties are universal and inviolable."
132 No. 1782.
133 No. 1785.

to exist and has, indeed, been greatly sharpened. On the one hand, the encyclical *Veritatis Splendor* says, "The Church puts herself always and only at the *service of conscience*".[134]

On the other hand, there has been a constant insistence that people must conform their thinking to the teaching of the Church. There are and have been many issues where this has been relevant, though the two critical ones have been contraception and the ordination of women. While the latter question does not belong to the field of moral theology, it does involve the moral question of whether conscience has the right to hold a view contrary to that of Church teaching. The two questions together have frequently become the litmus test of orthodoxy and loyalty.

An Assessment

The Catholic Church has at times been like a rock standing against a powerful flood of popular trends. It has at times been a lone voice asking some of the questions that need to be asked. It has been prepared to be reviled in order to stand up for things it believes are truly important for the good of all people. It has shown a good and right concern that people should do the right thing, because it knows that doing wrong things is not the way to moral growth. It has striven hard to base morality on objective principles rather than on subjective thoughts and feelings. It has devoted much energy to the manner of determining right and wrong actions, and many principles have been evolved over the centuries that are of enduring value.

At the same time, there are several major weaknesses.

- Because of an emphasis on right and wrong actions, there has been the tendency to place at the centre of morality the doing of right actions rather than the building of relationships. There has been too much of the attitude of "getting into heaven by avoiding wrong actions".

- There has been the tendency to stress the doing of right actions in and of themselves, and to downplay the importance of the individual taking personal responsibility for each action. It must be said that the teaching authority within the Catholic Church has not always respected the role of conscience. Indeed, it has sometimes seen conscience as the enemy of authority rather than its essential ally.

- Morality has been too much based on the pursuit of justice and has not given sufficient attention to the idea that love is essential to true morality. It has consequently tended to separate morality from spirituality in a way that is not helpful.

- Because the Bible does not give us clear and simple guidelines

---

134 No. 64, emphasis from the text itself.

concerning right actions, it has not been given a sufficiently important place as a source of moral thinking.

- The natural moral law as a source of moral thinking has been taken too far. This is particularly true in relation to sexual morality, where a restricted and purely physical view of what is "according to nature" has come to dominate and to push aside the quite radical views of Jesus on the subject. This tendency has been taken so far that the entire concept of natural law has at times come into disrepute and now needs to be rescued.
- Rather than look to improve the arguments it has used in its documents; Church authority has often done no more than insist repeatedly on the authority of the person issuing the document. (These last two criticisms go together. If one's overriding concern is that people do the right thing, a person will tell another the right thing as authoritatively as they can. If a person has an equal concern that they take responsibility for their actions, they will still make statements, but will rely more on the arguments presented than on authority.)
- In all of this, the teaching authority in the Church has relied too heavily on the wisdom and moral sense of a few people and has been lacking in its efforts to make its moral statements reflect a true consensus of the whole Church. It has not known how to value and make use of dissenting opinions, no matter how honestly they were offered.

Church authority has had a fear that any weakening in its stance would lead to an irresistible flood of people doing whatever they wanted to do. But it has relied too much on authority and too little on argument, and because of this it has lost much of its credibility. There is a profound conviction in the minds of many people that the teaching authority has been wrong on certain key subjects in the areas of power and sex, and this has profoundly weakened its credibility. The sad irony is that this loss of credibility has contributed to some of the very things the teaching authorities has most feared.

So where should Church authority go from here? We may perhaps answer this question by contrasting the Bible and Church authority. As I have already noted, the story of the Bible is that of people having to struggle to know the right thing to do despite a lack of clear statements. Struggling to determine the right thing to do and actually doing it were both seen as essential elements of that story. It was by this combination that people grew in moral stature and, as a broad plan, it came from God. Church authority, on the other hand, has frequently sought to spell out in detail the right thing to do in every circumstance, so that morality was then reduced to doing what Church authority had told us was right. In briefest summary, God always treated adults as adults, while the Church has too often treated them as children.

G: RESPONSIBILITY VERSUS DIFFERENCE

Dialogue with the Community

If a trusted and expert mechanic said that the brakes on my car could fail at any moment, I would be foolish to drive away without having them repaired, even if I myself could not see anything wrong with them. It is simply good sense to listen to such a person, for the mechanic is more knowledgeable and experienced in this matter than I am. If this principle of taking good advice is true in all areas of life, is it not true also in the field of morality?

It is not possible for individuals to shape their consciences on all matters entirely on their own, any more than every individual can be simultaneously an expert mechanic, nuclear scientist, medical doctor and professor of literature. No individual can possibly have the knowledge, experience and wisdom to do this, and those who attempt to do so will inevitably, and often unthinkingly, borrow much of their morality from some other source. It makes much more sense for people openly to admit their need for others in this field and humbly to join with these others in the search for truth.[135]

On serious and complex questions, it makes sense to look at the principles that the Christian community has painfully elaborated over many centuries. There have been two thousand years of Christian history and we can learn much from the best of the collective wisdom of that experience.

Just as a Christian must be in dialogue with God through the scriptures and prayer, so the same Christian must be in constant dialogue with the community of the Church. As need arises, I am in dialogue with a mechanic concerning my car, my doctor concerning my health, my dentist concerning my teeth, and so on. It does not make sense to call oneself a member of a church community and not be in constant dialogue with that community on moral matters. Within this community, conscience can never be an entirely autonomous ethical sense. It is, rather, the place where the individual seeks to combine the collective moral wisdom of the community and his/her own experience and insights.

One of the great writers on the subject of conscience, John Henry Newman, had this to say:

> The sense of right and wrong, which is the first element of religion, is so delicate, so fitful, so easily puzzled, obscured, perverted, so subtle in its argumentative methods, so impressible by education, so biased

---

135 "Through loyalty to conscience Christians are joined to other people in the search for truth and for the right solution to so many moral problems which arise both in the lives of individuals and from social relationships. Hence, the more a correct conscience prevails, the more do persons and groups turn aside from blind choice and try to be guided by the objective standards of moral conduct." *Gaudium et Spes*, no. 16.

by pride and passion, so unsteady in its course, that, in the struggle for existence amid the various exercises and triumphs of the human intellect, this sense is at once the highest of all teachers, yet the least luminous; and the Church, the Pope, the Hierarchy are, in the divine purpose, the supply of an urgent demand.[136]

It must be admitted, however, that the attempt to balance these different aspects of ethical discernment has not always been successful. There has long been a perceived conflict between conscience and the teaching authority of the Church. On the one hand, people are encouraged to educate and inform themselves and take responsibility for their decisions. On the other hand, whenever they do this and come to a conclusion different from that of the pope, they can be told that they must immediately and always assume that the error lies within themselves.

Dialogue between Conscience and Authority

If we take seriously the teaching of St Thomas Aquinas, and the Vatican Council's statements on the role of conscience, and the statements of both the Catechism of the Catholic Church and the encyclical *Veritatis Splendor*, it should follow that the task of Church authority in the moral field is that of assisting consciences. It should do this with deference to conscience as the place of final decision and it should do it with humility, for Church authorities are also human beings struggling to understand the divine.

This view of the role of Church authority in relation to conscience is reinforced by what has been constantly said here concerning the importance of both doing the right thing, and taking personal responsibility for one's actions. Taking personal responsibility means that the final decision must belong to the individual – and Church authority cannot do more than assist. The aim of the entire process is moral growth and the only way Church authority can foster this is by assisting conscience.

There is a twin danger in the idea of Church authority assisting conscience. For individual persons the danger is that of speaking of conscience when they have not done the work necessary to justify the use of this word, when they do no more than go along with the crowd or decide what they would like to do and call that "conscience". This is a constant danger for every single person and much that is called "conscience" does not deserve that name.

The danger for Church authority, on the other hand, is to think, that they alone have a responsibility and an authority to teach in the name of Jesus Christ. Therefore, if people had formed their consciences correctly, they would agree with us. If they don't agree with us, they can't have formed their consciences properly and must be in bad faith.

---

136 Letter to the Duke of Norfolk.

There is a constant tug-of-war between these two forces of Church authority and conscience and the truth must be found in the middle. In this middle way individuals would willingly recognise how easy it is to be led astray by forces within themselves and would freely acknowledge how much they need all the help they can get, for in the long struggle to seek goodness in one's very core there is no room for pride. In this same middle way, however, Church authorities would willingly recognise that they cannot usurp conscience but only assist it.

In other words, what is needed is not a fight between conscience and Church authority to see who gives orders to the other, but a constant dialogue between two parties who both want the best possible outcome for the individual. And that best possible outcome must include the individual taking personal responsibility for the decision. If the individual does not take personal responsibility, it cannot be the best possible outcome.

Some Elements of the Dialogue

a) The Force of Arguments

In fact, and in practice, the effectiveness of any document setting out moral teaching will always depend first and foremost on the power of the arguments contained in the document. The authority of the writer will never be able to make up for a lack of power in the arguments. A document containing powerful and persuasive arguments written by a person with little authority will always be more convincing than a document lacking persuasive arguments written by a person with great authority. If the arguments in a document fail to convince even people of good will, no amount of authority will make up for this. This has been the problem with the papal documents on contraception and on the ordination of women, for in both cases the arguments given have not even come close to convincing people of good will.

A system of documents based on authority rather than arguments could be justified only if the sole issue were that of doing right things. But if it is equally essential that people take responsibility for their decisions, such a system has no legitimate basis. If people are convinced by the arguments put forward, they will make a decision based on personal conviction and will be ready to take responsibility for the decision. If they are quite unconvinced by the arguments presented and do something only because of the authority of the person who wrote the document, they will not take true responsibility for the decision and accordingly will not grow.

b) The Importance of Authority

Despite what has just been said, authority does matter. If I am sick, I want the opinion of a qualified doctor rather than the opinion of someone ignorant of medicine. Sometimes I might want a second medical opinion or a referral to a specialist, but it is undeniable that in most matters authority does count.

I must, of course, decide whether I will accept the word of the doctor. There will be many factors involved in this decision, and one of them will usually be whether the doctor takes the time to explain to me exactly what is wrong and what needs to be done. In other words, I will have most faith in those authorities who do not rely on authority alone, but who attempt to lead me as far as possible along the road of making my own informed decision.

People who insist on being their own doctors are heading for trouble, and people who think they need no help in solving all moral problems run the danger of being both arrogant and foolish. I must, however, learn to trust the moral authority and I cannot be ordered to do this, any more than I can be ordered to trust a doctor. I will in fact have greater trust in a moral authority that does not rely on authority alone but attempts to take me as far as possible along the road of making my own informed decision.

c) The Power of Collective Wisdom

In assessing a moral authority, one of the criteria will usually be whether the opinion expressed represents the collective wisdom of the whole community or only the private wisdom of an individual or group, no matter who that individual or group may be. As a matter of fact, rather than theory, the documents of the Second Vatican Council carry a greater weight with Catholic people than documents written by a pope alone.

This point needs further comment. The Second Vatican Council published a document on what it called "The Means of Social Communication", that is, the media. In the opinion of most people it was an inadequate document. In other words, even the collective wisdom and massive authority of a general council were not enough to save a document when the arguments contained in it were not persuasive.

Something similar is true of the Council's document on religious nuns and brothers, and there is widespread agreement that some later documents on the same subject published by different popes have been superior to it. In these cases, in other words, the documents of individual popes have had more authority than the document of a council, for always and in all circumstances the major force of a document comes from the persuasiveness of the arguments contained in it.

d) Infallible Advice?

It is a contradiction in terms to speak of infallible advice to conscience. If a statement is presented as infallibly true, it is no longer advice.

Over the centuries popes have sometimes made infallible statements on dogmatic matters, on what people should or should not <u>believe</u>, but no pope of the past ever attempted to make an infallible statement on a moral matter – on what people should or should not *do*. Moral statements can be more or less certain and they can be made with more or less authority. But if they are to respect the essential role of conscience in moral growth, they must stop short of infallibility.

We grow by making our moral decisions before God alone and taking responsibility for them. Claims of infallibility block this process, for they seek to force us into the field of obedience rather than responsibility.

A Positive Role for Church Authority

The world of today often seems to present to people, a dogmatic and authoritarian church on the one hand, and on the other hand, the total freedom of the individual, and then ask: Which of these two do you prefer? To this I must reply: Do we need to choose either of these extremes? Can not a greater truth be found in the middle?

In that middle ground the decisions we make will always be ours and we alone will take full responsibility for them. Only in this way can we grow to become all we are capable of being. A church, or for that matter any other authority, must at all times respect this fact. The role of any authority is to assist conscience in its proper role.

On the other hand, moral problems can be both complex and subtle, so that a true moral sense has no room for arrogance or pride. It is wise to admit that in resolving moral problems we need all the help we can get. I see four roles for the Church in doing this.

a) Educating for the Use of Conscience

The first role is to assist people to educate themselves in the fields of conscience and moral principles.

In relation to *conscience*, the Church should help people to understand what is and what is not conscience, how it works, how one forms a conscience properly, and the dangers to be aware of in the difficult and subtle world of moral decision-making.

In relation to *moral principles*, the Church must not present a long series of statements beginning with "Thou shalt not", for a negative morality cannot be an adequate basis for a person's life. It must be a positive morality, consisting of positive principles such as: How can I best witness to truth and justice in this situation? How can I best help to bring peace and understanding between these persons in conflict? What can I do in this situation that will best help both others and myself to grow towards perfect love? In this situation how can I best strengthen the relationships between God, my neighbour and myself?

Since such principles require a profound sense of realism and honesty, the Church should then seek to give to people the best spiritual-moral insights it can from the scriptures, the great saints and the whole Christian tradition. The better people are educated in the field of moral principles, the better they will be able to make moral decisions and the more they will grow.

b) Guidance in Moral Matters

The second role I see for the Church is to present its position on many issues that commonly arise in the lives of people. In doing so, the Church must not rely simply on the moral authority of its leaders. Rather, it should always present the arguments in favour of its position as fully and as fairly as it can, that is, it should rely above all on the force of its arguments.

Indeed, I believe that in all such statements the Church should first present as fully and as fairly as it can the case against its own position. If it does this, it will truly be assisting people to make mature decisions in conscience before God alone. There is one obvious condition.

> Your exposition of your opponent's beliefs should be so accurate, so true to his beliefs, that he will gladly sign his name at the bottom of your exposition as a witness to its accuracy.[137]

If the Church acquired a reputation for putting the arguments against its own views as powerfully and as clearly as they can be put, its credibility would soar dramatically. If people were able to say, "You will never see the arguments in favour of this action put more clearly than they are in the document of the Church", then they might really start listening to the moral arguments the Church gives against that action.

There are, of course, different degrees of certainty in moral matters. At one extreme, it is impossible to think of any reasons in favour of rape, paedophilia or ethnic cleansing, and a church document would state its condemnation of such actions without wasting unnecessary time on contrary arguments. At the other extreme, where certainty is not possible, the Church might do little more than list the arguments on each side and leave it to people to make their own decisions. In between these two extremes it might, after fully and fairly presenting the arguments on both sides, explain why it finds the arguments on one side more convincing than those on the other.

In accordance with what was said earlier, I also believe that the Church should do all that is possible to ensure that its statements on moral matters reflect the collective wisdom of the whole Christian community rather than the wisdom of only a few people living in Rome.

c) Protecting the Community

The third role is a more negative one, but necessary. A community must protect

---

137 Donald Nicholl, "Wrestling with Truth", *The Tablet*, October 9, 1993, p. 1292.

its members against the decisions of individuals that harm other people, even when they are made in conscience. Just as the state will imprison a person who commits murder, so a Church community must dismiss from a teaching post a person who displays racial bias against certain students. Because harm is being caused to people, neither the state nor the Church will accept conscience as a defence. There are serious difficulties and dangers in this field, but it cannot be ignored.

d) Encouraging People

The fourth role I see for the Church is the important one of giving constant encouragement to people to believe in God's love and assistance, to have the courage to face the challenges that confront them, and to make all the conscience decisions they need to make. The Church should encourage people not to seek an easy way out, but to grow through challenges towards all they are capable of being. It can encourage them to have faith that they can grow to heights they have not dreamed of.

Freedom and Responsibility

If considered as a *system*, there are two difficulties with the idea of morality that I have presented here. The first is that it runs the risk that many people will take their ideas of morality from public opinion, from what everyone else is doing. "I can't really be bad if most people are doing the same as I am" is in practice a powerful and influential argument. Conscience is a more difficult and demanding idea than is often realised, and it is easier and more comfortable to do what everyone else is doing rather than take the personal responsibility that conscience demands.

And yet the Christian faith speaks of a person who died on a cross because of an infinite love for all people. If most public opinion would want to rise above the moral level of Lamech, it would stop far short of the level of God's love for us. Much public morality struggles to rise to the level of respect for the dignity of other people, and in practice all too often falls back to the level of whether others are seen as useful to us or not. There is always a serious danger of the community adopting a comfortable level of morality that asks little of us.

The second major problem is that we live in an age of individualism, and personal morality can override the need for public morality. As I noted above, a community must protect its members against at least some of the conscience decisions of others that harm them. Thus, the state must decide, for example, the speed at which it will allow people to drive their cars in different circumstances, while the Church must decide, for example, certain criteria for being in a position of speaking in the name of the Church. If we are not to descend into chaos, public morality is important.

When these two problems are put together, the danger is that the "easier way" becomes public morality, and there appear to be many examples of this already happening.

These are serious dangers and yet we will not and cannot grow merely by being obedient; we must take personal responsibility. If this creates problems, we must attempt to deal with them, but we must always retain the importance of taking responsibility for our actions. It would be the task of the Church's ministers to remind people "in season and out of season", by words and even more by actions, that a comfortable morality does not produce the level of growth that God desires for them.

I, and I alone, am finally responsible for who I become. It would be a pity if, at the end of my life, I had to say to God, "Lord, I must confess that I largely ignored the death of your son on the cross and I consistently followed the easier way." What God wants is growth and that must involve a truly responsible use of freedom.

Everything that I have said is based on the conviction that freedom and responsibility must go together. The aim of morality is that people should grow to become all they are capable of being. Freedom without responsibility is the surest way to prevent growth, while responsibility cannot be exercised without freedom.

Placing freedom and responsibility together is once again a middle ground between the two extremes of unlimited freedom (I decide to do something and that makes it morally right for me) and responsibility without freedom (don't think, just obey). The terms of the debate in our modern society are all too often either total obedience or unlimited freedom, but both are dead ends that allow no growth and no escape. The only road that opens us to true growth is that of freedom and responsibility taken together.

As children grow up, their parents must gradually stand back and allow them to make their own mistakes and learn from these mistakes. If the children abuse their freedom, the parents can only hope that the day will come when they see that their actions are not contributing to their growth, health or happiness, and consequently they will want to change. It is important that, through all of this process, however long it takes, the parents keep their relationship with their children, so that the children will know they are there and will turn to them when they experience the need. A church should act in the same way.

H: MORAL SYSTEMS

There are different ways of approaching moral dilemmas, so there are different moral systems, that is, different methods and principles according to which individuals may assess whether or not their actions are in accord with right conduct and will lead towards real goodness. The following example may help.

In the parable of the Good Samaritan[138] the priest and the Levite who "passed by on the other side" were not straw men, set up only to be knocked down, that is, they did not pass by simply because they were uncaring, but because there was a conflict of laws. Their dilemma was that contact with the dead was forbidden[139] and, since such laws had their origin in hygiene at a time when contagion was poorly understood, they cannot be simply dismissed. Because the priest and the Levite moved around the community more than others and could spread contagion more widely, there were special laws concerning them.

The parable says that "a certain person" was going down from Jerusalem to Jericho, but does not specify that he was a Jew. The robbers stripped him of his clothes, so that his nationality could not be seen from this source. They left him "half-dead". We may assume that the victim lay in a heap on the side of the road and that it could not be seen from a distance whether he was alive or dead, and whether he was a Jew or pagan.

The situation created a real dilemma for the priest and the Levite, for it created a conflict between laws telling them to help a neighbour and laws forbidding them to do anything that might spread contagion. In fact, commentators tell us that Jesus chose his case well, for many different laws were relevant to the situation and many of the detailed provisions of the oral tradition of the scribes had to be considered.

> In order to resolve the doubt whether the man was alive or dead, the priest would have to come within four cubits. If he were dead, the priest would thus be defiled. A priest must not 'overshadow' a corpse. If he bends over a dead body, even in ignorance of its existence, he may escape guilt, but not, of course, defilement. Poking a stick would not avoid this. An overhanging rock would, if the priest came within its shadow, extend the radius of defilement even beyond the four cubits. Yet the Torah obliges us to avoid transgression and defilement... The true positive commandment (to love one's neighbour) was conditional and could not overcome the unconditional commandment not to defile. But the strength of the opposing commandments would be a matter for tradition, and to some extent for personal preference. In a situation of doubt, however, which was the priest's situation ... preference must be given to that which is certain ... Justification for the priest's defiling himself, however, should he wish to do so, was not wanting. To save life he might do so, that is, he must have the intention of saving the life

---

138 Luke 10:29–37.
139 Leviticus 21:1–4; Numbers 6:9; 19:11–13; 31:19,24.

of a living person... Much depends on the inclination with which one approaches such a dilemma.[140]

The parable is a good example of an ordinary person suddenly confronted with a complex legal situation and having to make a quick decision. A modern parallel might be that of a doctor torn between recommending a certain course of action and the fear of a malpractice suit. For the scribes such situations were a real dilemma, for their moral system was a legal system in that the answers to all moral problems had to be found in the law of Moses.

The answer of Jesus, on the other hand, was that, at least in the case he presented, assistance to a neighbour in dire need was more important than the dangers from possible contagion to others, especially since these dangers could be minimised by undergoing the cleansing that the law imposed in such cases. This cleansing would be most inconvenient and costly, but it was always available. He presents as a Samaritan, not burdened by the provisions of the law, going straight to the heart of the matter and immediately doing what was required.

On many moral issues Jesus and the scribes would have reached the same conclusion, but this example shows that the *means* by which they reached that conclusion, the *moral system* they followed, would have been profoundly different. It would be incorrect and quite unfair to the scribes to say that they attended only to externals, for it is clear that they had a strong appreciation of the importance of inward dispositions. Nevertheless, their elaborate legal system of morality could prevent a person from acting by making it "safer" to pass by on the other side.

It was not necessarily the complexity of the scribes' method that was the issue between them and Jesus, for moral judgements can be very complex and the means of reaching them can be arduous and painstaking. The parable of the Good Samaritan is based on the twin commandment of love of God and love of neighbour, but this is a very broad commandment and it is not always easy to apply. It is legitimate to attempt to state what love of God and neighbour might mean in various particular circumstances. It is naive to interpret the biblical word "heart" solely in terms of feelings and then to say that, armed with a heart and the twin commandment of love of God and neighbour, we need nothing more in order to resolve all moral dilemmas instantly.

Jesus upheld the Ten Commandments and they are already a spelling out of the basic principle of love of God and neighbour. They imply that, if you wish to love God and neighbour, you should not kill or steal or commit adultery or bear false witness. If you then wish to obey the commandment of not killing anyone, you have to decide when and in what ways it is legitimate to defend

---

140 Cf. J Duncan M Derrett, *Law in the New Testament*, Darton, Longman and Todd, London, 1970, pp. 211–216.

yourself or another person against an attacker. This will lead to questions concerning the criteria for a just war, and this in turn will lead to questions of the morality of building up stockpiles of weapons. By the time you arrive at the morality of possessing nuclear weapons, the argument will have become highly complex. It is perfectly legitimate to analyse such questions in detail and to think about them carefully and deeply.

It is obvious that, the further we move away from the basic principle of love of God and neighbour, the more dangerous is the ground we tread. There is universal agreement that love of God and neighbour is a good thing, but the fiercest arguments rage over whether the holding of nuclear weapons could ever be a good way to express that love. This does not lessen the need to think about such questions nor destroy the process by which we arrive at answers. It simply expresses the dangers inherent in a situation where all kinds of objective and subjective factors complicate the basic principle of love of God and neighbour. Always and in all circumstances we must remember the basic principle that we are applying, but there is a permanent tension between the simplicity and beauty of that basic principle and the complexity and, at times, ugliness of the situations to which we must apply it.

Jesus was pointing to these dangers when he implied that the scribes had gone too far in attempting to spell out the detailed consequences of the divine laws. They had created a structure so vast and so complex that its basis in divine law could not always be recognised.

In this, Jesus was also objecting to the restrictions on the individual's own sense of right and wrong. Every Jew knew that he or she was to "keep holy the sabbath day". Did they really need someone to spell out thirty-nine different things they were not to do, with six sub-categories under each heading? Was there no room for diversity according to the circumstances of each individual? I am well aware that the community aspect of such observances is important, but there is a balance that must be struck, and, in the mind of Jesus, the weight of the system had destroyed that balance. To walk a few steps more than the prescribed distance could never be made equal to the basic command of observance of the sabbath.

These examples tell us that the answers we come to in the moral dilemmas that face us will depend to a significant extent on the *moral system* we are following.

I: ABSOLUTE VALUES VERSUS INTENTIONS AND CIRCUMSTANCES

Before we look at particular systems, we must consider the moral relevance of circumstances and intentions.

The teaching authority of the Catholic Church has long insisted that, in so far as is possible, our moral reasoning should be objective rather than subjective, that is, it should be based on the action a person performs – what that person actually does – rather than simply on what goes on inside the head of the person performing the action. An objective system permits a far greater consistency of action, both for individuals and for the community. This concern for an objective basis to morality, however, has led to a dispute over the centuries concerning the moral relevance of both intentions and circumstances.

Intentions exist in our minds rather than in what we do externally, and this is where the problems arise. There are times when a society will rightly insist that intentions are irrelevant. For example, if a person takes an oath to tell the truth in court, but privately says, "I don't intend to honour or respect this oath", society will rightly say, "We don't care what your private intention was. Publicly you took an oath to tell the truth and we will hold you to that." On the other hand, most people hold that in most actions whether a person *intends* good or harm must surely count for something, irrespective of the action performed, so they maintain that in most circumstances intentions must be at least one factor in our consideration of the morality of an action.

The danger is that intentions take us into a subjective morality, for we would be the sole judge of whether our intentions were right. The man from an example earlier in this paper who massacred his perceived enemies might well claim that his intentions had been pure. Indeed, throughout history some terrible wrongs have been done in the name of good intentions, and misguided good intentions still cause serious problems today:

> Example 9: I have already mentioned the "stolen generation" of Australian Aborigines who were forcibly taken from their families and given to white people to bring up because it was wrongly thought that this would help them to prosper in a white society. At the end of the Second World War British children were taken from their parents by force or deceit and sent out to Australia because it was thought that this would give them better opportunities. Until quite recently babies were frequently taken from unwed mothers because it was believed that this would be better for the babies. It is easy to add to this list.

Thus the problem is that, on the one hand, intentions must surely count for something, but, on the other hand, if intentions become the sole or even dominant basis of morality, we would have all the dangers of a subjective morality, where it was hard to have any consistency and where it would be all too easy to deceive ourselves.

The problem concerning the moral relevance of *circumstances* is similar. On the one hand, human acts are never performed in the abstract; they are always concrete acts, and so always have circumstances. On the other hand, which circumstances are considered morally relevant must involve some subjective judgement.

Some comments on this matter are easier to make, some more difficult. I shall deal with the easier ones first and then look at those more difficult.

Circumstances and Intentions Changing the Object

What? (the Object)

In any moral system, objective or subjective, the first and most important question must always be "What am I actually doing?" We cannot possibly answer any moral questions until we have answered this question. If this is not the first question, it is hard to see that we are talking about a moral system at all. At least to this extent, every moral system must be objective.

> Example 10: When the first human beings walked this earth, they must have had profound fears of many things, both known and unknown. The message they needed to hear at that time was, "Fill the earth and subdue it."[141] Today, on the contrary, the human race faces a dramatically different situation, for human beings have so multiplied and subdued the world that many of its precious resources are seriously threatened. Today it is a very different message that needs to be heard.

Both attitudes depend on the answer given to the question, "What kind of world do we live in?" In the first case, the early human beings saw the world as a fearful place where they needed to assert themselves against the many things that threatened them. In the second case, human beings see the world as a limited place that cannot sustain endless development and waste. Each attitude has many consequences concerning what is considered moral or immoral in the use of the world's goods.

Thus, in approaching a moral question, the very first question should be, "What are the objective facts here?" Even at a pre-moral level, we should treat things according to our understanding of what they are. It is basic common sense to put gasoline into a car and give oats and hay to a horse, but not vice versa. At a moral level we should always treat people according to who they are. For example, we should treat a woman as a woman and a child as a child, and it can be morally wrong to treat a woman as "one of the boys" or a child as an adult.

There are times when it takes a high degree of honesty to answer this

---

141 Genesis 1:28.

question of exactly what we are doing, for we can be good at disguising the honest answer from ourselves.

> Example 11: A person who drives when intoxicated can say that he is "going home to look after his family". People who throw empty cans into the bushes can say they are "tidying up". People who destroy the reputations of others can say they are "telling the truth". Adolf Hitler said, and possibly at times even believed, that he was doing no more than creating "living room" for his people.

Why? (Intentions)

Even in an objective moral system intentions can be morally relevant because they can change the object, the "*what* is being done".

> Example 12: If one person invites another to a meal, but the intention is to deceive and steal from the other, the intention (why) has changed the object (what). "What" the person is doing is deceiving and stealing, and the invitation to the meal is no more than a means to this end. Thus, a bad intention (deceiving and stealing) can make a right action (inviting to a meal) wrong.

A good intention, on the other hand, can mean that, even though an action remains in itself a wrong action (note: not "intrinsically evil", just "in itself wrong"), no moral fault is committed.

> Example 13: In the extraordinarily difficult and complex task of parenthood, parents can make honest mistakes in their dealings with their children and, with the best of intentions, do things that are not good for them. The children may in fact suffer harm, but the good intentions of the parents mean that no moral fault has been committed.

In What Circumstances?

The circumstances in which an action is performed can also affect the morality of the action, once again because they can change the "what".

> Example 14: Driving a car at 100 kph is acceptable on a highway, but not in a crowded shopping centre. Here the external circumstances have changed the answer to the question of "What am I doing?", for I would no longer be simply "exercising my right to freedom of movement", but also "endangering the lives of other people."

Most circumstances can be summed up in the questions: Who? How? Where? And when? Intentions, however, concern the question "why".

With What Foreseeable effects?

A foreseeable effect is a circumstance, but it deserves special mention.

> Example 15: A certain person is known to drink heavily at every party he attends and then to drive home while intoxicated. Do I have any moral responsibility in deciding whether to invite him to a party? After all, the decisions and the actions are his, not mine. Nevertheless, can it not be argued that the foreseeable effect of his attending the party changes the "what I am doing" if I invite him? If he in fact drank too much and killed someone while driving home, would I not share some responsibility for this death?

Are There Alternative Actions?

This is another circumstance that deserves special mention. In the example just used, if I make effective arrangements for someone else to drive this person to the party and home again, does this not once again change the "what" I am doing? An alternative action has changed the morality. On the other hand, the priest and the Levite in the parable had to choose between two courses of action, in both of which the "what" appeared to be wrong: abandon a neighbour in need, or risk spreading contagion. No other alternative was available, and a choice had to be made.

The Means and the End

We now come to the far more difficult questions. Can a good intention make a wrong action right or, as this is usually expressed, can the end ever justify the means?

> Example 16: It is learned that a bomb has been planted at a railway station somewhere in the city and primed to explode at peak hour. One of the terrorists has been captured but refuses to say where the bomb is. You are the Commissioner of Police and you are asked, "May we torture the terrorist to extract the information and save the lives of many innocent people?"

> Example 17: You live in a country which is persecuting and killing an ethnic minority. You are hiding a family of such people in the attic of your house. The Secret Police knock at the door and demand to know

whether any members of this minority are living there. What is the most moral answer you can give?
- a) Yes
- b) No
- c) I decline to answer
- d) Those (expletives deleted) so-and-sos. You think I'd have one of those bastards in my house? They're filth etc. etc.

Example 18: You work for a large international aid agency. It has put together a package to help a very poor country. You strongly approve of most provisions in the package, believing that they will bring the first real hope in years to many destitute people. But you notice that one provision demands the forced sterilisation of all women after they have had one baby. Do you vote for or against the package?

"Why, who, how, where and when" changing "what" cannot resolve these questions. In each case, it is true, your intentions would be good, for you would be seeking to help people, but in the first case you would be torturing, in the second lying and in the third voting for forced sterilisation, and no intentions or circumstances would change these facts. Despite this, there is more to be said.

Moral Absolutes

The Catechism of the Catholic Church, reflecting a long history within that church, says,

> There are acts which, in and of themselves, independently of circumstances and intentions, are always gravely illicit by reason of their object; such as blasphemy and perjury, murder and adultery."[142]

A little earlier, the Catechism speaks of "behaviour that is intrinsically disordered, such as lying and calumny."[143]

There has been much debate on this subject over the centuries. Are there "moral absolutes", actions that are so wrong that no intentions or circumstances can make them right? The Catechism gives the examples of blasphemy, perjury, murder, adultery, lying and calumny.

The inclusion of murder highlights the problem. The Catechism was unable to name killing as a moral absolute, for there are well known exceptions (self-defence, a just war), so it spoke of murder instead. However, *it is precisely circumstances and intentions, and nothing else,* that distinguish murder from a justified

---

142 No. 1756.
143 No. 1753.

killing. In both cases, one points a gun at someone and pulls the trigger, and it is only circumstances and intentions that distinguish the two cases. It follows that murder is not a moral absolute that is independent of intentions and circumstances.

If lying could never be permitted, I would have to answer either "yes" or "I decline to answer" to the Secret Police, with the consequent death of the innocent family. The problem is that at least 99 per cent of the human race would say that this is not the most moral answer in the circumstances.

Perjury (telling a lie under oath) would have to be taken even more seriously, but it is possible to change the example slightly:

> Example 19: I am in court as a witness and have already taken an oath to tell the truth. The judge then asks me whether I know the whereabouts of any members of this ethnic minority that is being persecuted.

Concerning adultery, there is a well-known example from the Communist era in Eastern Europe.

> Example 20: In occupied territory a man has been arrested and will most probably "disappear" forever. His wife goes to the enemy general to plead for his life. The general tells her that he will release the man if she agrees to have sexual intercourse with him. From heaven five scholars and six saints have observed this and are furious with the general, for his action is not the occasional wrong action of a basically good person, but a genuinely mortal or death-dealing sin, the act of a truly bad person. They appreciate the terrible, impossible dilemma in which the woman has been placed. While they have their private opinions as to what she should do, they are not judgemental, and will accept whatever decision she makes.

Blasphemy has the difficulty that for the most part it is a cry of anguish and anger at the perceived injustice of evil and suffering in the world. I believe in a big god who understands such cries and is not offended by them, so blasphemy does not make for a very good example.

I grant that it is virtually impossible to justify calumny (telling lies about another person in order to destroy character and reputation). I believe that we could add rape and paedophilia as actions impossible to justify in any conceivable circumstances. Even here, however, intentions and circumstances will enter in, determining, for example, the borderline between rape and consensual sex or between calumny and a truthful statement.

In the light of all this, we must ask whether it is useful to speak of such acts as "moral absolutes" or "intrinsically disordered acts", or whether they should be approached in another way.

Values and Disvalues (negative values)

Many moral theologians today would not argue cases directly in terms of intentions or the end justifying the means, but on another basis. They would speak of values and disvalues (a word invented by moral theologians, but useful, so I shall use it here). Values are good moral qualities of a person such as truthfulness, honesty, faithfulness, justice and kindness. Disvalues are bad moral qualities such as falsehood, dishonesty, unfaithfulness, injustice and unkindness.

These moral theologians would argue that, if we wish to talk about moral goodness at all, we must in all our actions strive with all our might to have the presence of values and the absence of disvalues. Indeed, this is at the heart of the whole moral endeavour. In extraordinary circumstances, however, they would argue that we may permit the presence of a smaller disvalue for the sake of a greater value.

The second case given above (Example 17) is the one to which this idea would most clearly apply. The value is that of saving the life of the family in hiding, the disvalue is that of untruthfulness. In this case saving the family by denying its presence in your house would win the approval of almost all people, but it is important to recognise that there are two serious problems associated with it.

The first is that, however great your justification may have been, you have consciously allowed a disvalue into your life, and you must not treat this as unimportant. I said earlier that in any moral field the first wrong action is the hardest to commit, while later actions will be far easier. Here, with strong justification, you have allowed the disvalue of untruthfulness into your life and, whether you like it or not, this will make it far easier to allow it into your life again, and on later occasions the justification might not be nearly so great. You must not allow a disvalue into your life lightly and you would have to be very careful about the effect it had on you.

The second problem is that in this solution you have moved away from an objective morality towards a subjective morality, for you have used your own personal judgement to determine that the value is far greater than the disvalue. In the given case this may be obvious, but there are many other cases where it will not be nearly so obvious. Once you have entered into the field of the subjective, it can be very hard to find a firm basis for moral action and it can be all too easy to convince yourself that someone else's "foul lie" is your "tiny disvalue for the sake of a much higher value".

> Example 21: Without his wife's knowledge, a man has been gambling and has lost money. To explain the loss of money he tells her that he has been robbed on the way home. He convinces himself that this is a

small disvalue for the sake of a greater value. But will his wife see it in the same light when she finds out the truth? Or will she feel that she has been deceived and lied to, that her dignity has not been respected, that their relationship has been cheapened, that, if he was truly interested in higher values, truth and honesty would have been a far better response?

There is much to be said for a system based on values and disvalues, but the dangers inherent in it must never be minimised. Indeed, it must be stated openly that it is a highly dangerous path and it is inevitable that in following it many people would become lost.

It is here that we must remind ourselves of the basic concepts of morality spoken of in the first sections of this paper. If the overriding concern is "to do right things", a system of values and disvalues will be seen as highly dangerous, and a system of absolutes will be considered safer. But if we go back to both God's insistence in the Bible that the people of Israel should grow by struggling in uncertainty, and to the idea of both doing right things and taking personal responsibility, then it is the system of moral absolutes that begins to look less adequate. These issues we must now address.

J: PARTICULAR MORAL SYSTEMS

In the field of moral reasoning there are today certain differences of opinion between moral theologians. I must stress yet again, however, that the seeking of goodness is the one fundamental concern in all of this. This may help us to tolerate certain differences of opinion and method in determining the rightness and wrongness of actions, for theologians are unanimous in considering that in all our actions we must seek goodness in our lives. Any moral decision that is not a seeking for goodness is automatically wrong, and this may help us to distinguish between cases. For example, the person telling a lie in order to protect the family from the secret police is seeking goodness, while the man lying to his wife about his gambling would find it hard to make the same claim.

We must also remember that all the evidence indicates that it is God's plan that we should grow by struggling in the midst of uncertainty, so the lack of certainty in moral theology is not simply a failure on the part of moral theologians, but something that is inherent in the nature of human life and is itself part of God's plan.

I shall now mention five different moral systems that are followed by different groups of people.

A Legal Morality

Legalism is less popular than it once used to be, but is still accepted by a number of people. It emphasises external actions conforming to objective principles and rules. It tends to ask that authorities of church and state should codify all moral conduct into clear laws and would then judge morality by obedience to these laws.

Among the followers of legalism there are many sincere people who genuinely seek goodness in their inmost being, but one must say that they achieve this goodness despite rather than because of the system of moral reasoning they have adopted.

The system has the advantage that people do not have to struggle with difficult decisions in conscience and usually know clearly what they should or should not do. It can also give its adherents the good feeling that they are succeeding in the moral struggle because they are obeying all the laws.

On the other hand, it pays attention only to external actions and fails to give sufficient attention to inward dispositions and motives. Its followers do not sufficiently take responsibility for their own actions, for they are obeying laws rather than taking personal responsibility. It can contain the convenient assumption that, if there is no law forbidding something, then one may do it without further thought. It seriously harms moral life by reducing the role of conscience to a decision to obey the law, and growth in goodness is never as easy as that. Furthermore, laws tend to ride roughshod over the details of situations and legalism forces complex and subtle situations to fit into the mould of some general law.

Not all people are seeking for genuine goodness in their inmost core. Legalism can frequently go together with belief in an angry god and, where this is true, it will certainly stunt growth.

A Subjective Morality

In some zoos artificial environments have been created to enable visitors to see nocturnal animals. When it is in fact daytime, most lights are turned out so that the animals will think it is night-time and come out. When it is in fact night-time, the lights are turned on so that the animals will think it is daytime and go to sleep. When the visitors come, the *objective* truth (reality) is that it is daytime, but the *subjective* truth for the animals (perceived reality) is that it is night-time. They are in fact mistaken, but they follow their subjective belief and come out at a time when visitors may see them.

Subjective truth is important. It has been said without cynicism that there are three stories of every broken marriage – his, hers and the truth. He can see the reality of the marriage only through his eyes and she can see it only through her eyes, while the full story probably involves more than either of them alone is able to see. On most subjects even well-meaning people can argue heatedly, not seeing each other's subjective truth, let alone the whole objective truth.

In many matters our subjective truth is the only truth we have, and we have no choice but to base our thoughts and actions on it. This applies to the moral field as much as anywhere else. We must remind ourselves of the words of Aquinas that conscience must seek the good as it perceives it. Even when mistaken, it must be followed because it presents its judgements as good and one is obliged to do what is good.

A powerful movement today has gone further than this, however, and says that we cannot know objective truth, that subjective truth is all we have and all that matters. It says that we should give up all attempts to know objective truth, and especially to base our moral decisions on objective truth.

It therefore bases morality on subjective decisions and on principles that are "right for me". The individual becomes the sole judge of right and wrong, without reference to any objective moral standard, and this judgement is frequently based on feelings and on instant reactions to events. It tends to say: "You have your truth and I have mine. You must decide whether a certain action is right for you, as I have decided that it is right for me." We are reluctant to admit that an individual might not see all relevant moral aspects of a situation.

In large part this attitude is a reaction against legalism and the excessive controls of the past, so that many people now say, "Nobody may tell me what to believe or what to do. I shall decide that for myself. I will not commit myself to any religious faith or moral system. I shall choose my own moral principles from whatever source I wish."

Just as for legalism, so under subjectivism there can be sincere people who seek goodness in their inmost being. They are the proof that the search for goodness in the core of one's being is the all-important factor in a moral life. Once again, however, one must say that they achieve this goodness despite, rather than because of the system of moral reasoning they have adopted.

The system has some serious disadvantages. It can take a whole community hundreds of years to develop a coherent moral system. Individuals cannot hope to do this on their own, for no one can possibly have that degree of knowledge and wisdom. In practice, therefore, those who follow subjective ideas borrow from many other sources, and how good their moral reasoning is will depend on the sources from which they borrow. Within this system it is not easy to have any consistency of action.

Not all people are seeking for genuine goodness in the inmost core of their being. For those who are not, subjectivism is marvellously convenient, for under this system it is easy to talk oneself into whatever one wishes to do. Indeed, it can be a means of avoiding the moral struggle altogether. It can easily go together with belief in a soft and indulgent god who does not challenge anyone to anything, and it can easily lead to a practical form of atheism in which I am the sole judge of morality for myself.

Despite these limitations, subjectivism has become very widespread in our community. A person who does not think about the matter will almost inevitably fall into this method. There is much in our society and in the media that fosters the most unthinking form of subjectivism.

> A public culture that trivialises what is important, sensationalises what is unimportant, and promotes gross sentimentality over genuine feeling is narcissistic… So are the social cultures that promote individualism and addiction.[144]

There is a need to develop a moral system that, against subjectivism, does everything in its power to follow objective standards, while at the same time, against legalism, insists that individuals take personal responsibility for their own decisions and actions.

An Absolute Morality

This is the traditional method of moral reasoning followed by the teaching authority of the Catholic Church and it is still the quasi-official method.

It holds that there are moral absolutes, that is, things that are always wrong, and that there are no circumstances that can make them right. In relation to the three examples given at the beginning of this section, it would say that torture is always wrong, telling lies is always wrong and forced sterilisation is always wrong.

This system would hold that "the end cannot justify the means", that is, it is never right to do something morally wrong in order to achieve a good purpose.

The system has the advantages of clarity in most matters and of a firm commitment to doing what is right despite the difficulties it might create for oneself. It is firmly committed to an objective morality.

It has the disadvantage already mentioned that it is most difficult, indeed impossible, to identify moral absolutes that are independent of circumstances and intentions, for there are no actions without circumstances and intentions.

Absolutism can in practice deny any role of conscience and give rise to an external conformity to the moral absolute. It can, therefore, come too close to legalism.

For these reasons absolutism will never be a satisfying answer to subjectivism. If it is the only answer offered, subjectivism will continue to thrive.

K: Proportional Morality

N.B.: the term "proportionalism" covers a wide range of views, some more acceptable, some less. The brief statements made here are necessarily very general.

---

144 Stephanie Dowrick, *Forgiveness and Other Acts of Love*, Viking, 1997, p. 75.

The proportionalists are those who speak of values and disvalues. They hold that there are very few, if any, moral absolutes, that is, things that are always and, in all circumstances, wrong. They hold that telling lies is usually wrong, and they give no support to wholesale lying, but they see circumstances in which it could be right to tell a lie. They hold that the total action of the person in its full context should be considered, especially in relation to its foreseen consequences. They then ask whether in a particular case there can be a *proportionate* reason for performing an action that in most normal circumstances would be wrong.

In the second example concerning the family in hiding, they would support the fourth answer of a vehement and intemperate denial of the family's presence. They would point out that the law persecuting the minority group was unjust and immoral and they would stress that the Secret Police had no moral right to the knowledge they asked for. They would then say that it would not be enough to say "no", you would have to swear and shout and convince the police that it would be pointless to search, that there was no chance that you would be harbouring such people. They would say that all the circumstances of the situation provided a proportionate reason for making a statement that was not objectively correct.

The obvious advantage of this system is that it allows us to take into account the whole concrete situation in all its details. If this is considered essential in order to make a proper judgement of a real situation, then no other system is required or possible.

The disadvantage is that, if absolutism is seen as too close to legalism, proportionalism can be seen as too close to subjectivism, for the judgement that a value outweighs a disvalue in a particular case is a subjective judgement. The example of the Secret Police and the minority group is clear enough, but what about the man who lied to his wife about losing money by gambling? Would it not be too easy for this person to become convinced that there was a proportionate reason for not telling the truth? Those who follow proportionalism have worked to present objective criteria to distinguish between different cases, but others would not accept that they have succeeded.

A Morality Based on Persons

One of the first sources of morality is the dignity of human beings and their potential for goodness. Personalism takes up this idea and argues that whatever most respects the dignity of human beings and best releases and supports their potential for holistic growth is morally right, while whatever harms the dignity of human beings and limits and suppresses their potential for holistic growth is morally wrong.

There are two essential conditions. The first is that all moral principles drawn from a consideration of the dignity of the human person must consider the whole person, not just this or that aspect of human activity. A true moral theology must be holistic and must always seek to plumb the depths of the human person rather than make superficial judgements about what is considered good for an individual here and now.

The second condition is that every possible effort must be made to see that personalism steers a middle course between an objective and a subjective morality. On the one hand, we must admit that it is virtually impossible to maintain a system of moral absolutes, for it is not possible to deny the relevance of circumstances and intentions. We must, therefore, admit the presence in human affairs of values and disvalues and of the need to make decisions even though they will contain subjective elements. Significant elements of proportionalism must come into such a moral system. Indeed, it may be seen as a particular form of proportionalism.

On the other hand, we must do all in our power to follow objective standards rather than be overwhelmed by the subjective. If we are to say that it can sometimes be right to lie, we must do all we can to have some objective standards by which to distinguish between one lie and another rather than rely solely on the subjective judgement of the person concerned. We must be aware of the very serious dangers involved in allowing a disvalue into our lives, no matter how small the disvalue and no matter how great the justification may seem.

For these two conditions to be fulfilled and, therefore, for personalism to gain acceptance as a moral system, we must strive to have a highly developed understanding of the holistic good of the human person. For example, each individual is capable of developing in seven different fields: physical, intellectual, emotional, social, artistic, moral and spiritual. We need to decide exactly what we mean by each of these seven terms, how they vary in understanding and relevance from one individual to another, how we are to strike a proper balance between them and how we determine the relative importance of each in the life of each person.

The teaching authority of the Church has shown that it is open to much of what personalism has to say and has itself done much to develop the central importance of the human person.

Are there dangers in personalism? Yes, there are two obvious dangers. The first is a selfish idea of what is good for the person (me), the second is subjectivism. Is there any answer to these dangers? Yes. They are not so much dangers of personalism itself as of what people can do to it, and those who would abuse personalism will probably abuse whatever system is put forward. The real answer is responsibility. I am responsible, my decisions will form my moral identity, and this matters.

The situation is, however, a difficult one. If, in the name of personalism, the teaching authority of the Church were even to hint that there could be extraordinary circumstances in which it might be lawful to tell a lie, there is the real danger that this would be interpreted as opening the door to subjective judgments. Subjectivism is an enormously powerful force in today's world and even the slightest opening of the door could lead to a flood sweeping through the house, washing away every trace of objective criteria of right and wrong in human behaviour. The many false and selfish ideas of self-fulfilment, of doing things "my way", that are prevalent in the Western world show that modern society often does not have a very deep idea of what constitutes true human development and moral goodness.

To develop personalism as a coherent and satisfying moral system in this atmosphere will not be easy, but the work must continue. While Western society is in danger of drowning in a sea of moral superficiality, absolutism is not a credible response to subjectivism, and only personalism can provide a satisfying answer. Furthermore, it will not be possible to have a true dialogue with the people of today on the basis of absolutism, while it will be possible on the basis of personalism, for there is much that the Church and the people of today share in common on this topic. In the first case given above, if you order the torture, your intention would clearly be the good intention of saving the lives of innocent persons. But torture is still torture and there are a number of questions you would need to ask yourself:

- Can it be morally right to destroy a human being through torture, even for a good motive?
- If we justify torture in this one case, on what basis do we condemn it in other cases?
- Have we not opened the doors to subjective assessments of when it is lawful?
- Apart from the effect the torture would have on the terrorist, what about its impact on the other human beings involved, such as ourselves? What effect would it have on us if we had used this method? Would we have descended to the same level as the terrorists themselves?
- If we used torture, would not our country have joined the ranks of those countries in the world that use torture? What sort of company would we be keeping and would we like it?
- By what moral right could I ask someone else to apply the torture if I was not willing to do it myself?
- There is the alternative of closing every train station in the city until the bomb is found. This would cause massive disruption to vast numbers of people, but is it better than using torture?

In this case the personalist would most probably reach the same conclusion as the absolutist and would disagree with anyone who said that there was a proportionate reason for using torture.

In the second case, the personalist might agree with the proportionalist and disagree with the absolutist. The absolutist would say that lying is wrong and one cannot use a right end to justify a wrong means. The personalist would claim that on quite objective grounds one can build a very strong case for saying that answer d) provides for the dignity, not only of the family you are hiding, but also of yourself and even of the Secret Police.

In the third case, we would probably have to say that none of the three systems really resolves the case for us. The only choice you have is to approve or not approve the total package. If you approve, women will be forcibly sterilised. If you don't approve, no one in that country will be helped. You would probably find that there was a dispute within the absolutist camp, with some saying that you were using a right end to justify a wrong means, while others were saying that you should use a quite different moral principle, that of double effect (that is, the one action has two effects, one right and one wrong). This latter group and the proportionalists and personalists would say that you will simply have to weigh up all the factors and decide where is the greatest good and the least evil. This will not be an easy question, for you would have to remember that, if you seem to approve of forced sterilisation on one occasion, you could be in a weak position to object to it on another occasion. You would have to seek a means by which you could vote in favour of the package but at the same time register your public disagreement with and protest against the objectionable element.

In the Encyclical Letter *Humanae Vitae*, Pope Paul VI said, "It is never lawful, even for the gravest reasons, to do evil that good may come of it, or in other words, to intend directly something that of its very nature contradicts the moral order, and which must therefore be judged unworthy of man, even though the intention is to protect or promote the welfare of an individual, of a family or of society in general." (No. 14) This is a clear expression of an absolutist approach to morality.

On the other hand, the entire eighth chapter of the Post-Synodal Apostolic Exhortation *Amoris Laetitia* of Pope Francis is an appeal for a personalist approach to morality, especially in regard to the many complications that can arise in family life.

In recent centuries an absolutist approach to morality has certainly been more prevalent in the Church, but it is not a dogma. To turn it into dogma would be simply one more example of pressing infallibility.

L: A CASE STUDY

Example 22: A *young woman* lives in a village next to a river infested with crocodiles. Her fiancé lives in a village on the opposite bank. One day she is feeling depressed and wants to see him. She approaches the *boatman* in her village and offers him the money to row her across. He replies that he will only do so if she will first have sex with him. She goes to see the village *headman* to complain about the boatman, but he tells her not to bother him because he is busy making a boat. She is now even more depressed and, in this state, agrees to have sex with the boatman. He then rows her across to the other side. She now feels both depressed and guilty and starts crying. Her *best friend* comes across her and asks what is wrong, and she confesses everything. The best friend wants the fiancé for herself, so promptly tells him the whole story. The *fiancé* is angry and comes and beats the woman.

Each of the five has done something wrong. List the five people in the order of the greatness of their wrong and give the reasons for your choice.

It will quickly become evident that there are no absolute answers and that your response will contain subjective elements. Indeed, your answers will probably say as much about you as they do about the five people in the story. Despite this, it is important that you do your best to give objective reasons for your choices.

You will quickly find that, in order to make a proper assessment, you will want more details about each of the wrongs. Can you suggest details you would need to know?

It is obvious that the girl has had a very bad day: she has been used and abused by the boatman, dismissed as unimportant by the headman, betrayed by her best friend and beaten and rejected by her fiancé. Does your sympathy for her cause you to judge her more leniently?

In what ways would you need to take local values and culture into account?

Are some of the wrongs mortal and others "only" venial (a lesser sin)?

How would the order of wrongs be judged by a legalist? An absolutist? A subjectivist? A proportionalist? A personalist?

Have you enjoyed discussing the moral situation of these people with whom you are not involved? Do you consider yourself superior to these "simple" people? They may, in the eyes of some, be "simple" people, but they still have to make moral decisions before they act. What help can you give them?

CONCLUSION

It may upset some people to hear that, even after two thousand years, there is disagreement over something as basic as the moral system we should follow in deciding between right and wrong. At the conclusion of this chapter, therefore, we must come back to some essentials.

Moral Choice

Example 23: An elderly lady is walking ahead of a boy. She reaches into her handbag for a handkerchief, but in taking it out a fifty-dollar note falls unnoticed onto the footpath. The boy is instantly faced with a moral choice, for he can either call the lady's attention to the note and give it back to her, or he can quickly put it in his own pocket and disappear.

The boy has a choice, and it is only because he has a choice that he can perform either a right or a wrong action.

> Example 24: As he instinctively bends over to pick up the money and before he has made any decision as to what he will do with it, he notices a policeman two metres away watching the whole incident. He quickly calls for the attention of the woman and gives the money to her.

The presence of the policeman has affected the boy's choice, so his action is no longer a particularly right action. It is certainly not a wrong action, but because the element of coercion has entered the picture, it has no particular morality to it.

If he could not choose wrong, he could not choose right. God wants goodness in the lives of human beings, so God must allow for the possibility of badness.

This choice between right and wrong, and ultimately between goodness and badness, is at the heart of the struggle in which we are all engaged throughout our lives. The moral struggle in the hearts of human beings was the first reality of human life that Jesus confronted, and it was the cause of his last battle on the cross. Jesus would die on a cross to show us that the struggle was worthwhile.

Knowing and Doing

One version of the Church of seventy years ago is that, by listening to Church authority, we always knew what was the right thing to do, and the moral struggle consisted solely in doing what we knew to be right. In fact it never was that simple and, in fairness, the teaching authority of the Church never said it was that simple.

As we all know only too well, it is often difficult to do things we know to be right and avoid things we know to be wrong. St Paul knew this two thousand years ago.

> I can will what is right, but I cannot do it. For I do not do the good I want, but the evil I do not want is what I do.[145]

Despite this, doing the right thing is often the last and easiest part of the moral

---

145 Rom.7:18–19.

struggle. The more difficult part can be that of deciding what is the right thing to do.

If I cannot present a neat moral system, agreed to by all, this does not mean that moral theology has failed. It means first of all that the subject is an extremely difficult one and that the seeking to know what is right is an important and indeed essential part of the moral struggle. I have continually insisted that God wants us to grow to become all we are capable of being and it is only through this struggle to know what is right that we can grow. If all moral problems were as simple as "2+2=4", we would not grow in the same way.

The constant search for truth and the constant openness to truth are more important than the possession of truth. The sincere search to know where moral goodness is to be found is more important than any neat list of moral rules. The search for answers to questions of evil and suffering in the world is more important than any answers we may come to. The search for God is more important than any ideas of God we may have. The Bible is a search, morality is a search, the spiritual life is a search, God is a search, and life itself is a search.

The Search for Goodness

We need a moral system, but it must always be subservient to the seeking of true goodness in the innermost core of our being. Our success in the moral struggle depends less on the moral system we follow and more on whether we are in all things seeking goodness in the core of our being. The six levels of moral living mentioned earlier remain and we should always strive for the higher levels. For a Christian goodness is ultimately to be found in imitating the life of Jesus Christ.

> The Pharisees always knew that goodness was more than obedience to law, but what they taught came too close to a quantitative concept of morality. By obeying each rule one earned marks and, if one tried particularly hard, one could even hope to score one hundred. But Jesus taught that goodness is wholly qualitative, for it consists in the effort to reproduce in one's own life the quality of God's love. On the cross Jesus showed the full quality of that love and, impossible as it may sound, we are actually meant to bring that quality of love into our own lives.[146]

---

146 Geoffrey Robinson, *A Change of Mind and Heart*, Parish Ministry Publications, Sydney, 1994, p. 556.

CHAPTER 17
THE SMELL OF THE SHEEP

THE INTERMEDIARY

There have always been intermediaries between human beings and their god(s), specialists who would strengthen, manage, and smooth the relationship.

The type of intermediary has depended on the type of god being worshipped. All people have within them both profound fears and insatiable longings. Throughout human history the fears have led to ideas of an angry god and the longings to ideas of a loving god. When people finally reached the idea of the one God of the whole universe, the two concepts were often confused in the idea of a god who was sometimes angry and sometimes loving. To this day children can receive many contradictory ideas about God from many sources while growing up.

Paradoxically, the angry god was seen as being too close and the task demanded of the intermediary was that of keeping this god at a distance, while the loving god was seen as too distant and the task demanded of the intermediary was that of bringing the god closer.

In our own day there has been a strong reaction against the angry god, but, like most reactions, it has gone to an opposite extreme. In an analogy, it has gone all the way from parents who beat their children into submission to parents who spoil their children. For many people it has produced the idea of a god of indulgent and unintelligent love who asks nothing of us.

I suggest that a Christian intermediary should consistently seek to present a god who, like a good parent or teacher, loves deeply and unconditionally but, precisely because of this love, wants people to grow to become all they are capable of being and so is not afraid to challenge them.

Much thought needs to go into the type of god one is presenting through every word spoken and, more importantly, every action performed. Anything else said about priests must never leave this basic truth behind.

ALL PRIESTHOOD

The literature concerning all forms of priesthood in all religions would say that there are four pillars, four essential tasks of priesthood. A priest must:
a) Offer gift and sacrifice to their god.
b) Pray to the god for the people, both in public and in private.
c) Proclaim the message of their god to the people.
d) Build a community based on shared religious values.

a) Gift and Sacrifice

The first pillar flows from a recognition by the people that their god is the source of all life and wellbeing. Throughout human history people have expressed this recognition by freely giving back to their god part of the harvest or other gifts received. They supply the gifts and then turn to their intermediary to make the gift and sacrifice.

For Catholics the Mass is the perfect sacrifice, but it is essential that on our part it contain more than the offering of the small amount of bread and wine used in the sacrifice or the smallest amount of money one can decently put on the plate. It must express the idea of giving back to God part of the gifts the whole congregation has received, so it should always contain some significant gift of time or money for those in need. If it does not do this, the perfect sacrifice of Jesus Christ remains, but it is not a true sacrifice on our part.

b) Prayer

Because of their role as intermediaries, priests will have a prominent role in the public worship of the community. One of the major roles will always be to offer public prayers to their god on behalf of the people.

This must absolutely not consist solely in asking favours of their god. There should always be five aspects to all prayer and they are summed up by the letters of the word: ALTAR.

> **A**doration
> **L**ove
> **T**hanksgiving
> **A**sking
> **R**econciliation

If prayer consists solely in asking for favours, it is leaving out essential elements of our relationship with our God. Asking for favours cannot fully express a love relationship, so it will breed false ideas of God and a false religion. Even in that part of our prayer that deals with asking, we should always ask for the good of the community and the good of the whole world before asking for our own personal good.

I find that the official prayers of the Church at Mass place far too much emphasis on ourselves getting into heaven, and too little on our reaching out to others and helping them. They ask that God do things for us; they do not ask God to help us from within ourselves to do things for others. We have spent much energy on the translations of the prayers, and not nearly enough on their essential content.

There is also the public prayer that all priests are to say each day, the Divine Office or Breviary. Some years ago, I met an Episcopalian bishop and saw that he was praying from his Anglican breviary, and I asked him whether it was an obligation for him to pray the breviary every day. He said that it was and told me that the obligation came from his ordination ceremony when he had publicly accepted the obligation to pray for God's people. I could not help thinking that this was a far better and more inspiring basis for the obligation than the law in the Code of Canon Law that obliges Catholic priests to say their breviary. So I have introduced this idea into every ordination to diaconate or priesthood I have celebrated since then. I have handed the candidates a copy of the breviary and publicly, before the congregation, asked them whether they will make this prayer each day for God's people.

I have done this with the serious reservation that the truly essential element is that priests actually pray for God's people rather than that they recite without thinking the words of a book. This is always a danger, and I doubt that even Mother Teresa was always thinking about the meaning of the words she was reading. Most priests work in a parish and gradually get to know different people and something of their joys and sorrows, their hopes and desires. And it is part of their bounden duty as priests to bring all of this and the needs of the whole world into their adoration, love, thanksgiving, asking and reconciliation rather than simply recite words.

c) Proclaiming the Message of the God

There is much that could be said about this pillar of the priesthood but let me limit myself to three things.

First, my faith is faith in a person and his song – the person of Jesus Christ and the story of his life and death and resurrection. We can get so tied up with creeds and catechisms, commandments and going to Mass, that we forget that what our faith is really all about is our personal relationship with Jesus Christ. So by all means priests should proclaim the truths, the moral rules, the worship and the community, but they should also make sure that always and in every way the person and the song are at the very centre of all they proclaim.

The second thing to say under this heading is that their whole life, that priests' whole way of living, will always be the most important message they proclaim. They can stand before the congregation in church and deliver the greatest homily there ever was, but if, as soon as they have left the altar, they show themselves to be rude and ungracious, their beautiful homily will count for nothing, for their actions will be giving a more powerful and more negative homily. Their life is their message.

The third thing is that the more they study the scriptures, the more they understand the sheer excitement of the gospels, and the more they can make the story of Jesus live in the hearts of their hearers. If they feel that they are too busy to spend time studying the scriptures, there is something very wrong in their priorities.

d) Building a Community Based on the Message

The last pillar is that of building both individuals and a whole community based on the message of God. This work will occupy most of their time, and it will take a lot of study, imaginative thinking and hard work. At times it can be sublime, such as when they are baptising new members into the community. At other times it can be very pedestrian and involve learning many things that they were never taught in the seminary, such as how to unplug the drains in the boys' toilet, how to deal with the countless acts of administration that a parish generates, and how to respond to the clashes of personality that can occur. There will be many moments when priests will need to remind themselves, "I'm doing this for the kingdom of God."

COLLABORATIVE MINISTRY

The Letter to the Ephesians says: "And to some his gift was that they should be *apostles*; to some, *prophets*; to some, *evangelists*; to some, *pastors* and *teachers*; to knit God's holy people together for the work of service to build up the body of Christ" (Eph 4:11–12; cf. Rom 12:6–8; 1 Cor 12:8–10, 28). These gifts are given to different persons, so the people should never expect their priest to possess all of them and the priest should never dream of claiming to possess all of them. The task of the priest is not to be the sole one exercising all of these different gifts, but to recognise and draw them out from the community and thus ensure that all roles are present in the community.

THE UNIQUE ROLE OF THE PRIEST

If I were to go to listen to a piano concerto of Beethoven's, I will at first be aware of all the sights and sounds of a concert hall. But if the pianist is very good, there can come a moment when I forget all these things and am caught up into direct contact with Beethoven himself speaking to me through his music. The pianist has fully succeeded when to me the only people present in that hall are myself and Beethoven. The pianist could then paraphrase the words of Paul and say, "I live now, not I, but Beethoven lives in me."

It is Beethoven alone who can sustain this moment, for it is his genius, inspiration and divine spark that make it possible. If the pianist suffered a sudden memory blackout, the music would crash to a halt, for there is no one else in that hall who can supply Beethoven's greatness.

There is the paradox, however, for that the moment when I have forgotten the very existence of the pianist is that pianist's supreme moment, the moment in which the pianist is most completely everything he or she is capable of being. There will have been decades of hard work, sacrifice and dedication behind the performance, for it is never achieved easily, but it is that moment of greatness which I am referring to.

This is the ideal for the priest in celebrating Mass and in preaching. In the homily, at the consecration or at any moment during the Mass, it is good if the people forget all about the priest and have the experience of Jesus himself speaking to them, Jesus taking bread and wine and saying, "This is my body, this is my blood." The priest has fully succeeded in his role if the people go beyond him and are in direct communion with Jesus. His mission is accomplished, if the priest can say, and the people believe, "I live now, not I, but Christ lives in me"(Gal 2:20). It is Jesus alone who can sustain the greatness of the Mass or homily and his input is required at every second, for there is no one else in the Church who can supply his greatness. And yet the moment of seeming oblivion is the priest's greatest moment.

Above all else, people expect in their priest a person who is in touch with God, who listens to God and speaks with God, who is a familiar of God like Moses, who reflects God, who makes God present.

BUILDING PRIESTHOOD

If you want a good priest, first find a good Christian; and if you want a good Christian, first find a good human being. It is not possible to have a good priest unless the person is first a good Christian and a good human being. Time spent on being a good human being is never wasted.

I hope that all priests have met non-religious people who have learned to be instinctively courteous, polite, truthful and caring, and I hope that they have seen how others respond to them and respect them. We cannot expect people to appreciate supernatural virtues if the basic natural virtues are not in place.

Throughout more than thirty years as a bishop I have heard many complaints about priests, and I could not help noting that very few were about failures in their priestly duties. Overwhelmingly they were about failures as human beings.

SIMPLICITY, FIDELITY AND SERVICE

Money, sex and power have always been seen as the three most significant factors in leading people astray. The Church responded to these dangers by imposing poverty, chastity and obedience on priests and religious, and then urging the laity to imitate them as best they could.

In our own day, there have been far too many cases of sexual abuse for priests and religious to be collectively seen as models of chastity. The Church is too rich for them to be collectively seen as models of poverty and there is far too much argument and dissension for them to be collectively seen as models of obedience. In any case, poverty, chastity and obedience will never be modelled well for laypersons.

Today we need a new paradigm, one that is valid for all Christians and in which priests and religious can regain credibility and become true models for all. With this in mind a number of writers have suggested we need an emphasis on the three paradigms of simplicity, fidelity and service.

Simplicity indicates a world in which we seek what we genuinely need rather than what we merely want. We have learned that it is simply not possible for all people to have everything they want, and not only because the limited planet on which we live cannot support this. And Jesus warned us of the dangers of what he called *pleonexia:* it is usually translated as "avarice" or "covetousness", but the word literally means "the desire for more" (Luke 12:15). Whether we are poor people or billionaires, we all seem to want more than we have, and this insatiable "desire for more" can become a monster leading us astray. "Simplicity", supporting the concept of being content with what we need, expresses the ideal better than "poverty". It is a virtue that priests and religious could model for the world, for it is a virtue that the entire world desperately needs.

Fidelity is a much richer idea than merely "not being unfaithful". Not being unfaithful is negative, while true fidelity demands many positive elements. It applies well beyond the field of sex and implies that I want to be faithful to all that I am and wish to become in all fields of life. Priests and religious who are truly faithful to their word, their promises, their beliefs, their vocation and their relationships, could become genuine and inspiring models.

Service, in the Christian understanding, refers to all power as being the power to serve. There is no other legitimate basis for power. Whether we are talking of a president or a parent, power is best seen as power to serve the good of those over whom it is exercised. If priests and religious genuinely understand power as power to serve, many of the evils of clericalism will disappear.

THE SPIRITUAL AND THE SOCIAL

For nearly two thousand years the parish was not only the spiritual centre of the village, but in most cases also the social centre, for the church was where one went to meet people and most social activities started from there. Whether people went to the church for purely spiritual reasons, or purely social reasons, or a mixture of both, they were there, and the priest could exercise a spiritual role in their midst.

In many parishes, at least in urban areas, the car, the television and the telephone have in a few short years changed all that, for the car has made people mobile in seeking social activities, the television has entertained them at home, and the telephone has enabled each person to develop a personal social network of friends. Many parishes are no longer the centre of social life and probably never will be again. Those parishioners not strongly motivated by religious reasons are simply not present any longer, so the priest cannot exercise a spiritual role towards them. This is arguably the biggest single change in parish life in 2000 years.

In all of these many parishes, the priest now faces the daunting task of creating a spiritual centre without the benefit of it being a social centre. Bishops, priests and people must all adapt to this seismic shift.

THE ART AND SCIENCE OF LEADERSHIP

There was a scribe who came to Jesus and asked, "Which is the first commandment of all?" (Mark 12:28). He wasn't simply asking the question about which commandment in the law of Moses was the most important, but the scribe went beyond in asking, "If you look at all the laws and all the wisdom of all the sages of all nations and cultures in the world, what is the most important commandment you will find, and what is its nature?" This question makes the answer of Jesus all the more powerful, for he says in effect, "You can search all the wisdom of all the wise persons of all places and times, and you will never find anything more important than the commandment which is contained in the prayer you already say every morning and every evening of your life: 'Hear, O Israel, the Lord your God is one, and you shall love the Lord your God with all your heart, and all your soul, and all your mind, and all your strength. And you shall love your neighbour as yourself'." That is the greatest commandment, and its nature is not that of command and obedience, but of love.

It follows that the priest is not to be a ruler, but a leader, for that is the essential nature of a commandment of love. We cannot be 'ordered' to love others; we must be led towards this. All priests must carefully study and practice the art of leadership. There have been and still are too many priests who have known only the art of ruling.

Much work has been done in recent years on the art and science of leadership, and excellent courses in leadership are readily available. Every priest should do such a course and it should be part of all seminary training. Such a course will typically include topics such as:

- setting goals
- balancing the development of task, team and individual
- leadership styles
- qualities of a leader
- methods of decision-making
- problem solving
- group dynamics
- personal relationships
- helpful and destructive behaviour
- motivation
- resolving conflict
- the challenge of change
- coping with stress, and
- time management.

Needless to say, a mere course would be useless unless it involved teaching a change of heart and mind and was enthusiastically put into practice.

Catholic people of today will no longer accept a priest as their ruler but do look eagerly for a leader. Sound leadership is the only style of governance that will enthuse and inspire people, and it is the only style that will help them to develop a sound conscience. The development of a sound conscience is one of the most essential changes required in the priesthood.

PROFESSIONALISM

Many times in recent years a priest has said to me, "But I have never sexually abused anyone, so why should I have to change?" I have to reply that the Church will never put this problem behind it unless there are serious changes in the lives of all priests.

If priests want to blame someone for this, they shouldn't blame popes or bishops. They should put the blame squarely where it belongs: on all those fellow priests who have moved so far from the person of Jesus Christ that they have sought sexual gratification by abusing the most helpless and innocent among us.

I know that many priests can reject the very word "professionalism" as though it could not apply to priests. But the word derives from the original concept of the three "learned professions", divinity, medicine and law. Virtually all other professions have adopted the idea, and it is priests who now stand out for their failure to be true professionals.

Making changes for the better – to become more professional – is a concrete and practical step that can be taken in the overall task of overcoming abuse and we need to remind ourselves of it constantly. It involves steps such as:

- a psychological assessment
- an acceptance that human development is an essential basis for spiritual development
- an appraisal every five years
- a supervisor
- obligatory in-service training
- a code of conduct
- a heeding of all signs of radical unsuitability for priesthood.

"TAKEN" OR "TAKEN UP"

The Letter to the Hebrews contains the sentence, "Every high priest chosen from among mortals is put in charge of things pertaining to God on their [mortals behalf] behalf, to offer gifts and sacrifice for sins" (Heb 5:1).

The Greek word translated as 'chosen' is *lambamenos*, but it was translated into Latin by St Jerome as *assumptus*, taken up, and persisted in that form for many centuries. *Lambamenos* simply means 'taken' and implies that a hundred people are standing there and one of these, exactly like the other ninety-nine, is taken or chosen for a particular role. One is chosen to be a farmer, another a teacher, a third a bus driver, a fourth a shopkeeper, a fifth a priest ... so that all the needs of the community may be met.

Assumptus, on the other hand, means 'taken up' and implies that the priest is somehow taken up above the others and placed in a special situation. This is a false translation, as is shown by the following words, "He is able to deal gently with the ignorant and wayward since he himself is subject to weakness" (5:2).

The false meaning associated with this translation persisted for most of the Church's history and was part of the training of every seminarian. In places it even developed into the claim that priests were 'ontologically' different from other people, that is, different in their very being.

For the health of the Church, it is quite essential that we go back to the original meaning of *lambamenos* to denote one who is taken or chosen for a particular role without in any way being taken up above the others.

Priests are exactly like other human beings. If we ever forget this, if we take away their humanity, we are bound to run into serious problems.

Countless Catholic people have experienced in priests an attitude of being taken up above others and being superior to them. It is exactly the kind of unhealthy idea that can contribute to abuse, and sexuality is only one of the areas in which priests can think that they are special, unlike other human beings and not subject to the restrictions that bind others. The privileges of this mystique will always be attractive to many inadequate personalities. The mystique also gives priests privileged access to minors and a powerful spiritual authority over them, making it so much easier to abuse.

If the governing image of how to act as a priest is tied to the ideas of lordship and control, an unhealthy domination and subservience will be present. If the idea of being called "Father" should be taken from the gospels, where it is invariably used as a term of intimacy and affection, and not from the Roman concept of the *paterfamilias*. Otherwise unhealthy and dangerous attitudes will remain established.

Pope Francis has used the marvellous image that all priests are chosen for the role of pastors or shepherds and should "have the smell of the sheep about them". This is far from priests having a "messiah complex", where they believe that God is calling him or her to be, as it were, a messiah: a chosen one who is called to some special mission and is, therefore, above the rules that apply to ordinary mortals. In such cases, if sexual abuse does not occur, some other form of abusive behaviour will. Every single priest needs to admit that the messiah complex is a real temptation that must be carefully and rigorously thrust aside.

Spiritual power is arguably the most dangerous power of all. In the wrong hands it assumes the power to make judgements even about the eternal fate of another person. It needs a sign on it at all times saying, "Handle with extreme care". The greater the power a person exercises, the more need there is for checks and balances before it is used, and accountability after it is used.

One of the saddest sights in the Church today is that of some young, newly ordained priests insisting that there is an "ontological difference" between them and laypersons, and they enthusiastically embrace the mystique of a superior priesthood. Whenever I see young priests doing this, I feel a sense of despair, and wonder whether we have learned anything at all from the revelations of abuse.

Part of the mystique is the inability to accept failure and vulnerability. Priests can feel that, because they have been "taken up", they must be perfect. When they realise that they cannot achieve this, they can settle for merely appearing to be perfect. Perfectionism is always dangerous, and it is particularly dangerous in a field as vast as the spiritual and the moral, where perfection is simply not possible for a human being. Feeling that one must appear to be perfect, even when one knows that one is not, and being unable to admit to failure and weakness, is an unhealthy attitude. Inherent in it is the covering up of faults that do occur and a split between the private individual and the public persona. Truly there must be room for a painful struggle towards maturity, with many mistakes along the way.

I will always remember feeling apprehensive when I had to confront a priest over his consumption of alcohol, and being greatly relieved when he freely admitted the problem. But then, just when I thought I had succeeded in my mission, the real problem arose. The priest could freely admit to me that his drinking was out of control and welcome my assistance, but he could not bear the thought that the people of the parish would find out. He had always tried hard to be perfect, and he could not live with the idea that the people would become aware of his failure and weakness. We talked this over at length, but I eventually felt that I had no choice other than to agree to a solution that would see him accept help without the parishioners becoming aware of any problem.

I contrast this with another priest whose alcoholism was so public that it could never have been hidden from the parishioners. This continued until one day the devoted housekeeper who had looked after him for many difficult years fell seriously ill. He immediately stopped drinking, joined Alcoholics Anonymous and looked after her attentively for two years until she died. He remained sober and became a wonderful apostle to those who had a problem with alcohol. When he died, he had one of the biggest funerals I can remember, as people responded to this "wounded healer" whose story moved them.

The first priest could not climb down from his pedestal of perfection, while the second had long since abandoned all ideas of pedestals and had a far better understanding of who and what he was. It was this second priest, with all his obvious weaknesses, who, after he had stopped drinking, could be more authentic and could better present the message of Jesus Christ.

Sadly, priests can be made to feel that superiors, people in their parish, the media, and the community at large, will also demand that they be perfect and will strongly criticise any lack of perfection. They can be made to feel that what would be described as an understandable failure in another person would be called "sickening hypocrisy" in them. These expectations can cause them to show externally a level of perfection that they know they do not possess. In both priests on the one hand, and in the community on the other, there needs to be change in the expectations that are present. Priests are ordinary human beings and, if either they or the community forget this, one kind of problem or another will be caused.

A major reason why the revulsion against the Catholic Church over abuse has been so great is that for centuries the Church presented itself as the great and perfect moral guide. It presented as a guide that could tell everyone else what to do and threaten eternal punishment for anyone who did not bow down and obey. And now this Church – which so vaunted its own perfection – has been shown to have a rottenness at its core. Now it is only natural that when the school bully is brought low, the whole school rejoices!

If we are ever to come out of this crisis of abuse, there must be a far greater humility. We need to adopt the Second Vatican Council's idea of "the pilgrim people of God": a community of ordinary, struggling people seeking to find their way towards God and making many mistakes during that process. This is the kind of community that God created in the People of Israel in the First Testament, and we would do well to imitate this model. The Church can help the world only if it works from within it, not if it tries to be above it.

It is never easy to change an ethos or mystique, but this one – of the Church seeing itself as being above all else – *must* change, for it denies the essential humanity of the priest and so establishes a series of false relationships at the heart of the community. Priests are ordinary human beings. This ought to be obvious to everyone; but authorities, priests and Catholic people all need to consider more closely this obvious fact. Also, I find that wherever there are priests trying to climb down from their pedestal, there are always not only Church authorities, but also many Catholic people insisting that they climb right back up again. The insistence that priests be perfect, or at least appear to be perfect, is very real. An extraordinary number of people believe the naïve idea that "priests are celibate, so they don't really have sexual desires and feelings the way the rest of us do". Of all the causes of abuse, this mystique of the priesthood would have to be put high on the list, and there will be much work involved in overcoming it.

CHAPTER 18
OBLIGATORY SANCTITY

Recently an Anglican bishop in England complained that his priests were too keen on applying for the "best" [read 'easiest'] parishes and were unwilling to move to working-class areas. He said that while it had taken two years to find a rector in a low-income parish in the north of the country, there had been abundant applicants for a wealthier parish in London. I can understand why a priest with a wife and children might want a good environment and good schools for the upbringing of his children, so a married clergy brings its own problems in relation to the preaching of the Christian message. But is this sufficient reason to impose a law of celibacy on priests, or is it merely exchanging one set of problems for another?

Most of this chapter is not about priestly celibacy as such, but about obligatory celibacy. It is not about whether it is good that priests should be celibate, but about whether there should be Church laws decreeing that only unmarried persons may be ordained; that, once ordained, they may not marry; and that any marriage they purported to enter into would be invalid unless a pope reluctantly granted them permission to leave the ministry of the priesthood and marry.

I have few problems with voluntary celibacy (as long as it remains truly voluntary) and I believe that there have been countless admirable examples of celibate priests. If I have problems with a law saying that all priests must be celibate, I would have even greater problems with a law saying that all priests must be married. Nothing that I say in the rest of this chapter should be used to weaken these statements. The sole question here is whether there should be a law demanding celibacy of priests.

I note that most arguments in favour of the present situation are in fact arguments in favour of voluntary celibacy, but I find these arguments unconvincing when applied to obligatory celibacy. There is a large gap in an argument that says that, because many people would consider voluntary celibacy be a good thing for priests, it is right to have a law imposing celibacy on all priests. There are few arguments put forward specifically in favour of the law commanding celibacy for all, and yet this must be the focus of all debate on the subject.

A) AVAILABILITY

A common argument put forward in favour of celibacy is that a priest has committed himself entirely to God and to God's people. He is said to be , so it is said, "married" to God, and he is expected to be faithful to God, just as a husband and wife are expected to be faithful to each other.

In this understanding, if a bishop tells a priest that an emergency has arisen in a parish at the far end of the diocese and he needs the priest to go there, the only question the priest will need to ask is, "What time does the train leave?" In other words the expectation is that being married to God, and no other, there will be no one and nothing that he cannot leave behind immediately.

The danger here lies in confusing an ideal with a law. Yes, it might be an ideal that every priest was fully available in this way, and it is certainly convenient to authorities in the Church that all priests should be so available, but is this sufficient ground for making a law that every priest must be available. Is it an attempt to turn an ideal into a reality by force of law? To say that the priest is married to the Church is at best an analogy rather than a reality, and it is a most imperfect analogy.

It may be argued that all priests make themselves available by freely taking on the priesthood knowing that it contains this requirement of celibacy, but there is a vast gap between the ideal of voluntary celibacy for a priest and the lived reality of lifelong celibacy. The right to marry is one of the most fundamental of all human rights, and to take away permanently the very right to a valid marriage by saying that the individual once freely surrendered this right, will inevitably lead to many problems in the priesthood.

> For a number of priests and religious, celibacy becomes an unattainable ideal that leads to living a double life and contributes to a culture of secrecy and hypocrisy. It can lead to emotional isolation, loneliness and depression.

No one has ever asked priests how many of them have lived a truly voluntary celibacy and how many of them have remained celibate solely because a law told them they had to if they wished to remain priests. It seems basic to me that authorities in the Church should know the answer to this question. It might be thought by some that authorities have not asked this question because they fear the answer they might receive and so prefer not to know.

B) THE NEED FOR THE EUCHARIST

Most people accept that the world's population cannot continue to rise at the rate it has, and that they share in the responsibility to ensure that in the future this rise is limited. It follows that, while in former times there were many families with four or more children, now, if we are to be responsible, because of the rise in world population and a far greater sense of the limits of this planet, there are more likely to be only two or at most three children. (This is in the Western world, of course.) It is a well-known finding of many anthropologists that in many countries where food is a long-term scarcity and people die of malnutrition or starvation, that they have more children in the hope that a larger number will survive and care for their parents. And it is only common sense that parents of larger families are more likely to approve of one child becoming a celibate priest than are parents with only one male child. To add to this, the widespread revelations of sexual abuse have caused many parents to have extreme doubts about their son becoming a celibate priest. These two facts alone are likely to lead to a shortage of priests.

It is not possible to say that the many difficulties young people of today have with the churches and with religious belief will soon disappear. One may hope that there will be more vocations to priesthood, but there are no realistic grounds on which to assert with any confidence that this will happen. It is pure wishful thinking to say that these are short term problems that will soon pass away, and the Church cannot afford to base itself on wishful thinking in this matter.

Demanding more and more work by older and older priests is not a solution to this need. Short term answers such as importing priests from Asia and Africa are not going to give more than temporary relief, and they cause their own problems. Inevitably – even in the near future – Asia and Africa may themselves be influenced by these same two factors.

It is already true that, because of this shortage of priests, people in a number of places are being deprived of the Eucharist. This situation will only become worse. And yet the Second Vatican Council calls the Eucharist "the source and summit of the Christian life". Is it lawful to continue to insist on celibacy for priests if this means that the Eucharist will not be available to more and more Catholics? Must we not say that Church authorities have a strict obligation to ensure that the Eucharist is available to all members of the Church, and that they are failing in their strict duty if they allow something such as celibacy to stand in the way?

The question of priestly celibacy must now be discussed within a new and most probably permanent situation.

C) BETTER PERSONS

If you want a good priest, first find a good human being. The one builds on the other, and you simply cannot have a good priest if that person's priesthood is not built on first being a good human being. So the question is relevant – does obligatory celibacy help people to become better human beings, or does forced celibacy get in the way of becoming a better human being?

I suggest that there is no simple yes/no answer, for it depends on the individual. Nevertheless, several factors can be considered.

Human beings are social animals. Their very DNA is programmed in this way. And it is natural for them to seek a special relationship with one other individual. To insist on celibacy for a whole group of people is to go against tens of thousands of years of conditioning and to place them in a situation their very DNA was never programmed for.

Given sufficient motivation, a young man might be prepared to take on a life without genital sex. But no young man in his right mind should be prepared to take on a life without love. There is no motivation that is adequate for this. And yet many priests appear to be living a life with too little love in it. Training for priesthood often accented celibacy and the protection of celibacy in the priest's life. In this training, celibacy was often presented in negative terms, that is, as a series of things the priest was not to do. Women were presented as dangers to celibacy, and there was little taught about cultivating a priest's own feminine side, or about what a priest might learn from women in this process. There is the also the suggestion that some priests will not know how to find love without sex becoming involved. The Church certainly spoke about loving God and about God's love for human beings, but it rarely spoke about priests finding love in the people around them. A life without sufficient love does not make people better human beings. On the contrary, it gravely harms the whole development of a person.

A husband and father has many practical and daily recurring demands on his obligation to love his wife and children. A priest is also obliged to love, but it lacks that same daily practicality and concreteness. Unless the priest is very careful, this lack of specific, practical and daily demands can cause the love itself to weaken.

Divine love is never meant to do away with human love, but to complement it. There is no contradiction between the two loves, as is easily seen in the marriage of a good Christian couple. A priest who has no human support or love around him is unlikely to be a good human being, and so is unlikely to be a good priest. Divine love would be sufficient only if it were overwhelming and spilled over into a profound love of people. This brings us to the heart of the problem. Celibacy is so unnatural for human beings, so against their DNA formed over tens of thousands of years, that it requires a form of heroism and sanctity to live it without being harmed by it. But can heroism and sanctity be demanded by law? Can any law ever legitimately say, "You shall be heroic and saintly."

Almost all the priests I have ever known at least started out as very good people, filled with high ideals and desires. The priesthood came to them as a pre-wrapped package, and they either accepted the package and were ordained, or they did not and left the seminary. But then those who were ordained had to live the daily reality of priesthood. In this process they inevitably unwrapped the package and looked at the different elements contained there. One of these elements was celibacy, and large numbers discovered that, while priesthood was still attractive, celibacy was not. As an empirical fact, many thousands or tens of thousands found themselves living an unwanted, unaccepted, unassimilated celibacy. This created a very dangerous situation, like a volcano on the brink of eruption. In our day we have seen what this has contributed to.

Heroism and sanctity are hard, very hard, and most priests fall short of the highest ideals. This does not mean that they are failures, nor that they have betrayed their calling. It simply means that they are human beings who have not reached the highest ideals they once set for themselves. To demand, by force of law, that all priests reach and live the very highest ideals is unrealistic and will lead to many problems.

The sexual abuse of minors is not the only significant problem that can arise. There is also a significant amount of alcoholism among priests as they seek escape from the overwhelming sense of loneliness and isolation that celibacy can give rise to. Careerism, the desire for human advancement within the Church, is another problem that can be created. The desire for absolute authority in one's parish or diocese, and the inability to pay attention to the desires and needs of others, is also a consequence of the frustration of desire that is inherent in celibacy. These are all expressions of the desire for human recognition and comfort as priests struggle with the demands made of them.

As a bishop, I received many complaints about priests. I could not help noticing that very few were about priestly failings (failing in their strictly priestly duties). Overwhelmingly the complaints concerned human failings such as being rude, high-handed, and not listening.

Celibacy can make an individual a better human being if it is combined with an overwhelming love of God and neighbour, but it will not make a whole large group of people better persons, for the chances that every last priest will live a life of heroic virtue are nil.

Celibacy is a charism, a gift of God, but it is an individual charism, not a community charism, and it cannot be coerced by law.

D) SEXUAL ABUSE

Celibacy is not the sole cause of the sexual abuse of minors that has been revealed in the Church. The amount of abuse by married men, including married priests in other Christian churches, is clear proof of this. Furthermore, a voluntary celibacy based on a passionate love of God and people is not unhealthy.

It is not celibacy itself, but obligatory celibacy that has been the problem, for it has led to many thousands of priests worldwide embracing priesthood but discovering, sometime after ordination, that they could not embrace celibacy, no matter how hard they tried. Religious may not have had the same laws, but there were powerful psychological factors preventing them from leaving.

It is not even the desire for sex that is the major factor leading to abuse, but the insatiable human longing for love. Priesthood and religious life are structured in such a way that it is very difficult for a priest to find the love that is the deepest longing of every human heart. As a bishop I have sat with strong men and witnessed their anguish and tears because of their inability to cope with a profound sense of loneliness. Because of the loveless way they felt they were forced to live, the desire for love became distorted into a desire for sex and found its outlet in the problems we have seen. No matter how much priests try to sublimate their desire for love into a desire for divine love, the human being behind the priest cannot be satisfied. Celibacy cannot be imposed by law on a whole category of people. If anyone attempts to do so, the result will be the catastrophe we have witnessed and are still witnessing.

Celibacy was imposed because of a genuine desire that the Church be as divine as possible, but this ignored the fact that if we try to be too divine, we can fail to be properly human.

The Church cannot afford to maintain the law of celibacy on the basis that it has not been empirically proven that celibacy causes abuse. Rather, so great is the crime of the abuse of minors, so massive the harm caused, and so contrary is the very idea of abuse to everything Jesus stood for, that the Church must abolish the law of celibacy unless it can be empirically proven that there is no link between obligatory celibacy and sexual abuse. And this simply cannot be proven.

The Hippocratic oath for doctors begins by saying, "At least do no harm." If we can do good things, that is a wonderful bonus, but if we can't, then at least do no harm. If priestly celibacy has achieved great things, that is a wonderful bonus, but first comes the obligation to do no harm.

The idea that unwanted celibacy is a major cause of abuse is extremely widespread, so widespread that, if the question of obligatory celibacy were put on the table for discussion, the world would acknowledge that the Church was at last being serious in confronting the problem. But if we are told that the question of celibacy may not even be discussed, as Popes John Paul, Benedict and Francis have done, the Church loses all credibility on the subject and is not seen to be serious about overcoming abuse. On such a basis, the Church will never put the past behind it.

E) FAMILY

The vast majority of people are born into and raised in a family and then form a family of their own. Most of human life is lived in family. To minister to all of these people and assist them in their moral and spiritual lives surely requires an understanding of family life. To seek to offer moral and spiritual help without having the experience and knowledge of family life is a certain recipe for many difficulties.

The most obvious example is surely that parents are instinctively quite fierce and ferocious in protecting their children against anyone who would harm them. It has become evident that all too often priests and bishops have not shared this fierceness in protecting children from sexual abuse. All too often they have put the good of the offender or the good reputation of the Church before the good of the child victim. There are too many things that they have not previously seen in the situations that have confronted them.

F) CELIBACY IN ITSELF

Up to this point this chapter has been concerned with the obligatory celibacy of priests, for a legally enforced celibacy has special dangers and requires a special justification. But recent events indicate that there must be some comment on celibacy itself.

Religious brothers and nuns take vows of celibacy but are not bound by the same law of obligatory celibacy as priests and can more easily obtain permission to marry. They would still have to leave religious life and enter into a whole new way of living, but at least this is possible. One might hope that those tempted towards sexual abuse might avail themselves of this possibility.

The Royal Commission into abuse within institutions in Australia, however, has produced staggering statistics concerning religious brothers. The Commission spoke of a figure of 7 per cent for priests against whom an allegation of abuse had been made. But for male religious the figure was startlingly higher. For the largest two orders of brothers the figure was 20 per cent and 22 per cent and for one smaller order the figure was an unbelievable 40 per cent.

This smaller order (the John of God Brothers) looks after intellectually handicapped children, and it is a well-known fact that the more powerless children are and the less chance there is of the abuse being revealed to others, the more abuse there will be. But this is not in any way an excuse and the statistics stand.

Such figures demand that celibacy itself, at least in any institutional form, be most seriously reconsidered. The entire issue deserves its place in this book and the whole question of religious life needs to be subjected to serious study.

CHAPTER 19
SEXUAL MORALITY

SEXUAL MORALITY IN THE BIBLE

The major difficulty in dealing with this topic is that the Bible contains several different ethics of sex, that is, several different criteria for making moral judgements, several different viewpoints for looking at the subject, several different questions that are asked. For example, a justice ethic will ask, "Is this action just?", while a love ethic will say, "It may not be unjust, but is it a loving thing to do?" Thus, these two ethics can come to opposing conclusions, with one approving and the other disapproving of the same action.

Ethics of Love, Justice and Goodness

There is certainly a love ethic in the Bible, the best example of where this can be seen being the Song of Songs. In fact, for centuries many people were so afraid of this poem's uninhibited glorification of sexual love that they believed it had to be an allegory of something else. However scholars today say that it is quite simply what it appears to be – a lyric rhapsody concerning the love of a man and a woman, with sexual desire as an obvious and natural expression of that love. It has been noted that the couple do not live in the same house[147] and so are not married, and yet their love is clearly sexual.[148] Despite the fact

---

147 Song of Songs 3:1–4, 5:2–8.
148 See again 3:1–4 and, indeed, the whole poem.

that God is never mentioned, both Jews and Christians have always included this book in the Bible.

Among other statements in the Bible reflecting a love ethic, we may include the following:

> When a man is newly married, he shall not go out with the army or be charged with any public duty. He shall be free at home one year, to be happy with the wife he has married. (Deut 24:5)

> Rejoice in the wife of your youth,
> A lovely deer, a graceful doe.
> May her breasts satisfy you at all times;
> May you be intoxicated always by her love. (Prov 5:18–19)

> I will take you for my wife forever; I will take you for my wife in righteousness and in justice, in steadfast love and in mercy. I will take you for my wife in faithfulness... (Hos 2:19–20)

> I remember the devotion of your youth,
> the love of your bridal day. (Jer 2:2)

In the prophet Malachi we find what may be called an ethic of both justice and love taken together:

> You cover the Lord's altar with tears, with weeping and groaning because he no longer regards your offering or accepts it with favour at your hand. You ask, "Why does he not?" Because the Lord was a witness between you and the wife of your youth, to whom you have been faithless, though she is your companion and your wife by covenant... For I hate divorce, says the Lord, the God of Israel. (Mal 2:13–16)

And, of course, on the very first page of the Bible we find what may be called a "goodness ethic":

> So God created humankind in his image,
> In the image of God he created them
> Male and female he created them.

> God blessed them, and God said to them, 'Be fruitful and multiply, and fill the earth and subdue it'... And God saw everything that he had made, and indeed, it was very good. (Gen 1:17–28,31)

These beautiful sayings are an integral and important part of the biblical tradition. And yet, in a book that tells the story of a journey and reflects every part and every level of that journey, the other side of the love ethic could not fail to be present. Thus, the author of the Book of Ecclesiastes, who finds little that is good in any human being, says,

> One man among a thousand I found,
> but a woman among all these I have not found.[149]

The Bible was written by men and inevitably contains many brutal comments on women.

> Like a gold ring in a pig's snout
> is a beautiful woman without good sense.[150]

The same book of Proverbs paints a very masculine picture of the perfect wife as a woman who is constantly working from before dawn to well after dusk, while her husband seems to spend most of his time sitting with the elders at the city gates.[151]

The most damaging remark comes from the book of Ben Sira (Ecclesiasticus) in a classic misinterpretation of the *story* of Creation,

> From a woman sin had its beginning,
> and because of her we all die.[152]

Both the good and the bad comments that come out of ethics of love, justice and goodness are, however, rare when compared to the far more frequent sayings that come out of two other ethical viewpoints: the purity ethic and the property ethic.

The Purity Ethic in the First Testament

The purity ethic asks, "Is this thing or action ritually clean or unclean?"

To be a Jew did not mean only to profess a certain faith, but also to belong to a particular people. So, the *Torah* was not only religious law, but the basic law of Israel in all areas of life. Since Israel placed a very high value on being distinct from other peoples, the laws that made them different had a value greater than their intrinsic worth. High among these were circumcision, Sabbath observance

---

149 Ecclesiastes 7:28.
150 Proverbs 11:22.
151 Proverbs 31:10–31.
152 Book of Sirach 25:24.

and the purity laws.[153] They became an important part of the national identity during times when there was immense pressure to abandon this identity and merge with other peoples.[154]

The rationale of the purity laws appears to be that God's holiness calls for the completeness and purity of all creation. Only that which is complete and only that which is pure, that is, not a mixture of kinds, may be offered to God or stand in God's presence.[155] The particular rules were a spelling out of these two principles of completeness and purity, and were meant to be practical, everyday things that raised the mind to a meditation on God's completeness and purity.

In relation to completeness, for example, only an unblemished animal could be offered to God and only an animal that had a divided hoof and chewed the cud was considered complete, and hence clean. Since blood was considered the life force of a human being, a menstruating woman was considered incomplete and therefore unclean. On the part of the man, an emission of seed was considered a diminution of the life principle, so he too became unclean.

In relation to the second idea, that of purity, it was forbidden to sow two different crops in the same field or to use two different types of thread (for example cotton and wool) in the same cloth. Homosexuality was forbidden because the man playing the female part was both male and female at the same time, and so a mixture of kinds.[156]

Some of these purity laws could be justified on rational grounds (such as the laws concerning witchcraft, adultery, incest, and leprosy), but others reflected particular cultural ideas of what made something "complete" (for example that only an animal that had a divided hoof and chewed the cud was complete), or they reflected the instinctual ideas that every nation has and that are not subject to rational analysis (some peoples eat snails, dog-meat or certain insects, while others recoil from them).

It can be seen that the purity code of the First Testament puts three separate "states of being" – sinful, clean and dirty – in close proximity. However they are separate, for "sinful" refers to a moral offence, "unclean" refers to ritual uncleanness such that a person could not, for example, enter the temple while

---

153 Though individual purity laws are scattered throughout the five books of the Torah, the two most substantial collections are found in Leviticus 11–16 and 17–27.
154 The most famous stories can be found in the Second Book of Maccabees. These are the stories of Eleazar (6:18–31) and the mother and her seven sons (7:1–42),.
155 This insight comes from the anthropologist Mary Douglas, whose study of purity codes in many cultures led her to see the unity of those in the Bible. See *Purity and Danger: An Analysis of Concepts of Pollution and Taboo*, London, Rutledge and Keegan Paul, 1966.
156 "If a man lies with a male as with a woman, both of them have committed an abomination." (Leviticus 20:13.)

unclean, and "dirty" refers to the instinctual reaction that different cultures have to different things.

Nevertheless, the three ideas were put so closely together in the purity codes that it was easy to cross from one to the other. If a couple had intercourse, they had to "bathe in water"[157] in order to become "clean" again, so it was easy to think that something dirty had happened. If menstruation was unclean, it was easy to think of it as dirty, and since the woman carried the contagion to any chair she sat on or object she touched, it was all too easy to conclude that she herself was dirty, at least at the time of her periods. The menstruating woman, without the slightest fault on her part, was considered to be lacking in holiness, that is, she was in "a state of being incompatible with the holiness of the Lord and hence prohibitive of any contact with him."[158]

Indeed, it was easy to think of females as more unclean than males at the best of times; after giving birth to a male child a woman was unclean for seven days, but after giving birth to a female child she was unclean for fourteen days.[159]

It was also easy to start thinking that there had to be some moral stain on the menstruating woman if she carried the contagion of uncleanness everywhere she went and passed it to every object she touched. The forms of sexual activity that were forbidden under the purity laws were adultery, incest, homosexuality, bestiality, and intercourse with a menstruating woman. It is obvious that this listing could suggest that the menstruating woman was just as guilty of some form of wrongdoing as the persons in the other four categories.

The Purity Ethic in the Second Testament

It is clear that Jesus set aside the purity laws: "Thus he declared all foods clean", says the Gospel of Mark.[160]. Indeed, it seems that he went even further and denied that these laws had come from God in the first place. For Jesus they were too external a measure, while what mattered for him was purity of the heart. It is unlikely, however, that Jesus made a crystal clear statement abolishing the purity laws, yet this was the firm and clear conclusion the writers of the Second Testament reached from their observation of all that Jesus had said and done.

Jesus abolished the purity laws across the board. He did not abolish only those concerning foods, while retaining those that spoke of leprosy, witchcraft

---

157 "If a man lies with a woman and has an emission of semen, both of them shall bathe in water, and be unclean until the evening." (Leviticus 15:18)
158 *The New Jerome Biblical Commentary*, Geoffrey Chapman, London, 1989, p. 68.
159 Leviticus 12:2–5.
160 Mark 7:19.

or sex.[161] Therefore if any of these things were still to be considered wrong, it would have to be on some grounds other than the purity ethic.

Despite this, the matter becomes more complicated because Jesus himself on occasions followed the purity laws, such as when he sent the leper to the priests to be examined.[162] This tendency to still follow some of the purity laws became stronger in the followers of Jesus, and Paul may serve as an example of this. Paul was a Jew and had been brought up according to a strict observance. Inevitably, he had acquired a level of instinctual reaction against those things that were forbidden because they made a person unclean. He thus found himself in the difficult position of defending mightily the freedom of his Gentile converts from the requirements of the purity laws while observing most of them himself. He developed his teaching on the strong and the weak, and this teaching was reflected in the Council of Jerusalem in the year 50 CE.[163] The answer given by this council to the question of following the purity laws was a compromise and a postponement. It was a compromise because it asked Gentile converts to observe a modified purity code, and it was a postponement because the provisions made were less than completely clear and could be interpreted in different ways by different groups.[164] This request of Gentile converts to observe a modified purity code became a step in the longer process of transition to freedom from the purity laws, but it also served to reinforce the idea that the purity laws had not entirely disappeared.

The most common day-to-day problem that would have faced the new Christian community was whether Gentiles and Jews could share a meal together. Therefore the statements about food laws are more frequent and more explicit in the Second Testament. No replacement argument was ever given for abstaining from these foods, so if they were no longer forbidden by virtue of the purity laws, they were not forbidden at all. This possibly left an

---

161 He touched the leper (Mark 1:41) and allowed the woman with a flow of blood to touch him (Mark 5:25–34), in both cases without appearing to be concerned by issues of being clean or unclean.

162 Mark 1:43–44.

163 See Acts 15:28–29. "For it has seemed good to the Holy Spirit and to us to impose on you no further burden than these essentials: that you abstain from what has been sacrificed to idols and from blood and from what is strangled and from fornication."

164 L William Countryman, *Dirt, Greed and Sex, Sexual Ethics in the New Testament and their Implications for Today*, Fortress Press, Philadelphia, 1988, p. 71. There were some difficulties with the phrase "what has been sacrificed to idols", but the major difficulties were with the requirement to refrain from *porneia*. In the NRSV this word is variously translated as "unchastity", "fornication" and "immorality". It derives from the verb *pernemi*, "to sell", and so indicates "bought sex" or "harlotry". Elsewhere it is used in the figurative sense of idolatry. No one can really explain with certainty what the word is doing in a list of things that were permissible in themselves but were to be avoided because of the sensitivities of the Jewish converts, nor can anybody explain what the word means in this context.

ambivalence in relation to those parts of the purity code where some other argument could be given against certain actions, and this applied particularly to sexual matters. If a whole community has been told for centuries that certain sexual actions are wrong, and is now told that those same actions are still wrong, but not for the reason they were formerly thought to be wrong, the argument will be too subtle for many people to grasp. The fact that these actions are still constantly proclaimed as wrong will, in the minds of many, serve to perpetuate the idea that aspects of the purity code remain in force. This feeling will be all the stronger if the reasons now given for why the actions are wrong are not always overly convincing. Following the example of Jesus, the early Christians had to abandon the purity ethic, but it may be said that they did not find a clear replacement sexual ethic.

Philo of Alexandria

To understand how these ideas affected Christian history, we must go outside the Bible for a moment. Philo of Alexandria, a contemporary of Jesus (13 BCE – 45–50 CE) was a Jewish philosopher who was familiar with Greek philosophy and living in a Gentile world. Some of these Gentiles were attracted to the Jewish religion but found its purity laws an insurmountable barrier. So Philo tried to explain the purity laws in terms that Gentiles could accept. He found that this was impossible in relation to the food laws, but that he could find common ground when speaking of the purity laws concerning sex. From Plato he took the duality of body and soul and the necessity for human beings to free themselves from the sensual element, while in accordance with the Stoics he regarded indulgence and pleasure as hedonistic and animalistic and exalted self-control and orderliness.[165]

The Stoics often described what is morally right as "according to nature", so Philo could appeal to "nature" as something that would justify his religion's antagonism towards certain sexual acts. He therefore argued that the purpose of sex was to beget children, so to sow seed in a menstruating woman was like "sowing seed in a swamp", while homosexual sex was like "sowing seed in a desert".[166]

This work of Philo had two unintended effects. Firstly, for the Jews who listened to him, it changed the nature of the purity laws, for the sexual laws

---

[165] That these ideas were primitive in nature can be seen from the following quotation: "Philo considers the blame as lying in most of these cases not with the soul but with the balance of the elements of fire and moisture in the body when 'the moisture is sluiced in a stream through the genital organs, and creates in them irritations, itchings and titillations without ceasing'." William Loader, *The Septuagint, Sexuality and the New Testament*, William Eerdmans, Grand Rapids, Michigan, 2004, p. 13.

[166] Countryman, pp. 59–61.

were no longer simply purity laws, but also "natural laws". Secondly, because his whole purpose in writing was to explain the reasonableness of the purity laws, the Gentiles who accepted his arguments would find it difficult not to take on certain aspects of a purity law. Philo was read with respect by a number of Christian thinkers including Clement of Alexandria, Origen, Gregory of Nyssa, and Ambrose, and his ideas passed with much acceptance into Christian thinking. And following this an ethic of what is "according to nature" began to replace the purity ethic.

The Property Ethic in the First Testament

The property ethic is a form of justice that begins by asking the question, "Whose property is it?"

> (In the Bible) marriage is assumed to be the calling of every human being. Virginity is a tragedy; infertility a curse. God's blessings are given through the process of procreation.[167]

In this context, the family, not the individual, was the basic unit of society in the ancient world. It consisted of a male head who possessed one or more women as wives or concubines, and children who would either carry on the family (sons) or be used to make alliances with other families (daughters).

The male head ruled the family, but this does not mean that he was a completely free agent, for he, too, was the servant of the family, with the serious task of maintaining and increasing the family's wealth and public standing in the community. The other members of the family were the property of the male head, and the wives and concubines were his sexual property.

It was difficult for a love ethic and a property ethic to co-exist. Even a man who began his marriage on the basis of a love ethic could easily find that he later moved to a property ethic.

There is little evidence of significant development in this ethic between the writing of the Torah and the time of Jesus. Apart from the waning of polygamy and an occasional protest against the abuse of divorce, the Torah's definition of sexual property was the one which Jesus and Paul found to be current in their own time.[168]

The Property Ethic in the Second Testament

As I shall explain in the next chapter, Jesus was truly radical on the subject of divorce and taught a completely new understanding of marriage in the process.

---

167 Luke T Johnson, "The Biblical Foundations of Matrimony", *The Bible Today*, March/April 2003, p.114

168 Countryman, op. cit., p. 156.

The rest of the New Testament, however, did not keep up with him.

In a number of his letters, Paul was quite convinced that the Second Coming of Jesus was an imminent event. In these letters, especially 1 Corinthians, he saw little point in seeking to change ancient, deep-seated and hallowed family structures. Jesus had given no detailed ideas concerning a new family structure to replace the old, so the work involved in such an enterprise would be immense and any changes proposed would certainly arouse fierce anger and opposition. What was the point if the world was about to end?

Paul's advice to people was, therefore, to stay as they were. If they were married, they should stay married. If they were single, they should stay single. If they were about to get married, the choice was theirs. They did nothing wrong if they got married, but they were probably better off if they did not. His overriding concern was that people should be able to wait on the imminent coming of the Lord without distraction. There was simply no time for Christians to be making sweeping changes in the life of the world, and any attempt to do so would itself be a distraction.[169]

Paul was, therefore, quite conservative in his attitudes towards many family matters and the role of women in society and in the Church. It is possible that this was his natural disposition but, since he believed that the end of the world was about to occur, it is hard to judge him severely.

An extreme view in the Second Testament is represented by the First Letter of Peter. Peter was greatly concerned by the public hostility to Christians that threatened to break out into serious persecution (2 Peter 4:12–19) and so was of the opinion that Christians should appear as respectable as possible. For this reason, he did not wish to see Christians seeking to overturn societal and family structures. Conservative family life was for him a necessity. He made a permanent principle out of a temporary need, converting Paul's provisional acceptance of traditional family structures into a principled insistence on them. The impetus of the radicalism of Jesus on this point has here very nearly disappeared.

Conclusion

While there are statements concerning sex in the First Testament that come out of an ethic of love or justice or goodness, they are overwhelmed by the far more frequent statements that stem from motivation out of the ethics of purity and property. In the gospels Jesus radically rejected both the purity ethic and the property ethic. The rest of the Second Testament rejected the purity ethic concerning foods, but for a variety of reasons it did not entirely abolish the idea of purity laws as they applied to sexual matters and it seriously compromised Jesus' radical rejection of the property ethic. As a result, neither the purity

---

169 See 1 Corinthians 7:25–31.

ethic nor the property ethic has been abolished from Christian thought. Philo of Alexandria's ideas concerning the need for control of passion and the "natural" purpose of marriage continue to be influential in Catholic thinking, though there is no trace of an ethic of what is "natural" in the gospels.

There is a need, therefore, for a new and serious study of the Bible in relation to all matters sexual, with a view to regaining and renewing the radicalism of Jesus himself on these questions.

It is extraordinary how little Jesus said about sex when compared with virtually every other founder of a new religion in history. There is much to think about in this absence of any detailed instructions on this subject. There is no reason to think that Jesus was unworldly or prudish, that he was not aware of the importance of sex and how it can both build human relationships and complicate and disrupt them. It is safer to conclude that he saw no need to single out the topic for particular comment. In this the Christian world has not followed his example. And yet, if people followed his ideas in all aspects of their lives and approached other people with the same frame of mind as he did, they would find the answers to their questions about sex. Surely the basic rule for all sexual relations should be the same as the basic rule for all Christian living: "This is my commandment: love one another as I have loved you."[170]

HOMOSEXUALITY[170]

The thesis of the second section of this chapter is in three parts:
1. There is no possibility of a change in the teaching of the Catholic Church on homosexual acts unless and until there is first a change in its teaching on heterosexual acts.
2. There is a serious need for radical change in the Church's teaching on heterosexual acts.
3. If and when this change occurs, it will inevitably have its effect on teaching on homosexual acts.

PART ONE

There is no possibility of a change in the teaching of the Catholic Church on homosexual acts unless and until there is first a change in its teaching on heterosexual acts.

The constantly repeated argument of the Catholic Church is that God created human sex for two reasons: as the means by which new human life is brought into being (the procreative aspect) and as a means of expressing and fostering love between a couple (the unitive aspect). The argument then says that the use

---

170 John 15:12.

of sex is "according to nature" only when it serves both of these God-given purposes, and that both are truly present only within marriage, and even then only when intercourse is open to new life, so that all other use of the sexual faculties is morally wrong.[171]

If the starting point is that every single sexual act must be both unitive and procreative, there is no possibility of approval of homosexual acts. The Catechism of the Catholic Church deals with the question with quite extraordinary brevity: "(Homosexual acts) are contrary to the natural law. They close the sexual act to the gift of life. They do not proceed from a genuine affective and sexual complementarity."[172]

If this is the starting point, there is little else to be said. There is no possibility of change concerning homosexual acts *within* this teaching, and it is futile to look for it, for homosexual acts do not possess the procreative element as the Church understands that element. If teaching on homosexual acts is ever to change, the basic teaching governing all sexual acts must first change.

PART TWO

There is a serious need for radical change in the Church's teaching on heterosexual acts.

In an ideal world, a man and woman are drawn to each other by love; they marry and have children, and then over many years they help these children to grow to maturity in their physical, intellectual, emotional, social, artistic, moral and spiritual lives, so that they may be ready, in their turn, to found their own families.

In normal circumstances the growth of the union between the parents and the growth to maturity of the children go together, so I have no problem with the idea that marriage and family as institutions of the human race have both a procreative and a unitive aspect.

---

171 The most important papal document on sexual morality of the last century, the encyclical letter *Humanae Vitae*, expressed the argument thus: "Such teaching, many times set forth by the teaching office of the church, is founded on the unbreakable connection, which God established and which men and women may not break of their own initiative, between the two meanings of the conjugal act: the unitive meaning and the procreative meaning. Indeed, in its intimate nature, the conjugal act, while it unites the spouses in a most profound bond, also places them in a position (idoneos facit) to generate new life, according to laws inscribed in the very being of man and woman. By protecting both of these essential aspects, the unitive and the procreative, the conjugal act preserves in an integral manner the sense of mutual and true love and its ordering to the exalted vocation of human beings to parenthood." (Pope Paul VI, encyclical letter *Humanae Vitae*, July 26, 1968, no. 12.)

172 The Catechism of the Catholic Church, no. 2357.

But to move from this to the idea that every single act of intercourse must contain both the unitive and the procreative aspects is an enormous leap rather than a modest and logical step, and I have five serious difficulties with it.

The First Difficulty: A Sin Against God

The first difficulty is that through this teaching the Church is saying that all use of sex that is not both procreative and unitive is a direct offence against God because it is a violation of what is claimed to be the divine and natural order that God established. This raises two serious questions, one concerning nature and the other concerning God.

The Question concerning Nature

If this divine and natural order exists in relation to our sexual organs, should it not exist in many other areas of human life as well? Should not the Church's arguments concerning sex point to many other fields where God has given a divine purpose to some created thing, such that it would be a sin against God to use that thing in any other way? Why is it that it is only in relation to our sexual organs that this claim is made, and not for any other part of our body or any other human activity?

The Question concerning God

Striking a king or president has always been considered a more serious offence than striking an ordinary citizen. In line with this, it was said, the greatest king by far is God, so an offence against God is far more serious than an offence against a mere human being.

Because all sexual sins were seen as direct offences against God, they were, therefore, all seen as most serious sins. Sexual sins were seen as being on the same level as the other sin that is directly against God, blasphemy, and this helps to explain why, in the Catholic Church, sexual morality has long been given a quite exaggerated importance.

For centuries the Church has taught that every sexual sin is a mortal sin.[173] In this field, it was held, there are no venial sins. According to this teaching, even deliberately deriving pleasure from thinking about sex with anyone other than one's spouse, no matter how briefly, is a mortal sin. The teaching may not be proclaimed aloud today as much as before, but it was proclaimed by many

---

173 See Noldin-Schmitt, *Summa Theologiae Moralis*, Feliciani Rauch, Innsbruck, 1960, Vol.I, Supplement *De Castitate*, p. 17, no. 2; Aertnys-Damen, *Theologia Moralis*, Marietti, Rome, 1956, vol.1, no. 599, p. 575. The technical term constantly repeated was *mortale ex toto genere suo*. The sin of taking pleasure from thinking about sex was called *delectatio morosa*.

popes,[174] it has never been publicly retracted, and it has affected countless people.

This teaching fostered belief in an incredibly angry God, for this God would condemn a person to an eternity in hell for a single unrepented moment of deliberate pleasure arising from sexual desire. This idea of God is totally contrary to the entire idea of God that Jesus presented to us, and I cannot accept it.

My first questioning of Church teaching on sex came, therefore, not directly from a rejection of what the Church said about sex, but a rejection of the false god that this teaching presented.

The teaching has also been at the heart of the poor response of the Catholic Church to revelations of sexual abuse. For too many Church leaders it was the sexual act and pleasure involved in abuse that was the great mortal sin, while any harm caused to the minor was lesser, for the sexual sin was a sin against God, while the harm to the minor was merely an offence against a human being.

Furthermore, there is a long history of sexual sins being easily forgiven in confession, with the person being then completely restored to the situation before the offence, and this thinking contributed to the moving around of offending priests. Abuse was seen as a sexual sin, and was to be treated like any other sexual sin. Many Church leaders have been very slow to see that this type of thinking is totally wrong and dangerous, for it seriously downplays the harm done to the minor and the indignation of God at this harm. It has created a profound flaw at the heart of the Church's response to abuse.

The Second Difficulty: A Teaching Based on Assertions

The second reason for why change is needed is that the statements of the Church appear to be simple assertions rather than careful arguments.

Both the unitive and procreative elements are foundational aspects of marriage as an institution of the whole human race, but does it follow that:

- They are essential elements of each individual marriage, no matter what the circumstances?
- That they are essential elements of every single act of sexual intercourse?

For example, a particular couple might be told by medical experts that any child they had would suffer from a serious and crippling hereditary illness, and so decide to adopt rather than have children of their own. Are they acting against God's will? Another couple might decide that they already have several children and that they are both financially and psychologically unable to add to their family. On what basis is it claimed that they would be acting against God's will?

---

174 For example, Clement VII (1592–1605) and Paul V (1605–1621) said that those who denied this teaching should be denounced to the Inquisition.

There are always problems when human beings claim that they know the mind of God. So is the statement that it is God's will, and indeed order, that both the unitive and procreative aspects must necessarily be present in each act of sexual intercourse a proven fact or a simple assertion? If it is a proven fact, what are the proofs? Why do Church documents not present such proofs?[175] Would not any proofs have to include the experience of millions of people in the very human endeavour of seeking to combine sex, love and the procreation of new life in the midst of the turbulence of human sexuality and the complexities of human life? Is an ideal being confused with a reality?

If it is only an assertion, is there any reason why we should not apply the principle of logic which states that what is freely asserted may be freely denied? If it is no more than an assertion, does it really matter who it is who makes the assertion or how often it is made? Where are the arguments in favour of the assertion that would convince an open and honest conscience?

The Third Difficulty: A Morality of Physical Acts

The third argument is that the teaching of the Church is based on a consideration of what is seen as the God-given nature of the physical acts in themselves, rather than on these acts as being actions of human beings. And the Church's teaching continues to be this at a time when the whole trend in moral theology is in the opposite direction.

As a result, the Church gets into impossible difficulties in analysing physical acts without a context of human relations. For example, some married couples find that there is a blockage preventing the sperm from reaching the ovum, but that in a simple procedure a doctor can take the husband's sperm and insert it into the wife in such a way that is passes the blockage and enables conception. But the Congregation for the Doctrine of the Faith condemned this action because the physical act was not considered "integral", even though the entire reason for the intervention was precisely that the couple wanted their marriage to be both unitive and procreative.

The Church's arguments concerning sex are based solely on the integrity of the physical act in itself rather than on the physical act as an expression of a human intention.

The Fourth Difficulty: The Idea of "Natural"

It was God who created a world in which there are both heterosexuals and homosexuals. This was not a mistake on God's part that human beings are meant to repair; it is simply an undeniable part of God's creation.

---

175 In recent years there has been an appeal to anthropology, but I have not seen a clear statement of how anthropology demands that every act of intercourse include both the unitive and procreative purpose.

The only sexual acts that are natural to homosexuals are homosexual acts. This is not a free choice they have made between two things that are equally attractive to them, but something that is deeply embedded in their nature, something they cannot simply set aside. Homosexual acts come naturally to them, heterosexual acts do not. They cannot perform what the Church would call "natural" acts in a way that is natural to them.

The only exercise of freedom there is for the homosexual is in choosing to move from denial to acceptance of their condition and, through this, choosing to be who and what each of them is.

Why should we turn to some abstraction in determining what is natural rather than to the actual lived experience of human beings? Why should we say that homosexuals are acting against nature when they are acting in accordance with the only nature they have ever experienced?

The Church claims that it is basing its views on "natural law", but a natural law based on abstractions is a false natural law. Indeed, it brings the whole concept of natural law into disrepute. God created homosexuals and we must live with this fact.

The Fifth Difficulty: Not Based on the Teaching of Jesus

The fifth difficulty is that the entire idea of the necessity for both the unitive and procreative element in each act of intercourse is not based on anything Jesus said or implied, but comes from ideas outside the Bible concerning acts that are said to be natural and acts that are said to be against nature.

Of course, philosophical thinking is justified and necessary in relation to sexual morality, as it is in every other field, but for Christians it must always have some foundation in the scriptures, and this is singularly lacking in relation to sexual morality.

The Dilemma

In the light of these five difficulties we are left with the fact that the Catholic Church is propounding a teaching that, on logical grounds, has had little appeal to people, even those favourably disposed. Even within the Church most people no longer accept it, especially among the young. Western society as a whole has rejected this teaching and gone to a position that is in many ways an opposite extreme.

The Middle Ground

If we decide to leave behind an ethic that sees non-procreative sex in terms of a direct, and always mortal, offence against God, emphasises physical acts rather than persons and relationships, derives its idea of what is natural from abstract philosophical argument rather than human experience, does not come from the gospels, and is based on an assertion rather than a logical argument, where should we go?

I suggest that the answer is that we should move to an ethic that:
- sees any offence against God as being brought about, not by the sexual act in and of itself, but by the harm caused to human beings
- speaks in terms of persons and relationships rather than physical acts
- draws its ideas of what is natural from experience
- draws consciously and directly on the gospels, and
- builds an argument on these foundations rather than on unproven assertions.

From God's Point of View

If it is impossible to sustain an entire sexual ethic on the basis of direct offences against God, all the evidence tells us that God cares greatly about human beings and takes a very serious view of any harm done to them, through sexual desire or any other cause.

> If any of you put a stumbling block before one of these little ones who believe in me, it would be better for you if a great millstone were hung around your neck and you were thrown into the sea (Mark 9:42)

> Then they will answer, "Lord, when was it that we saw you hungry or thirsty or a stranger or naked or sick or in prison, and did not take care of you?" Then he will answer them, "Truly I tell you, just as you did not do it to one of the least of these, you did not do it to me." (Matt 25:44-45)

In these two quotations Jesus identifies with the weakest persons in the community and tells us that any harm done to them is a harm done to himself. I suggest that this harm done to people is the real sin in matters of sex, and the only sexual sin that angers God.

I suggest, therefore, that we should look at sexual morality in terms of the good or harm done to persons and the relationships between people, rather than in terms of a direct offence against God.

Following from this, may we say that sexual pleasure, like all other pleasure, is in itself morally neutral, neither good nor bad? It is rather the circumstances affecting persons and relationships that make this pleasure good or bad, for example it may be a good pleasure for a married couple seeking reconciliation after a disagreement, a bad pleasure for a man committing rape.

The Church v Modern Society

To take this further, if we go beneath the particular teachings of the Catholic Church on sex and come to its most foundational beliefs, I suggest that there is a fundamental point on which the Church and modern Western society appear to be moving in opposite directions.

In its simplest terms, the Church is saying that, because love is all-important in human life and because sex is so vital a way of expressing love, sex is serious, while modern society has become more and more accepting of the most casual sexual activity, even when in no way related to love or relationship. For many people sex is in itself just "a bit of fun".

On this basic point I find myself instinctively more in sympathy with the views of the Church than with those of modern society. It was actually the effects of sexual abuse on minors more than anything else that convinced me that all sex is serious.

Do not Harm v Love your Neighbour

Precisely because I see sex as serious, capable of causing both great good and great harm, I cannot simply conclude that all sex is good as long as it does not harm anyone. I would never want to put the matter in those simple terms, for I have seen far too much harm caused by this attitude.

"Do not harm" is a negative phrase, and inevitably contains within itself the serious risk of brinkmanship, that is that, with little thought for the good of the other person involved, one may seek one's own pleasure and, in doing so, go right up to the very brink of causing harm to another. In a field as turbulent as this, countless people basing themselves on such a principle will go over that brink.

If we turn to the gospels, Jesus said "love your neighbour" rather than "do not harm your neighbour". Love implies more than the negative fact of not harming. It implies a genuine respect for the other and positively wanting and seeking the good of the other. The essential difference between the two is that an attitude of "do no harm", while good as far as it goes, can still put oneself first, while "Love your neighbour" must put the neighbour first, or at least on the same level as oneself.

In applying this principle of Jesus, we must take the harm that can be caused by sexual desire very seriously, and look carefully at the circumstances or factors that can make morally bad the seeking of sexual pleasure that involves harm to others, to oneself or to the community. Some of these factors are: violence, physical or psychological; deceit and self-deceit; harming a third person (for example a spouse); treating people as sexual objects rather than as persons; trivialising sex so that it loses its seriousness; failing to respect the connection that exists between sex and new life; failing to respect the need to build a relationship patiently and carefully; and failing to respect the common good of the whole community.

It will be seen from all of this that, even though I see sexual pleasure as in itself morally neutral, I have serious difficulties with the idea that "anything goes". In reacting against one extreme, there is always the danger of going to the opposite extreme. I believe that this is what modern society has done in relation to sex.

A Christian Ethic

I suggest that the central questions concerning sexual morality are:

> Are we moving towards a genuinely Christian ethic if we base our sexual actions on a profound respect for persons and the relationships between them that give meaning, purpose and direction to human life, and on loving our neighbour as we would want our neighbour to love us?

> Within this context, may we ask whether a sexual act is morally right when, positively, it is based on a genuine love of neighbour, that is, a genuine desire for what is good for the other person, rather than solely on self-interest, and, negatively, contains no damaging elements such as harm to a third person, any form of coercion or deceit, or any harm to the ability of sex to express love?

> Is the question of when these circumstances might apply, and whether and to what extent they might apply outside marriage, one for discussion and debate by both the Church community and the wider community? Is this question calling us – each individual – for decision and responsibility before God, other people and one's own deeper self?

Many would object that what I have proposed would not give a clear and simple rule to people. But God never promised us that everything in the moral life would be clear and simple. Morality is not just about doing right things; it is also about struggling to know what is the right thing to do. It is not just about doing what everyone else around us is doing; it is about taking a genuine personal responsibility for everything we do. And it is about being profoundly sensitive to the needs and vulnerabilities of the people with whom we interact.

I believe that there is normally a far better chance of a sexual act meeting the requirements I have suggested within a permanent vowed relationship than outside such a relationship. But I could not draw the simple conclusion that inside a vowed relationship everything is good, while outside that relationship everything is bad. The complexities of human nature and the turbulence of sexuality do not allow for such simple conclusions.

The 1968 encyclical *Humanae* Vitae was a genuine watershed in the relationship between papal teaching and Catholic people, for it was the first time in the history of the Church that the Catholic people as a whole heard a solemn pronouncement of a pope on a matter of faith and morals, paused to relate it to their own experience and knowledge, and then collectively said a firm "No." We must not underestimate the permanent importance of this moment. It led to the near universal conviction that popes and bishops can be wrong, especially on sex, so people have to make up their own minds on matters such as pre-marital sex, gay sex, divorce, the ordination of women, and anything else dealing with either sex or gender. The tidal wave of sexual abuse of minors by priests and religious then came in to reinforce these ideas strongly. I cannot see the slightest possibility of the Catholic people as a whole ever returning to the current hierarchical teaching on sexual morality. If the gap between the two is to be bridged, it must be on the basis of mutual acceptance of a middle ground. And it is here that I hope I have pointed the way in fruitful directions.

PART THREE

If and when this change occurs (in the teaching concerning heterosexual acts), it will have its effect on teaching on homosexual acts

If we apply what I have just said about heterosexual acts to homosexual acts, several things follow.

Negatively, I could not accept for homosexual acts, any more than I can for heterosexual acts, that "anything goes", or that morality can be based on self-interest or on nothing more than the brinkmanship involved in the idea of "not harming" another person. I would ask that homosexual persons be as conscious as heterosexual persons of how easily thoughts about sex can be directed solely towards self-interest and lead to harm. I could not applaud a deliberate lifestyle of many transient sexual partners, anymore than I could applaud this in heterosexuals, for I cannot see how this could be reconciled with everything I have said in this chapter.

Positively, it would follow that sexual acts, whether heterosexual or homosexual, are not, in and of themselves alone, offensive to God. This means that sexual acts are pleasing to God when they help to build persons and relationships, and displeasing to God when they harm persons and relationships. Since I seek a specifically Christian ethic, I would always hope that it be based on a genuine loving, or willing the good of the other, rather than on self-interest or self-gratification.

If Church teaching were based on persons and relationships rather than on what is considered "according to nature" in the physical act, consideration of homosexual acts would exist in a whole new world and would have to be rethought from the very beginning.

In short, if you wish to change the Church's teaching concerning homosexual acts, then work to bring about change in its teaching on all sexual acts.

SCRIPTURE

There are statements in the Scriptures that appear to condemn homosexual acts. There are five in particular, two in the First Testament (Genesis 19 and Leviticus 18:22) and three in the Second (Romans 1:26–27, 1 Corinthians 6:9–10, and 1 Timothy 1:9–10). While there are difficulties in interpreting all five, they cannot simply be brushed aside.

In reading these statements there are three points to keep in mind. The first is that we must be very careful of language. The First Testament calls homosexuality an abomination, but in that Testament the word "abomination" is used 138 times and for many different things, including the eating forms of seafood such as prawns (or shrimp) that do not have fins and scales.[176] Rather than take the meaning of the word "abomination" from a modern dictionary, we should see it as a technical word in the law of ancient Israel deriving from ideas concerning what is ritually clean and unclean. In the same vein, *porneia* should not be translated as "fornication", *epithumia* means "desire" not "lust", and the meanings of *malakoi* and *arsenokotai* are uncertain.

The second factor is that, at the time these parts of the bible were written, there was little of even the limited understanding of homosexuality that we possess today. It seems that it was believed that all persons were in fact heterosexual. Homosexual acts were, therefore, seen as the deliberate choice by heterosexual persons of homosexual actions. Granted the fears that can be aroused in heterosexuals by homosexuality, it is easy to understand why someone such as St Paul could not understand heterosexual persons performing homosexual actions, was thoroughly uncomfortable with the idea, considered these acts "unnatural" and condemned them. All statements in the Scriptures concerning homosexual actions must be read against this background of a lack of understanding of homosexuality.

The third factor is that the bible is essentially the story of a journey, the spiritual journey of the people of Israel. As such, it has a beginning, a middle and an end. If Jesus represents the end of the journey, we may see its beginning in a person such as Lamech in Chapter Four of Genesis, who demanded seventy-sevenfold vengeance for any wrong done to him. The Bible does not

---

176 "Everything in the waters that has not fins and scales is an abomination to you." (Leviticus 11:12)

contain only perfect statements of eternal truth, but also statements of every stage of this very human journey, including many words and actions that we are definitely not meant to imitate (such as Jephthah sacrificing his daughter to fulfil a vow in Judges 11:29–40). Statements concerning a subject such as homosexuality must be seen within the context of this journey. For instance, the statement on homosexuality in Leviticus 18:22 comes from a purity ethic that Jesus would later explicitly reject, so it cannot be seen as the final word of God on this subject. Indeed, these references need to be relegated to the ethical dustbin along with similar prescriptions for the stoning of women for adultery.

The statements on homosexuality in the Second Testament do not give convincing reasons for their prohibitions, leaving us with the feeling that they are a relic from the purity laws.

It seems that, when the Church began to treat sexuality in terms of natural and unnatural acts, the purity ethic of the First Testament heavily influenced its attitude towards homosexual acts. In short, it is hard to build too great an edifice on these texts.

It remains true that the entire field of sexual morality is in urgent need of being studied again from the foundations up. Homosexuality has been the direct focus of this second half of the present chapter, but the same questions apply to contraception, premarital sex, masturbation, and sexual morality in general. All of these subjects need to be radically revised.

GAY MARRIAGE?

This question deserves special consideration. It is complicated by the fact that it is usually posed in the simple form: Are you for or against gay marriage? I believe that this is putting at least three questions into one, and we are more likely to find satisfying answers if we ask the three questions separately.

The first question is: Should gay couples be able to enter civil unions authorised by the State, and should these civil unions be given protections and privileges similar to those available to heterosexual couples? I believe that the answer must be a resounding yes, for anything less would be unjust discrimination.

The second question is: Should the Catholic Church accept such unions, allow them to be celebrated in church and recognise appropriate rights? If everything I have said in this book were accepted, then I believe the answer should be another yes.

The third question is: What name should be given to these unions? I find this a more difficult question, for there are two sides to the question and no simple answer can be given.

On the one side, calling such unions "marriage" would involve a revision of a definition of what marriage is that is thousands of years old, and this should not be done lightly. I see two dangers in particular in doing this.

Firstly, marriage has traditionally been seen to have three elements: permanence, fidelity and openness to new life. These elements help to give stability both to marriage and to the very important function of raising children. These elements have been under attack and have been weakened in our society, but even now it remains true that on their wedding day most couples still hope and intend that their union will last for life; most still expect fidelity; and most still see the bearing and raising of children as a natural part of marriage. These are still assumptions that most heterosexual couples bring to any talk of getting married. But homosexual couples – who might or might not be open to raising children – will certainly as a whole have different elements to this. However, 'marriage' has long been seen in most societies as something peculiar to a man and a woman, primarily because of the sex act which is an act which can cause co-creation of new life.

The Latin word *comes*, meaning companion or partner, but also containing the word "marriage", in recognition of the fact that, if this particular form of companionship or partnership does not contain all elements of marriage, it does contain many of them, especially the element of love expressed through sexual union. If such a word were accepted, many problems would be overcome.

The idea is not entirely novel, for the Ancient Romans had different names for different types of recognised marital unions, e.g. *connubium, consortium vitae, contubernium, confarreatio*.

On the other hand, we must never forget that there has been massive, severe and humiliating discrimination against homosexuals for thousands of years, causing untold harm to millions of individuals. It has led to many, many suicides. This discrimination, strongly reinforced by religious teachings, has powerful roots in the community and no change in the law is going to make it go away quickly.

I appreciate that gay people are insistent on the word "marriage", for I appreciate that they are convinced that nothing less than this word would give them the recognition they both need and demand. I am sure they fear that any other word would even be used as a new form of discrimination.

As I have said, there is no simple answer to this dilemma. A new name would go a long way, but I understand that many gay people would not be ready for this, for their concerns, based on a long history of discrimination, would be too great. It is probable that we must first overcome the massive prejudices and then perhaps a new name could be considered. The end of prejudice is, after all, within our power.

I would hope that we can keep the idea of a new name open, but in the meantime, if we are to put an end to the unjust, harmful and disgraceful discrimination of the past, I see no alternative to endorsing the use of the name "marriage" for homosexual unions.

I believe that we must see the certain evil of gross harm and injustice against homosexuals as a more pressing concern than the use of the term 'marriage'.

CHAPTER 20
A UNION OF EQUALS

THE BACKGROUND

The Old or First Testament of the Bible tells the story of a journey, the spiritual journey of the people of Israel. This journey contains the bad as well as the good, the distinctly unedifying as well as the edifying, lessons about what not to do as well as what to do. When the Bible says, "An eye for an eye, a tooth for a tooth", we must not see this as a direct order from God telling us what to do today, but as a particular and early moment in a long journey, a moment we were meant to leave behind.

In the First Testament we may see the people of Israel passing through six levels:
- superiority and vengeance
- getting even, justice without mercy (an eye for an eye)
- acting on the basis of usefulness to oneself
- respecting the dignity and rights of all (Ten Commandments)
- loving as you love yourself (the Beatitudes), and
- loving as God loves.

To move from superiority and vengeance to loving as God loves is a long journey. It was a long journey for the people of Israel, it is a long journey for the whole world, and it is a long personal journey for each one of us. It is a journey that is never completed, and we can easily take steps backwards as well as forwards. Indeed, if someone offends us in a serious matter, some of us can fall all the way back to the level of vengeance in a single moment.

All human institutions, including marriage, have been involved in this journey. In its beginnings human society was not based on the individual but on the family, so a community was not a collection of individuals but a collection of families. Each family was ruled by the male, and his wives, concubines, children and servants were all his property. His wives and concubines were his sexual property. Because his wife was his property, he could divorce her as easily as he could sell a donkey he no longer wanted, and the wife had little more say in the matter than did the donkey.

This property model of marriage dominated throughout the entire world for thousands of years. For that immense period of time women were constantly oppressed, but it is also true that these attitudes meant that men constantly missed out on many of the most important things in life. The whole human race paid a massive price for the property model of marriage.

Ancient ideas about wives as property entered deep into the very fibre of males. They are still strong in many cultures today and are far from dead in our own society. Every time we hear of a man killing his wife and children so that they will not become the property of another man, these ideas are surely at work. Every time we are confronted with the sheer enormity of domestic violence, we are reminded of this past.

Because the property model of marriage was so universal, there is much in the Bible concerning marriage and women that reflects the early parts of this journey. I give just two examples.

Perhaps the most damaging remark concerning women in the Bible comes from the book of Ecclesiasticus 25:24, which reads: "From a woman sin had its beginning, and because of her we all die." This is a classic misunderstanding of the story of Adam and Eve, but it has been quoted many times and has done much harm.

The other example comes from the book of Job, where Job defends himself before God stating he is an honest and just man, saying that if he has taken another's property, let another take his property. In applying this, he says, "If my heart has been enticed by a woman, and I have lain in wait at my neighbour's door, then let my wife grind for another, and let other men kneel over her" (31:9–10). He is stating that he will give his wife to others to have sex with her. To us this sounds horrendous, but he was simply taking for granted and applying the principle that she was his property.

Most of the statements and laws about marriage in the First Testament are based on inequality, most of the marriages we encounter there were unequal marriages. The inequality involved in the idea of women being the property of their father first and then their husband is pervasive in the whole of the First Testament.

Despite this, that testament also contains three key instances where the story moves to higher ideals for marriage. They are key because they concern nothing less than the three most important concepts in the entire Bible: creation, covenant and redemption. They remind us that the Bible is the story of a journey and that, for all the failure to understand that we find there, the ideas of Jesus did not come out of nowhere.

CREATION

There are two stories of creation at the very beginning of the Bible, and readers can sometimes be confused by the fact that the earlier story (Adam and Eve) has been placed in Chapter Two while the later story (the seven days of creation) has been placed in Chapter One of Genesis.

The earlier story, written several centuries before the later one, contains the words, "God formed man from the dust of the ground, and breathed into his nostrils the breath of life; and the man became a living being." (Gen 2:7) The story starts with the man, because that is certainly where ancient society sees civilisation as starting. The fact that in the story God breathed into his nostrils the breath of life gave great dignity to the man in relation to other forms of life on earth, and yet it left him in a state of restlessness and dissatisfaction because, though he had the divine breath in him, he was also made from "the dust of the ground" and so could not be fully united to God.

In order to assist him in this situation God said, "It is not good that the man should be alone; I will make him a helper as his partner" (Gen 2.18), and the word used for "helper", *ezer*, does not imply a subservient helper, for in the First Testament it is used also of God as our mighty helper.

All the animals were brought to the man and he gave each one its name (2:19–20), implying, in Jewish understanding, that he both understood their nature and had power over them. Precisely for these reasons, however, the animals did not satisfy him – "but for the man there was not found a helper as his partner" (2:20).

So God formed a woman and brought her to him, and this time he could not give her a new name, but only his own name, *ish*, with a feminine ending, *ishshah*. He could not understand her depths as he did the animals, for she had the same divine breath in her as he did; and he had no power over her, for with that divine breath she was his equal. The words, "Therefore a man leaves his father and his mother and clings to his wife, and they become one flesh", immediately follow, implying that the man did find true satisfaction in the woman and that this happened precisely because, unlike the animals, she shared the same divine breath and so was his equal.[177] She could satisfy him,

---

[177] I have taken this interpretation from the book, *The Promise to Love*, by Wilfrid J Harrington OP, Geoffrey Chapman, London, 1968).

but only because she was in fact his equal, and only if she were treated as his equal.

It is obvious that this story represents great progress in the journey of the people of Israel, for it goes against all the basic structures and attitudes of the society of its time. It tells us the story of God's plan that the first two human beings, equal in God's sight, would form a covenant between them on which the whole story of the human race would be based. Unfortunately, it remained a story and did not succeed in changing deeply entrenched structures and attitudes. Despite this, it remains permanently significant that this powerful story stands at the beginning of the Bible, part of the story of Creation itself.

In the later story in Chapter One of Genesis, written several centuries later, God created human beings on the sixth day.

> So God created human being (adam) in God's image;
> in the image of God, God created adam;
> male and female God created adam.
> God blessed adam, and God said to adam,
> 'Be fruitful and multiply,
> and fill the earth and subdue it... (c.f. Gen 1:27–28)

Human being (*adam*) is the summit of God's creation and *adam* is essentially both male and female. The charge to fill the earth and subdue it was given to the man and woman jointly and equally. There is no hint that it was really the male who was to "fill the earth and subdue it", while the female was to do nothing more than give birth to the babies and walk along meekly after him.

Adam was created in the image and likeness of God. This likeness was obviously not physical or photographic, but expressed a deep spiritual reality, for *adam* alone had received the divine spirit of life, *adam* alone longed for the infinite.

Once again this remained a story and did not change the basic structures of society. Despite this, these two stories, essential parts of Israel's journey and placed at the very beginning of the Bible, still have much to say to us today. As we shall see, it was to these two stories that Jesus referred to in his own statements on marriage.

COVENANT

In seeking to bring salvation to the world, God freely chose one people to be the carrier of the divine message to the whole world and made a solemn agreement or covenant with them. This covenant became the central fact of Israel's existence and the basis of its identity as a nation. It was not a nation defined by geographic boundaries; it was a people defined by its covenant with God.

One of the tasks of the prophets was that of constantly calling the people of Israel back to this covenant with God from the many ways in which they had gone astray, and in doing this they made use of many images and parables. Beginning with the prophet Hosea (8th Century BCE), one of the main images they used was that of marriage. The aspect of marriage the prophets insisted on was not the contractual element of marriage with its rights and obligations, or even the fruitfulness of marriage, but it was the love aspect, that aspect that had to fight so hard for its very existence in a world where the property model dominated. These prophets wished to stress that God's covenant obligation was a freely chosen obligation of love, and they knew of no better image to express this than the image of marriage.

In Chapter Two of Hosea there is a long poem about Israel as God's faithless wife and God's continuing love for her, ending with:

> I will now allure her, and bring her into the wilderness, and speak tenderly to her ... I will take you for my wife forever; I will take you for my wife in righteousness and in justice, in steadfast love and in mercy. I will take you for my wife in faithfulness ..." (Hos 2:14,19–20).

Jeremiah has God calling the people back to faithfulness with the words, "I remember the devotion of your youth, the love of your bridal day" (Jer 2:2). He also says:

> The days are surely coming, says the Lord, when I will make a new covenant with the house of Israel and the house of Judah. It will not be like the covenant I made with their ancestors when I took them by the hand to bring them out of the land of Egypt – a covenant which they broke, though I was their husband, says the Lord. But this is the covenant I will make with the house of Israel after those days, says the Lord. I will put my law within them, and I will write it on their hearts; and I will be their God, and they shall be my people. (Jer 31:31–33)

Ezekiel says:

> I clothed you with embroidered cloth and with sandals of fine leather; I bound you in fine linen and covered you with rich fabric. I adorned you with ornaments: I put bracelets on your arms, a chain on your neck, a ring on your nose, earrings in your ears, and a beautiful crown upon your head ... You grew exceedingly beautiful, fit to be a queen. (Ezek 16:10–13)

Third Isaiah uses the same imagery:

> For your Maker is your husband, the Lord of hosts is his name; the Holy One of Israel is your Redeemer, the God of the whole earth he is called. For the Lord has called you like a wife forsaken and grieved in spirit, like the wife of a man's youth when she is cast off, says your God. For a brief moment I abandoned you, but with great compassion I will gather you. In overflowing wrath for a moment, I hid my face from you, but with everlasting love I will have compassion on you, says the Lord, your Redeemer. (Isa 54:5–8)

The prophet Malachi says:

> You cover the Lord's altar with tears, with weeping and groaning because he no longer regards your offering or accepts it with favour at your hand. You ask, "Why does he not?" Because the Lord was a witness between you and the wife of your youth, to whom you have been faithless, though she is your companion and your wife by covenant … For I hate divorce, says the Lord, the God of Israel. (Mal 2:13–16)

Against the background of their times, this use of the image of marriage to express the covenant inevitably meant that the prophets also made important statements about marriage, for it was impossible for marriage to say something about the covenant without the covenant in return saying much about marriage. Stressing the love element in the covenant had the effect of stressing the love element in marriage.

The obligations of the people under the covenant were specified in a whole series of laws and a basic obedience to these laws was necessary, for one could hardly speak of loving God unless one showed this by a whole series of practical actions expressing that love, and this included a basic obedience to the law. Despite this, the obligation of the covenant was essentially more than the mere total of the specific obligations. It was essentially a personal love relationship with God. A mechanical fulfilling of specific duties in obedience to law would have created an empty religion, for religion must involve the heart and one's whole being if it is to come to life.

Marriage, too, brings with it many specific obligations, some small, some large, and they cannot be ignored. After all the talk of love, someone has to peel the potatoes, dispose of the garbage, wash the clothes and repair the broken window, and a person who consistently ignored all of these specific tasks could hardly speak of love. Marriage is, however, essentially more than the mere total of these specific duties. It is essentially the relationship itself, and a mechanical fulfilling of specific duties would create an empty marriage, for marriage, like the covenant, must involve the heart and one's whole being. Marriage and covenant had much to say about each other, as long as marriage understood as covenant was far removed from the property model.

REDEMPTION

In the two stories of creation and in the idea of covenant there are some beautiful and enduring statements about marriage. Despite this, the entrenched structures did not change, so Jesus was confronted with a contradiction between the beautiful words and the entrenched structures, for they simply could not be reconciled.

Divorce

The practice of divorce in the Israel in which Jesus lived was very different from that with which we are familiar today. It would be a serious mistake to think of divorce as practised in Western society today and imagine that this is what the gospels are referring to whenever the word "divorce" is used. There are two major points of difference.

The first is that the husband alone had the right to divorce. The wife had no rights of appeal and, indeed, few rights of any kind at all. The only way in which she herself could secure a divorce was by putting pressure on her husband to divorce her.

The second is that there were no civil courts decreeing divorce, and no legally binding provisions for custody or maintenance. Indeed, there were no obligatory public procedures at all, and the matter was ruled by custom passed down within the tribe, clan or family. The most common requirement that did exist was the handing over to the wife by the husband of a certificate of divorce in the presence of two witnesses.

The grounds of divorce were very broad. From very early times ancient Israel was an honour-shame society, that is, one in which the honour of the male in the eyes of the community was of the utmost importance, and anything that was seen as bringing shame on him was treated with great seriousness. It followed that, if a man believed that his wife had brought shame on him by some extramarital sexual action, divorce was seen as obligatory, as the only means of restoring his honour.[178] By the time of Jesus there were very few restrictions on the husband's power to divorce.

It followed that the position of women in relation to marriage was precarious. And a woman divorced by her husband had no standing in the community and could easily find herself destitute.

---

178 In the story told in the Gospel of Matthew, Joseph would have stood out from the crowd when, "being a righteous man and unwilling to expose her to public disgrace, (he) planned to dismiss her quietly." (Matthew 1:19) For other men the public disgrace of the unfaithful wife would have been seen as an essential part of the restoration of their own good name.

We must see the statements of Jesus concerning divorce primarily in relation to this world of first century Israel. Only then can we apply them to our own time.

Adultery

The general understanding of adultery for us now is that it is voluntary sexual intercourse between a married person and someone other than their spouse. Before we decide, however, that this is the meaning we must give to the term in the gospels, we need to consider two facts.

The first is the one already mentioned, that the man was the lord of his wife and she was his property. As a result, adultery was essentially the violation of a *property right*. If a married woman had intercourse with any man other than her husband, it was always adultery, for it violated the property rights of her husband. If a man had intercourse with a married woman, it was also adultery, for he had violated the property rights of the woman's husband. But if a married man had intercourse with a single woman, it was not adultery, for the property rights of no husband were violated. Thus, the term "adultery" had little to do with the breaking of a promise or with harm to a love relationship, but rather related to the stealing of the "property" of a male.

The second fact is Matthew has reported Jesus as saying:

> You have heard that it was said, "You shall not commit adultery." But I say to you that everyone who looks at a woman with lust has already committed adultery with her in his heart. (Matt 5:27–28)

For Jesus, sin existed in the mind and heart, and the external action was simply the result of the sin that had already occurred in the mind and heart. Thus, when divorce was contemplated, Jesus saw the adultery as occurring long before the formal divorce and remarriage, and long before any act of sexual intercourse had occurred. Adultery had occurred as soon as a man said to himself, "I know this woman is married, but I want her and I'm going to do all I can to have her."

THE GOSPEL OF MARK

Mark 10:2

"Some Pharisees came, and to test him they asked, 'Is it lawful for a man to divorce his wife?'" The scene is presented as one of confrontation – "to test him" – with the Pharisees seeking ammunition to use against Jesus. For this reason, each of the verses 3–6 begins with the word "but", implying a continuing argument between the two sides. The question at hand concerned an issue (the very fact of divorce) where the Pharisees thought they were on certain ground, for, as already noted, in ancient Israel divorce was simply a fact of life, not really queried by anyone.

The basic First Testament text on divorce is to be found in Deuteronomy 24:1-4. It simply accepted divorce as a fact of life and added two requirements: the husband had to write out a bill of divorce and give it to his wife before two witnesses, and he could never marry her again once she had married another man. It says much that this text, dealing with the rare case of a man wishing to remarry his first wife after he had divorced her and she had been married to another man, became the standard text on divorce in the First Testament. It was the standard text because there was so little else on the subject. Divorce was a given, a fact of life.

Mark 10:3

"He answered them, 'What did Moses command you?'" Instead of giving his own view, Jesus followed the constant scribal practice of answering a question with a question, taking the Pharisees back to the basis of their own beliefs in the law of Moses. His choice of the word "command" was a tactical move, for the direct answer to this question would be that all that Moses had commanded was that, if a man divorced, he must give a written bill of divorce and may never marry the same woman again.

Mark 10:4

"They said, 'Moses allowed a man to write a certificate of dismissal and to divorce her.'" Instead of saying what Moses *commanded*, the Pharisees spoke of what he had *allowed* and, in doing so, they were tacitly admitting that Moses had not commanded divorce. If divorce occurred, it was the people's, or at least the men's, own choice.

Mark 10:5

"But Jesus said to them, 'Because of your hardness of heart he wrote this commandment for you'." In the First Testament the term "hardheartedness" refers to the insensitivity that comes from continual disobedience to God.[179]

---

179 The Greek word for this, *sklerokardia*, is still used in modern medicine. "When Jesus affirmed that Moses framed the provision concerning the letter of dismissal out of regard to the people's hardness of heart, he was using an established legal category of actions allowed out of consideration for wickedness or weakness. What is involved is the lesser of two evils ..." William L Lane, *The New International Commentary on the New Testament, The Gospel of Mark*, Wm B Erdmans, Grand Rapids, 1974, p. 355. " ... hardness of heart is a major biblical theme. Since in biblical anthropology the heart is the source of understanding

The force of the verse is that the people had for so long been disobedient that they had lost their sensitivity to God, so that Moses had been able to do no more than salvage what he could by imposing some minimum restrictions.

Mark 10:6

"But from the beginning of creation ..." The Pharisees had asked Jesus if divorce is lawful and by this they were questioning if it is lawful according to the law that came from God through Moses? In his answer Jesus took the radical step of reinterpreting this law by asking them questions. Basically he was asking them if the law of Moses on this point was a true and full reflection of the mind of God? And it was this question, not theirs, that he would now answer.[180] It is crucial to note that the entire argument of Jesus in this passage in Mark's Gospel is based on his appeal – from a situation created by human insensitivity – to the original intention of God.

"God made them male and female." These words are a quotation from Genesis 1:27, stating that from the original intention of God human beings are essentially both male and female, with all their natural attraction and complementarity. That human beings were both male and female was part of the creation, and, as I have already noted, the charge by God was given to them jointly and equally.

Mark 10:7

"For this reason a man shall leave his father and mother and be joined to his wife, and the two shall become one flesh." This verse also contains a quotation from Genesis, but this time from the earlier account of creation in the second chapter of Genesis (2:24) in the story of Adam and Eve. I have already commented on this passage, noting that its essential message is that the equality of the couple was part of the creation itself. In the mind of Jesus this was, therefore, the original divine plan of marriage, and it was only in the security of this plan that marriage could fulfil its role in overcoming the restlessness of the human condition (Gen 2:18) and bringing a lasting happiness to people.

As Jesus grew up, he saw all around him a system of marriage that did not reflect this divine plan, and for two major reasons. Firstly, marriage in the

---

and judgment as well as emotions, hardness of heart involves closing off one's mind and emotions from the truth." John R Donoghue and Daniel J Harrington, *The Gospel of Mark*, Sacra Pagina Series, The Liturgical Press, Collegeville, 2002, p. 293.

180 "The error of the Pharisees lay in their losing sight of this distinction (between an absolute divine command and a divine provision to deal with situations brought about by men's 'hardness of heart') and so imagining that Deut 24:1 meant that God allowed divorce, in the sense that it had his approval and did not come under his judgment." Augustine Stock OSB, *The Method and Message of Mark*, Michael Glazier, Wilmington, 1989, p. 265.

society around him was a relationship of dominance-subservience based on the idea of women as property, and for this very reason it created across the whole of society a form of marriage that would not and could not fulfil the deeper needs for which marriage had been created by God "in the beginning". Marriage can be either a relationship of power and authority between unequal partners or a relationship of respect and love between equal partners, but it cannot be both, and it cannot move backwards and forwards between the two at different times.

The rights acquired in a wedding ceremony are either rights to property and ownership by the husband, or they are mutual rights to such things as justice, caring, respect and love, but they cannot be both. If they are rights to property, then the marriage contract is really between the father of the bride and the husband. It is a contract in which the father gives his property rights over his daughter to her husband, and she is simply the property or object that is passed over. It is only in a relationship of love and respect that the woman has something to give to her husband, so it is only in this case that the marriage is a true contract between the two of them. Furthermore, even if love is the basis on which a couple first enter a marriage, the fact that in Jewish law the man had dominance over the woman and could resort to power at any time placed severe strains on the love relationship. In Jewish law the authority of the husband was always there, and the wife's position was weak.

The second reason follows from the first. One can always dispose of property, so if a man thinks of his wife as mere property, then she is easily disposable. Where there is gross inequality, divorce will always flourish. The questions of equality, marriage and divorce could not be separated, so in answer to a question concerning divorce, Jesus responded by first insisting that the original plan of God concerning marriage had been based on equality.

We know that Jesus recognised rights in women that the society around him did not and there are many scenes in which he showed a profound respect for their dignity. The power of men over divorce, the idea of a wife as property, the weak position of women in relation to marriage and the destitution of many divorced women, constituted a system that Jesus found abhorrent, for it was contrary to his deep concern for justice and love. In responding to a question concerning divorce Jesus saw the need to attack this system and reform the entire understanding of marriage on a basis of equality. Without this reform of the entire system, it would never be possible to give an adequate answer to the specific question he had been asked concerning divorce.

Mark 10:8

"... so that they are no longer two but one flesh." The words concerning one flesh have their mystery, but would seem to include a number of elements: the unity of flesh in sexual intercourse, the couple becoming a unity before both the law and the community, their mutual love and common journey towards God, the two becoming one in their child, and the idea that marriage is such that part of the very being of each married person is the relationship to the other, so that to exclude this relationship is to deny part of one's own being.

Mark 10:9

"Therefore what God has joined together, let no one separate." I suggest that there are two possible interpretations of the words of this verse. The first is the interpretation given by the Catholic Church at the Council of Trent and held to be infallibly binding for all time.[181] In this interpretation what "God has joined together", and human beings may not separate, is each individual marriage. The words of Jesus would then imply that, in every single marriage ceremony, God joins the couple together in a divine bond that neither partner can ever break.

The problem with this conclusion is that it does not follow from the argument that has gone before it, for that argument had not concerned divorce, but the divine plan for satisfaction and fulfilment through a relationship of equality and complementarity. The word "therefore" in verse 9 would be meaningless. Indeed, if this is a law concerning a divine bond, then the entire argument just given by Jesus is irrelevant, and one would have to query why that argument is there at all, for it neither explains nor adds anything to the statement concerning a divine law. Having just given women a whole new status in marriage, Jesus would be leaving the abandoned wife in her predicament and doing nothing to help her. He would be doing nothing to redress the serious inequities that were present in marriage as it was practised in the society around him. He would not even be doing anything to curb divorce, for as long as marriage was unequal, divorce would flourish. He would, out of nowhere, be suddenly introducing a divine law that has no parallels to it anywhere in the gospels. While it has massive ecclesial authority behind it, there are serious problems with this interpretation.

The second interpretation is based on taking literally the word "therefore" in

---

181 "5. If anyone says that the marriage bond can be dissolved because of heresy, or irksome cohabitation, or because of the wilful desertion of one of the spouses, anathema sit ... 7. If anyone says that the church is in error for having taught and for still teaching that in accordance with the evangelical and apostolic doctrine (cf. Mark10:1; 1Cor.7), the marriage bond cannot be dissolved because of adultery on the part of one of the spouses, and that neither of the two, not even the innocent one who has given no cause for infidelity, can contract another marriage during the lifetime of the other; and that the husband who dismisses an adulterous wife and marries again and the wife who dismisses an adulterous husband and marries again are both guilty of adultery, anathema sit." Quoted from *The Christian Faith in the Doctrinal Documents of the Catholic Church*, edited by J Neuner and J Dupuis, Collins Liturgical Publications, London, 1983, p. 529.

verse 9, that is, by insisting that the words, "What God has joined together let no human being separate" are a logical conclusion from what has been said in the argument just given. May I suggest that, if we take the word "therefore" seriously, what God, in the mind of Jesus, had joined together "in the beginning" was the two ideas of marriage and equality, while all around him Jesus saw that human beings had separated the two, substituting instead the two ideas of marriage and inequality. In terms of the biblical story, putting together marriage and equality was the sole force that would take away the man's loneliness and give him a true partner. This is what God had joined together and no human beings were ever to separate. At this point the entire passage becomes one coherent whole, with a logical argument and a logical conclusion.

If I may dare to rewrite the words of Jesus in a manner that people of today might better understand:

> "It was because of your continual rejection of God that you misunderstood God's thinking about marriage and gave to men the right to divorce their wives whenever they wished. But from the beginning of creation God created human beings male and female and gave them a joint mission to build up the world. They were to leave father and mother and set up a new family based on their equality and their free commitment to each other. The two ideas of marriage and equality must always go together, and no one may ever separate them. Because they are equal, the couple become one in their sexual union, in their child, and in their common journey through life; they become one before the community and in the fact that part of the very identity of each lies in the relation to the other."
>
> Later, in the house, the disciples were asking him again about this matter. He said to them, "The idea that a wife is nothing more than the property of her husband comes solely from human beings and is offensive to God. From what I have said about equality, don't you see that when a man, without any pressing reason, divorces his wife and marries another, he commits adultery against her. And if she divorces him and marries another, she commits adultery."

Against the background of his own time, this was extraordinarily radical thinking, and yet, as Jesus saw it, it reflected the mind of God.

In all talk of marriage in the modern world the accent always seems to be on love. But there is something more fundamental in marriage than love, namely respect. A marriage can survive if the couple no longer love each other, but it cannot survive if they no longer have even the most basic respect for each other. Respect based on equality, on a belief in the basic dignity of every person

– this is the most necessary and fundamental aspect of any marriage. In seeking to bring about a profound restoration of the entire institution of marriage Jesus unerringly focused his attention on this crucial element, so conspicuously absent across the whole of the ancient world.

For two thousand years people have understood the words, "Therefore what God has joined together, let no one separate", to refer to the two individuals, and the Council of Trent gave a most powerful backing to this idea. However, the words do not actually speak of the two individuals; this is a conclusion that human beings have drawn. May I dare to suggest that this understanding needs to be looked at again.

Several times in the Gospel of Mark, Jesus changed a question he was asked and then insisted on answering the changed question rather than the original one. This is exactly what he had done in verse 6 of this same scene, as I noted above. The reason he did the same thing here in verse 9 is that, if we ask the wrong question we will never find the right answer. In this case the original question was a wrong question because it assumed that men alone could divorce and that women were mere property. Jesus could not agree with these assumptions and so insisted on changing the question. In its essence, they had asked, "What is divorce?", while Jesus insisted that the real question was, "What is marriage?" It was this question that he then sought to answer, and he gave no direct answer to the question concerning divorce, leaving his hearers to draw their own conclusions from what he said about marriage. This, too, was in accord with his usual practice, for he never wanted simply to win an argument, but always strove to get his opponents to think again about a matter.

I suggest, therefore, that what Jesus was speaking about here was what God had "from the beginning of creation" intended marriage to be, and some of the powerful and compelling *moral* consequences that flow from this. For Jesus, marriage in the mind of God based on equality and it is precisely for this reason that it is essentially permanent. The equality comes from God's creation, the permanence comes from the solemn and binding commitment that equal partners make to the marriage in accordance with God's plan for their fulfilment and happiness. There is even a form of indissolubility in marriage, but only in the sense that, without powerful reasons, neither partner is free to leave the marriage without being untrue to both themselves and their partner.

Mark 10:10

"Then in the house the disciples asked him again about this matter." The original tense for 'asked' is more accurately rendered 'were asking'. The questions of the disciples were not polemic, but came from a genuine desire to understand, so in his reply Jesus did not seek to confront them as he had the Pharisees. At the same time, the imperfect tense of "were asking" implies that the disciples were slow to accept the answer given them by Jesus and kept asking their questions.

Mark 10:11

"He said to them, 'Whoever divorces his wife and marries another commits adultery against her'." The last two words ("against her") are of great importance, for by his use of these words Jesus was proclaiming that the violation of the rights of a wife was also and equally adultery. This was a logical conclusion from the argument he had just given concerning equality, but it was also a truly revolutionary idea, for it meant that for Jesus a wife had such rights and was, therefore, not the mere 'property' of her husband. This overturned the entire basis on which the family, and hence the whole of society, had been built for thousands of years. In its social impact it is arguably the most revolutionary statement in the whole of the gospels, for it demanded a completely new ordering of all of society. It is a small wonder that the disciples were slow to grasp the vast implications of what Jesus was saying. It is unspeakably sad that even two thousand years later the followers of Jesus have still not caught up with his radicalism on the matter of the equality of male and female. The sheer amount of domestic violence in our societies is perhaps the clearest sign of this failure to grasp what Jesus was trying to say.

In the conversation with the disciples, I suggest that they brought up obvious points such as, "Yes, all these beautiful things you are saying about equality and fulfilment are good and nice, but what about the hard reality of when a marriage is bringing only pain and misery." The response of Jesus was to take his argument further. We might summarise his earlier argument in verses 6–9 in this way, "You will have a far happier and more fulfilling relationship if you in all things treat your wife as your equal and commit yourself fully to the relationship." In verse 11 the argument goes further and is based on strict justice and I suggest it might be this: "It is not just a matter of your happiness. Your wife is truly your equal and has the same rights as you do. You believe that, if she starts looking outside the marriage for a more acceptable partner, she is committing adultery against you. Well, if you start looking outside your marriage, you will be equally committing adultery against her."

Unlike legal consequences, however, moral consequences must always be estimated within the total context of all the circumstances of each marriage. There will, therefore, be circumstances which allow of a new marriage, for there will be circumstances that do not involve any form or degree of adultery. I shall return to this point.

Mark 10:12

"And if she divorces her husband and marries another, she commits adultery." It was Roman law that first gave to a wife the right to repudiate her husband, and commentators see this verse as a conclusion drawn by the Christian community from the words of Jesus rather than as a saying that came directly from Jesus himself[182].

Conclusions from Mark's text

I believe that in this passage Jesus made it clear that he wanted far more than to make changes to divorce practice. He wanted to do away with the entire *system* of both marriage and divorce then in practice and with the attitudes that went behind the system. I believe that any interpretation that has him doing less than this fails to see the full force of the passage.

Jesus was confronted with a situation where the males in the community were collectively the lords of marriage as a social institution and each man was then lord of his own marriage, with a broad power to divorce his wife. Women were mere property and had no say in the matter. Jesus rebelled against these attitudes, asserting that they came from 'hardness of heart' and that they had not been the original intention of God. He insisted that it is God who is the sole lord of marriage, so all people, male and female, must seek to be true to those things that are inherent in marriage as God created it.

He said that God in the beginning created human beings male and female, and created them in such a manner that their greatest happiness and growth, their best chance of learning to live creatively with the restlessness of the human condition, are to be found in committing themselves unreservedly and *as equals* to a lasting union in accordance with a divine plan, and in then doing everything in their power to make sure that the union in fact flourishes and lasts. Each of the couple, therefore, has a powerful *moral* obligation towards the other.

In other words, what Jesus could not agree with in this scene in Mark was a *system* that he saw as an *adulterous system*, understanding the word 'adulterous' in the sense I have already indicated. For men to consider themselves lords of their marriage and free to divorce and remarry as it suited them, without any consideration for their wife, was, in the mind of Jesus, to be already deeply immersed in an adulterous mindset. In accordance with everything we know about him as a person, Jesus strongly attacked this system and replaced it with both an insistence on the essential equality of the couple and the profoundly

---

182 This verse in effect has the church saying to women under Roman law, "Don't start getting legalistic and claiming that what Jesus said doesn't apply to you because, against his Jewish background, he spoke only of men. It applies to you too."

challenging ideal of regaining the original purpose of marriage as expressed in Genesis.

Jesus was greatly concerned with what had happened to marriage in Jewish society and wished to restore it to what it had originally been in the mind of God. If we judge by all we know about him from four gospels, it is surely far more likely that he saw the solution in the equality of the couple rather than in a divine law forbidding all divorce, no matter what the circumstances.

THE GOSPEL OF MATTHEW 5:31-32

> It was also said, "Whoever divorces his wife, let him give her a certificate of divorce." But I say to you that anyone who divorces his wife, except on the ground of unchastity, causes her to commit adultery; and whoever marries a divorced woman commits adultery. (Matt 5:31-32)

The context of the saying being considered here is that of the Sermon on the Mount (5:1-7:29) and, in particular, the section contained in 5:17-48. It begins by saying, "Do not think that I have come to abolish the law or the prophets; I have not come to abolish but to fulfil."[183] Over the following twenty-eight verses (21-48) Jesus then spells out what he means by "not come to abolish but fulfil"[184] in a series of sayings in the form, "You have heard that it was said ... but I say to you ..."

> You have heard that it was said to those of ancient times, "You shall not murder" ... But I say to you that if you are angry with a brother or sister ..." (Matt 5:21-26)

> "You shall not commit adultery ... But I say to you that everyone who looks at a woman with lust ..." (27-30)

---

183 "The ethical teaching of Jesus that follows in this sermon ... has such a radical character and goes so much against what was the commonly accepted understanding of the commands of the Torah that it is necessary at the outset to vindicate Jesus' full and unswerving loyalty to the law." Donald A Hagner, *Matthew 1-13*, Word Biblical Commentary, Word Books Publishers, Dallas, 1993, p. 103. "These were the words of a strict Jewish Christian community seeking to maintain absolute obedience to the letter of the Law, probably in opposition to a more liberal interpretation such as those represented by Stephen (cf. Acts 7:48ff., 8:1) and later by Paul (Gal. 2:2-6, 11:6; Acts 15), Edward Schweizer, *The Gospel according to Matthew*, SPCF, London, 1975, p. 104.

184 "When considered in itself, the opposition of 5:17 allows us to say that 'to fulfil' is contrasted with 'to abolish', that is, to dismantle, tear down, and thus make invalid, annul ... Fulfilling means, therefore, having a constructive attitude towards Scripture and considering it important, not null." Daniel Patte, *The Gospel according to Matthew*, Fortress Press, Philadelphia, 1987, p. 72.

> It was said, "whoever divorces his wife ... but I say to you ... (31–32), [and] 'you shall not swear falsely'... "but I say to you, do not swear at all ...." (33–37)
>
> "An eye for an eye and a tooth for a tooth." ... "But I say to you, if anyone strikes you on the right cheek, turn the other also ..." (38–42)
>
> "You shall love your neighbour and hate your enemy. But I say to you, Love your enemies (43–47)"
>
> "Be perfect, therefore, as your heavenly Father is perfect."(48)

Though most commentators call these sayings "antitheses", the word fits the rhetorical pattern but not the content. In some cases, Jesus expresses agreement with the biblical teaching but urges his followers to go deeper or to the root of the commandment (murder>anger, adultery>lust, retaliation>non-resistance). In other cases, Jesus' teaching can seem to go so far as to make the biblical commandment useless (divorce, oaths, love of neighbour.)[185]

Furthermore, the sayings concern different orders of law from the Torah: while the first two concern the Ten Commandments, the others do not and, indeed, there was no law forbidding divorce itself.

The first thing that appears to be clear is that, while Jesus is quoting laws from the First Testament, he is not simply replacing them with new laws. He is leaving the laws in place ("not abolish") and then expressing moral principles that show the more perfect way to observe the value that is behind the law ("but fulfil"). To be perfect as the heavenly Father is perfect or to turn the other cheek are not new laws. We are not morally deficient if we fail to be as perfect as the heavenly Father and we are not breaking a law if we swear an oath in court or fail to turn the other cheek and allow someone to strike us a second time.

> Interpreters of these verses must be careful not to translate into legal statute what is presented as an evangelic counsel. That is, it ought not to be treated differently than the other antitheses, none of which has been or can be converted into law.[186]

The new sayings of Jesus go beyond the external action demanded by the law to moral principles concerning the internal attitudes that lead to the breaking of the law.[187] In this they may be called prescriptive ideals, that is, they are

---

185 Daniel J Harrington SJ, *The Gospel of Matthew*, Sacra Pagina Series, The Liturgical Press, Collegeville, 1991, p. 90.
186 Douglas R A Hare, *Matthew*, John Knox Press, Louisville, 1993, p. 54.
187 "Common to most is the sense that righteous behaviour has to do with the heart and with

ideals, not laws, but they are prescriptive, for we are meant, and indeed obliged, to strive after them. I do not commit sin if I fail to have warm feelings for my enemies, but I do fail as a follower of Jesus if I do not even see loving my enemies as an ideal that calls to me with genuine power and urgency. I do not fail morally if I am not as perfect as the heavenly Father, but I do fail as a Christian if I do not see being as perfect as the heavenly Father as a goal that might guide and inspire me in my life.

Furthermore, the language of this section needs to be taken into account, for it is Semitic language and therefore is concrete rather than abstract and involves what our modern Western minds would consider serious exaggeration or overstatement, even extravagance. It is a language that appears to be typical of the person of Jesus, for example:

> If any of you put a stumbling block before one of these little ones who believe in me, it would be better for you if a great millstone were hung around your neck and you were thrown into the sea. (Mark 9:42)

> It is easier for a camel to go through the eye of a needle than for someone who is rich to enter the kingdom of God. (Mark 10:25)

> Why do you see the speck in your neighbour's eye, but do not notice the log in your own eye? (Matt 7:3)

> So therefore, none of you can become my disciple if you do not give up all your possessions. (Luke 14:33)

> It is easier for heaven and earth to pass away, than for one stroke of a letter in the law to be dropped. (Luke 16:17)

> "Whoever comes to me and does not hate father and mother, wife and children, brothers and sisters, yes, and even life itself, cannot be my disciple." (Luke 14:26)

It is obvious that these sayings cannot be taken in a slavishly literal manner.

This type of language abounds in the context of the series of prescriptive ideals that surround the sayings on divorce. There we are told by Jesus not to be angry, though in fact we have no direct control over our feelings whenever a serious wrong is done to us and cannot prevent feelings of anger. We are told that if we say to someone, "you fool", we "will be liable to the hell of fire",

---

attitude rather than with mere conformity with external prescription." Brendan Byrne, *Lifting the Burden, Reading Matthew's Gospel in the Church Today*, St Paul's Publications, Sydney, 2004, p. 58.

though no one would take this literally. We are told not to look at a woman with lust, though the very continuance of the human race demands that there be sexual desire. We are told that, if our eye causes us to sin, we should tear it out and throw it away, and no church has ever suggested that we should take these words literally. We are told that we should never swear oaths, and yet both church and state routinely administer oaths. We are told to turn the other cheek, to give a cloak as well as a tunic and to walk a second mile, though no one interprets these as literal obligations. We are told to love our enemies, though once again we have no direct control over our feelings. Finally, we are told to be perfect as the heavenly Father is perfect, though this is manifestly impossible, and we will never come even remotely close to living up to this ideal.

The saying on divorce comes in the middle of these prescriptive ideals (31–32) and this context cannot be ignored. It would surely be nonsense to say that the statements surrounding this one are all prescriptive ideals, not laws, but that the one on divorce is a strict law rather than a prescriptive ideal. It would be nonsense to say that all the surrounding statements use exaggerated Semitic language, but this one uses only literal language.

It follows that the saying on divorce must also be seen as a prescriptive ideal rather than as a law. The message must surely be that people are not necessarily committing sin if they divorce, for there are cases where it is justified, but they are failing if they do not see permanency as a powerful and binding ideal, something that they must strive for with all their might.

These considerations strongly reinforce the idea that the words contained in Mark 10, and that I commented on in the last section, are forceful statements of moral obligation rather than statements of law.

Matthew goes further than Mark, for Mark had spoken only of the case where the man had divorced his wife and married another. Matthew refers to two other cases. In the first he has Jesus saying that, if a man divorces his wife, he is causing the wife to commit adultery, presumably by marrying another man. In the second case, he imagines a man marrying a woman who has been divorced and speaks of this as adultery on his part. Mark had placed the accent on the act of divorcing a wife, while Matthew looks to the remarriage after the divorce, not by the man who divorced his wife, but by the woman who is divorced and by the man marrying her.

The two statements in Matthew 5:32 appear harsher than those of Mark, for they might seem to include the woman divorced by her husband and left destitute, but we must keep firmly in mind the fact that in Matthew they are presented as prescriptive ideals. It follows that Jesus is not saying that either the wife or the second man is necessarily committing sin through a second marriage. What, then, is the prescriptive ideal he is pointing to? I shall return to these questions later.

EXCEPT FOR UNCHASTITY

In this passage we must also consider the extra phrase introduced by Matthew both here and in chapter 19 that I shall consider next: "except in the case of *porneia*." The word *porneia* can cover any form of sexual impropriety and is better translated by the broad word "unchastity".

In understanding this phrase I believe that it is important that we do not see Jesus as only agreeing with those (a fairly small minority) who believed that divorce was permitted only in the case of adultery by the wife, for then his taking the high ground by twice referring back to the will of God in the creation would be meaningless. His reply would no longer be radical or revolutionary,[188] and it would still include the idea that only men could initiate divorce and that women had no rights in the matter. In other words, Jesus would still be approving the *system* of marriage and divorce then in practice. It seems to me that the very essence of this scene in Matthew is that Jesus was asked to decide between two schools of thought and gave an answer that was more radical than either. I believe that we are on far firmer ground if we see Matthew as being fully as radical as Mark, and this essentially demanded a rejection of the entire *system* of marriage and divorce then in practice.

> That Jesus was demanding a fidelity to marriage and a commitment to pledged love that went beyond the expectations of his contemporaries of whatever school of thought is obvious from the reaction of his disciples.[189]

There is an immense literature on the meaning of the exceptive clauses, and most explanations can be reduced to two. Common to both is that the words do not come from Jesus himself, but were added by the early Church.

> If the Matthean exceptive clause had been a part of the original form of the prohibition, it is extremely difficult to understand how and why Paul, Mark and Luke would all have come up with absolute forms of the prohibition.[190]

The first explanation is that the words are a true exception. One version of this (among many) is that it is possible that Jewish followers of Jesus might have accepted his ideal of returning to God's original intentions in creating

---

188 "The addition (of the exceptive clause) not only softens the ethics of the kingdom, but it also stands in tension with the absolutism of v.6, weakens the argument of vv.7–8, and makes the disciples' comments in v.10 and Jesus' statements in vv.11–12 less appropriate than would be the case of an absolute prohibition of divorce." Hagner, op.cit., vol. 2, p. 549.

189 Michael Fallon MSC, *The Gospel according to Saint Matthew*, Chevalier Press, Sydney, 1997, p. 261.

190 John P. Meier, op.cit., Vol. IV, p. 104.

marriage, and even accepted that women had rights, and (with great difficulty under the strong influence of the powerful personality of Jesus) that they even had equal dignity and rights. But, with a lifetime of a culture of honour-shame behind them, they simply could not bring themselves to accept that a man should remain with a wife guilty of adultery or some other serious sexual impropriety. That was altogether too much, and the weight of their cultural heritage was too powerful. In this interpretation the early Church, through Matthew, is allowing for this attitude.

This interpretation presupposes that Matthew realised that the words of Jesus had been a statement of powerful moral obligation, to which there can in serious circumstances be exceptions, rather than a divine law about an unbreakable bond, to which there can be no exceptions.

The other explanation of the exceptive clause is that it refers to a marriage within the forbidden degrees of kinship laid down in the First Testament. These laws went beyond those of most other nations, so it was always possible that Christian converts from paganism might already be in a marriage that was forbidden by Jewish law, and hence that would scandalise Jewish converts. The Jews considered such a marriage to be a *porneia*, an unchastity, and believed that in these circumstances divorce was not divorce at all, but the putting aside of a wife whom one should not have married in the first place. The exceptive clause would then have been an addition by the early Church to cover situations that had arisen and were causing scandal to Jewish converts. Chapter 15 of the Acts of the Apostles tells the story of the First Council of Jerusalem, when the early Church introduced laws precisely in order to avoid scandal for Jewish converts. There are, however, some serious problems with this interpretation[191], and I personally favour the first explanation.

THE GOSPEL OF MATTHEW 19:1–12

> Some Pharisees came to him, and to test him they asked, "Is it lawful for a man to divorce his wife for any cause?" He answered, "Have you not read that the one who made them at the beginning made them male and female, and said, For this reason a man shall leave his father and mother and be joined to his wife, and the two shall become one flesh? So, they are no longer two, but one flesh. Therefore, what God

---

191 "1) The context does not indicate at all that Matthew wants to take *porneia* in such a narrow sense and to refer his exception only to the former Gentiles. 2) Correspondingly, no single Church father and no single interpreter up until the modern time would have understood what he was truly concerned about. 3) In Leviticus 18 the word *porneia* is missing. 4) *Parektos logou porneias* is a clear reference to Dt.24:1, but then it must deal with the reasons for the divorce of legitimate and not with the invalidity of illegitimate marriages." Ulrich Luz, *Matthew 1–7, A Commentary*, Augsburg Fortress, Minneapolis, 1989, pp. 304–305.

has joined together, let no one separate.' They said to him, 'Why then did Moses command us to give a certificate of dismissal and to divorce her?' He said to them, 'It was because you were so hard-hearted that Moses allowed you to divorce your wives, but from the beginning it was not so. And I say to you, whoever divorces his wife, except for unchastity, and marries another, commits adultery.' (19:3–10)

It is impossible to imagine that Matthew would here in chapter 19 be contradicting what he himself had said in chapter 5 of his own gospel. It is equally impossible to think that Matthew, using the same language, quotations and arguments as Mark, would wish his readers to reach a conclusion different from that of Mark. The sayings must absolutely be harmonised, and this present scene must be seen in the light of the earlier two.

The question asked by the Pharisees assumes the inequality of husband and wife ("Is it lawful for a man to divorce his wife for any cause?"). There could be no simple yes/no answer to a wrong question such as this, so the first necessity was to change the question. Jesus did this by going back to the same two quotations from Genesis that Mark had referred to, emphasising the equality of the couple. He then said that "for this reason", that is, because they are equal, they become "one flesh", implying that the becoming "one flesh" was dependent on their equality.

At this point the Pharisees introduced the law of Moses, attempting by this to claim that Moses had given a broad power to men to divorce. Jesus replied that Moses had only allowed, not commanded, divorce, and had done so only because of people's hardheartedness. The conclusion was the same as in Mark, "Whoever divorces his wife and marries another, commits adultery." Though the words "against her" are not stated explicitly, they are implicit, for adultery has to be committed against someone, and it is clearly the wife who is intended. Once again, the statement that a man could commit adultery against his wife was startling, radical and revolutionary in its implications.

The conclusions I drew from the Gospel of Mark can be drawn from this passage also, for it contains the same essential argument: a call back from the current *system* of marriage and divorce to God's original intention in creating marriage, the same two quotations concerning the equality and complementarity of man and woman, and the radical conclusion that the man could commit adultery against his wife.

Equally with Mark, it is the condemnation of a *system* of marriage and divorce that all too easily involved an adulterous mindset and harmed the very purposes for which marriage had been created "in the beginning". Matthew echoes Mark in having Jesus make a powerful call for equality, love, justice and respect in marriage and a powerful condemnation of "easy" divorce, but the phrase "except for unchastity" makes it clear that this is not a blanket condemnation of all separation and divorce under all circumstances. The words of Jesus are not a law forbidding divorce, but a powerful statement of the moral obligations that arise from a wedding ceremony between two equal parties. The couple places their lives and happiness into each other's hands, and that gift must be treated with the greatest possible respect.

THE GOSPEL OF LUKE 16:18

> Anyone who divorces his wife and marries another commits adultery, and whoever marries a woman divorced from her husband commits adultery. (Luke 16:190)

This saying is in language very similar to Matt 5:31–32, so that most scholars believe that both texts come from the Q document that lies behind much of Matthew and Luke.

As it stands in the Gospel of Luke, the saying has its difficulties, for the context does nothing to assist us. Beginning in chapter 15 we have a series of parables (the lost sheep, the lost drachma, the prodigal son and the dishonest steward), then we have four sayings that do not appear to have any direct connection either to the parables or to each other, and then we have another parable (the rich man and Lazarus).

The saying on divorce is the fourth of the sayings in the middle of these parables. The first saying may be seen as connected to the parable of the unjust steward immediately preceding it, for it speaks of love of money. But the second deals with the kingdom taking the place of the law and the prophets, and the third with the fact that no detail of the law will be abolished.[192] The fourth then deals with divorce.[193] So far as can be seen, the saying stands on its own without any particular context.[194]

---

192 "The second set of sayings in this Lucan editorial unit preceding the parable of the rich man and Lazarus has almost nothing to do with material possessions or ambitious esteem before other human beings, topics of Jesus' comments in vv.1–15." Joseph A Fitzmeyer, *The Gospel According to Luke,* Anchor Bible, Doubleday and Co., New York, 1985, Vol. 2, p. 1114.
193 "The third saying in this editorial unit seems to move to an entirely different topic – even less related to the general theme of ch.16 than the sayings on the law in the two preceding verses – viz. the prohibition of divorce (v.16)." Joseph A Fitzmyer, op.cit., p. 1119.
194 In the commentaries I have studied there are many attempts to give a unity to these sayings, but no two seem to agree. Brendan Byrne expresses a common opinion when he says, "It is hard to account for the series of sayings lying between the two parables in this chapter. The sayings seem disconnected, both with the wider context and among each other." *The Hospitality of God, A Reading of Luke's Gospel,* St Paul's Publications, Sydney, 2002, p. 134. Furthermore, the middle two sayings are not at all clear in themselves and there is much debate over their meaning. Commentaries that are most helpful in understanding

This lack of context creates problems for an interpreter. There is, however, no reason to think that the Gospel of Luke wishes to contradict the gospels of Mark or Matthew. Good practice in biblical interpretation would rather say that we should interpret the brief statement without a context in Luke in the light of the longer statements, with the context given in both Mark and Matthew. We may conclude that Luke is also speaking the language of moral obligation in justice and love rather than law. To dismiss a wife because a man has met another woman he prefers, and to leave his wife and the children of the marriage without a man, in a world that was built on families, was a violation of respect, justice and love and, therefore, in the eyes of Jesus it was adultery. If to the words of Luke we add all that the same author says about the *person* of Jesus, we must once again see Jesus insisting, with all the force at his command, on the rights and equal dignity of the woman and on the moral obligations that flowed from this.

In common with the first saying on divorce in Matthew (5:31–32), Luke also has Jesus speaking of the man who marries a divorced woman. Once again, I shall leave comment on this point until after we have looked at the statement of Paul.

THE FIRST LETTER TO THE CORINTHIANS 7:10–15

> To the married I give this command – not I but the Lord – that the wife should not separate from her husband, but if she does separate, let her remain unmarried or else be reconciled to her husband, and that the husband should not divorce his wife.
>
> To the rest I say – I and not the Lord – that if any believer has a wife who is an unbeliever and she consents to live with him, he should not divorce her. And if any woman has a husband who is an unbeliever, and he consents to live with her, she should not divorce him …
>
> But if the unbelieving partner separates, let it be so; in such a case the brother or sister is not bound. It is to peace that God has called you …

This letter of Paul to the Corinthians was written around the year 54–55 CE, some fifteen years before any of the gospels, so it is the first testimony to the teaching of Jesus on the subject of divorce.

Paul introduces the topic by saying that he is answering some questions that the Christian community in the city of Corinth had referred to him ("Now

---

other parts of Luke's Gospel seem to be at something of a loss here. See, for example, Luke Timothy Johnson, *The Gospel of Luke*, Sacra Pagina Series, The Liturgical Press, Collegeville, 1991, pp. 250–251, 254–255.

concerning the matters about which you wrote ... 7:1).[195] What follows has been described as similar to listening to one end of a telephone conversation,[196] and Paul had no idea that his simple reply to a letter would one day be considered part of the New Testament and analysed in minute detail. We would love to know the exact questions he was asked, but there is considerable difficulty in determining this.[197]

This creates a problem when we come to the question of divorce. In verses 10 and 12 Paul appears to create an antithesis: "To the married I give this command – not I but the Lord .... To the rest I say – I and not the Lord". But who are "the rest"? They are not "the unmarried", for this would not make sense of the text. It is possible that "the married" means those in a marriage of two Christians, while "the rest" indicates Christians in a mixed marriage with a non-Christian, but this is far from certain.

It appears that the particular case referred to Paul concerns the situation of a Christian whose non-Christian spouse has left and sought a divorce. In his answer, it appears that Paul first quotes his understanding of what Jesus had said ("not I but the Lord"), and then gives his own application of this teaching to the particular case that the community had referred to him ("I and not the Lord").

In presenting his understanding of what Jesus had said, Paul is close to what the gospels will later say. He is unusual in speaking first of the wife leaving her husband, and this implies a practice of divorce different from that of the Jewish world in which Jesus had spoken. It reflects the fact that he was writing to Christians in the Greek city of Corinth who had been influenced by Greek and Roman practices of divorce. It is also possible, of course, that this was the particular case that had been referred to him.

In applying this teaching of Jesus to the case presented to him, there is no scriptural basis on which to claim that Paul understands himself to be quoting a law laid down by Jesus and then, by virtue of some claim of delegated divine authority, either changing that law or dispensing from it (the so-called "Pauline Privilege"). It surely makes more sense to say that Paul is quoting the serious moral obligation, the prescriptive ideal, of which Jesus had spoken in relation

---

195 "The matters which they raised can be gathered in part from Paul's introducing them with 'now concerning'; by this criterion they included: marriage and divorce (7:1), virginity (7:25), food offered to idols (8:1), spiritual gifts (12:1), the collection for Jerusalem (16:1), and Apollos (16:12)." *1 and 2 Corinthians*, edited by F F Bruce, New Century Bible, Oliphants, London, 1971, p. 66.

196 "Paul was asked some definite questions, and he answered them; he was not concerned with developing a full theology of the subject." Dennis Murphy MSC, *The Apostle of Corinth*, Campion Press, Melbourne, 1966, p. 166.

197 It is most probable that he is quoting or at least summarising the first question when he says in 7:1, " It is well for a man not to touch a woman."

to marriage and divorce ("not I but the Lord") and is then applying that moral obligation to a particular situation that had arisen in Corinth ("I and not the Lord"). In this application he says that a Christian should not initiate a divorce, but that if the non-Christian partner leaves the marriage, "let it be so."

In the circumstances presented Paul appears to acknowledge that the words of Jesus do not constitute a law or an absolute prohibition of divorce. This saying of Paul, therefore, supports the idea of moral obligations and prescriptive ideals rather than laws, for if Paul saw the words of Jesus as a universal law, it is impossible to understand how he could have claimed the authority to dispense from it. He refrains, however, from spelling out the details of his answer, for in saying, "let it be so", he does not speak explicitly of remarriage. I suggest that he implies that on that subject his readers should listen to what Jesus had said about powerful prescriptive ideals.

REMARRIAGE

Perhaps recent history shows us why Jesus stopped short of making a law, but did use such forceful and extravagant language in speaking of an ideal. For many centuries in the Christian world all divorce was forbidden, and this caused most serious hardship for large numbers of individuals. Then civil divorce was introduced, at first on very restricted grounds, but eventually, and inevitably, on virtually any ground. The attitudes created by this practice have in their turn affected the manner in which many people approach marriage and the expectations they bring to it, leading to further divorce. Through these attitudes, many people, including many children, are badly hurt. The present situation, in which the very institution of marriage itself seems to be in danger, can hardly be seen as an ideal by anyone.

I suggest that it is at this point that we can perhaps see why Jesus spoke, not only of the man who divorces his wife and marries another (Mark 10:11; Matt 19:9; Luke 16:18), but also of the woman who is divorced and the man who marries her (Mark 10:12; Matt 5:32; Luke 16:18). We have seen in our own day that when divorce thoroughly permeates the thinking of a community, and marriage is so little respected that very large numbers of people dispense with it entirely, one of the effects is that married persons are no longer seen as "off limits". If one is attracted to a married person, the fact of the marriage often seems to be of little concern in pursuing that attraction. In the thinking of Jesus, such a person has adulterous desires and gives adulterous effect to them, and the married person who responds has equally adulterous desires. Often the other partner is left with little choice other than to agree to the divorce.

In the texts we have been considering, it is obvious that Jesus has gone well beyond the formal act of adultery and has spoken of persons as adulterous when their thinking was adulterous. I have already noted that verse 5:32 of

Matthew must be interpreted in the light of verse 28, where "looking at a woman with lust" is seen as adultery.

In this sense, the man who has invaded a marriage and the married woman who has responded to him are already adulterous before any act of intercourse has taken place, and certainly before any remarriage occurs. At all times it was not law or external actions that concerned Jesus, but the violation of a solemn commitment based on respect and love and the important rights that flowed from this in justice.

I suggest that it was this "culture" of divorce in his own day that Jesus was seeking to confront. He would not forbid divorce altogether, for this would cause unbearable hardship for some, and in any case, he had not come to promote a system in which morality was based solely on law. But, with the divorce practice of his own time and place before his eyes, he would have nothing to do with the idea of divorce on any terms and without concern for the harm caused to others or to the institution of marriage itself. The culture of divorce around Jesus was powerful and he had to break through it at all costs and make people think. His response to this dilemma was to call people back to God's original intention in creating male and female and to speak the language of prescriptive ideals, powerful and binding moral obligations that his followers must treat with the utmost seriousness. He would never be content with paying lip service to the idea of permanency while in practice condoning a lax attitude, and so in forceful Semitic language he insisted on total seriousness by presenting the most radical ideal and challenge possible.

When Jesus said, "If your right eye causes you to sin, tear it out and throw it away", he did not mean this to be taken literally. On the other hand, he certainly did not want anyone to think that it was mere exaggeration and could be ignored. By means of this forceful and concrete language he was saying, "If something has become an obstacle between you and God, get rid of it. Do whatever you have to do but get rid of it. Be radical. Treat the matter with the utmost seriousness and accept no compromise. " Instead of using more abstract statements like these, the Semitic Jesus used the more graphic and deliberately shocking pictorial language of tearing out an eye to express the same idea.

I suggest that when he said three verses later, "Whoever marries a divorced woman commits adultery" he was again using graphic and even shocking pictorial language to express as forcefully as possible the idea that when a marriage is ignored in the pursuit of desire, there is a most serious danger of committing adultery in the heart.

He was insisting that marriage is to be taken with the utmost seriousness, that the words "for better for worse ... 'til death do us part" are to be said with all one's heart and soul and being. He was reminding us that we are shaped by the promises we make and the way we stand by them, for they enter into our being and make us the persons we are. He was stressing that, more than almost anything else in human life, the commitment given on a wedding day both expresses and shapes the very persons we are.

He was aware of just how much of their happiness and well-being individuals place in the hands of another person on a wedding day, and was insisting that their partners accept this gift as a most sacred trust. He was pointing to the most serious danger of both individuals and whole communities stepping on to the slippery slope that leads to the breakdown of the very institution of marriage.

At the same time, he was acknowledging the seriousness of the difficulties that can arise in marriage. He was acknowledging that situations can occur where separation and divorce are the only intelligent and proper solution. He did his best to combine these two sides to the argument by means of a prescriptive ideal and a commanding, even shocking challenge.

THE IDEAL

Once we begin to speak the language of prescriptive ideal and commanding challenge rather than law, the vast variety of particular situations that can arise must be taken into account. The words of Jesus, as applied to a man who abandons his wife solely in order to marry a younger woman, cannot be applied without further thought to, for example, a woman with young children abandoned by a husband and left destitute.

What was the ideal, then, that Jesus was speaking of in his words about remarriage? Let me start with a case I have met in pastoral practice. A couple married, but six months later the wife was involved in a car accident that caused serious brain damage and left her unable to communicate or even recognise people. I met the couple some thirty years after this and found that the man had not divorced and remarried but was still devoted to his wife and looking after her every day. He was not a Catholic, so Catholic teachings were not part of his thinking. But he loved his wife and had committed himself to her "for better for worse, for richer for poorer, in sickness and in health, till death do us part." I have no desire to make a law for all people out of this free decision of one person, but must we not admit that there was much that is admirable and even heroic in his fidelity? Had not this man in some manner regained the creation?

We may add the not uncommon statement of separated or even divorced persons that "I couldn't go out with anyone else yet. I still feel married." When a total commitment was given on a wedding day, many people do not find it easy to leave a marriage behind, no matter what has happened.

When people today talk about divorce, they usually start from the moment when a marriage has completely broken down and ask, "How should we respond compassionately to this situation?" But Jesus wanted his followers to put this situation into a context. He wanted to ask them, "How do you as a young person make sure you yourself are as fully prepared for marriage as your age allows? How should you choose a partner? How seriously do the two of you prepare for your wedding day? How totally do you commit yourselves to each other in that ceremony? How do you live your married life? How do you handle the difficulties that arise? How much are you affected by the culture of divorce around you and how do you respond to it? Do you truly share Christian ideals for marriage and how hard are you willing to work to achieve them? Have you really tried all other alternatives before you even look at separation and divorce?" Only in this light can the question of remarriage be seen in context. Only then is the ideal of Jesus still alive. The only people not profoundly hurt by the breakdown of a marriage are those who put little into it in the first place. Jesus was radical and those who genuinely seek to follow him need to be radical too.

In the light of these considerations, it would seem that for a follower of Jesus, divorce could be accepted in only three situations:

- when there is a genuine conflict between the obligations towards a marriage partner and other even more serious obligations, such as basic obligations towards children, the duty to preserve one's own life and sanity, basic obligations towards God;
- when, despite all efforts, including the seeking of assistance from others through counselling, the living of anything that could be called "married life" has become an impossibility, beyond the powers of the two individuals concerned;
- when a marriage partner has departed, and it is virtually certain that he/she will not return.

It is in interpreting these three criteria and applying them to a particular situation that the strength of the challenge of Jesus would have to be kept firmly in mind.

Is this combination of prescriptive ideal and radical and shocking challenge more in conformity with everything we know about the *person* of Jesus Christ than the idea of his using divine authority to decree a law? Is it in conformity with the story of his own life and death on a cross? On this basis can we reconcile the words of the gospels with all we know about the *person* who spoke them?

CONCLUSION

Some fifty years ago the theologian Edward Schillebeeckx wrote a book titled *Marriage: Secular Reality, Saving Mystery.* The title is profound and suggests a whole new way into the future. It suggests that marriage is first and foremost the often messy secular reality that it is, varying greatly according to culture and with countless individual forms, and that the task of the Church is to turn this secular reality into a saving mystery, both for the individual couple and for the community as a whole.

In line with this, Pope Francis has recently warned us to stop creating niches or boxes and then spending much time and effort determining into which box we will fit a particular marriage.

> Jesus expects us to stop looking for those personal or communal niches that shelter us from the maelstrom of human misfortune, and instead to enter into the reality of other people's lives and to know the power of tenderness. Whenever we do so, our lives become wonderfully complicated.[198]

Jesus understood how "wonderfully complicated" people's lives can become in "the maelstrom of human misfortune" that can be involved in marriage, and he spoke to this complicated world.

Throughout the many cultures of the world, marriage is first and foremost that messy, complicated and immensely varied secular reality that it is, and it defies neat boxes. The task of the Church is to take that messy reality and to do all in its power to assist couples to turn it into a saving mystery according to the mind of Jesus, both for individuals and for whole societies. In this task the idea of the equality of the couple will be central to all of the Church's endeavours.

---

[198] *Amoris Laetitia* (The Joy of Love), Post-Synodal Apostolic Exhortation on Love in the Family, March 19, 2016, no. 308.

CHAPTER 21
EXCLUDING THE FEMININE

THE THEOLOGIAN Elizabeth Johnson
speaks of a church
in which all power is in the hands of men,
all the dogmas, teachings, laws,
customs and even attitudes
are those of men,
all authority is in the hands of men,
all the imagery is masculine,
and, after all the talk,
God is still fundamentally seen as male.
Indeed, even men's ways of being human beings
have been seen as normative for all human beings.
Women have had no voice in articulating
the Church's doctrine, morals or law.
Banned from the pulpit and the altar,
their wisdom has not been permitted
to interpret the gospels,
nor their spirituality
to lead the Church in prayer.[199]

---

199 See Elizabeth A Johnson, *The Quest for the Living God*, Continuum, New York, 2007, ch. 5, 'God Acting Womanish'.

David Ranson says that
this absence of women
from any positions of influence
has led to a serious underestimation
of desire, imagination, dreaming and prophecy.
There is a failure to appreciate adequately
the importance of such things as
sensitivity, touch, attentiveness,
vulnerability, hospitality and compassion.
These attitudes can take away
the natural warmth and spontaneity of love
and leave goodwill as a vague term
not directed at anyone or anything in particular.
Simplicity can become confused with minimalism,
self-mastery seen largely in terms of physical discipline,
obedience equated with conformity
and chastity reduced to control and lovelessness.
In cultures built on a masculine energy
that is not balanced by the feminine,
there can be a growing incapacity for
genuine interior reflection,
an inability to relate with intimacy,
a dependence on role and work for self-identification,
and the loss of a humanising tenderness.[200]

The author Sandra Schneiders says
that in looking at the Church,
Christian feminists do not limit themselves
to negative criticism,
but have an alternative vision to present.
This vision is characterised by
equality,
relatedness
and empowerment
rather than hierarchy,
individualism
and power.
It seeks to restore to unity
all those things that have been divided
by a patriarchal mindset,

---

[200] I am here indebted to an unpublished paper of Father David Ranson OCSA, a lecturer at the Catholic Institute of Sydney.

e.g. spirit and body,
transcendence and immanence,
culture and nature,
the rational and the intuitive,
intelligence and emotion.
It rejects stereotypes of both men and women
and seeks to replace them with wholeness.[201]

The very male liturgy of the Mass
consists overwhelmingly
of rational ideas poured out
in a vast torrent of words
over a largely passive congregation
by a hierarchical priest.
A liturgy that was a genuine combination
of the male and female
would be far richer.

A true equality
between male and female in the Church
would change the entire culture dramatically.
It is surely reasonable to assume that,
if women had been given
far greater importance
and a much stronger voice,
the Church would not have seen
the same level of sexual abuse
and would have responded far better
to this overwhelmingly male problem.

---

201 Sandra M Schneiders I.H.M., 'Feminist Spirituality', in *The New Dictionary of Catholic Spirituality*, edited by Michael Downey, The Liturgical Press, Collegeville, 1993, p. 395.

THE GOSPELS

Each of the four gospels goes its own way in telling the story of the resurrection, and it is not possible to put all these stories together into one cohesive and logical story. Despite this, there are certain elements that are consistent throughout the four.

The first is that all the male disciples abandoned Jesus and fled when he was arrested, and they were slow to come back again. Peter at least followed him into the court of the high priest, but then his failure was the most calamitous of them all as this leader of the twelve denied three times that he had ever known Jesus.

It was the female followers of Jesus who were more faithful and kept some measure of connection with Jesus through his passion. They did not belong to some different order of nature, so there was a measure of failure in them too, for they followed only "at a distance" (Mark 15:40, Matt 27:55, Luke 23:49). Part of the gospel story is that there were no human beings who did not fail Jesus in his passion. It is the Gospel of John alone that speaks of any followers standing "at the foot of the cross", and we may dismiss the idea that this is a literal account, for we know that the Romans never allowed relatives to stand near a crucified victim for fear that they would be so moved by the terrible sufferings that they would try to prevent the suffering, even by killing the victim.

The second common element among the gospels is that after the resurrection it was the women who became the agents of the story, for by and large the men were still nowhere to be found. There were occasions when the testimony of the women was rejected as an "idle tale" (Luke 24:11) and was believed only after it had been corroborated by the men, but it is undeniable that in the four gospels the women were the first witnesses to the resurrection. So apparently God had no problem with the idea of women as the foundational witnesses to one of the most important facts stated anywhere in the gospels: "He is risen. He is not here."

In light of this, it is surely hard to deny to women a significant and ongoing role in proclaiming publicly and officially the faith of the Church in the Risen Christ.

THE DOCUMENT 'ORDINATIO SACERDOTALIS'

Rather than seek to develop these thoughts further, I want to give one example that will show how thoroughly the presence and voice of women are excluded and, ultimately, why women are excluded.

> By the middle decades of the twentieth century, the rising social and political claims of women for equality began also to affect most Christian denominations. The discussion of the ordination of women

began in earnest ... There were nearly eight hundred articles and books written on this subject between 1960 and 2001, and interest in the subject does not seem to have waned since then.[202]

In 1994 Pope John Paul II wanted to put a stop to this increasing talk about the ordination of women to the priesthood, so he decided to publish a document that would have the maximum possible authority, and he knew that the support of the bishops of the world would assist in giving it greater authority. He prepared a document and then called to Rome the Presidents of the Bishops' Conferences from around the world. These Presidents were shown the document and then asked to endorse it in the name of all the bishops in their conferences.

The Presidents replied that they could not do this, for they could not speak in the name of all the bishops without first consulting them. They also asked for two changes in the text of the document. They asked that the phrase "having heard our brothers in the episcopal college" be omitted, for the consultation with the Presidents alone did not add up to this. They also asked that the word "irrevocable" be omitted.

(My account of these events comes from the verbal report given soon afterwards to the Australian bishops by its then Vice-President, Archbishop John Bathersby of Brisbane, who had attended the meeting in Rome.)

The document was published[203] with no reference to consultation with the bishops and with the word "irrevocable" replaced by the words "and that this judgement is to be definitively held by all the Church's faithful."

My interpretation of these events is that Pope John Paul II wanted his document to have the maximum possible authority and so wanted the support of the bishops but was unwilling to consult all of them because he could not guarantee their response. I believe that, had he asked them, the majority would have supported him, but a number would not have. I do not know how large that number would have been, but the point is that neither did he, and he was unwilling to take the risk. I further believe that a significantly larger percentage of the bishops, almost certainly a majority, would not have supported the use of words such as "irrevocable" or "infallible", and this is surely indicated by the request of the Presidents that such words be omitted.

The dilemma for the Pope was that he could not publish his document with any hope that it would achieve the desired result of stopping even talk of the ordination of women if any noticeable number of bishops voted against it, and if a majority did not want any reference to infallibility. How could a pope claim the document was infallible and that it should, therefore, stop all discussion, if

---

202 Gary Macy, *The Hidden History of Women's Ordination, Female Clergy in the Medieval West*, Oxford University Press, 2007, p. 10.
203 John Paul II, Apostolic Letter, *Ordinatio Sacerdotalis*, May 22, 1994.

Catholic women could reply, "But a significant number of your own bishops don't agree with you, and most of them refuse to call the teaching infallible?"

Instead of consultation with the bishops, it was arranged that the Prefect of the Congregation for the Doctrine of the Faith, Cardinal Joseph Ratzinger, should in the following year publish a Response to a Doubt in which he said that:

> This teaching requires definitive assent, since, founded on the written Word of God, and from the beginning constantly preserved and applied in the Tradition of the Church, it has been set forth infallibly by the ordinary and universal Magisterium.[204]

The use of the word "infallible" here means that the Presidents of conferences were overruled and the word "infallible" was used, so that John Paul II and, later, Ratzinger himself (as Benedict XVI) could say that even talk of the ordination of women was forbidden.

The cardinal referred to two factors. The first is "the written Word of God", which is presumably a reference to the fact that no women are recorded as being among those present at the Last Supper. But the fact that none are recorded as being present is not proof that none were present. The gospels are clear that a group of women accompanied Jesus throughout his travels and there is no hint that Jesus ordered segregation at mealtimes or specifically excluded women at the Last Supper.

The second factor is his appeal to the constant tradition of the Church over two thousand years. I find this a weak argument, for in appealing to the dead bishops of the past, it excluded the living bishops of the present and, over the centuries, all too many of those past bishops had extreme negative views concerning women that today appal us.

There is an abundance of lurid statements to draw on from statements from the past. For example:

> I speak to you, O charmers of the clergy, appetizing flesh of the devil ... you, poison of the minds, death of souls, venom of wine and eating, companions of the very stuff of sin, the cause of our ruin. You, I say, I exhort you women of the ancient enemy, you bitches, sows, screech-owls, night owls, she-wolves, blood suckers, who cry "Give, give without ceasing".[205]

---

[204] Congregation for the Doctrine of the Faith, Concerning the Teaching Contained in *Ordinatio Sacerdotalis, Responsum ad Dubium*, October 28, 1995.

[205] Peter Damian, c. 7 of *Contra Intemperantes Clericos* in PL145:410A-B, translation by Anne Llewellyn Barstow, *Married Priests and the Reforming Papacy: the Eleventh Century Debates*, Texts and Studies in Religion, 12, Edwin Mellon Press, New York, 1982. The text available to

Today we would say that this writer has serious problems and is in urgent need of psychological help!

Rather than quote more of this type of statement, I prefer to add quotations from two sober canonists who were doing no more than quoting the reality of their times. Both acknowledge that for many centuries there had been women deacons, but Theodore Balsamon (12th century) then says,

> But the monthly affliction banished them from the divine and holy sanctuary.[206]

Matthew Blastares (14th century) says,

> They were forbidden access and performance of these services by later fathers because of their monthly flow that cannot be controlled.[207]

This continuing influence of the ancient purity laws of the First Testament, at least those concerning women, has never disappeared, even though it causes most Christian people of today to cringe in shame.

When looking at Tradition, it is not only the quantity, but also the quality that must be considered. Some years earlier, Joseph Ratzinger himself had written:

> Not everything that exists in the Church must for that reason be also a legitimate tradition; in other words, not every tradition that arises in the Church is a true celebration ... of the mystery of Christ. There is a distorting, as well as legitimate, tradition ... Consequently, tradition must not be considered only affirmatively, but also critically.[208]

All that I said in the last chapter concerning the teaching of Jesus on the subject of the equality of men and women, and the failure of the Church to live up to his radicalism, needs to be kept in mind in considering the two thousand year tradition of the Church on the issue of ordination.

It is a small wonder that Hans Küng responded to the Reply of Cardinal

---

me is that of Gary Macy, *The Hidden History of Women's Ordination, Female Clergy in the Medieval West*, Oxford University Press, 2007, p. 113.

206 Kevin Madigan and Carolyn Osiek, *Ordained Women in the Early Church: A Documentary History*, John Hopkins Press, Baltimore, 2005, p. 137.

207 Madigan and Osiek, op.cit, p. 138. I have quoted both these sources from Gary Macy's chapter in the book *Women Deacons*, Paulist Press, New York, 2011, pp. 31–32.

208 Joseph Ratzinger, "The Transmission of Divine Revelation", in *Commentary on the Documents of Vatican II*, vol.3, edited by Herbert Vorgrimler, Herder and Herder, New York, 1969, p. 185.

Ratzinger by writing in an open letter to his friend, "Joseph, how could you? You're far too good a theologian for this!"

The conclusion I have drawn from these events is that the declaration of papal infallibility in 1870 has now developed to the point that, in the Vatican, papal authority and infallibility trump all other issues. Popes of the past could not have been wrong in not ordaining women and that had to be the end of the matter or all papal authority would be called into question. So there could not even be any discussion, not among Catholic people throughout the world, and not within the Vatican itself. The only question remaining was how to suppress the talk by Catholic people on this subject. If this meant subjecting the desires, dignity and rights of women to the needs of papal authority, then so be it.

Since I believe that the exclusion of women from all positions of influence in the Church has been a significant causal factor in sexual abuse, this decision also means that the protection of papal authority and infallibility has been more important than eliminating sexual abuse.

It has also meant that, under the present system of governance within the Church, infallibility and collegiality are as incompatible as oil and water. The understanding of infallibility applied by Pope John Paul II in this case demanded monarchy. On any controversial issue a pope could never guarantee that he would obtain that very high degree of consensus from the bishops that infallibility would demand. As long as this kind of infallibility reigns, there will be no room for collegiality.

And if the pope is not listening to the bishops, then even less will he be listening to the whole Church. This in turn means that there will be no seeking of the opinion of women on any subject of importance, let alone on a subject such as sexual abuse where they might well have some strong things to say about how the popes themselves and all the men around them have acted.

As I showed in the last chapter, it was precisely on the question of the role of women that the Church failed to live up to the radicalism of Jesus, so surely arguments of the Church seeking to prove that women are not equal to men in a particular field such as ordination would need to be especially strong. The Church has singularly failed to give such arguments. And this is the point: it does not have to be proven that women can be ordained; it would have to be conclusively proven that they cannot, and the Church has come nowhere near doing this. The very weakness of the arguments given is a powerful argument in favour of women being ordained.

CHAPTER 22
ABORTION IS NOT A SIMPLE QUESTION

A number of countries have in recent times held a referendum on questions such as gay marriage, divorce, abortion or euthanasia. In all cases the relevant government has been particularly requested that the question posed be as simple as possible, but in doing this it has created problems for many of its own citizens.

This appeared to be evident in the recent referendum in Ireland on abortion. A number of people in the media proclaimed the result to be a rejection of Ireland's Catholic past and an embrace of a secularist future, but I doubt that this expresses the struggle that many thinking Irish people had in deciding how to vote. I suspect that many were most sympathetic to victims of rape or incest but were profoundly uneasy with the idea of saying that a foetus is a nothing. The question asked did not allow them to make such distinctions. If we are to make serious progress, we must make every effort to get away from simplistic questions.

At a meeting in 1991 the cardinals of the Church asked Pope John Paul II "to reaffirm with the authority of the successor of Peter the value of human life and its inviolability, in the light of present circumstances and the attacks threatening it today".[209]

---

209 Encyclical Letter, *Evangelium Vitae*, no. 5, p. 9.

The crucial question was whether, not just some form of human life, but an actual human person, is present from the first moment of conception, so that to carry out an abortion would be to terminate the life of a human being. The question is both important and urgent, and it would be very convenient to have a clear and simple answer.

But is it really possible to have this clear and simple answer? If one gives such an answer, do the arguments given in support add up to the certainty one desires? Or is authority being used to go further than the arguments can go?

The Pope's answer was to quote two statements from the Congregation for the Doctrine of the Faith which go within a whisker of saying that from the first moment of conception the embryo is a new person, and then add that the matter is so important that we must assume the presence of a living person lest we run the risk of killing one.[210]

I feel that this reply is a less than satisfactory foundation on which to base the very strong teaching of the Church on abortion, with its absolute statements and its penalties of excommunication.

Long ago the Church seems to have decided that all its statements on moral matters had to be crystal clear and simple, giving exact and specific guidance and allowing no room for vagueness or doubt. It thought that this was its duty and, in fairness, it is probably true that this is exactly what many people demanded of it. And yet human affairs are so complex and subtle that it is not always possible to give a simple answer.

Abortion is not a simple question. Simplistic answers on both sides are automatically wrong and misleading. Abortion gives rise to many acutely difficult moral questions. I believe that this must be our starting point.

A couple come together in a sexual act, and a single sperm penetrates an ovum. The pregnancy starts there and ends nine months later when a baby, a new and separate person, is born. What happens over these months is obviously a **process**, and no-one can say with certainty at what point in this process of development a separate human being is present.

The pro-choice lobby may feel that it is on certain ground in saying that at the moment of conception what is present is not a separate human being, but they would have to admit that with each passing day after that their certainty of this dissolves more and more into uncertainty. The pro-life lobby would no doubt declare its certainty that at the moment of birth what is present is a human person, but would have to admit that with each day going back in the pregnancy before that its certainty dissolves more and more into uncertainty. Neither arguments nor authority can solve this problem for either side.

If we are ever to move towards agreement, people from the pro-choice

---

210 Op.cit., no. 60, pp.107–108.

lobby who admit the weakness of their own arguments would need to meet with people from the pro-life lobby who admit the weakness of their arguments.

Even then, if progress were to be made, the pro-choice lobby would have to show that it was not ignoring the new life that is being created, and the pro-life lobby would have to show that it had a genuine empathy for the near-impossible situations in which women can be placed.

The most we can say is that, in the earliest stages of the pregnancy, there is less chance that a separate human being is present, while in the later stages there is more chance. But no-one knows with certainty, and no-one has found any clear criterion of proof that can be applied.

I therefore have serious problems with both the pro-life and the pro-choice lobby, for they both appear to claim a certainty that is simply not possible. This certainty of many people on both sides appears to be strident and is counterproductive.

WHETHER TO INCLUDE OR NOT

I felt the temptation to ignore this seemingly insoluble question and pass it on to others so that I might gain some real clarity in my own mind. But then I thought that the title of this book, *Towards the End of my Days*, would be empty if I was merely picking and choosing the questions I considered. Abortion is too important for me to ignore it.

And yet I am painfully aware of all the insensitive things men, and in a particular way priests, have said on this subject. Abortion is something that affects women in a profound and intimate way, while men can afford to stand at a distance from it. For a woman a pregnancy binds her to nine months of carrying the child, the trauma of the birth and then the profound commitment of every moment of seven thousand six hundred and seventy days and nights until the child turns twenty-one, a massive and enduring task. For even the best of men it is never quite like that.

Laws are black and white, but women's lives are many shades of grey. When all a male has to offer is a black and white law, a woman can feel that what he says is quite unreal and does not even touch the reality of her life.

In speaking of divorce, I quoted words of Pope Francis concerning the manner in which Jesus understood how "wonderfully complicated" people's lives can become in "the maelstrom of human misfortune" that can be involved in marriage and family. Unwanted pregnancies are a particularly turbulent part of this maelstrom.

ALL LIFE IS PRECIOUS

I start from the belief that all human life is precious. I believe that how far a society has progressed as a whole society in respecting all human life is the single most important criterion of civilisation. One society is civilised because it places a high value on every human life, while another society is uncivilised because it does not do so and life is cheap. I believe that this is the single most important criterion of civilisation, and no number of universities or art galleries can replace it.

Respect for human life can never be taken for granted, for it is always at risk and the desire to base our actions on what is of advantage to ourselves is a constant. The work to preserve human dignity and the rights that flow from it must be unceasing.

Our concern to protect human life, dignity and rights must extend from the beginning of life to its end. It would be wrong to fight loudly against abortion while being far weaker in our defence of human life at any other time in life or in any other circumstances. And the work to protect the dignity of human life must include the quality of life as well as the fact of life, for it would surely be wrong to be loud in our defence of life, but without any real concern for its quality.

SAVING AS MUCH LIFE AS POSSIBLE

Imagine that you are the only doctor in a town a long way from the next town and far from the nearest hospital. One night at a level crossing on the outskirts of the town, a train smashes into a bus and the train itself is derailed. You race to the scene to find a situation of total chaos, with people dead or dying with many different kinds of injury. You have the help of citizens, but you know that you are the only trained medical person present and that there will be no ambulance or other expert medical help for at least an hour.

I suggest that you would quickly adopt the principle of saving as much life as possible, though this would involve many hard and most unpleasant decisions. You might decide that one person is so seriously injured that he/she cannot be saved, so you might ask other people to offer whatever support they can while you move to others who can be saved. If you found two people, a child and an elderly person, with an equally serious injury, but had time to save only one, you might instinctively save the child. At every moment you would have to make hard decisions about life and death.

In these circumstances I believe that people would agree overwhelmingly with the principle of saving as much life as possible. The decision to save the child rather than the elderly person would show that the quality of life inevitably comes into this equation.

Let me now apply these principles to five different cases of abortion. They will not cover all possible circumstances, but they will at least give an idea of the direction in which I believe we should be heading.

Case 1: The Holiday

A young married couple desire a baby and the wife becomes pregnant. Then the couple is offered an all-expenses-paid overseas holiday. The wife has an abortion and they go on the holiday. Another couple want a boy. As soon as they find that the foetus is female, they arrange an abortion. Though a large majority of women seeking an abortion do not fall into such categories, both cases are real.

Human life is precious, so it must be defended. A holiday or the gender of a foetus is surely grossly inadequate as a reason for an abortion. I cannot help the feeling that civilisation in this country took a step backwards on those two days.

Case 2: The Conflict Situation

In 2010 in Phoenix, Arizona, a pregnant woman was brought into a Catholic hospital with complications. The best experts available in the city studied her case and concluded that they simply could not save the baby. If, however, they did nothing and let nature take its course, the mother would also die, and she had other small children for whom she was responsible.

The matter was referred to the Ethics Committee of the hospital, where Sister Margaret McBride suggested that it was better to follow the principle of saving as much life as possible and favoured the abortion of the doomed foetus. The local bishop promptly excommunicated her because she had proposed the direct killing of a foetus.

Let us imagine something that would never happen. Imagine that the doctor turned to me and said, "You are a bishop, and this is a Catholic hospital, so you take the responsibility. See this tube that I'm pointing out to you. If you take this scalpel and cut it, the baby will die but the mother will be saved. If you don't cut it, you can sit here and watch both mother and baby die." I would feel the responsibility powerfully, but I know that I could not simply sit there and do nothing, for that would violate something very deep within me. I would take the scalpel and cut the tube.

I believe that saving as much life as can be saved is the humane and right decision to make in this situation.

Case 3: The Accident

A pregnant woman was driving her car when another car smashed into it, causing her to miscarry. The woman was a supporter of abortion but was upset when she found that she could not sue the driver for the loss of her child, for the foetus had no standing in law. She received considerable support for new legislation that would cover future cases while still allowing abortion, but then found that the new legislation was strongly opposed by the abortion lobby.

From their point of view, the abortion lobby was right to oppose this legislation, for legal abortion essentially demands that the law not recognise the foetus as human. If a new law had granted other women the right to sue in similar circumstances, the entire case for abortion would be drastically weakened.[211]

At its best, feminism occupies the moral high ground in relation to the Catholic Church because it is faithful to the real-life experiences of real women, but at its worst it has abandoned the moral ground altogether by saying that the foetus is a nothing.

The woman knew that the loss of her baby (and this is the language every woman uses in these circumstances) was far more important to her than the damage to her car. An outsider, through criminal negligence, had caused her grave harm. She could sue for part of that harm, the damage to her car, but not for the far greater harm caused through the loss of her baby, for in law there was nothing there to lose. At this point abortion law is in conflict with the overwhelming experience of pregnant women.

This case of the car accident must give people much to think about concerning the whole question of abortion.

Case 4: The Child Rape Victim

In 2008 in the city of Recife in Brazil an eight-year-old girl was found to be pregnant by her mother's *de facto* partner. The mother arranged an abortion. When the facts became public, the Archbishop of the diocese excommunicated the mother.

Behind the attitude of the Archbishop there appears to be the thinking that every single woman who has an abortion is exactly like the couple in case 1 above who had an abortion in order to go on a holiday.

We absolutely cannot afford to think in abstract categories but must make every effort to appreciate the real-life situation of those concerned.

I can only imagine the feelings of the mother in this fourth case as she saw her eight-year-old child in this impossible situation, and I know that I have not the slightest desire to cast stones at her. The Church must be a church of mercy, and mercy must be based on our understanding of the real-life situation.

Case 5: The Good Catholic Woman

A good Catholic woman, following faithfully the teachings of the Church on contraception, has given birth to seven children. Her husband demands sex when he wants it and leaves everything else to her, so she finds herself

---

211 This law is named as "Zoe's law" and was before the State Parliament of New South Wales, though I have heard nothing about it now for several years.

pregnant with an eighth child. The husband is shiftless and spends too much money on cigarettes, alcohol and gambling, so there is never any money to look after the children. The woman finds herself chronically tired, at the point of desperation, on the verge of a breakdown, and with the overwhelming feeling that 'she is drowning'. She knows that, if she stops to think, she will be unable to do anything, so at the earliest possible moment and without informing her husband that she is pregnant, she goes to a clinic, has an abortion and has her tubes tied. She returns home filled with guilt and with the conviction that she can never be forgiven.

Even Catholic morality would say that a person can reach such a point of desperation that they are no longer responsible for their own decisions. I would hope that any confessor would treat this woman with compassion and understanding, but I could never guarantee that this would happen. Even when compassionate to her, the Church would still declare emphatically that what she has done is in itself mortally sinful and capable of causing automatic excommunication.

I have acknowledged that it is impossible to exclude considerations of the quality of life from any situation of abortion. Despite this, I am most hesitant about any arguments that put the quality of life before life itself. If society went down that track, it could find itself condoning the elimination, before or even after birth, of any baby considered "defective". I have seen at close quarters the heroic sacrifices that parents have to make for a "defective" child, but I have also seen many such children living happy and fulfilling lives. I have a profound objection to a society deciding that those considered "defective" would be "better off dead". This is not civilisation as I understand it or want it. So I could not accept that an abortion would be legitimate in this fifth case for the sole reason that the quality of life of the eighth child would be less than ideal.

I am more impressed, however, by the argument that the total collapse of the mother, necessitating an extended stay in a psychiatric hospital and a possible permanent inability to care for any of her children, would not be good for anyone. So I have great reservations about simply applying pre-conceived rules to her situation.

I suggest that how we answer this fifth case will depend on our understanding of how morality works. In doing this, I will refer to one article in particular.[212] It is not an article in which the author, Joseph Parkinson, puts forward his own ideas, but rather a survey by a competent moral theologian of the aftermath of the encyclical *Humanae Vitae*, quoting documents from the teaching authority in the Church, both universal and national, and showing the development of understanding concerning the role of conscience and the areas of consensus reached.

---

212 *Humanae Vitae II:* Conscience, Contraception and Holy Communion, *Australasian Catholic Record,* July 2013, Vol. 90, no. 3, pp. 297–310.

There is a dispute in the Catholic Church concerning conscience that goes back more than sixteen hundred years. St Augustine said that, if conscience says one thing while Church authority says another, one should follow Church authority, for it is the higher authority and far more likely to be right. St Thomas Aquinas, on the other hand, said that one should listen most carefully to what Church authority says and give it great weight, but that, in the end, if conscience believes Church authority is wrong, at least for the particular case, then the person should follow conscience.

This dispute has never been fully resolved, though the trend has been more and more towards conscience, as Parkinson's article shows. For myself, I agree with the statement of Pope John Paul II in his encyclical *Veritatis Splendor* that, "The Church puts herself always and only *at the service of conscience.*"[213] (The emphasis is from the original.)

Because of the conflict between the views of Augustine and Aquinas, however, this statement is in conflict with much of the practice of the Church over a long period. On countless occasions the Church or its representative has not sought to assist conscience, but rather told conscience what conclusion it must come to. If the Church is to be "always and only at the service of conscience" on a subject such as abortion, then it may by all means put forward many of the principles that I have suggested in this chapter, but it must stop short of statements that seek to compel conscience. 'Compelling conscience' cannot be called 'assisting conscience' however, for it is rather like taking over from conscience and pushing it aside.

In the fifth case I have proposed there are matters for conscience to consider:

- The woman sought an abortion at the earliest possible moment, and there is the question of whether at this early stage there was a human being present. The papal statement is an assertion rather than a proven fact, so there must be room for conscience to disagree.

- There is an ancient principle in morality which assumes that that no one can be bound to the impossible,[214] and for this woman in all the concrete circumstances of her life one may argue that an eighth child is impossible.

- Indeed, to speak of conscience at all presupposes a calm intellectual consideration of all circumstances. But this woman's decisions are not calmly intellectual; they are decisions deep within her very being, her gut, her entrails. They have not been reached lightly but are the final step in a long and most painful process. They are decisions of a good Catholic woman, intensely desiring to be faithful to the teachings of

---

213 No. 64.
214 *Ad impossibile nemo tenetur.*

her Church but fighting for her very sanity and unable to go a single step further.

I suggest that in this case the final decision cannot be made by anyone other than the woman herself in conscience before God. The Church may invite her to consider a number of principles it has proposed, but it must stop short of interfering with conscience, and it must not bully her. Filling people with feelings of guilt if they make a decision different from that of Church authority is a form of bullying.

When we cannot find a neat solution to a moral problem, we have no choice except to turn to conscience. If I cannot agree with a pregnant woman who simply asserts without proof that there is nothing more than her own body there, I can agree that in the final analysis it is she alone who must determine what she will actually *do* about her situation, for this is exactly the role of conscience.

On the one hand, the woman must take responsibility for her decision, for that is an essential part of conscience. Indeed, it is simply not conscience if one does not take responsibility, or if one does what one wants and calls that conscience. On the other hand, her sense of despair and desperation must be included when talking about her ability to take responsibility. There must be both compassion and humaneness in our attitude.

I realise the dangers inherent in what I have put forward. If one allows the slightest breach in the dyke, the entire structure can give way and the sea sweep in to flood the land and drive everything before it. If one gives an inch, even in this extreme case, there is the danger that almost any reason could be seen as justifying an abortion. I suggest that this is a major reason why Catholic morality has been so absolute on so many questions, including abortion.

Despite all the difficulties, it is no solution to propose absolute principles that fail the test of humaneness, allow no room for conscience, and do not respect the almost infinite variety of circumstances that human nature gives rise to. There must come a moment in this whole discussion when we leave it to God to make the judgements rather than grandly inform people that our judgement is God's judgement.

The moral struggle for goodness does not consist only in doing right things, but even more importantly, in the struggle to know what is the right thing to do in the confused circumstances in which we must live. There will always be the temptation to choose the easier way, and people who do this are diminished by their choice. Despite this, it is through the struggle to know and do the right thing that we grow as human beings. We will most probably make many mistakes along the way, but the struggle to both know and then do the right thing is the way to growth that God has created for us. If we try to substitute

Church authority for a large part of this struggle, we actually inhibit the growth of people.

We have a long way to go in this debate, and the very first step must be a profound change in basic attitudes. As long as the two sides keep hurling accusations at each other, no progress will be made. Physical or moral violence used to prevent a woman from accessing a clinic is always wrong, and unwarranted pressure is counterproductive. On the other hand, conscience is a serious concept and it must not be cheapened by turning it into nothing more than *what I want to do*.

For myself, I hope I feel a deep compassion for this woman, and all like her. I would do all I could to bring her some measure of healing. I would like the teaching authority within the Church to be far more aware than it is of its own significant role in bringing the woman to this point of impossible choice. At the same time, I would try to keep strong my own respect and concern for all human life. I would mourn the small life that has been lost (whatever this life was that early in the pregnancy), though I am sure that this particular woman would be a long way ahead of me in doing this already.

CHAPTER 23
EUTHANASIA IS NOT A SIMPLE QUESTION

Just as for abortion, so I find that in relation to euthanasia there are no simple answers. Like abortion, euthanasia gives rise to acutely difficult moral problems, and I find that the arguments put forward on both sides can be simplistic.

There are two questions that must be addressed. The first is the theological question of whether God would under any circumstances approve of euthanasia. The second is the practical moral question of whether it is possible to have the desired positive effects of euthanasia without also introducing most serious and quite unacceptable negative effects.

THE THEOLOGICAL QUESTION

I am not satisfied with the traditional argument that God created human life, God alone is the master of human life, so God alone can take away human life.

God creates human life through human beings, in partnership with them, as God does so many things in partnership with human beings. In fact, as I read it, this is a major part of the story of the Bible: God creating the world, giving it into the care of human beings, and working with them as a partner. I see no reason to exclude questions concerning the end of life from this partnership.

I am, however, equally dissatisfied with the argument that: "I have the right to determine the time and manner of my own death; this is my right and it concerns no one else." For God all human life is precious and to be treated with reverence. A decision to end a human life must always be seen as a major decision and is never to be taken lightly.

In making a decision for euthanasia, God would always want us to take into account the good of the whole community. We are not just individuals who act together with others only when, for purely pragmatic reasons, we freely choose to do so. On the contrary, we are essentially parts of a living community; we need each other, and we grow more surely when we all work together to make the community grow. Today the world around us appears to stress individual rights and give them precedence over community needs, but a community cannot survive in a world in which the rights of each individual always trump those of the community, and so we must balance the two.

Every human being is part of God's plan, and each of us has an obligation to reach beyond ourselves and do all we can to help the whole human race to grow. For almost all people, for almost all of the time, this would rule out suicide, for suicide would be a refusal to fulfill our obligation towards our fellow human beings.

Euthanasia involves the State cooperating in and enabling a death, and what the State does is a matter of community rights. We all have a right and responsibility to ensure that what our State does will not harm others.

But what about those who are suffering from such a degree of unmanageable pain that none of us would have the right to criticise them if they wanted euthanasia, for none of us could possibly guarantee that we would not cry out for euthanasia ourselves if we were suffering from the same degree of unmanageable pain? Do not such persons have the right to say, "Lord, I've done all I can usefully do for others, but now I can go no further. You speak of mercy, but there has never been a time when I have needed mercy as much as I need it now."

Where is the proof that, in entrusting the world to human beings, God withheld this authority from them and insisted that they bear the pain? To bear that degree of pain for any length of time would require the heroic virtue of a saint, but sanctity must always be a choice, for no one ever can or ever will be compelled to be a saint.

In an earlier chapter I said that my thinking about sexual morality changed, not because of any change in my thinking about sex, but because I could not believe in a god who would condemn a person to an eternity in hell for doing no more than taking pleasure in thinking about sex. Here, too, I could not believe in a god who insisted on the very last ounce of suffering from a dying person. Fortunately for me, that is not the kind of God I believe in.

The conclusion I have drawn is that God does not absolutely forbid all euthanasia under all circumstances but does want us to treat all human life with the greatest seriousness and always to be aware of the common good of the whole community.

THE MORAL QUESTION

Wherever euthanasia is permitted, there is always the danger of outside factors coming into the equation. For example, there have been situations where a doctor, without even consulting the patient, can decide that a patient's life is "no longer worth living". And (possibly only for reasons of convenience or money) relatives can decide that "granny's time has come".

These and many other pragmatic questions can be involved in any situation where euthanasia is proposed as a solution. There can be real questions concerning whether the patient is making a free decision or, indeed, any decision at all.

Euthanasia has been available for some time in a small number of places in Europe and North America. The situation in these places gives rise to a number of questions:

- Is it true that in these countries/states the number of cases of euthanasia has steadily increased since euthanasia was introduced and there has been constant pressure for an extension of the grounds on which it is legal?
- Is it true that the passing of the original law was the threshold event, and that once that threshold had been crossed, there has been an inevitable and constant pressure to extend the law?
- Is it therefore true that the passing of the law is only the beginning, not the end?
- Is it true that things that were positively excluded at the time of the original law are now under serious consideration?
- Will there not be a constant pressure towards euthanasia on demand?
- Will not individual desire inevitably seek to triumph over community need?
- Must we not make a very strong distinction between cases where a patient asks for euthanasia for him/herself and cases where anyone else, anyone at all, asks for, let alone decides, the issue?
- What does the evidence show concerning the danger to groups such as indigenous Australians or the very poor, where other people might apply their own values, attitudes and prejudices in "suggesting" euthanasia?
- What guarantees can be put in place to ensure that those with a long-term illness are not pressured into asking for euthanasia?
- There are people who can see no immediate way out of a temporary problem such as a period of depression, being bullied at school, or a broken love affair, and people going through these crises are often easily suggestible. These are common causes of suicide. What steps

have been taken to ensure that such people receive proper assistance without euthanasia being seen as the first response?
- How effective have safeguards been in these countries that allow medically assisted death?

Three authors have recently produced an interdisciplinary study of the legislation in Belgium.[215] In a book review in *The Tablet*[216] the reviewer John Keown quotes one of the contributing writers, Prof. Etienne Montero, as saying:

> Once euthanasia was legalised in Belgium, in 2002, experience demonstrates that it is an illusion to believe that euthanasia can be permitted as a narrowly circumscribed, well-defined, exceptional practice to which 'strict conditions' apply, and which is under rigorous control. Once euthanasia is allowed, the limiting conditions established under the law fall away, one after another, and it appears practically impossible, to maintain a strict interpretation of the statutory conditions and to prevent the extension of the law.

The opinion of one writer does not resolve a difficult issue, but the conclusions of this book must be taken most seriously.

CONCLUSION

If I bring all my conclusions together into one place, I would express them in this way:
- God works together with human beings in partnership, and there is no convincing proof that God excludes matters concerning the end of life from this partnership.
- There is no convincing proof that God insists on the last drop of pain from a dying person.
- The taking of a human life is always a major matter, never to be done lightly.
- Individual choice must not be allowed to abolish all considerations of the good of the whole community.
- Our first response should always be to improve and spread palliative care so that a genuine alternative to euthanasia is available. Work to move beyond opioids should be encouraged. At the same time, palliative

---

215 *Euthanasia and Assisted Suicide: Lessons from Belgium*, edited by David Albert Jones, Chris Gastmans and Calum MacKellar, Cambridge University Press, 2018.
216 December 15, 2018, pp. 17–18.

care does not meet the need in all cases, and not all countries have this response available to them.
- To draft any law on the subject raises a whole host of difficult moral questions.
- It is extremely doubtful whether any law, no matter how well drafted, can prevent all problems.
- Any law on the subject is a threshold event, and a continuing role for the legislator becomes even more essential after that threshold has been crossed.
- At the same time, we cannot resolve the practical moral problems, no matter how serious, by an inhumane law that does not allow euthanasia in even the most extreme cases. We cannot allow a person to suffer endless excruciating pain in order to resolve our own problems for us.
- All important decisions of principle should always be made by the community rather than by any one individual, whether patient or doctor.

I would be against giving authority to doctors to make decisions. At the very least, I would wish to see the State establish tribunals or boards which could consider individual cases in accordance with written criteria. There would have to be checks on the work of these tribunals or boards, and periodic reviews by outside persons.

CHAPTER 24
THE PLACE OF MARY IN THE CHRISTIAN WORLD

The sole purpose of the gospels is to tell the story of Jesus, and everything else is subjected to this. The writers were not concerned to give information about other persons for their own sake, not even Mary. Rather, like everyone else in the gospels, she is used solely to express truths about Jesus.

We should never forget the sobering fact that the first gospel, that of Mark, mentions Mary only twice and neither reference is flattering. On the first occasion (Mark 3:20–21, 31–35) she appears to be included among those relatives who did not understand Jesus ("He has gone out of his mind") and who remained outside the community of his followers. Indeed, Mark deliberately contrasts the family "outside" with the disciples "inside" (3:32–35). In this story Mark wished to stress that it was faith in Jesus that made a person a member of the community he was founding, and no one, not even his closest relatives, had a right of entry without faith. On the second occasion (6:1–6) the people of Nazareth expressed the view that the son of someone as ordinary as Mary could hardly be a special person ("Is not this the carpenter, the son of Mary …?"). Here Mark wished to stress that the greatness of Jesus did not come from his human origins. For whatever reason, Mark did not use Mary in any positive manner.

Matthew softens Mark's idea of Mary as someone outside the community. He also gives his infancy story, which adds material about Mary, though it is more concerned with showing the fulfilment of prophecies than to give information about Mary for her own sake.

Luke gives a consistent presentation of Mary as a young woman caught up into a divine plan, given very little explanation and having to live by faith.

> She was deeply disturbed by these words and asked herself what this greeting could mean. (Luke 1:29)

> As for Mary, she treasured all these things and pondered them in her heart. (Luke 2:19)

> As the child's father and mother were wondering at the things that were being said about him ..." (Luke 2:33)

> They were overcome when they saw him, and his mother said to him, "My child, why have you done this to us? See how worried your father and I have been, looking for you." ... But they did not understand what he meant. (Luke 2:48–51)

Luke's Gospel also has the *Magnificat*, to which I shall return later.

On the other hand, Luke repeats a theme close to that of Mark when, to a woman who blesses his mother, he writes that Jesus replies, "Blessed rather are those who hear the word of God and obey it!" (Luke 11:28)

John places the entire public ministry of Jesus between two incidents in which Mary is present, the wedding feast at Cana (John 2:1–11), called "the first of his signs", and the giving of Mary and the beloved disciple to each other from the cross (John 19:25–27), one of the last of his signs. Both scenes, however, while they certainly say things about Mary, are primarily about Jesus and his work, and they appear to be as much about the importance of marriage and family as they are about Mary for her own sake.

The Acts of the Apostles tell us that, after the Ascension of Jesus, the remaining eleven apostles "were constantly devoting themselves to prayer, together with certain women, including Mary the mother of Jesus, as well as his brothers" (Acts 1:14), so Mary, joining in prayer and awaiting the Holy Spirit, was seen as part of this earliest Christian community.

From this meagre information a complex and often extravagant story developed. Artists, sculptors and poets as well as theologians and preachers all contributed. Popular piety often went far beyond the limits of official teaching and the sober gospel stories were often in stark contrast to the extravagances that developed from them. Exaggeration, and even a heresy or three, came to be looked on with indulgence if their purpose was to praise Mary. It was clear from very early times that Mary represented something that touched a very deep chord within the Christian soul.

The Protogospel of James (mid-second century), a "gospel" that the Church never accepted as genuine, gives us alleged biographical information about Mary that has entered popular tradition. This information includes the names of her parents, her living in the temple, the miraculous choosing of Joseph as her husband. This desire to "expand" on the gospels in order to give Mary a greater part in the gospel story goes back to a very early time.

From the third or fourth century comes the enduring prayer *Sub tuum praesidium*, "… suffer us not to be in adversity but deliver us from danger …" in which Mary is already addressed as a power in her own right.

At the Council of Ephesus in 431 she was proclaimed *theotokos*, Godbearer or Mother of God, though the term has always remained controversial and a cause of division. Since Jesus was God and Mary was the mother of Jesus, there is a sense in which she can be called mother of God, or at least "bearer of God". On the other hand, a mother essentially pre-exists her child, so there are serious dangers in the title.

From the sixth century comes the great prayer of the Greek Church, the *Akathistos*. It eulogises Mary's role in the salvation of the world, and in poetic language it attributes to her certain power and activity that belong to God alone. It is a beautiful hymn, used to this day in the Orthodox churches, but its poetic imagery goes well beyond sober theology.

In the middle ages this tendency grew stronger. God was often presented as a stern king and judge, and the more this happened, the more Mary came to be seen as the gentle female presence, balancing and tempering the sternness of God. She came to be seen as a mediator (and even the mediator) between a human race lost in sin and a distant and often angry god. She herself became an idealised human and something more than human. She was often described as though she possessed all virtue and knowledge, all beauty and goodness. The medieval ideas of courtly love were applied to her.

Prayer to Mary became increasingly popular. For example we have the Ave Maris Stella, the Salve Regina, the Hail Mary, the litanies, and the Rosary.

The Reformers of the sixteenth century reacted strongly against this whole tendency and insisted that there could be only one mediator between God and humanity, Jesus Christ. In their zeal to abolish exaggerated elements, they ran the real risk of losing that deep reality that Mary had always represented in Christian history. As on so many other matters, the two sides were quickly driven to the extremes of their positions: many of the reformers eliminated Mary entirely, while she became a rallying symbol for the Catholics.

In the seventeenth century in France an intense devotion to Mary grew, but it was sentimental, exaggerated and even heretical, particularly in the concept that one *must* go through Mary to reach Jesus. This devotion declined in the eighteenth century with the rise of the spirit of rationalism, but it became strong again closer to our own time, especially in the period between the two papal declarations: the Immaculate Conception in 1854 and the Assumption in 1950. During these times sodalities, processions and the crowning of statues were all popular.

During this same period alleged apparitions of Mary (at Lourdes and Fatima, for example) also played a significant part. In theology the accent was on her special privileges (mother of God, free from sin, assumed into heaven), rather than on the gospel idea of a young woman caught into a divine plan and having to live by faith. There was even talk of further privileges (co-redeemer with Christ and mediatrix of all graces), though these were in fact rejected by Church authority.

If we look a little more deeply at this history, we can perhaps better understand why certain developments occurred.

GENTLENESS IN GOD

There are both fears and longings within every person. The fears have led to ideas of a god of justice, the longings have led to ideas of a god of mercy. The two have always co-existed and they have rarely been harmonised. Frequently both ideas were taken to extremes: the just god became harsh, while the merciful god became soft and indulgent.

In much of Christian (and especially Catholic) history, this contradiction – between fears and longings, justice and mercy, a harsh and an indulgent deity – led to the popular ideas of a male, rather stern supreme being with a gentle female figure beside him: Mary, who had a unique ability to soften his harshness.

In this process the very exaggerations of popular Marian devotion reflected the true insights that justice and mercy must be harmonised, and that God cannot be adequately presented in stern and male language and imagery. If the official Church frequently presented a harsh and demanding deity, the popular church put Mary up there together with this deity in order to accent the gentleness of God. Devotion to Mary has often been an implicit criticism of an overly institutional, overly rational and overly male church, and of an overly stern and demanding deity. Popular devotion has been wrong in attributing quasi-divine aspects to Mary, but only because it has been profoundly right in insisting on the gentleness of God.

Many Protestant churches have also seen God as harsh and male and, wherever this has occurred, the absence of a gentle female figure has not improved them.

The only way out of this dilemma is to come to the idea that God contains both the male and the female, and is neither harsh nor soft, genuinely combining justice and mercy and hence loves us and wants our growth but for this very reason is not afraid to challenge us to further growth. If we could come to a better understanding of God, the popular need to make Mary quasi-divine would disappear. Then, at long last, Mary would no longer have to carry the impossible burden of being the bearer of softness and gentleness in God and would finally be free to be herself.

In other words, if Mary is to have her proper place in the Christian world, we must first revise our ideas of God.

CULTURAL EXPECTATIONS

In every age the image of Mary has tended to reflect the dominant cultural expectations concerning women. For example, in the fifth century the monastic and ascetical life flourished, so the idea of Mary as virgin received strong emphasis. In the Middle Ages the ideals of courtly love were applied to Mary. In more recent times there was an ideal of the submissive woman, placed on a pedestal and living in a private world of beauty and harmony, but with no real contribution to make outside her family. Much of the imagery of Mary has been at pains to conceal or even deny her sexuality. In a church where celibate males have had a powerful influence, many ideas concerning Mary have been based on a greatly idealised version of those males' own mothers.

However, any form of idealised woman does not help real women, who have too often been presented with the contrast between themselves and the unreachable ideal of Mary as the perfect woman, without sin or fault, virgin and mother. To be both virgin and mother is not an option open to real women, and to present this as in any way an ideal is harmful.

THE SECOND VATICAN COUNCIL (1962–65)

In the closest vote taken at the Council, it was decided to include a treatment of Mary as part of the treatment of the Church rather than have a separate document concerning her alone, that is, to insist that Mary is part of the Church, not someone separate from and above the Church. The closeness of the vote shows the division between two ways of approaching the subject of Mary.

The council stated with crystal clarity that Jesus Christ is the sole mediator between God and the human race, and in its document there is a clear movement towards a Marian theology that is based on the gospels, sees Mary as part of the Church, is open to the sensitivities of other churches, and which leads to sound pastoral practice.

The main concern of the Council, however, was to correct past ideas and it did not always set a creative direction for the future on this topic. In particular, it set no guidelines for authentic popular devotion. It was the document of Pope Paul VI, *Marialis Cultus*, in 1974 that attempted to do this. It renewed the lost dialogue between theology and popular devotion. It then set four guidelines for devotion: it should be based on the gospels, harmonised with the liturgy of the Church, open to the sensitivities of other churches and avoid images that glorify a restricted and passive role for women.[217]

THE SIGNS OF THE TIMES

It is perhaps surprising that both liberation theology and feminist theology have shown some opening towards Mary.

Liberation theology accents the *Magnificat* and sees Mary presented there as a strong and determined woman, a spokesperson for the poor and oppressed.

> The Almighty works marvels for me.
> Holy his name ...
> He puts forth his arm in strength
> and scatters the proud-hearted.
> He casts the mighty from their thrones
> and raises the lowly.
> He fills the starving with good things,
> sends the rich away empty.

This Mary was anything but timid and submissive. If her older cousin needed her, she would instantly travel though the hill country, despite her own pregnancy. She would always speak and act for those who needed her.

Feminist theology was at first negative towards Marian theology, strongly rejecting the sweetly submissive stereotypes found there. More recently there has been a cautious and tentative discovery of positives, as long as we begin with the gospels and the teaching of Vatican II. This theology stresses the feminine qualities of God and believes that, with these firmly in place, strong positive statements can be found in "Mary of the *Magnificat*" and "Mary the woman of faith", struggling to be faithful despite a lack of understanding.

Liberation theology and feminist theology look at the world around us in their search for the liberation of the poor and oppressed and the proper place of women in the world. They are not the only viewpoints, but they are valid viewpoints. In the Church of the future Mary must be relevant to the poor and oppressed and she must be relevant to women.

On the other hand, much of the continuing and widespread popular devotion to Mary tells us that, through both its structures and its teaching, the Church is still proclaiming to many people a god who is too stern, too male, too authoritarian and too distant. It follows that in the hearts of many people Mary still has something of the old quasi-divine role of making real the gentleness of God. After all, if the cause of a problem still exists, it is unlikely that the

---

217 *Marialis Cultus*, February 2, 1974, AAS 66 (1974), pp. 113–168, nos. 29–37.

problem itself will disappear. Thus, Mary must still be set free to be herself. Popular devotion would also warn us that religion cannot be coldly rational, but must contain warmth, closeness, light and colour and, yes, even a dash of sweetness now and then. It warns us that official religion should never leave the people behind.

THE SYMBOLISM OF MARY

If the exaggerations and "pious heresies" of the Catholic Church are out of place, so is the total rejection of Mary, for it is clear that Mary has been an exceptionally powerful symbol within Christian history from its earliest times. There has been far too much real substance consistently there for two thousand years for it all to be simply swept aside.

It seems to me that the future on this subject needs to be concerned with exactly what it is that she represents. I have suggested that it is wrong to use her to imply that God is male and lacking in gentleness, and it is wrong to imply that only Mary can convince this stern deity to give us what we ask for. But if we reject ideas such as these, where do we turn?

I am sure there are many answers to this question. Here I name five.

First, she is a model of the person who must live by *faith*. The Gospel of Luke is quite powerful on this point. Mary is the person who was closer to Jesus than any other human being, but who then had to follow an extraordinary son as he left home and followed paths that were at the same time inspiring, strange and dangerous. Eventually she had to follow him to his death on a cross. Since we must live by faith every day of our lives, this example is a powerful one. If the mother of Jesus had to live by faith, how can we be exempt?

Second, she is Mary of the *Magnificat*, standing up for the poor and the weak, and ready to travel to wherever she is needed, despite the difficulties for herself. She is the great advocate of social justice. So great has been the accent on her gentleness that this aspect of Mary has seldom received the attention it should.

Third, the figure of Mary clearly draws much strength from her *motherhood*, for this is one of the most powerful symbols the world possesses. There is great power in the scene in John's Gospel where Jesus, dying on the cross, says to his mother and the disciple whom he loved, "Here is your son," and, "Here is your mother." It surely justifies Christians in seeing her as a spiritual mother. If we do not need this mother in order to come to the loving God whom we can approach directly, we can, in all the difficulties we meet, often feel a closeness to her and a need for her assistance.

While we must freely acknowledge the exaggerations and even heresies that have abounded in the Catholic Church, the attitudes of some Protestants have at times been perhaps too rational and lacking in feelings. Yes, Jesus is the only person capable of being the bridge between God and the human race, but it would be wrong to conclude that God forbids us to feel a closeness to special saints who help us to come to Jesus. The fact that God is as close to us as our own selves and that God possesses infinite kindness and gentleness does not mean that we weak human beings cannot feel closer to a mother figure such as Mary and need her assistance.

Fourthly, while it is wrong to limit her to the gentle female figure softening the stern male God, she is a constant reminder that it is not sufficient to speak of God in male terms, and that we need female as well as male language and imagery in order to speak about God. There is much in the language of the Church that needs to change.

Fifthly, Mary must not be reduced to the role of a powerful intermediary asking God for favours on our behalf, for our interest in her would then be solely in what we could get out of God through her, and we would not be seeing her as a person in her own right. All prayer should contain elements of adoration, love, thanksgiving, asking and reconciliation, and all prayer to Mary should be nothing more than a means of expressing these same five attitudes towards God through her and with her. Only then does our asking for favours have a proper context, and our asking would always be conditioned by the words of Mary herself: "Be it done to me according to your word." The clear criterion for prayer to Mary should be whether our prayer brings us closer to God or in some manner puts Mary between us and God.

At the wedding feast of Cana, we have the only example of a prayer offered to Jesus by Mary. It is not even a request but a simple statement of fact and contains the minimum number of words: "They have no wine". Mary knew the heart of her son and knew that further words were superfluous. Her response is the only answer to prayer that she ever gave in the gospels, "Do whatever he tells you to do." She has no answer of her own but speaks only of total fidelity to Jesus. If we take this prayer and response as the model of all prayer, then she will surely be someone who brings us closer to God rather than gets between God and us.

As I have sought to follow these lines of thinking, I have gained a greater appreciation of Mary for, in the words of Sally Cunneen, "I feel I am joining a long list of doubters, seekers, and petitioners who have been drawn to this real woman at the centre of the mystery linking God to life on our planet."[218]

Let me end by presenting an image that I would love to see become more popular. In paintings and in sculpture Mary is usually presented either as a sweetly submissive figure or as the mother of a baby or very young child. I have already noted that her sexuality is frequently concealed or denied. We are told that she is the mother of the Church and our mother, and yet art almost never presents her as the loving mother of adult children. The only exceptions are those statues and paintings known as the *Pieta*, where an impossibly young

---

218 *In Search of Mary, The Woman and the Symbol*, Ballantine Books, New York, 1996, pp. 337–338.

Mary holds the body of her Son taken down from the cross. I know of no picture or statue that presents an older woman, with an ample bosom and a lined and wrinkled face that reflects profound, life-long struggles, standing there facing us with the warmest possible smile of welcome on her face, and her arms thrown as wide open as they can be to embrace adult children returning to their parents' house after a long absence. We know that, the moment she has embraced us, she will immediately lead us to her son and show us (if we need this assurance) that God's welcome is as fervent as hers. In my imagination, the right hand of this statue is already slightly turned away towards her son behind her, to indicate that she is leading us to him. Do we not need this image, not to take the place of all other images, but to be added to them as a necessary complement?

CHAPTER 25
THE SECOND VATICAN COUNCIL

Since the book, of which this is one chapter, has at this point been written for myself alone, I feel at liberty to base the chapter overwhelmingly on my own personal summary of one book, *What Happened at Vatican II*, by John W O'Malley.[219] To this I have added some comments from the person I believe was the single greatest and most influential expert at the council, Fr Yves Congar, in his book, *My Journal of the Council*.[220] Furthermore, I was a student in Rome from 1955 to 1965. Needless to say, I had no role in the council, but I was there, I heard many of the stories and met or listened to a number of the people involved. This undoubtedly influenced my thinking and I have dared to include a number of personal comments in this chapter, always in italics.

Where there is the slightest doubt, the ideas come from O'Malley, not from me.

Pius XII wrote forty encyclicals, four of them being major. The first three were quite progressive and opened up the fields of biblical studies, the mystical body, and the liturgy. Then he turned conservative and wrote *Humani Generis* in 1950, condemning many things and seeing problems everywhere, so that there was a return to the concern with Modernism.

I arrived in Rome as a student in 1955 and found that Scripture studies were very slowly opening up, that the theology of the mystical body was inspiring, and that there was much talk about development in the liturgy (though these

---
219 Harvard University Press, Cambridge, Massachusetts, 2008.
220 ATF Press, Adelaide, 2012.

developments had little influence in the seminary where I lived and we had to read about them, as it were, under the covers). At the same time I was required to take an oath against Modernism on no less than seventeen occasions. On the eighteenth I stated that, if I was not believed after seventeen affirmations, the problem was theirs, not mine.

There were also condemnations of something called "la nouvelle theologie" (a disparaging term meaning "this novel theology") which abandoned the philosophical language of the recent past and sought to express theology in more biblical and pastoral language. These condemnations led to the silencing of such great theologians as Congar, Chenu, de Lubac and Rahner, all of whom would play a significant part in Vatican II.

The Council would be a clash between all of this history and the forces that had created the modern world. After one hundred and seventy years of a largely negative response to events, the church would finally begin to come to terms with the Enlightenment, the French revolution and the modern world.

ISSUES BEHIND THE ISSUES

Following from this history, there were three pervasive issues behind the issues at the council, three underlying issues that were present in every single discussion. They represent three permanent tensions in any society: continuity versus change, the centre versus the periphery, and the legal versus the pastoral.

Continuity versus Change

The first issue concerned the circumstances under which change is possible and appropriate in the Church. The Church is essentially conservative, in the sense that it draws its very lifeblood from its belief in the permanent validity of the message it received from Jesus, and it must always proclaim this message in all its fullness. On the other hand, the past must not so bind the present that it is impossible to move forwards in any field when it is essential that we do so. A proper balance must be found between these two forces of proclaiming the message of Jesus and not being so bound to the past: how to be faithful to Jesus and at the same time relevant to the modern world. When does evolution become revolution? This permanent tension in the Church was made far more acute by the definition of infallibility in 1870. The new council did not oppose it directly, but it did raise many issues that queried the truth of earlier statements, and so implicitly raised the question of infallibility.

The solution the Council found to this dilemma was in the combination of two words, one Italian and one French. The Italian word was *aggiornamento*, meaning bringing up to date. The French word was *ressourcement*, meaning going back to the sources. The council sought to bring the Church up to date, not by confronting the immediate past head on, but by going back to a far older tradition based on Scripture and the teaching of the ancient Fathers. The argument behind this was that if it was not always thus in the past, it need not always be thus in the future.

It followed a principle that one writer has called "discontinuity for the sake of a greater continuity", that is, in attempting to reconcile opposing views the Council often reached back behind a particular formulation of truth to an earlier and greater truth. For example, the Council went behind the more static categories of the Church as a perfect society to a more dynamic concept of a Pilgrim Church on a journey and involved in history. It went behind the second millennium's emphasis on hierarchy to the first millennium's greater balance between hierarchy and community. It went behind 1000 years of exclusively clerical decision-making on all matters of faith to revive the ancient idea of the *sensus fidei*, the sense of faith of the whole people of God. It went behind 1000 years of teaching that the bishops' power of governance came from the Pope to the idea that all the bishops' power comes from ordination. It went behind some 1500 years of teaching that only truth has rights to the idea that it is people who have rights, even when they are in error. It went behind much of both the first and second millennium to a rejection of the idea of Christendom. It went behind Gregory VII's virtual rejection of the bishops in his confrontation with the Emperor to a teaching concerning the College of bishops as an equal holder of supreme power within the Church. It went behind the Council of Trent and the whole counter reformation to an appreciation of the independent reception of the great tradition by the separated churches and to open dialogue with them. It went behind the same Council of Trent and Counter-Reformation to a better balance between Scripture and tradition in the life of the Church. It went behind the attitudes and style of Gregory XVI, Pius IX and Pius X in their condemnations of modernity to the sentiments expressed in the first sentence of *Gaudium et Spes*: "The joy and hope, the grief and anguish of the people of our time, especially of those who are poor or afflicted in any way, are the joy and hope, the grief and anguish of the followers of Christ as well. Nothing that is genuinely human fails to find an echo in their hearts."

Among the experts it was Congar, with his massive knowledge of the early Church, who led this trend, while among the bishops it was Maximos IV Saigh who most consistently invoked ancient traditions to challenge the status quo, and he thus opened up for the council fathers a new breadth in the choices they had before them.

This discontinuity with the immediate past for the sake of a greater continuity with the whole history of the Church, this bringing up to date by going back to the sources, sums up much of the Second Vatican Council. It was the council's method of dealing with the weight imposed by the idea of infallibility. It was not always successful, as we shall see, but it did express very well the spirit of the Council.

The Centre and the Periphery

The second issue behind the issues concerns the relationship between the centre and the periphery, between the Vatican and the individual dioceses, between unity and diversity. Within the Council and outside the Council there has been a constant tension between the Roman Curia and the bishops, and there have been tensions between the pope and bishops. As we shall see, there were even some conflicts between the pope and Council. There was among the bishops a deep resentment against high-handed actions by many members of the Roman Curia and, as we shall see, this had a direct effect on many matters at the council.

The Legal versus the Pastoral

The third issue concerns the model according to which authority should be exercised, and the style of the Council. In recent times, we have had very good examples of different styles in Popes John Paul and Benedict on the one side, and Popes John and Francis on the other side. In the same way there has been a dramatic difference between the style of Vatican II and the style of all earlier councils. The Emperor was present at the Council of Nicaea, and this set the tone for councils as imitations of Roman procedure. Councils were legislative bodies like the Roman senate – they made laws. Their canons consisted largely of words of threat and intimidation, of surveillance and punishment, words of a superior speaking to an inferior or even to an enemy. They consisted of power words, the most powerful and constant being "let him be anathema". They dealt with external actions and words.

Against this, the second Vatican Council used equality words such as *people of God*, *collegiality*, *co-operation*, *partnership*, *dialogue*, *conversation*. It used humility words such as *pilgrim* and *servant*. It used words expressing change, such as *progress, development and evolution*. It used interiority words such as *charisma, conscience* and *the call to holiness*. Words such as these could not have appeared in the canons of earlier councils. In this language is to be found much of "the spirit of the Council", the overriding vision that transcends the particulars of the documents. The statements are presented as open-ended, that is, subject to further development. By these changes the Council redefined what a Council is. It adopted the language of persuasion, reconciliation of ideas, invitation and inspiration. To a large extent it put the bishops beside those they were speaking to rather than above them.

The documents must be analysed according to this literary form. This is where many difficulties have arisen. Because of the long history of councils, many people have read the documents as though they were laws, when in fact the Council was trying very hard to move away from such language.

IMMEDIATE PREPARATION

On 25th January 1959 Pope John XXIII announced a new Ecumenical Council. It was a complete shock to everyone, for the entrenched idea in the Vatican was that papal infallibility meant that there was no more need for councils. In response, Cardinal Montini (later Paul VI) commented: "This holy old boy has really put the cat among the pigeons."

There are three reasons why I consider John XXIII one of the greatest of the popes. The first is that for him the gospel truly meant what the word itself means, "good news". This good news filled him with joy, and he constantly radiated a true Christian joy to all around him. The second reason is that the greatness of his office was never allowed to obscure his humanity. The wholeness and goodness of a most likeable human being shone through everything he did. The third and most important reason is that he had the humility to know that he did not have all the answers to the problems facing the Church as it entered the new and difficult world of the 1960s. And so it was with his heart first and his head second that he instinctively turned to the collective wisdom of the whole Church and called a council.

Two thousand eight hundred bishops were invited to the council and 2200 came. At Vatican I there had been 750, while at Trent there were a mere 22 bishops at the first session and even at later sessions there were never more than 200. If a new council were held now, there would be more than five thousand bishops. Figures concerning costs were never published but, if transport and accommodation were included, it would have cost many millions of dollars. Five thousand pages of suggestions for the council were received from the bishops.

It was the first media council. Let us hope that it will be the last totally male council. Let us also hope that it will be the last overwhelmingly European council: even though 64 per cent of the bishops were from outside Europe, the council was almost exclusively the story of Europeans debating issues arising out of European history.

The most controversial issues at the Council would be Scripture, religious liberty and conscience, collegiality, and the Jews. The council would produce sixteen documents: four constitutions, nine decrees and three declarations. All four of the constitutions would be important, the nine decrees would have varying degrees of importance and even two of the three mere declarations would turn out to be of great importance: those on non-Christian religions and on religious liberty.

FIRST SESSION (1962)

On 11 October 1962 more than 2000 bishops in full vestments and mitre processed from the Apostolic Palace through St Peter's Square into the basilica.

It was a sight that had never been seen before and quite possibly will never be seen again.

Pope John gave a rather lengthy speech, much of which gained little attention, so it was only later that it was realised that there were some most important ideas in it. In particular, John looked forward to the future rather than back to the past. He decried the prophets of doom and in this he was implicitly rejecting much of the 19th century. He made a clear distinction between a truth that is permanent, and the manner in which it is expressed, which can change.

There was drama at the very first session. The bishops were told that they had to elect 16 members to each of 10 commissions. They replied that they had just arrived in Rome, knew no one, and couldn't elect the commissions. So the matter was deferred. An important point was involved here, for the organisers of the Council had no interest in bishops' conferences and yet those conferences were essential to the working of the Council, for they were the means by which the bishops came together and discussed the various issues that arose.

Many expected that the Council would be over by Christmas and would involve little more than confirming the documents that had been prepared by various commissions. The Cardinals of the Curia were the presidents of the various commissions and each of them was highly defensive of his own document.

It is also important to be aware that the regulations for the running of the Council were quite poor. They lacked many essential details and so allowed much room for disagreements. This would prove to be a problem. They did not clearly define the scope and limits of the authority of the various bodies responsible for different aspects of the council's business. The relationships of these bodies to one another, to the assembly of bishops and to the pope, were often so vague that they could not be clearly presented in any organisational chart.

It soon became obvious that within the council there was a powerful and vociferous minority and a large but unorganised majority. The clash between the two would take up much of the time of the council.

Among the most famous names of the minority were Cardinals Ottaviani, Ruffini, Siri, Larraona and Santos, Bishop Carli, and non-bishop experts such as Tromp, Fenton, Parente, Piolanti and Garofalo. (The last three taught me, and one of my greatest revelations at the council would be to hear my professors being roundly criticised and outvoted. Congar: "Garofalo, who was sitting beside me, is a very self-satisfied and mediocre man." And yet, he was Rector Magnificus of the university I attended. Of the eleven names I have quoted, seven were Italian and this was no accident. Much of the opposition came from Italy and, in particular, the Curia. There was a certain sense of ownership of the Church there.

In the late 1950s the first American Cardinal was appointed to the Roma Curia, Cardinal Strich. He set sail for Rome but became sick during the voyage and died before he reached his destination. I can still remember the anti-American jokes that broke out among the Curia, all along the line that God was intervening "to prevent such a calamity from occurring".

Some of the most famous names of the majority were Bea (Germany), Willebrands (Netherlands), Frings (Germany), Suenens (Belgium), Konig (Austria), Phillips (Belgium), Maximos IV Saigh (Melkite, Lebanon), and the non-bishop experts Congar, Chenu and de Lubac from France, Rahner and Ratzinger from Germany, Küng from Switzerland, Schillebeeckx from the Netherlands, and on one subject Murray from the USA. The best organised on this side were the Belgians from the university of Louvain, and Congar joked that it should be called 'The Council of Louvain sitting in Rome'.

It can be seen from this that non-Europeans were rather marginal, and that it was to a large extent a conflict between Southern and Northern Europe. Bishops from Asia, Africa and South America had their concerns (such as how to be a Christian without being European), but they tended to be pushed aside.

I came to realise that my entire training for priesthood came from the minority side, and that a much richer and broader theology existed outside it. This would be a significant part of the journey of my years as a priest.

Congar in his journal several times uses the phrase: "The perfect is the enemy of the good." He argued that at this council no one was going to get everything he wanted, so he was prepared to let pass by him many things that he did not think were perfect. Küng, on the other hand, showed less willingness to compromise and, as a result, achieved less than Congar.

LITURGY

Pope John wanted to start with a more pastoral topic and chose the liturgy. He had organised for a draft on the topic to have been prepared by several groups numbering 65 persons under the leadership of Professor Annibale Bugnini (who had taught me). It was a good text that would undergo little change before being approved by the Council. The president of the commission was Cardinal Gaetano Cicognani, who was in poor health, so he had not played an active part. However, he then read the completed document, didn't like what he read and refused to sign it. An appeal was made to Pope John, who in turn appealed to the president's brother, Amleto Cicognani, the Cardinal Secretary of State, who in turn convinced his still-reluctant brother to sign.

Gaetano Cicognani then died and was replaced by a Spaniard, Cardinal Larraona, who also didn't approve and so was a poor chairman. He sacked Bugnini and replaced him with someone who had not been on the commission and knew nothing of all the work that had gone to produce it. Bugnini was also sacked from his teaching positions in Rome. The Council was indeed made up of very ordinary human beings. Some people would pray in a most fervent manner to the Holy Spirit, but then didn't really trust the Spirit to guide the council and worked to gain their own ends by less than spiritual means.

Most speakers approved of the document. Outside the basilica some bishops from the new churches of Africa and Asia held press conferences, insisting particularly on cultural adaptation of the liturgy. They had their impact, though it was a pity that they did not feel able to say these things in the Council itself. As always, one of the most trenchant inside the Council was the Melkite patriarch Maximos IV. He said (paraphrased),

> The almost-absolute value assigned to Latin in the liturgy strikes us from the Eastern church as strange. Christ after all spoke the language of his contemporaries. In the east there has never been a problem about the proper liturgical language, for all languages are liturgical. The Latin language is dead. But the church is living, and its language must also be living because it is intended for us human beings and not for angels.

The speeches went from October 22 to November 13, with many speakers repeating earlier material. The regulations contained no provision for putting a stop to debates, so the speeches went on until eventually an appeal was made to Pope John and he intervened. There was drama during the speeches. At one stage Ottaviani criticised the use of any language other than Latin, the idea of concelebration and the whole style of the document. He went over time and was rung off but ignored this until he was rung off again and the entire Council started applauding. He stormed out and boycotted the Council for two weeks.

The document was approved overwhelmingly, by a vote of 2162 to 46. It was remarkable how little the document had changed from the original draft document. There were some sentences that certainly needed more work, for example, "Let the rite and formula of the sacrament of penance be revised so as more clearly to express the effect of the sacrament." It would take much more than this to revive the sacrament of penance. Latin was retained in the Mass, but some parts of the Mass, for example, the readings, were allowed in the vernacular. Then after the Council, by its own internal logic this became extended to the whole Mass. It is worth noting, however, that it was not the Council itself that made this dramatic change.

A new committee was set up to implement the document and it was Bugnini who was resurrected to chair this committee. Opposition to him, however, had not gone away and he was appointed as papal Nuncio to Iran, where no one celebrates mass in Latin. It is hard not to see this as a malicious act, a classic application of an old Vatican principle: *Promoveatur ut amoveatur* – Let him be promoted so that he may be removed.

This first document to be discussed and approved did establish certain principles. It was the first application of the idea of *aggiornamento* through *ressourcement*, of bringing up to date by going back to the sources. For example, greater lay participation in the Mass, the greater significance of the Liturgy of the Word, and communion in the hand, were a return to ancient practices. Secondly, it allowed some measure of adaptation to local circumstances. Thirdly, through this document the bishops of the Council began the process of realising that they were in charge and could actually determine the future of the church. Fourthly, it greatly encouraged the active participation of the congregation in the Mass, compared to what had been in place in preceding centuries. On this point however, there is still much more work to do. I believe that, to far too great an extent, the Mass still consists of thousands upon thousands of words being poured over a passive congregation.

SOURCES OF REVELATION

As one of the non-Catholic observers commented: "At this point the dam broke", for the fate of the whole council would to a great extent depend on this document.

Ottaviani reappeared to present the draft for implementation of the document on the liturgy. He began by claiming that, because his document had been approved by the Pope, it could not be changed by the Council. Looking back afterwards, it was statements like this that most strongly galvanised the bishops to resist what he was saying. He went on to say,

> You have heard many people speak about the lack of a pastoral tone in this draft. Well, I say that the first and most fundamental pastoral task is to provide correct doctrine. The Lord's greatest commandment is precisely that: teach all peoples. Teaching correctly is what is fundamental to being pastoral. Those who are concerned with a pastoral style can later give the church's teaching a fuller pastoral expression. But take notice: Councils speak in a style that is orderly, lucid, concise, and not in the style of the sermon or a pastoral letter of some Bishop or other, not even in the style of an encyclical of the supreme Pontiff. This style of Council discourse is sanctioned by its use throughout the ages.

The secretary of the commission, Garofalo, confirmed this idea by saying, "Everybody knows that the principal task of an ecumenical Council is to defend and promote Catholic doctrine. A Council cannot renounce its duty to condemn errors." It may be seen that all three issues behind the issues were in play here.

The draft they presented was truly a summing up of all the ideas of the past, almost as though Pius XII had never written his encyclical on biblical studies. It contained five chapters. The first stated that Scripture and tradition are two distinct sources. The second chapter dealt with inspiration and said that God, the principal author, moved the human author to write what he intended. Thus, the Bible is entirely free from error, in both religious and secular matters. The third chapter dealt with the Old Testament and said that the whole reason for the Old Testament and what gives it its momentum is movement to the New Testament. The fourth chapter dealt with the New Testament and condemned the calling into question of the historical accuracy of the Gospels' accounts of Jesus' words and deeds, even in the infancy narratives. The fifth chapter dealt with Scripture in the life of the Church and the authority of the magisterium was an overriding theme.

(One of my university professors, Mariani, had presented us with a 600-page Latin text Latin text seeking to prove the Mosaic authorship of the five books of the Pentateuch by disproving the theory of an author named Wellhasusen, who was the first to introduce the idea of the four sources: Jahwist, Elohist, Deuteronomic and Priestly.)

Two Cardinals (Lienart and Frings), supported by many others, stood up and said: *Schema non placet*. This did not mean that they disagreed merely with some ideas in the document, but that they rejected the entire document as not being in any way an adequate basis for discussion. They wanted the entire document taken away and a new one written from the beginning. It was one of the most dramatic moments in the whole Council. It did not come out of nowhere. For some weeks there had been reports by Rahner, Ratzinger and Schillebeeckx circulating around Rome. The major problems concerned the idea of two separate sources, new methods of exegesis, fundamentalism, and the language of the draft.

The Council for Christian Unity had been set up by Pope John as a formal body of the council. It had tried again and again to dialogue with Ottaviani, but he had refused. So now the secretary of the Council of Christian Unity claimed that the document was anti-ecumenical. Thus, one body set up by the Pope was rejecting the work of another body set up by the same pope.

After a number of speeches, a vote was taken as to whether the draft should remain or be completely replaced. This vote was put to the bishops on the twentieth of November but in the unfortunate form: should the discussion be interrupted? This meant that a yes vote was a vote against the draft, while a no vote was a vote in favour. Confusion reigned until the bishops finally understood that yes meant no and no meant yes. 1368 voted to reject the entire draft while 822 voted to continue discussion of it. This was a clear majority, but it was 100 short of the required two-thirds majority. The next morning, however, there was a note from Pope John, referring the whole matter to a new mixed commission from the Doctrine of the Faith and Christian Unity.

The subject of the sources of revelation would have an extremely troubled history for the next three years and the document would be approved only in the last days of the Council in 1965.

THE MASS MEDIA

By now there were only two weeks left of the first session and everyone was rather washed out after the drama concerning revelation. It turned out that there were only three days of discussion of this document and it was then approved. This document on the implementation of the liturgical reforms is generally considered to be the weakest document of the entire Council in showing how little the bishops understood the mass media. Meanwhile there was chaos in the press office. In accordance with good Roman tradition there had been the attempt to keep everything secret, even though the media had an intense interest in what was going on. There were constant leaks and there were articles and books claiming to tell what was really going on in the Council.

THE CHURCH

Even though there was little more than a week left, the Council moved on to the next scheduled draft. This happened to be the draft document on the Church, one of the central questions of the entire Council, so all the tension and drama was stirred up again. Ottaviani introduced the draft this time by saying,

> The concern of those who prepared the draft was that it be as pastoral and biblical as possible, not academic, and that it be done in a form comprehensible by everybody. I say this because I expect to hear the usual litany from the fathers of the Council – its academic, it's not ecumenical, it's not pastoral, it's negative, and other things like that. Further, I'll tell you what I really think. I believe that I and the speaker for the commission are wasting our words because the outcome has already been decided. Those whose constant cry is "Take it away! Take it away! Give us a new draft!" are now ready to open fire. I'll tell you something you may not know even before this draft was distributed. Listen to me! Listen to me! - even before it was distributed, an alternative draft had already been produced. Yes, even before the merits of this draft had been looked at, the jury has rendered its verdict. I have no choice now but to say no more because, as Scripture teaches, when nobody is listening, words are a waste of time.

The document presented was 82 pages long and contained 11 chapters. The first chapter was entitled the Nature of the Church Militant. It worked from the top down, with a strong emphasis on obedience to authority, especially papal authority. A little cowed by Ottaviani's words, the responses were more mild, but the speakers still saw major difficulties. For example, Frings said that the draft was not Catholic for it did not reflect the universal church. He said that the Council must rise above the ideas of the 16th and 19th centuries and place the Church in a wider context. He said that the draft reflected the manuals still current in many seminaries. (Here were Cardinals criticising what I had been taught a few years earlier and doing so just one kilometre away from St Peter's!)

Seventy-seven speeches were given, until there were only a few days left. Then after talking with Pope John, Cardinal Suenens of Belgium said that what the Council needed was a central theme that would lend a basic orientation to everything. He suggested "The Church of Christ, Light of the World." The first part of this statement suggested that the Council should look at the inner life of the Church, while the second suggested it look at the Church's relationship with the world. Hence, he said, there should be three dialogues: with self, with fellow Christians, and with the world. After this talk there was prolonged applause. It achieved three things. Firstly, it meant that the Council was no longer dealing with scattered documents but with one central theme. Secondly it meant that the drafts needed more than a simple touching up, they needed to be in accord with this central idea. Thirdly his speech sowed the seeds of a new document not yet mentioned, a document that would become *Gaudium et Spes*, the document on the Church in the Modern World. On the next day Cardinal Montini supported Suenen's idea and his support was important.

John announced the formation of a co-ordinating commission that would look at all documents.

Pope John then gave his final speech, and it was poignant, for it was the last time that most of the bishops would see him.

BETWEEN SESSION ONE AND TWO

The bishops returned home hopeful but frustrated. They were hopeful because many good things had happened, and they had a sense that something of massive importance was taking place. They had come to realise that they were not a rubber stamp and were, indeed, creating history. They were gratified by the attention the council was receiving in all countries. But they were frustrated because there were 70 documents to be studied and only two had been finalised. There had been over 600 speeches but a certain number of these were banal and repetitious. More importantly, a series of speeches is not really a debate. Pope John had appointed the Curial Cardinals as heads of each of the preparatory commissions and this meant that the Council was essentially dealing with a series of extremely conservative documents. And yet in one way this did have a powerful positive effect, for many bishops, who were struggling with the massive step up of being part of a universal council, said to themselves, "I don't know what I want, but I know that it is not these conservative documents." Congar in his journal says that the negative documents also had the positive effect of making people who wanted change look really seriously at their own arguments and seek to improve them.

Much hope was placed on the co-ordinating commission, and it did fill a real gap in the organisation of the council. By the end of January, this group had reduced the 70 texts to 17 and had handed down directives about the form and substance of the documents. In a real sense it made the Council possible.

Within some particular commissions the discussions were very stormy. In the commission dealing with the document on revelation there were nine very stormy sessions, until the document was rejected and the preparation of an entirely new one was begun. This new document would not, however, be ready for the second session and would come up only at the third.

The commission on the Church was also stormy. The chapters were reduced from 11 to 4. The document was given the new title, "On the Mystery of the Church." Such had been the dissatisfaction with the conservative draft presented earlier that by now no less than nine new drafts were being circulated. The group decided on the one created by Bishop Phillips from Louvain. This was met with a bitter attack from Ottaviani, Browne and Tromp, who said that the commission had gone beyond its powers in rejecting the original draft and substituting Phillips'. When it became obvious that the majority favoured the new, they launched into a bitter attack on the text, calling it dangerous and relativistic. If this was not bad enough, the discussion then moved on to the most controversial topic of all, that of collegiality.

There were still gaps in the regulations. There was a council of presidents, a group of four moderators, a co-ordinating commission and a secretariat, and it was not at all clear what the relationship was between these four bodies, and which of these bodies was meant to be the intermediary between the pope and the council. In fact, all four acted as intermediary at different times and this created confusion. There was an even a more important question behind all this: Who ran the council – the pope or the bishops? Without ever seeking to resolve the theological question, John had in practice given the answer that the bishops ran the council and he would intervene only in exceptional circumstances. No one objected to the few interventions he made. But all that was about to change.

In June 1963 Pope John died, and everyone felt that the great inspiration for the Council had gone and would now have to be found elsewhere. The conclave that followed was stormy, for it was a struggle for control of the Council and hence for the soul of the Church. One of the Cardinals, Cardinal Testa, later said, "Hair-raising things happened at this conclave." The Cardinals eventually chose Cardinal Montini as the new Pope. He was not the first choice of the conservatives, who had earlier managed his removal from the Curia to Milan, but he was the compromise candidate, for he was moderate and cautious.

Congar says of him (paraphrased):

> Cardinal Montini is an extremely intelligent and well-informed person. He creates a deep impression of holiness. He will take up John XXIII's programme, but obviously not in the same way and perhaps not altogether in his spirit. He will be much more Roman, more in the style of Pius XII. Like Pius he will want to decide things on the basis of ideas, and not simply let things evolve by themselves from openings created by a movement of the heart.

He made changes to the regulations, but he still left too many different bodies in place and with no clear lines of communication between them or with himself. This led to everybody trying to get his ear, and Paul let this happen, with very serious consequences. He would intervene in the Council far more than John had and would even use papal power to determine questions, even taking them out of the hands of the Council, for example, reform of the Curia. He wrote an encyclical on the Church at the very time this was a hot topic at the Council. Indeed, he sometimes seemed to be setting himself up in competition with the Council. He was concerned for papal power and appointed himself as a guardian of orthodoxy. He appointed himself as arbiter of procedural disputes, sometimes even in first instance. He even put in submissions as a Bishop, though a Pope really cannot do this. Increasingly it came to be felt that the true site of the Council was not the floor of the Council but the papal apartments. On the question of who runs the council, it time and again seemed that his answer was that the pope ran the council, and the bishops had little more than an advisory role.

SESSION TWO

The Church

It will be remembered that the commission had adopted the draft of Bishop Phillips and reduced the chapters to four. They were:
1. the mystery of the church;
2. the people of God;
3. the hierarchical constitution of the church; and
4. the call to Holiness.

Thus, the Church is first of all a mystery of divine presence in the world, then it is a pilgrim people, and only then does it have a form of government to direct its activity. The universal call to holiness is the essence of its work. It is not simply a community of people who have decided to come together for mutual benefit, but a communion of people who seek to share in the same divine mystery of God's presence in the world. Its strength is in the story of Jesus Christ, which is its foundation; its weakness is in the human beings who make it up, especially at the higher levels of its government. Its purpose is to draw weak human beings ever closer to the example of Jesus Christ, hence the universal call to holiness.

The strong vertical line of ruler and subjects was replaced by the horizontal line of the people of God. The word "subjects" was abolished altogether. The whole was presented in a far more pastoral style and language.

The call to holiness was radical. Holiness is what the Church is all about. From this point on, the idea of the call to holiness came to be part of every document of the Council. For some the great emotional block was the idea that, if holiness was for everyone, married people could even (shock, horror) have sex and still be holy!

The council then considered the relationship of the Catholic Church to other religions. There have been three questions. The first is: Can those who do not believe in Jesus and have not been baptised be saved? On this Vatican II endorsed a far more optimistic view and really settled this question.

The second question is: If they can be saved, are they saved through the practice of their own religion or despite it? On this the council was less definite but still positive ("The Catholic Church rejects nothing which is true and holy in these religions.") Work has continued and the Church appears to be moving towards a positive answer.

If through their religion, do these religions enjoy a positive meaning in God's plan of salvation for the whole human race? On the third question there has been movement towards an affirmative answer, but there has also been the response of Benedict XVI in *Dominus Jesus*. Work continues.

The council also raised the question of permanent deacons, but it intended married deacons, raising again the question of sex and holiness. It became disputed.

Under Chapter Three the council discussed collegiality and this became one of the most fiercely contested questions of the council, for it seemed to attack solemn statements of the First Vatican Council concerning papal power. That Council had said:

> And so, if anyone says that the Roman pontiff has only the office of inspection and direction, but not the full and supreme power of jurisdiction over the whole church, not only in matters that pertain to faith and morals, but also in matters that pertain to the discipline and government of the church throughout the whole world; or if anyone

says that he has only a more important part and not the complete fullness of this supreme power; or if anyone says that this power is not ordinary and immediate either over each and every church or over each and every shepherd and faithful, *anathema sit.*

This clash led to one of the most heated moments of the Second Vatican Council. Because the matter was so important, 119 speeches and 59 written submissions were allowed. The four cardinal moderators of the Council's sessions then met with the Pope to discuss how best to proceed. They agreed that they would draw up a number of votes on particular issues to guide the commissions in redrafting the text. They drew up eight questions but made the fatal mistake of not discussing them with the appropriate commission.

The questions were to be presented to the Council after Mass the next day, but during the Mass various observers saw urgent and animated discussions taking place between the moderators and the secretary of state. Then the moderator for the day announced without explanation that the vote had been postponed. It became clear that opponents had got wind of what was happening and had hastened to see Paul VI. Paul had at first endorsed the plan of the moderators, but had then, under pressure, gone back on this, even ordering that any ballots be burned, and he had then in practice communicated his decision to the moderators in a manner calculated to humiliate them.

Confusion reigned. During those days the place of the council was definitely in the papal apartments. Then five votes were put, but of the morning of the vote Congar in his Journal comments: "While chatting with several bishops, including some French ones, I was astonished to see how little they realised what is involved in the five votes that they are asked to cast today. They do not see clearly what is at stake doctrinally, the foundations. Strange business! Was it like this at Nicea and Chalcedon?" (*My Journal of the Council*, p. 404)

The result of the five votes was:
1. Should the draft assert that Episcopal consecration is the supreme grade of the sacrament of orders? 34 against.
2. Should the draft assert that every legitimately consecrated Bishop in communion with the other bishops and the Roman Pontiff is a member of the body of bishops? 104 against.
3. Should the draft assert that the so-called body or College of bishops in its evangelising, sanctifying and governing tasks [be] successor to the original College of the Apostles and, always in communion with the Roman Pontiff, enjoy full and supreme power over the universal church? 336 against.
4. Should the draft assert that the aforementioned power of the College of bishops, united with their head, belongs to it by divine ordinance and therefore not by papal delegation? 408 against.

5. Should the draft assert that it is opportune to consider the reinstatement of the diaconate as a permanent grade of sacred ministry, according to needs in different parts of the Church? 525 against.

(A sociologist once told me that it is pointless to hold a vote on any matter which gives to or takes away either power or freedom from a certain body, for the members of that body will always vote for the maximum power and freedom for themselves. We can see the same thing happening here. We should also note that the negative vote increased with each successive vote. We can further note that the question concerning the diaconate simply avoided the question of celibacy, and even so received 525 negative votes because many saw the question of celibacy as implicit. In the main the negative votes were large enough to give encouragement to the minority to continue with their fight.)

The Council then moved on to the chapter on the people of God, especially the laity. The comments were positive, but they had to deal with the tension between the vertical and the horizontal in the Church. Cardinal Siri asked that praise of the laity be toned down: "Encouragement is a good thing, but it should not go overboard." Despite these negatives the Council gave a massive boost to the role of the laity in the apostolate of the Church.

They then moved on to Chapter Four, the call to Holiness. Obviously, no one could possibly oppose this.

The question of the role of Mary in the Church arose. Was she so important that she should have a document of her own or was it sufficient to treat her as part of the Church? This became one of the most emotional and tenacious topics of the Council. There were many who wanted a new Marian dogma as the summit of the Council. Others wanted devotion centred on the liturgy and the Bible rather than on private devotions. Such emotion was aroused that it risked splitting the Council. Pope Paul was so alarmed that, together with the moderators, he decided to appoint two speakers: Santos and Koenig. They spoke and then a vote was held with only 40 votes difference between the positive and negative. It was the closest vote at the entire Council. (In his Journal Congar frequently comments on the persistence of this question of Mary in the different commissions. He also comments on the very high level of emotions that the question aroused.)

Bishops

This commission had not held a single meeting since the last session. Instead, any work done on it had been done by its secretary, Carli, and he had not even submitted what he had done to the commission. He took no account at all of collegiality and assumed that all powers held by a Bishop were a delegation from the Pope. He identified the Roman congregations with the Pope. Even members of the commission itself criticised the draft in the Council.

Ruffini warned of the dangers of bishops' conferences encroaching on the work of the Vatican, and the relationship between the two would in fact later become a serious problem.

Virtually the only progressive Italian Cardinal, Lercaro, spoke of the need for a structure to implement collegiality. That question, too, is still with us today.

Frings attacked the whole centralising tendency in the Church. He said the question is not what is delegated to bishops by the Pope, but what is reserved to the Pope for the sake of unity. There should be clear rules for congregations, including the Holy Office. No one should ever be judged without being heard. This last comment was met with applause. Ottaviani replied to Frings and demanded an apology, and the media loved it.

In the end, the commission was expanded and, rather than revise the draft, it wrote a new one.

ECUMENISM

It was a surprise to many that this subject was even being discussed, but Pope John had insisted on it. The draft statement came from the Secretariat for Christian unity. There was discussion and many small changes, but there was overwhelming support for the document. It was one of the great changes brought about by the Council. (In all the lectures on dogmatic theology from Piolanti, all I ever learned about other Christian churches came under the heading of "Errors". Remember that at this time it was still forbidden for Catholics to attend weddings or funerals in non-Catholic churches.)

Chapter Four of this document dealt with the relationship with the Jewish people, again put there by Pope John. This topic would have a far more difficult passage and would end up in a different document.

Chapter Five was on religious liberty. This became one of the most difficult questions of the entire Council and would also end up in a different document.

With this the second session came to an end. If it provided no finalised documents, it had dealt with collegiality, ecumenism and religious liberty, all topics crucial to the Council. At the concluding session Pope Paul announced that he was soon to visit Israel and this would be the first journey outside Italy by a Pope in 500 years.

BETWEEN SESSIONS TWO AND THREE

In January 1964 Pope Paul visited Israel and there met with the ecumenical patriarch Athenagoras in an historic meeting (the first since 1445). This journey was the centre of world attention.

By this time everyone connected with the Council was tired and wanted the third session to be the last and worked towards this end. They were also concerned with the growing costs of the Council and with the absence of the bishops from their dioceses.

Within the commissions the document on the Church met the most opposition, because collegiality was seen as contrary to the first Vatican Council. How could collegiality be combined with the statements of that council?

In May Pope Paul wrote to the Council offering 13 "suggestions" for this document. This was the first of a long series of interventions that became known as "the red pencil of Paul VI". Furthermore, he had waited until the document was virtually signed and sealed before putting them forward. The commission replied to his suggestions but was obviously embarrassed at having to deal with "suggestions" coming from the Pope. His suggestions indicated the way he was thinking. For example, he wanted the text to say that the bishops would exercise their power "according to the prescriptions of the pope" and that the pope was "responsible only to the Lord".

In August that year he published his first encyclical on the Church at the very time when the Council was discussing exactly the same topic. The great positive of this encyclical was that it used the word "dialogue" 77 times, and the idea occupies two thirds of the entire document. From this the word entered almost every document of the Council and became a *leitmotiv*. On the other hand, the encyclical said that, while Paul "wanted the council to have full liberty in its deliberations, he would at the proper moment and in the proper manner express his judgement on them".

Meanwhile the commission on revelation was processing 2481 recommendations. The document on bishops was totally rewritten in the light of the document on the Church. On the subjects of the Jews and religious liberty there was fierce debate. Work also began on the document on the Church in the modern world, but there were several different texts, including one from the Polish bishops through their spokesperson Cardinal Wojytla. His draft would be rejected.

Certain changes were made in the regulations, so that things would work a little more smoothly, but the papal apartments had begun to compete with the floor of St Peters as the Council's centre of gravity.

A few days before the Council resumed, Cardinal Larraona presented to the Pope a document signed by 25 Cardinals (16 from the Curia), saying that Chapter Three dealing with collegiality would be a mortal danger to the Church. These Cardinals insisted that the Pope should remove it and refer it to a commission of theologians. Paul responded sharply, but private interventions continued.

I will quote from Larraona's letter, because it sums up much about the minority's whole approach:

> Holy Father, in this moment of history that we consider heavy with consequences, we place all our confidence in you, who received from

our Lord the duty of confirming your brothers, the duty you generously accepted saying, "We will defend [the] holy Church from errors of doctrine and morals that inside and outside threaten its integrity and blind us to its beauty." The document put the full burden of the Council on the Pope's shoulders and foresaw catastrophe if he did not take radical action immediately, without recourse to the Council.

On the opening day of the third session there was another missive: experts were to answer questions asked by bishops, but not volunteer opinions. They were not to promote their opinions in any organised or public way through interviews or talks. They were not to criticise the Council to the media or communicate inside information.

THIRD SESSION (1964)

The third session opened with a concelebration by the Pope and 24 other bishops from 19 countries.

When the 25 Cardinals saw that Paul had rejected their idea, they wanted the debate on collegiality reopened. This was rejected, but a compromise was accepted: there would be three presentations in favour of the text, and one against, reflecting the earlier voting. This was a final concession to the minority. Franic spoke against the idea of power coming from ordination, against collegiality, and against married deacons. Then Koenig, Parente and Jimenez spoke in favour. The extraordinary one was Parente, for he had been a leader of those opposing change. What motivated him to change sides on this issue is hard to know. Larraona kept bombarding the Pope. All votes, including those concerning collegiality, passed by large majorities. The document and collegiality seemed secure.

RELIGIOUS LIBERTY

This document had now been separated from the one on ecumenism and it had been fully revised. This was a subject on which the minority believed that there simply could not be any change.

In earlier times the attitude had been that the people should follow the religion of their ruler. The teaching of the Church said that error has no rights, and this idea was contained in every Catholic textbook. The opposition to it began with the French philosopher Jacques Maritain, but then grew strong in the United States in accordance with the ideas of John Courtney Murray. The idea was condemned by Ottaviani in 1953 and Murray was told not to publish anything further. But then there was all the controversy that surrounded the election of the first Catholic President – John F. Kennedy – so the United States bishops were en masse in favour of change.

Their argument was that it is not truth that has rights, but people. They have the right to follow their conscience, even when they are in error. This idea went all the way back to the ancient truth that the act of faith cannot be coerced. Its supporters used the language of evolving, developing, progressing, but many saw it simply as changing earlier teaching. The first speaker was Ruffini, who said that there is only one true religion, so there can be no freedom of choice. He said that the document was designed for Protestant countries and would lead to unbridled license. He said it was not evolution but revolution. Lefebvre predicted ruin for the Church.

The document was supported by the Americans, by the bishops from Eastern Europe and from most English-speaking countries. After the speeches, the document was sent for revision, but it was obvious that there was still strong opposition. In fairness, one must say that, after all the talk of *ressourcement*, it was difficult to deny that this was an open change with a long-standing teaching. Together with collegiality, it is perhaps the clearest and most difficult case the Council considered concerning that permanent underlying issue of when change is evolution and when it is revolution, and whether *ressourcement* is a sufficient answer to infallibility.

THE JEWISH PEOPLE

The origin of this document was in an approach to Pope John by Jules Isaac, a man involved in Christian-Jewish dialogue. It took place in the aftermath of the Holocaust and of long Christian preaching against the Jews. The most inflammatory question was: Were the Jewish people responsible for the death of Jesus and, therefore, the death of God (deicide)? On the other hand, the question was also inflammatory to the Arab bishops at the Council, for they felt that in this the Vatican was moving towards recognition of the state of Israel.

There was a serious and open disagreement between Pope Paul and Cardinal Bea over the question of deicide. Bea wanted to absolve not only the Jews of today, but also the Jews of the time of Christ (other than some leaders). He said that it was only the leaders who had plotted the death of Jesus and that Jesus himself had said of the people, "They know not what they do." Eventually the draft said: "Let everyone take care not to impute to the Jews of our times what happened during the passion of Christ."

Nine days later Pope Paul dropped a bomb, definitely far more than his red pencil. He sent two letters to Cardinal Bea as prefect of the Secretariat for Christian Unity. He wanted a completely new commission for religious liberty. He took it out of the hands of the Secretariat for Christian Unity and added four conservative members, including Lefebvre. In the second letter he took the question of the Jews out of the hands of the Secretariat and wanted a mixed commission that would include Ottaviani. He wanted the question of the Jews to become a brief note in chapter 2 of the document on the Church.

Word of the letters reached the media, and there was a flurry of conspiracy theories. The bishops were also confused about what had happened and were asking themselves what was the point of having a Council if it could be set aside in this manner.

There was a flurry of letters and of personal meetings with the Pope. Within a few days the matter was settled by a return to the situation before the two letters. No-one apologised, and no one explicitly disowned anything that had been written, but Bea emerged with his texts firmly in hand. The affair was typical of a situation where messages were conveyed indirectly or through third parties, so that it became almost impossible to know how to interpret what was really going on and to whom to address questions or grievances. In practice, the solution was always to run to the Pope.

REVELATION

There had been significant changes since this document was last discussed two years earlier. For example, the earlier draft had implied that all revelation consists of doctrines expressed in a series of timeless propositions. This idea had held sway for centuries and was in every seminary textbook. The new draft said that what is revealed is not individual truths, but Truth itself, that is, God, both in acts and in words. Ultimately, this Truth is the revelation of the person and story of Jesus Christ. God is also the source of revelation, not Scripture and not tradition.

In the earlier document tradition had been presented as containing truths that Scripture did not contain. Moreover, tradition was the interpreter of Scripture, so that, though Scripture is inspired, its sense cannot be fully and certainly understood and made clear except by tradition. Scripture and tradition are equal, but, according to this older idea, tradition in practice has the more privileged role. The new draft put scripture first and said that tradition cannot contradict scripture.

For the minority there were also the questions of the Immaculate Conception and the Assumption. Unless there were truths revealed outside the scriptures, how could these two doctrines be maintained? And if you wanted high drama at this Council, just mention the word "Mary". Tradition containing truths not in Scripture could also be found in the documents of the first Vatican Council and in encyclicals from Pius IX to Paul VI. Thus there was also a deep suspicion of modern exegesis.

Despite this, the majority favoured the new document. There was much support for Chapter Six, which encouraged the reading of the Bible by all Catholics. The document would not resolve all problems, but it gave Scripture a whole new place and honour within the Church. At the end it was realised that the document had stood the test, so it needed to be refined, but not rejected. But there was still fierce opposition and it would have a difficult course.

LAITY

This was the first time this subject had ever been discussed at a Council, and it received general approval. This led to a far broader and more important role of the laity in the work of the Church. Needless to say, some bishops were negative. For example, Browne was concerned that "lay people are obliged to obey their parish priest". And a bishop named Bauerlein said: "The first and principal task of the laity is to beget children because of the shortage of vocations to the priesthood."

THE CHURCH IN THE MODERN WORLD

This was the first time that a Council had ever looked outwards in this way and certainly the first time a council ever said anything positive about the world. It dealt with:
- the human vocation
- the church in service to God and humankind
- how Christians should conduct themselves in the world; and
- some special responsibilities of Christians in today's world.

These responsibilities were:
- the human person in society
- marriage and the family
- the promotion of culture
- economic and social issues; and
- human solidarity and peace.

There were more than 150 speeches and it is impossible to summarise them. Some of the issues concerned a balance between the Church's human endeavours and its supernatural mission, a debate between a more positive Thomistic view of the world and a more negative Augustinian view, and calls for the condemnation of communism. Two bishops spoke strongly on a more positive role for women in the Church.

There were heated arguments on marriage, particularly concerning the so-called primary end of begetting children and the secondary end of the mutual support of spouses. The council eventually dropped this language of "primary" and "secondary" entirely. The Council made the consciences of the spouses the deciding factor for the number of children and did not explicitly reaffirm a condemnation of birth control. Then Cardinal Suenens said that a change in the teaching on contraception might be in order. He also said that the names of the commission set up by the Pope should be released so that the members might receive the most copious information and the whole people of God be represented. This was seen as a call for a referendum on the subject of birth control. Ruffini promptly demanded that Suenens should be removed as a moderator and a visibly angry Paul VI confronted Suenens, demanding a retraction.

Things seemed to be proceeding smoothly and constructively towards the end of this third session, but then, in the last week, there was a bombshell, a cyclone and an earthquake.

The bombshell was that Paul sent a list of 19 additions to the text on ecumenism and on this occasion insisted that they be accepted. At this point the text had been finalised and the bishops had already voted on each chapter, so that all that was left was the final vote. Some of the 19 additions were of little importance, others more important. What was at issue was the method the Pope had adopted of suddenly intervening at this very late stage and insisting on his changes. It was a sharp reminder that for Paul even a council was subject to him. Even a council was ultimately advisory. Many of the non-Catholic observers were quite upset by this display of raw papal power.

The cyclone occurred when Paul sent to the Council what was called a preliminary explanatory note to be added to the major document on the Church concerning collegiality. In it Paul seemed to be telling the bishops what their own document on collegiality meant. The language was highly technical and was opaque to many bishops. Even Ratzinger called it "a very intricate text" marked by ambivalence and ambiguities. Some claimed it changed nothing, but the minority was ecstatic. Ruffini informed Paul of his pleasure with this "most opportune note" and asked that it be attached to the main text itself. The note in fact gave those who opposed collegiality a tool they could and would use to interpret the chapter as a reaffirmation of the status quo. If there was anything about the note that should have given the leaders of the majority pause, it was the ready, even gleeful, support the note received from those council fathers who had done everything they could to scuttle collegiality.

(As an aside, Mary McAleese, former President of Ireland and eminent jurist, has written a book entitled *Quo Vadis: Collegiality in the Code of Canon Law*. In this book she analyses all the statements made by the Council and the code concerning collegiality and concludes that there is very little clarity. She says that the term collegiality has never been defined and that it is used in quite a number of different senses in different documents. She really concludes that the Church would now need to go back and clarify almost everything said at the Council and write a new document on this subject if collegiality is to become a reality in the Church.)

The earthquake came when the presidents announced that the vote on the document on religious liberty had been postponed to the next session on the grounds that the draft had been so changed that it was a new document. Paul endorsed this decision of the presidents. He was probably right in doing this, for the text was now far longer than before and so was in fact a new document. Paul was personally in favour of this document and did not want the later acceptance of the document questioned because of doubts about the legitimacy of the process. It was a procedural decision to settle an issue not of his making, but it occurred in the middle of the fireworks of what was being called "the black week" and was judged harshly. It also gave the hard-core minority another chance to attack the document.

Thus the third session of the council came to an end with a distinct frostiness between the Pope and the bishops. There was a strong feeling that the minority had been running to Paul to obtain things they could not obtain on the floor of the council, that he was listening to them, and that the Pope would freely override decisions of the council so that, even in council, bishops were no more than advisory.

And this atmosphere was not helped by the speech Paul gave at the final Mass of the session. He promulgated the three documents that had been approved – those on the Church, the Oriental churches and ecumenism. He gave ecumenism only the briefest mention and did not mention the Oriental churches at all. Concerning the document on the Church he said, "The most important word to be said about the promulgation of the Constitution on the Church is that through it no change is made in traditional teaching." He spoke of the Church as both "monarchical and hierarchical", though the document never uses this phrase and does not even mention the word monarchy. The Council had rather used the words "primatial and collegial". He then spent 40 per cent of the entire speech on chapter 8 of the document, the chapter concerning Mary. To everyone's surprise he announced that he was creating a new title for Mary as "mother of the Church". The doctrinal commission had repeatedly rejected this idea, both because it was not traditional and because it seemed to put Mary above the Church rather than see her as part of it. The entire speech appeared to be a deliberate assertion of his primacy. As he was carried out of the Basilica, the applause was less than spontaneous.

BETWEEN SESSIONS THREE AND FOUR

At the end of three sessions only five decrees had been promulgated, and there were still eleven to go. Despite this, there was an absolute determination that the fourth session would be the last. What could not be done there would never be done.

In line with this, the Pope made it clear that he would exercise a more active role in supervising the procedures and the outcome. He began seeking the opinion of many individuals on the various documents and began letting the commissions know how he wanted certain issues developed. This had three consequences. Firstly, each of the commissions was looking over its shoulder at what the Pope thought. Secondly, the central commission diminished in importance. Thirdly, direct appeals to the Pope inevitably increased. Congar several times commented, however, that though Paul was highly intelligent and a holy person, he did not have the theological expertise to take over from the council in this way.

Four documents had truly serious problems: revelation, religious liberty, the Jews, and the Church in the modern world. The problems regarding this last document were its sheer scope and the fear that there would not be time to develop it properly. There were also the contentious specific issues of birth control and nuclear stockpiling. The Germans and Wojtyla still thought it was too optimistic.

There were also heated discussions on the document concerning the Jews. The Arab bishops still saw it as a siding with the Jews against them. Maximos IV even threatened to leave the Council over the issue. Carli widely disseminated two articles in which he argued that saying the Jews were guilty of deicide is as least as true as calling Mary 'Mother of God'. Paul himself made this question of deicide far worse by a statement he made on Passion Sunday in a Roman parish, "The Jewish people not only did not acknowledge Christ when he came but also abused and killed him."

In the months before the Council reconvened, Paul started speaking of a crisis of authority and a crisis of obedience. He said, "Truths that stand outside time because they are divine are being subjected to a historicism that strips them of their content and their unchangeable character."

Then Paul published a document establishing the Synod of Bishops. The draft of the document on bishops had spoken of a body to help the Pope to govern the Church. Paul had misgivings about what the council might do with this idea, so he pre-empted it by writing his own document. While it concerned matters that were most important to the council, Paul did not consult the council concerning it, but simply presented the bishops with a finished document. The first response to his document was positive, but then commentators saw the repeated statements that the Synod was completely subject to the Pope and was only an advisory body. Collegiality was, therefore, cut off from any practical grounding. It was another blow to collegiality and pre-empted the role of bishops in future synods. This initiative of Paul must be seen together with the preliminary explanatory note and his speech to close the third session. Between them, they left little room for real collegiality.

THE FOURTH SESSION

The Pope's opening speech was more positive, and he announced that he would be speaking to the United Nations.

RELIGIOUS LIBERTY

There was still loud opposition to Paul's document on the Church – especially from Catholic countries. Paul's document on the Church. This raised the problem: how could the Pope speak to the United Nations if hundreds of bishops were still voting against religious liberty? Should a vote even be risked? There were, however, several more positive speakers. The most noticeable was Cardinal Beran, the recently released Bishop of Prague. He said that the burning of Jan Hus at the Council of Constance and then the imposition of Catholicism on the population of Bohemia had done immeasurable harm to the Church. He insisted that religion cannot be imposed on people, and his personal history gave great weight to his words. A vote was finally taken with 1997 in favour and 224 against. The Secretariat went to work making the final revisions to the document, harassed all the way by the minority and with frequent visits to the Pope. Paul told the Secretariat to listen to the dissenters in the hope of a near unanimous vote this time, but the final vote in November was virtually the same: 1967 against 249.

THE CHURCH IN THE MODERN WORLD

This document had to be finished at this session, and yet it was vast. It was still being criticised by many as too positive. The attitude of Ruffini is typical of a whole mindset, "The draft barely touches on the multitudes of vices and sins that corrupt large parts of society, especially nations that glory in their refined culture ... Nobody is ignorant that filthy morals contravening the natural law spread more widely every day, with new means of corruption constantly being invented."

This last clause was almost certainly a reference to the recently invented contraceptive pill. He also objected to the line in the draft that said that the Church in every age was stained with imperfections. Is this the way, he asked, to present Mother Church to the world? There was also much controversy about the ends of marriage and birth control. Paul forbade the Council to discuss the question of divorce. The discussions continued, and a multitude of amendments were proposed.

The Council had just moved on to the subject of war and peace when Paul made his dramatic and emotional plea, "La guerre jamais," to the United Nations. The Council took up the discussion of the question of a just war, with some saying that a just war is possible, while others said that war could never be justified. The most powerful speaker against all war was Ottaviani, and for the first time he received warm applause. The Council did not condemn stockpiles of weapons but spoke strongly of how destructive modern war is.

Time was so precious that the discussion had to be cut off, and 10 subcommittees were set up to go through all the proposals and revise the text. This was done and finally the document was ready. The document is one hundred pages long, and I cannot really give a few quotes that would in any way sum up its content. There is much that was not new, and some that was platitudinous. Nevertheless, taken as a whole, it is both a rich and a powerful document, with its constant calls for human dignity and for dialogue, mutuality, friendship, partnership and co-operation. It is the first time the Church has ever spoken out to the world in this fashion. In both its style and its content it is the antithesis of the negativity of the nineteenth century.

After some discussion on some more minor documents, there was a break of one week, a week of sessions, and another break of one week. The reason for this was to enable feverish work to take place in committees so that the documents could be voted on and finalised. There was also the fact that a spirit of fatigue had overtaken the bishops and they needed the break before the final push. At the vote on 16th October only 1,521 bishops had even turned up to vote.

After the two breaks came entire days of voting. Five documents were approved in one day.

Much diplomatic work had gone on behind the scenes concerning the document on non-Christian religions, especially the section dealing with the Jews.

Then there was an entire day of voting on the document on revelation. The major problem here still concerned the relationship between Scripture and tradition. Even in the last days the commission had to study 1500 suggestions for change.

Paul kept intervening on several subjects, and we even had the extraordinary situation of several commissions hiding from the council the fact that he had intervened, lest there be a return to the bad feelings at the end of the third session.

In the end, the document on revelation gave no room for fundamentalism, acknowledged the legitimacy of a critical study of the bible, recognised the wide variety of literary forms in the bible and gave great encouragement to the study and reading of the bible in the Church. It did not entirely solve the question of scripture and tradition.

The very last battle of the council concerned contraception. In the end the council did not condemn it, but, of course, three years later, Paul VI did.

Paul gave a last speech, saying that the Roman Curia would be the agent for the implementation of the council. He said, "There are no serious reasons for changing its structure." He warned against interpretations of the council that twisted aggiornamento into relativism.

Finally, there were several days of celebrations. There was the formal promulgation of all the documents. There was a ceremony with the Protestant and Orthodox observers at St Paul's basilica. There were many expressions of gratitude and mutual congratulations. And there was a final Mass in St Peter's Square with 2400 concelebrants, the last glorious fling of the Church Triumphant.

CONCLUSIONS

There had been two centuries of negativity and suspicion of the new. Behind the scenes a number of brilliant theologians had seen the limitations of this, and a number of bishops had spoken with these theologians. In Rome and Italy above all there were powerful figures opposing all change. Then more than 2000 bishops, all trained in the older forms and categories, and largely ignorant of the ferment beneath the surface, came together expecting a brief council that would approve all the draft documents and then go home.

The conflict between the two groups, especially the conflict between infallibility and *ressourcement*, provided the drama of the council, but the greater drama consisted in the way in which the 2200 bishops became aware of the conflict and slowly and painfully educated themselves over a period of four years. Resentment of the high-handed actions of the Curia was undoubtedly a factor in the Council. However, it is still amazing that ninety percent of these unprepared bishops consistently and insistently sided with the reformers.

There was no total victory for any side or any individual. If the council spoke of collegiality, it often did so without the necessary clarity.

The language of each of the documents is serene, with no hint of all the controversies and heated debates that were behind it. There is never an admission that anything has changed.

It is also important to realise that the documents of the council have many ambiguities and compromises. For example, the council said that "the whole body of the faithful ... cannot err in matters of belief,"[221] but it also said that, in coming to these beliefs, it must follow the teaching authority of the pope and bishops.[222]

In the same way, the council in one passage extols conscience, but in another passage can't get away from the idea that a good conscience will always follow the teaching of the pope.[223] In many ways the council was a beginning rather than an end.

Its solution to controversy was often to place statements from the two camps side by side without any real resolution between them. Despite all of this, among the irreversible fruits of the council are that:

- it saw the Church as a divine mystery and a pilgrim people rather than simply as a hierarchical institution
- it placed the Bible back beside the sacraments at the centre of Church life, and opened up the Bible to a deeper understanding
- it placed the pope into the context of the college of bishops
- it greatly promoted the active role of the laity

---

221 *Lumen Gentium*, no. 12.
222 See the whole text of both no.12 and no.25 of *Lumen Gentium* taken together.
223 Compare nos.16 and 50 of *Gaudium et Spes*

- it renewed enthusiasm for Christian unity
- it brought some settlement to ancient tensions between Christians and Jews
- it made landmark statements on religious liberty and conscience
- it brought the liturgy to the people, and
- it gave us a glimpse of what the Church could be, *and for the last fifty years it is this vision that has inspired my life and my priesthood.*

On each of the points I have just listed, we still have a long way to go, and yet we have already made considerable progress.

There are two ways to judge any movement in a society. The first is the very common one of judging the movement by the criterion of how far short it falls of where we believe it ought to be, and by this criterion many will see the results of the council as disappointing. The second, and more realistic, way is to judge how far a society has moved from where it used to be. Using this criterion it can be seen that vast change has already occurred within the Church, and the hope for more is alive and strong. The whole process of needed change may take longer than we hoped. It may not achieve everything we hoped for. But I believe that the Second Vatican Council is a work of the Holy Spirit and that it is still a work in progress.

CHAPTER 26
RELATIONSHIP WITH THE RELIGION OF ISLAM

When a Muslim terrorist deliberately explodes a bomb in a crowded place, is it Islam itself that is to blame? Is the major motivating cause a religious hatred and intolerance of people of other religions, deliberately fostered by their holy book, the Qur'an? Is Islam genetically prone to violence? A large group of people and much popular opinion would say yes. They would point to passages in the Qur'an that appear to foster violence against non-Muslims.

And yet the vast majority of Muslims do not implement the Qur'anic injunction to kill idolaters (sura 9:5). There are two reasons for this. The first is that the language used in the Qur'an, while always beautiful and poetic, is very frequently unclear, leaving itself open to more than one interpretation. In reading the Qur'an interpretation becomes just as important as text. It is possible to interpret certain texts as ordering the indiscriminate killing of unbelievers, but it is equally possible to interpret these texts as bearing a far more conciliatory message.

The second reason is similar to the first. In addition to the texts of the Qur'an, there is also *a living tradition*. In this tradition Islam has for centuries developed a sophisticated interpretation of Qur'anic texts, often using quite new political and social considerations in doing so. This tradition has, for example, laid down strict conditions as to who can declare a jihad and in what circumstances. This rich tradition must be studied before passing any judgement.

The situation is similar to that in the Bible where it is said that a couple should be put to death for adultery.[224] There is no evidence that the Jewish tradition ever took up this idea and put it into practice, and the Christian tradition positively rejected it. In all religions the tradition must be considered together with the text it is interpreting.

It is ironic that both Muslim extremists on the one hand, and extreme critics of Islam on the other hand, equally reject the tradition and attend only to the literal text of the Qur'an. In other words, both are equally fundamentalist. Our first positive step must be to do all we can to abolish fundamentalism in all three religions: Judaism, Christianity and Islam.[225]

FACTORS OUTSIDE THE QUR'AN

A major problem for Islam today is that powerful emotional factors outside the Qur'an are driving a number of Muslims to a desire for violence and hence to a fundamentalist interpretation of the Qur'an in order to justify or excuse the violence. The Qur'an then becomes, not the cause of the violence, but the justification and excuse for the violence.

I suggest that the major factors today within Islam leading to violence are an intense feeling of outrage and injustice, a sense of powerlessness against this injustice, a loss of pride in self and a desire to strike out against those perceived as causing the injustice.

For some Muslims a major cause of this sense of outrage is the situation in Israel. Whatever the historical facts may be, it is undeniable that there is a profound feeling among Muslims that a combination of Israelis, Americans and the West in general robbed them of their land and left them as powerless beggars in what should have been their own home.

They feel that the Christian West had for centuries had a Jewish problem that then came to a head in the Holocaust. They feel that, when the West became aware of the full horror of the Holocaust, it acted, out of its own guilty conscience, to solve its Jewish problem by dumping it on the Muslims through its assistance in the founding of the State of Israel and its takeover of Arab lands. So powerful is this sense of outrage among some Muslims throughout the world that there will be no solutions to worldwide violence unless and until there is a solution to the situation in Israel.

Even that will not be enough, for there are many other causes of this sense of outrage. These include a general sense of persecution by the West, extremes

---

224 "If a man commits adultery with the wife of his neighbour, both the adulterer and the adulteress shall be put to death." Leviticus 20:10.

225 For a good study of fundamentalism see Karen Armstrong, *The Battle for God, Fundamentalism in Judaism, Christianity and Islam*, Harper Perennial, London, 2004. After 350 pages of evidence, she concludes that the dominant cause of fundamentalism in all three religions is fear.

of poverty in the slums of the Middle East, unemployment, especially among the young, the loss of a sense of purpose and meaning in life, the abundant individual acts of discrimination and belittlement committed by Westerners, the stereotyping of Arabs as "baddies" in films and novels, and a general sense that the West looks down on them and despises them.

MUSLIMS IN WESTERN COUNTRIES

The situation of the millions of Muslims now living in Western countries must also be considered. While each individual is unique, in broad terms we may say that it takes four generations for individuals to be fully assimilated. Those who move to a new country as adults will always be, for example, Italians living in Australia, not really speaking the language and feeling somewhat alien in a foreign world. Their children (the second generation) will always be half-Italian and half-Australian and will feel conflicted between the two. Their children (the third generation) will be Australian children of Italian origin, largely assimilated but still probably marrying another Italian. Their children (the fourth generation) will be fully Australian, with a nod or two towards Italian heritage but probably by now intermarried with other cultures. While individuals may adapt more rapidly, this is the general picture and it is impossible to speed it up. We must accept it and work within it.

Even this presupposes that nothing goes wrong, yet there are many factors that can slow down the process, with religion certainly being one of these factors. It is no accident that the two groups that have been slowest to assimilate fully have been Jews and Muslims, for both strongly discourage intermarriage, insist on their own separate identity and condemn any abandonment of the religion.

Some years ago there was a series of rapes committed by Muslim youths in Sydney. Of course one must blame the youths, but I feel that it was necessary to blame also the older generation of Muslims who never committed such crimes themselves, but in the hearing of the young men constantly complained about how shamelessly the local young women dressed and constantly called them "whores". There was a riot in the suburb of Cronulla, and I did not think it was an accident that it was a beach environment where the differences between the swimming costumes worn by Muslims and those worn by non-Muslims were at their most extreme. In both cases first-generation migrants were strongly influencing the attitudes of those more assimilated, dragging them back.

If there is perceived discrimination, racial or religious hatred, unemployment or other hardships, the process of assimilation is likely to be further slowed down, and the individual is likely to continue to opt for the foreign rather than the local half of the equation. If the causes of their outrage continue, the outrage itself is unlikely to go away. It is pointless to say, "If they come here to live, they must learn English and become Australian." It is never as simple as that. It is no accident that so many terrorists are drawn from among the Muslims living in non-Muslim lands.

A NEW TRADITION

I have spoken of a tradition within Islam that was important in the development of the whole religion. This tradition was always most alive in the great centres of learning such as those of Al Azhar in Cairo in the Sunni world or those of Qom (Iran) and Najaf (Iraq) in the Shiite world. These great centres of learning helped to put the Muslim world far ahead of the Christian world for a number of centuries. The learning of the ancient Greeks was reintroduced to Europe through Muslim scholars, and fundamental inventions such as paper, soap and spices came from the Muslim world. Muslims rightly thought of Christians in their crowded and unsanitary cities as primitive. In those centuries Islam had much to teach Christianity.

Later on things changed, as the scientific revolution caused the Western world to catch up and then surpass the Muslim world in many fields. Unfortunately, Westerners were not slow to tell the Muslim world how superior they had become and how primitive they thought the Muslims were. Many modern problems began there, and it would be very helpful if people in the West were more aware of how their own ancestors acted, of how their prejudices and sense of superiority began to bite into the souls of Muslims.

In recent history we have seen the rise of dictators in many countries of the Middle East, coinciding with the rise of oil revenues. In country after country we have seen very rich rulers living a life of ostentatious wealth, while the ordinary people lived in great poverty. The people have felt powerless to change anything, but there has been a deep resentment that exploded whenever possible, such as in the hatred of the people of Iran for Shah Pahlavi, paving the way for the revolution of Ayatollah Khomeini; in the manner in which the people of Iraq put Saddam Hussein to death; the manner in which the people of Libya killed Muammar Ghaddafi; and the manner in which the people of Egypt sought to prosecute Hosni Mubarak. If the people of Muslim countries tend to blame the West for most of their problems, they are also well aware of the contribution of their own rulers.

One of the things these rulers had done was to use financial power to coerce the centres of learning into following the rulers' own ideas and preferences. That is, they sought to coerce the long and proud tradition itself to start interpreting the Qur'an in a manner that suited them. The centres of learning lost their independence, and the whole tradition of Islam began to move in a new and more dangerous direction.

A new interpretation of the Qur'an began to intrude, bringing about a seismic change in Islam. The most famous and influential form of this tradition is known as Wahhabism or Salafism, more strict and more intolerant of non-

Muslims than earlier traditions. It had two pieces of great good fortune. It started in an area of Saudi Arabia dominated by rulers who then became rulers of the whole country, the Saudi family, and it saw the spectacular rise of oil revenues, so that there was an abundance of money to spread its message. It is not coincidence that the attack on the twin towers of the World Trade Centre in New York was led by a wealthy junior member of the Saudi royal family, Osama Bin Laden. The Qur'an remained the same, but the tradition that interpreted it had become very different.

I AM GOD

There is then the fact that most of those who commit terrorist acts don't actually believe in God. They think they do, and they loudly claim they do, but they are in fact guilty of the error that occurs in all religions, when strong desires and emotions cause people to believe only in a god who in all things agrees with them. Ultimately, this means that they believe only in themselves, that they have become their own god, that they are seeking to create God rather than God creating them. Either God is, or I am God! This is a danger for all people in all religions, but it has been given a special place in the recent developments of the tradition of Islam.

A good example of this is the question of suicide. The Qur'an condemns suicide on no less than six occasions, but the Palestinians felt completely helpless and ineffective before Israeli military might until they discovered that suicide bombing provided them with a weapon that the Israelis and the whole world would listen to. They immediately began the process of using the new Wahhabist tradition to reinterpret the Qur'an, so that, despite the six specific prohibitions, it would not only allow but actually praise suicide, extolling the bombers as martyrs. The method was so spectacularly successful on 11th September 2001 that it has become the normal method of attack.

FORCE VERSUS CO-OPERATION

Force alone will never resolve the problems between Islam and the West. On the contrary, force used by the West will only increase the number of extremists within Islam and make the problem worse, while terrorist acts by Muslims will only harden the resolve of the West to fight against them rather than to understand them or dialogue with them.

Acts of interference by Western powers in the Middle East, whether military or diplomatic, overt or covert, have by and large been disasters, with next to no understanding of the multitude of different forces at work. They have been designed to fix one specific problem, but with little idea of how to deal with the many forces that this would unleash and with no clear exit strategy. They have naively believed that their own models of democracy would be embraced and would solve all problems.

To move forward, there are some things the Western world must do, and some things the Muslim world must do.

WHAT THE WEST MUST DO

The Causes of Conflict

Rather than dismiss all problems between Christians and Muslims as "religious", we must first study all the causes of the current difficulties.

For example, the conflict between Israelis and Palestinians cannot be dismissed as a conflict between two religions, with each side trying to convert the other to its beliefs. The two religions of Judaism and Islam lived side by side for centuries in Israel without trying to destroy or convert each other and there is no essential reason why they could not do so again.

The present dispute is first and foremost a conflict over land, with two peoples fighting over too little land for too many people. Israel is a small country, the land is poor land, and the numbers of people on both sides are continually increasing as more Jews flee to Israel, and the Palestinians in the refugee camps are brought into the equation.

Outgunned by the military forces of Israel assisted by the Americans, the Palestinians have turned to powerful religious forces in the community in their attempt to bring pressure to obtain more land.

There will be no peace until this land problem is resolved. It is only then that the religious element can begin to fade into the background. The so-called Two State Solution will not work as long as it is nothing more than an attempt to divide up too little poor land between too many people. To find a solution there needs to be more land available and it needs to have a measure of fertility.

I cannot see how this can be done without the Palestinian people becoming part of the country of Jordan, with vast and costly amounts of work being done, funded in large part by the West, in order to make water available so that significant parts of the soil of this new Jordan can be converted into more fertile land. This may seem like nothing more than an ignorant fool's dream rather than a vision that could ever be realised, but I see no other way to a solution that might actually work.

Syria is a most complex place. I lack the knowledge to attempt to explain the many factors that apply there and can only state that all of these factors need to be carefully studied before solutions are proposed. Simply taking sides and bombing each other is not a solution.

Education

If there is to be peace, the West must come to understand Islam far better than it does currently. I feel that this must begin with an understanding of just how advanced Islam was a thousand years ago when compared to the West. We need to understand better all the good things that came into the Western world from the Islamic world and we need to have a genuine respect for the level of culture they achieved. Today's stereotypes of poor, illiterate Muslims filled with violence, ignorance and hatred need to give way to a genuine appreciation of historical fact.

We need to show images of people exactly like ourselves speaking and acting in a prejudiced manner. We need to shatter the myth that "we" have always acted well, while "they" have acted badly. We need to be helped to enter into the minds of Muslims and see ourselves through their eyes. We need a greater appreciation of all that is good about Islam.

I would like to see a whole series of thoughtful documentaries that sought to present this history and this analysis of present situations. I would like to see a number of these documentaries become part of the curriculum in schools and universities.

WHAT ISLAM MUST DO

The Ummah

Islam has no history of councils, where the whole community comes together to determine common policy, but it seems that it must now find a way to listen to the *ummah*, the worldwide Islamic community, in determining a new interpretation of the Qur'an and in forming a new tradition that would walk beside and modify the Qur'an. Though Wahhabism, supported by Saudi money, has been growing, it still seems that a large majority of the Muslim world does not support it and would wish to see a more moderate interpretation and tradition. That majority needs to be given a voice.

If the great universities were set free from the financial power of secular rulers, they could contribute greatly to this tradition.

Forms of Government

There has been quite an unhealthy relationship between Islam and dictatorship. The dictators have been emperors, kings, sheiks, ayatollahs, generals, presidents and prime ministers with monarchical powers, but they have all amounted to one-man rule. There have been exceptions, such as in Indonesia in the last decade, but it has been a general rule. Far too often this one man has used force to eliminate opposition and has taken a very generous share of State revenue for himself, his family and his most ardent supporters, so much so that little has been left for the poor.

Muslim countries are unlikely to adopt Western forms of democracy, and it must be said that, while religion would certainly favour participatory forms of government, it does not seek to dictate any of the present forms of democracy. Islam must now find forms of government that involve universal participation, government in which people have a say in their own destiny and their own governance.

It is essential that governments in Muslim countries show far more concern for the poor and, indeed, for all ordinary citizens, that they have done in the past.

Where Religion Ends and Culture Begins

In all religions there are many practices that are held by some to be religious obligations, but on closer inspection are found to be no more than cultural expressions of the religion. Precisely because they are cultural, they vary from one country to another. Behind the practice there is a core value that derives from religious beliefs, but the practice itself is simply cultural and it is wrong to seek to impose it as religious obligation.

Veils and special clothes for women come into this category and it is important to distinguish between what is religious obligation and what is no more than a local and changeable cultural expression of religious beliefs. Modest clothing is held to be a religious obligation, but many of the particular forms to which so much attention is given are no more than local cultural expressions of this obligation. Female genital excision (mutilation) also comes into this category. Indeed, the entire imbalance between male and female in most Muslim lands comes from cultural as much as from religious values.

Peace is possible, but it will require serious change on both sides. If it costs large amounts of money, it will arguably be no more than is currently being spent on wars. Why is it that we always seem to be able to find the money for war, but not for peace? The answer to this question surely lies in the word "fear". Is it not time to move beyond fear towards more positive and more noble attitudes?

APPENDIX
THE STRUCTURE OF A COUNCIL

I suggest that the entire Church take part in any council, but in such a manner that the members of the Church contribute in different ways according to the particular expertise and experience that they have, and with different people playing different roles.

There are precedents in Church history for people other than bishops attending a council and having a vote. For example, at the Council of Florence (1435–42) three estates were present: bishops, abbots-religious, and 'lower clergy'. At the Council of Trent three laypersons, the Holy Roman Emperor, the King of France and the King of Spain, had considerable authority and a profound influence. John O'Malley says that the First Vatican Council in 1869 was the first council in the Church's history at which no laypersons were present. There is no reason why there cannot be significant numbers of non-bishops, especially laity, appointed as members of a new council.

There are four things in particular that must make a new council different.

1. Scope and Duration of the Council

The last three councils (Trent, Vatican I and Vatican II) looked at all aspects of the Church at particular moments in history. It may well be argued that, in seeking to do this, the Second Vatican Council tried to cover too many subjects in too brief a period of time. The consequence of this was that it left many matters unresolved and was distinctly ambiguous on a number of others, leading to conflicting opinions concerning how decisions were to be interpreted.

It is not necessary that a council look at all aspects of the Church at a particular moment in history. A new council could have a carefully limited focus and seek to answer only a limited number of specifically determined questions, or even only one question. However, it must then have the time to do its work thoroughly.

2. The Method of Communication and Discussion

Each session of the Second Vatican Council brought together in Rome more than three thousand people, including the bishops, theological experts, secretaries and ancillary staff. The number of bishops has grown much larger over the last fifty years, so the number of people travelling to Rome for a council today would be over six thousand. Bringing all these people to Rome and lodging them there for months on end would be both a logistical nightmare and massively expensive. And St Peter's Basilica itself would be too small for the daily sessions, at least in the form that was followed for the Second Vatican Council.

The essence of a council of the Catholic Church is that:

- While the initiative for the council can come from other sources, the unity of the Church is expressed through the calling of the council by the bishop of Rome.
- The subject matter of the council is clearly determined.
- There is a dialogue between the voting members of the council and the relevant experts in each field.
- Through this dialogue – and the sharing of information and opinions – the members have adequate opportunity to inform themselves on the issues.
- After members have informed themselves on the issues at hand, they then cast their votes.

It is not essential that council members all come together in the one place at the one time in order to do this, for abundant discussion can take place both at more local levels and through the use of modern electronic means of communication. Every effort should be made to ensure that all members of the council have available to them a personal computer and access to the internet. The majority of communication and access to materials could be through this means, as with most discussions.

3. The Participation of the Entire Church

Since we can, through the means of communication available, avoid the financial and logistical problem of bringing all members together in Rome, I suggest that there be abundant representation of the whole Church. I suggest that there be at least one non-bishop member for every bishop member.

The lay members could be chosen from among those who have done the equivalent of at least three years' full-time theological study at a recognised theological faculty. If there are not enough suitable candidates in a particular area with this qualification, the requirement could be lowered to the equivalent of at least two years' full-time theological study.

They should not be chosen from either the extreme conservative or the extreme progressive wing of the Church; that is, they should not be people who would possibly be more likely to start with preconceived answers, but people who would humbly seek God's truth on each question, and would be prepared to change their minds whenever the evidence led them to do so.

All appointments should be strictly on merit, so that the council might have the very best persons available to it. There has, however, been a long history in the Catholic Church of men being privileged over women in this as in every other field. Where two candidates are seen as equal, preference should, therefore, be given to a woman over a man, so that the number of women at the council might come as near as possible to that of the men.

4. The Presumption

At the very outset the council would need to decide where the presumption and the burden of proof lie. The presumption can lie in favour of what has been believed or done in the past, and then it would require a consensus or at least a majority to change that belief or practice. Or it can lie in favour of the freedom of the children of God, and then it would require a consensus or at least a majority to reimpose an existing obligation or to impose a new one. It would certainly seem that the presumption should here, as in all fields, be in favour of freedom. But in order to avoid confusion this must be one of the first questions the council decides.

SUGGESTED STRUCTURE OF A COUNCIL

Here, I am assuming a council that meets through the internet rather than through solemn meetings in Rome.

Furthermore, if a council is to discuss many topics, it would always be possible to divide the one council into several sections, so that each section discussed one of the topics. In this manner, the work of the council would proceed more smoothly, and no individual would be overburdened with work. In what follows I shall assume one single council, but the idea of, in effect, many councils working together or at least simultaneously should always be kept in mind.

I suggest three commissions at three levels to co-ordinate and carry forward the work of the council.

The Central Commission

The federations of bishops' conferences could nominate members to a Central Commission of the Council (e.g. four from Western Europe, two from Eastern Europe, four from Africa, five from South America, two from North America, and three from Asia and Oceania together, equalling twenty). There would be both bishops and non-bishops. Because of the great importance of this Commission to the entire work of the Council, the bishops would be asked to appoint the very best persons they have available. Every effort should be made to ensure that the Commission does not consist of twenty men but has the best possible gender balance.

The Central Commission would have the task of determining the detailed norms that would govern this Council and seeking the consent of the members of the Council for these norms. Within these boundaries, the Central Commission would then determine all procedural questions and all questions relating to the time to be allotted to each question discussed by the council at each stage of the process.

The Central Commission would also have the task of co-ordinating the work of the Regional Commissions.

The Central Commission would ensure that the members of the council were given the best information available in order to form their opinions and were fairly presented with both sides of each question. They would have the task of ensuring that the entire discussion was conducted in a Christian manner, avoiding all personal attacks and unbecoming language.

The Regional Commission

The members of the council within the jurisdiction of each Bishops' Conference would establish an office in their region (the Regional Office) and elect from the members of the council or from outside it, a commission (the Regional Commission). This Regional Commission would determine the manner and timeline of the work of the council to be carried out in that region and would co-ordinate all such work.

Smaller Bishops' Conferences would be free to join with other Conferences, setting up one Regional Office and one Regional Commission for their combined area. For example, the bishops of New Caledonia would be free to join with other French-speaking bishops around the world OR with the bishops of the South Pacific region.

The Local Commission

Each member of the council would publicly name a number of persons to work as a Local Commission in advising the member on all matters raised by the council and in assisting in consulting the people of that area.

Determining the General Topics

In any human endeavour, if we want the right answers we must first ask the right questions. Furthermore, if the statements expressing the questions are ambiguous or unclear or fail to address exactly the matter they are dealing with, confusion will result. Time spent determining and refining the right questions will in the end save time and energy for the whole council. It is, therefore, legitimate to spend adequate time on this aspect of the council.

The process could begin with the Central Commission drawing up a list of those broad subject areas that they believe should be discussed and decided by the council, and forwarding this list to the members throughout the world.

The members of the council could then consider the list of topics forwarded from the Central Commission and propose variations or additions. In doing this, they could, to the greatest extent possible, listen to the wisdom of the Church community around them in their area and use members of the Local Commissions in doing so. The changes the individual members propose would be sent to the Regional Office.

The members of the council in that region would consider the proposed variations and additions sent by individual members and vote on them, with only those that receive the support of two thirds of the members being forwarded to the Central Commission. This Central Commission would study the proposals from around the world and, in fidelity to the wishes of the members of the council, decide on which topics to include.

Determining the Particular Matters for Discussion and Voting

As soon as the general topics are determined, the members of the council could take up the work of determining the specific points to be voted on under each topic.

These points should be presented as statements expressed in one single sentence and containing one single idea, and should be framed in such a manner that they can be answered by:

- A = 'affirmative' (I endorse the statement.)
- N = 'negative' (I disagree with the statement.)
- C = 'change' (I generally endorse the statement, but I would prefer to see it changed as follows. if the change is not accepted, I still vote affirmative.)

- CC = 'conditional change' (I endorse the statement if the following change is included. If it is not included, I vote negative).
- U = 'unsure' (I do not know enough about the subject. Or the arguments on both sides appear to be equal and I cannot decide between them.)
- D = 'defer' (The arguments given on both sides are not sufficiently mature or complete, and the matter should be deferred to a later council.)

More complex ideas should be divided into several statements. In framing them, matters of style should give way to clarity and substance. Needless to say, a series of consecutive statements could go together as part of an argument on a particular topic, but they would remain separate statements, to be voted on separately. They could be called simply "the statements".

All members of the Church could be invited to be part of this process in accordance with the principle that the process is at least as important as the written outcomes. While any member of the Church could propose statements, those with a special expertise in a particular area would specifically be asked to do so. While any member of the Church could send in proposals, it would be highly recommended that ideas be refined by discussion with larger groups before being presented. On the one hand, the larger the number of people involved in a discussion, the greater the attention that ought to be given to the submission; on the other hand, a carefully researched submission by an expert in a particular field might be worth far more than a more superficial discussion between many people. The aim would always be to receive the best ideas, while at the same time finding a balance between an invitation to all to participate and the need to limit the amount of time necessary to read and evaluate all the material submitted.

The only proposals that would be considered would be those that come in the form of the statements as described above.

The members of the council in that region would then consider all the submissions made and draw up a list of statements under each topic. Only those statements that received the support of two thirds of the members would be forwarded to the Central Commission.

The Central Commission would then, by a majority vote, draw up a list of statements from all the submissions received.

The Learned Societies

Within the Church in most countries there are societies of persons with an expertise in a particular field of study, such as scripture scholars, historians, dogmatic theologians, moral theologians and canon lawyers. There are other groups of people who could also make an expert contribution in various fields under some subjects, such as doctors, psychologists, lawyers and social workers.

These societies should have their important role in the process of the council, in line with the idea of an ongoing dialogue between the voting members of the council and the experts in relevant topics. These societies or groups could be invited by the members of the council in that region to discuss those statements that come within their own particular field of expertise. Seven tasks could then be assigned to these societies and groups:

1. Assist in the work of choosing the topics and preparing the statements under each topic.
2. Select among the statements those foreseen as being more important or more controversial, and/or on which they feel that their own contribution will be most useful.
3. Discuss these controversial or key statements among themselves and become informed on these matters.
4. Prepare papers setting forth the major arguments for and against a particular statement and forward these papers to the members of the council in their region, at the same time making the papers publicly available.
5. Be aware of significant contributions for or against the statements made in other countries and make appropriate use of them, though without overwhelming the members with more material than they could fairly be asked to study.
6. Make themselves available to meetings of the members of the council in their region for discussion of the question.
7. Vote among themselves on all those statements that come within their field of expertise and publish the results at a time determined by their Regional Commission, under the overall direction of the Central Commission.

When the learned society concerns a church discipline (such as theology or scripture studies), appropriate members of other Christian churches could be invited to join the discussions – with a right to vote, but perhaps with their votes counted separately.

When the society concerns a secular discipline (for example psychology), religion would be irrelevant, both in regard to eligibility for membership and voting.

The work of the learned societies could have one other function, in that all private opinions from scholars should first be submitted to these societies. The Catholic people of the world would then know that anyone who sought to publicise private views through the media without first presenting them to the learned societies was most probably someone who could not convince his or her own peers.

The Central Commission would have the right to forward to the members of the Council a limited amount of selected material on particular questions.

Discussions

Each member of the council could be encouraged to hold open discussions in the place where they live – either personally or though the members of the Local Commission – and invite input from any who wished to attend, always remembering that the process of the council is just as important as the content.

At regional meetings the members of the council could then discuss those questions that they believe most require such discussion. They could take provisional and informal votes on various questions in order to determine which ones need the most study and discussion. They could invite experts or representative groups to attend their discussions and assist through their expertise.

Voting

At times determined by the Central Commission, the voting on each topic would take place. Different parts of the entire work of the Council could be brought to a vote at different times.

The first step would be to gather the votes of the learned societies from around the world bearing on that topic, collate them, then make public the results of the voting, so that the members of the council would be aware of the opinions of the experts in each field.

The members of the Council in the region would then discuss the questions among themselves.

At the appropriate time, the members of the council would then be invited to vote and to forward their votes, by a suitable and secure means, to the Regional Office, which would count them and in turn forward the results to the Central Commission.

Assessment of the Voting

The assessment of the vote requires the most careful consideration. The purpose of the council is to put the bishop of Rome in the position of being able to declare that "this is the faith of the Church on this topic at this point in its history". This will necessarily require a certain interpretation of the outcome of the voting and so clear principles need to be established.

To set a mark of 50 per cent and then divide the votes into 'passed' or 'defeated' on this basis seems inadequate when speaking of faith and morals. There should surely be a difference between a statement that receives 98 per cent support and another that receives only 52 per cent support. 98 per cent means that this is the faith of the Church, while 52 per cent means that the Church is divided down the middle and there is no clear faith of the Church that the bishop of Rome can proclaim. A vote of 52 per cent does not mean that the bishop of Rome can impose this belief on the other 48 per cent. Democracy may work like that, but on matters of belief the Church cannot.

The first step should be that the publication of the results would always include the percentage of the votes favouring each side, so that people may know the strength of the belief.

The second step would always be to interpret the results in the light of the question asked earlier: does the presumption lie in what has been proclaimed up to now, so that a change would require a consensus of the votes, or does the presumption lie in the freedom of the children of God, so that a consensus would be required to both impose or reimpose an obligation?

And when do we have a consensus? 52 per cent is not a consensus, nor is 55 per cent, nor is 60 per cent. It would seem that consensus begins to exist only when we have two votes in favour for every one against, that is, at 66.7 per cent. At 75 per cent, when there are three votes in favour for every vote against, we can be more confident of consensus. By 80 per cent, when we have four votes in favour for every vote against, consensus appears certain. When the vote is between 67 per cent and 75 or 80 per cent, we must look at just how important the question is, how deeply it affects the lives of people and how much heat there has been in the debate. If at all possible, the level of consensus should be established before the event. I do not wish to see the bishop of Rome given the power to decide what constitutes a consensus on his own authority alone, for that would put us back on the highway to monarchy and make councils irrelevant.

When a majority is in favour, but not a sufficient consensus, I would suggest three ways of proceeding:
- The question could be referred back to the council, where it could be further refined, with the questions rephrased or divided into a number of component parts, and a new vote taken.
- The bishop of Rome could declare that there is no consensus, so the matter remains an open one and people are free to follow their own beliefs in the matter.
- The matter could be deferred, possibly to be taken up again at a future council when thinking on the subject is more developed.

In matters of practice rather than belief, and where an immediate decision is needed, the Church may in some cases need to proceed on the basis of a bare majority. It should always remember, however, that a vote of 51 per cent for and 49 per cent against really means that the Church is divided down the middle and there is no agreement.

All decisions concerning the force of the vote must pass the test of credibility, that is, the People of God must be able to say, "Yes, this decision is not one person or one small group of persons imposing a minority will on the Church. Whether I personally agree with the decision or not, I admit that it is a conclusion that may legitimately be drawn from the voting according to predetermined principles."

There must also be respect for the principle that even a consensus vote on a particular matter does not mean that an individual who disagrees should be excluded from membership of the Church (although this may be a relevant issue in some instances). I refer to what I said in an earlier chapter concerning the Assumption of Mary and the exact manner of the Ascension of Jesus.

Expenses

There would, of course, be expenses associated with this council, though they should be less than would be incurred by a traditional council. One could anticipate that the Catholic people of the world would strongly support the idea of this council and would be willing to contribute to a collection (or even several over a period of time) taken up for this purpose.

To avoid adding to the destruction of a large forest, electronic communication would always be preferred to the printing of hard copies.

Through the entire process set out above, one could surely hope that the mind of the Church on the chosen topics would emerge. Then the bishop of Rome could proclaim, not a personal faith, but the "faith of the Church on this topic at this moment in its history".

Questions & Reflections

Questions Chapter 1a

1. I understand the word "infinite" to mean that I can write on a blackboard the number "1", and then after it continue writing noughts until I have filled that entire blackboard and then every other blackboard on earth, and then both sides of every piece of paper in the world, and then every wall or spare space on the entire planet, and then not merely have I not reached infinity, but I am actually not even one second closer to the beginning of time or one metre closer to the edge of the universe than I was before I started. Is a universe infinite in space or infinite in time a logical contradiction?
2. If the universe has truly had infinite time in which to develop, why is evolution not complete?
3. Many scientists have moved beyond the idea of a simple big bang in which nothing suddenly became something. They speak of a multiverse, of many universes stretching out in space and back in time to infinity. Do you believe that such speculations will eventually lead us to a satisfying explanation of the origin of our universe? Or do you feel that something else, something from outside, is needed?
4. Who is greater: a god who could create out of nothing the world we know today, or a god who could create a big bang, knowing that over billions of years, and without any further intervention, it would develop into the world we know today?
5. Do you feel that science and religion are in irreconcilable conflict on these issues? Where do you see a resolution to this conflict coming from? Can the two work together, with each fully respecting the other?
6. Do you see some end point or purpose in the evolution of the universe? What is it?

Questions Chapter 1b

1. How would you wish to rephrase these statements?
2. What statements would you wish to add or take away?

Questions Chapter 2

1. Is it worthwhile to speculate on questions of evil and suffering in this world or would we be better off just bowing before the mystery? Do our speculations cause more problems for us than they solve? Should this chapter be quietly abandoned altogether or is it good to have it, however inadequate, in this book?
2. Are there statements in this chapter that you believe are positively wrong and should be deleted? Why are they wrong?
3. Are there essential questions that you believe are not even mentioned in this chapter?

Questions Chapter 3

1. How would you wish to rephrase some of these statements?
2. What statements would you wish to add or take away?

Questions Chapter 4

1. Do you accept that the Bible is the story of a spiritual journey, with a beginning, a middle and an end?
2. Is there abundant evidence of human imperfection in the writers?
3. Does the Bible contain "insights that are at best partial and much that is far from sublime"?
4. Does the Bible contain any examples blatant worldly wisdom?
5. Does the Bible, in many places, contain racism, sexism and a failure to condemn slavery?
6. Does the Bible indicate that "God wanted a book containing a mixture of the divine and the human, and the story of a god who spoke to people, less by divine oracles from heaven, and more in and through the turbulence of the world around them"?
7. Does the Bible indicate that, "rather than directly reveal divine answers to all questions, God wanted human beings themselves to struggle slowly and painfully towards a higher understanding"?
8. Is there a strong tendency in the Bible to "talk in pictures"?
9. Do we need to accept that, in addition to scientific truth, there is also symbolic truth, such as in the story of Jonah?
10. Do you accept the presence of many different literary forms?
11. Do you accept that, with steps both forwards and backwards, there was a gradual progress in the people's understanding of God?
12. Do you accept what is said about inspiration in this chapter? If not, what would you insist on adding?
13. How would you wish to reword what I have said about the "essential truth" of the scriptures?
14. Is the "faith dimension" an essential element of the scriptures? In what ways must we take account of it?
15. How much truth is there in the statement that "every translation is a lie"?
16. Do you prefer translations that favour readability over accuracy? What do you lose by doing this?

QUESTIONS & REFLECTIONS

17. In reading the Bible, how should we attend to each of the following: history, social history, the text, the language, the traditions, the editing, the faith dimension, the literary forms, the relationship between the gospels and the community, and inspiration?
18. What should be our response to the anti-intellectual stream in Christian thought concerning the Bible?
19. In what spirit should we read the Bible?

Questions Chapter 5

1. The Trinity is a mystery impossible to speak about in human words. When we use human words, there is always the danger of doing more harm than good. Would you prefer to remove this chapter entirely from the book? Or is it possible to amend and improve it, so that it has a useful place in the book?
2. Which statements do you positively agree with? Which statements do you positively disagree with?
3. How would you improve the chapter?

Questions Chapter 6

1. I have listed four statements that I believe must be made if we accept that Jesus was fully human as well as divine. Do you disagree with any of the first three?
2. Are there any other statements that you believe should be added?
3. Which statement is more correct?
    - The gospels present a Jesus who always had divine knowledge.
    - The gospels present a Jesus who always had only human knowledge.
    - The gospels do not give us a clear answer on this question.
4. What are your comments on what I have said about the Council of Chalcedon?
5. What are your comments on the three statements that I have taken from the Catechism of the Catholic Church concerning:
    - The intimate and immediate knowledge the Son of God made man has of his Father;
    - divine penetration into the secret thoughts of human hearts;
    - the fullness of understanding of the eternal plans he had come to reveal?
6. To what extent is the Church free to adapt its structures to the needs of the times?
7. Even if we were to accept that Jesus freely chose to invite only the twelve male apostles to the Last Supper, would this prove that women should never be ordained?
8. What is your comment on the statement, "We are, after all, speaking of exactly what went on within the mind of Jesus, an individual unlike any other who has ever walked on this earth, a person within whom the divine and the human were bound together in a singular manner"?
9. Do you agree with the statement that, in the absence of crystal clear and

consistent evidence from the Bible, it is dangerous for any mere human being to claim to have certain knowledge of what went on within the mind of Jesus?
10. Do you agree with the statement that "it is not proven fact that Jesus determined for all time the details of his future Church with perfect knowledge and divine authority"?
11. Do you agree with the statement that, if the divine origin of any elements in the Church "could not be proven, we would have to conclude that God deliberately left the choices to us and that we are free to decide whether such elements should or should not be part of the Church of the future"?

Questions Chapter 9

1. What other elements must be mentioned even in a history as brief as this?
2. What are the most obvious defects in this very brief summary?

Questions Chapter 10

1. Is the Church losing the battle for the imagination?
2. Are popes, bishops and priests too close to being absolute monarchs?
3. Has the overall response so far to the scandal of sexual abuse been:
   a) adequate
   b) inadequate or
   c) catastrophic?
4. Was *Humanae Vitae* a watershed moment in the history of the Church, leading to a profound change in the way Catholic people see authority in the Church?
5. Do very large numbers of Catholic people now in practice see Church teaching on all matters involving sexuality and gender as largely discredited?
6. Does Catholic teaching on homosexuality perpetuate a discrimination that has harmed many lives?
7. Is it true that, "There are many deeply spiritual Catholic women who have abandoned the Church because of a profound feeling that there is no place for women there?"
8. Is it true that, on the subject of women, the Church is "in fact dragging along in the rear, reluctantly making small changes years after the rest of humanity has moved on"?
9. Is there "a broad impression of a church of rules in every area of life, rules laid down by a deeply tarnished authority and without any serious attempt to explain or persuade"?
10. Does "the necessity of right behavior dominate thinking at the expense of a love relationship"?
11. Has the Christian life too often "been reduced to a form of stoicism where people are driven by duty rather than drawn by delight"?
12. Is it true that "the hierarchy of holiness is still marginalised by the hierarchy of authority"?
13. Is it true that, "There is a morality of rules that leads to immaturity rather than growth?"
14. Is there "too little respect for the proper use of conscience as the only way to

QUESTIONS & REFLECTIONS

true growth"?

15. Is it true that, "There are too many teachings of the Church, particularly in the fields of sex, gender, marriage and family life, that are not seen as reflecting a God of love, for they are lacking in a basic humanity? " What examples would you give?
16. Is clericalism rampant in the Church?
17. Should the Church look again at pretentiousness and out of date titles such as Your Holiness, Your Eminence, Your Grace, My Lord, Monsignor?
18. Should the Church look again at pretentiousness and out of date forms of dress?
19. Does clericalism open the Church to careerism?
20. Does clericalism give an unhealthy authority to clerics?
21. Has clericalism "contributed significantly to sexual abuse by giving clerics power over minors and making them feel privileged and entitled?"
22. Does clericalism "reflect the idea of an authority that can tell people what to do rather than enter into intelligent conversation with them"?
23. Is there too great a contrast between the wealth of the Church and the simplicity of the life of Jesus?
24. Is it true "that the Church lectures civil society on the important social justice principle that all people must have a real voice in their own governance, but this principle does not apply anywhere in the Church – not the parish, nor the diocese, nor the universal Church"?
25. Is there a Sunday liturgy that still consists of too many thousands of words poured over a largely passive congregation?"
26. What should be done about Sunday sermons? Would you be for or against the idea of playing on Sundays the recorded sermons of the best preachers available?
27. Do you find that, "The prayers of the Mass are still overwhelmingly about getting into heaven rather than working to change for the better the lives of people in this world?"
28. Is it true that, "There are still too many aspects of liturgy that were invented in monasteries and then imposed on parishes?"
29. Is it true that, "For 95 per cent of Catholics, it is only when the Sunday parish Mass appeals to their imagination that the Church is appealing to their imagination, and not nearly enough creative thinking is being devoted to this priceless asset?"
30. Is there still too much condemning of words ending in "ism" (relativism, materialism, hedonism, individualism etc., etc.), and not enough appreciation of all that is good in the world? Is there too little willingness to enter into dialogue with the world, and too much of a tendency to lecture the world?
31. Is faith still too often presented as intellectual assent to propositions rather than as a personal response of love to God's declaration of love for us? Is there truth in the statement that, if people believe all the truths in the Creed, they are held to "have the faith", whether there is any love in their hearts or not? Does there often appear to be an obsession with right doctrine and right behavior rather than a response of love?
32. Are there far too many statements about God, and not enough expressing

the humble recognition that God is beyond our imagination and beyond all human words?
33. Is there still a lack of humility in the Church, despite sexual abuse? Is there still too much of the church of Constantine and the *Dictatus Papae?*
34. Is the Sacrament of Reconciliation a dead letter for most Catholics, and would it have to become a positive experience for them before it could be resurrected?
35. Can authorities in the Church still act with harshness and even ruthlessness in bringing people into line with their own ideas and wishes? Does a special harshness seem to be reserved for bringing into line those who have dedicated their lives to the Church in priesthood or religious life?
36. Has there been too much use of hard power and too little of soft power?
37. Has the Church been too "heavy"?
38. What factors would you add to what I have called the "deeper currents at work in society that are leading people away from all religious belief"? Would you wish to rephrase or amplify the factors I have mentioned?

Questions Chapter 11

1. In discussing the Eucharist, should we abandon the language of the Reformation and seek a new language to express a common faith?
2. Should we limit ourselves to a statement of those truths that are essential?
3. Should our understanding start with the phrases "This is my body" and "This is my blood"?
4. What conclusions should we draw from the presence at the beginning of Chapter Six of John's Gospel of the two stories of the multiplication of the loaves and of Jesus walking on the water? Do they have any relationship to the sayings that follow them?
5. In the whole of chapter six of John does the word "bread" have only the one meaning, or is there a development in its meaning?
6. In the early part of the discourse, does the meaning of the phrase "the bread that gives life" appear to be that of the message and person of Jesus as being spiritual food for people?
7. Does a change come over the discourse in verse 51? How do you understand that change?
8. If the people misunderstood what Jesus was saying, why did he not explain himself more clearly?
9. What significance do you see in the change from *phagein* to *trogein?*
10. His own followers "broke away and would not accompany him anymore." If their understanding of his words was false, why did he allow this?
11. Do you agree with the statement that, in relation to the Eucharist, the essential truth must contain the word "is" and must reject the words "is not"?
12. Do you agree with the statement that, after the words of the Last Supper have been spoken over the bread, we must in some manner be able to say and mean, "This is the body of Jesus"?
13. Is an answer to questions concerning the exact manner in which the bread

becomes the body of Jesus essential to our understanding of the Eucharist?
14. Can we hope to know the exact manner in which the bread becomes the body of Jesus? Is it even useful to pursue the question? Or should we simply bow before the mystery?
15. Does it matter if there is some diversity in the way in which people understand the manner of Christ's presence, as long as we all agree on "is" and reject "is not"?
16. Does the philosophical word "transubstantiation" help or hinder our understanding?
17. Is it ever legitimate to "canonise" a particular philosophical system? May words and ideas from that system ever become dogmatic assertions?
18. Are there things we should refrain from doing lest they give offence?
19. Is there anything that it is truly essential to add to the words, "This is the body of Jesus", provided we genuinely mean "is" rather than "is not"?

Questions Chapter 14

1. Is the Church caught in a prison of the past that it has created for itself?
2. Can any organisation continue to flourish without the "right to be wrong"?
3. Has the Catholic Church too often believed that it had such a level of divine guidance that it did not need the "right to be wrong"?
4. Are there examples of the Bible being interpreted in too literal or legal a manner?
5. Are there examples of interpretations of the Bible that should be revised in the light of more recent knowledge of biblical meaning?
6. Are there statements that take a text of the Bible out of its context in a manner that is not legitimate?
7. Are there statements that canonise a particular system of philosophy in a way that is not legitimate?
8. Are there statements that are not sufficiently aware that human words are inadequate carriers of divine truth?
9. Are there cases of a psychological inability to admit ignorance or error?
10. Is it legitimate to demand submission of mind and will to the words of a pope while brushing aside deeds that were far from the mind of Jesus Christ?
11. Are the recent revelations of sexual abuse in the Church and the response to them a major or a minor matter?
12. If they are major, how can infallibility be maintained in the light of the most fallible response to one of the greatest moral crises the Church has ever faced?
13. If infallibility means a divine assurance that the Church will not go astray in important matters, how has God allowed it to go so far astray on this matter of sexual abuse?
14. If infallibility is singularly absent in a crisis of this magnitude, what does the word mean?
15. On what basis can we separate words and deeds in this manner?
16. In assessing infallibility, must we look at the entire history of the Church?
17. Are there truths that are essential to the identity of the Christian Church, for example, "Jesus was a real person who lived on this earth"?

18. Do you agree with the statement that every truth that is declared essential creates a serious obligation, and such obligations should not be multiplied without very good cause?
19. Do you agree that the overriding principle must be that freedom should prevail?
20. Do you agree with the revised statement that "In essential matters unity, in non-essential matters freedom and in all matters love"?
21. Do you agree with the statement that, "The question then becomes one of finding the balance between the necessity of having clear statements of the beliefs that are essential to the identity of the Church and the need not to place more obligations on individuals than is absolutely essential?"
22. Are there solemnly defined truths in the Catholic Church that are not essential to the identity of the Church?
23. Is the Assumption of Mary one of these truths? Can you name others?
24. Are there defined truths that are essential in themselves, but not in the details of the manner in which they occurred?
25. Is the Ascension one of these truths? Can you name others?
26. Should the Church solemnly define truths that are considered certain but are not essential to the identity of the Church?
27. Do you agree with the statement that one of the truly essential beliefs of the Christian faith is that in all matters and at all times we must seek God's truth and goodness, that we are never free to believe whatever we wish, for we must always be seeking God's truth.
28. Do you agree with the principles set out in the quotation from St Augustine?
29. Do you agree with the statement set out by Pope Pelagius II in the letter drafted by the future Gregory the Great?
30. Was the Western Church justified in introducing the *filioque* clause into a Creed proclaimed by a universal council of the whole Church?
31. Do the combined authorities quoted in this section at least give rise to serious questions?
32. Did Jesus delegate something of his own authority to Peter?
33. Do you find a deliberate contrast in the Gospel of Matthew between what is said about Peter in 16:17-19 and what is said in 16:21-23?
34. Do you find significance in the fact that Jesus deliberately chose the passive name of "rock" for the leader of his apostles?
35. Do you find parallels between this and the story of the appointment of Saul in the First Book of Samuel?
36. Do you find significance in the fact that the words said about Peter in 16:19 are said about all the disciples in 18:18?
37. Article 20 of *Lumen Gentium* says that the bishops "have by divine institution taken the place of the apostles as pastors of the Church". Does this statement assume divine knowledge in Jesus and is this justified?
38. Did the early Church see Peter as answerable to the Church?
39. Does the singular role that the pope came to play in the Catholic Church come solely from the gospels, or does it also come from the influence of such things as the conversion of Constantine and the forces that led to the *Dictatus Papae?* Is there now a need to revisit these ideas?

QUESTIONS & REFLECTIONS

40. At the First Vatican Council are the gospel sayings quoted in support of infallibility made to bear too heavy a doctrinal and legal weight?
41. Do the three historical precedents quoted prove infallibility (Constantinople IV, Lyons II, Ferrara)?
42. Would the "Greeks", the members of the Eastern Churches, have accepted infallibility if this question had been specifically asked at any of these councils?
43. Does *Pastor Aeternus* represent an extreme response to a long debate concerning papal authority? Does the crisis of sexual abuse show the unacceptable dangers of this extreme response?
44. Can a pope infallibly proclaim papal infallibility unless we assume in advance that the pope is infallible?
45. Can a council infallibly proclaim infallibility unless we assume in advance that a council is infallible?
46. Do we still need to find a balance between cephality and synodality?
47. The Bible is the story of the spiritual journey of a people filled with confusion and conflict. In that story God placed the emphasis on search and responsibility leading to growth. Is it likely that God would now place the accent on certainty leading to obedience?
48. Infallibility appears to be based on the attitude that God would not allow the Church to be mistaken on matters seen to be important. Do we really have this level of knowledge of how God operates? Is it not possible that God has permitted Church authorities to err in order to break down the trust in human beings that would always be a temptation to the Church?
49. At a time when we are coming to realise that Jesus himself may have given up the privilege of perfect knowledge and have had to struggle through his life and mission with only limited knowledge, must we look again at claims which imply that the Church has access to a level of knowledge that even Jesus may not have had access to?
50. In discussions between different churches in recent decades it has become evident that there are many people belonging to other Christian churches who would seriously consider the idea of a Peter-figure in a future united Church, but would categorically reject the full claims of the Catholic Church on this matter, especially infallibility. Does the Church have a choice between Christian unity and these claims, or is it clear that it cannot have both, not now and, with overwhelming probability, not at any time in the future?
51. Is the following statement true: The Second Vatican Council (1962-65) faced a tension between the need to be faithful to its origins and the need to confront the pastoral problems posed by the modern world. The solution the Council found was in the combination of two words, one Italian and one French. The Italian word was *aggiornamento*, meaning "bringing up to date"; the French word was *ressourcement*, meaning "going back to the sources". The council sought to bring the Church up to date, not by confronting the immediate past head on, but by going back to a far older tradition based on scripture and the teachings of the ancient Fathers.
52. Is the following statement true: The Second Vatican Council followed a principle

that one writer has called "discontinuity for the sake of a greater continuity"[1], that is, in attempting to reconcile opposing views the council often reached back behind a particular formulation of truth to an earlier and greater truth?

53. Is the following statement true: In following the principle of "discontinuity for the sake of a greater continuity", the Second Vatican Council modified statements and traditions that had been in place for centuries and were claimed to be infallible. It did this despite the fact that with considerable heat and fury, "discontinuity for the sake of a greater continuity" was constantly and adamantly condemned by a number of members of the council.

54. Is the following statement true? The events addressed by the preceding questions point to the need for the principle that a later general council of the Church should have the authority to modify or clarify or adapt the teaching of an earlier general council in the light of developing knowledge and understanding.

55. Is this "authority to modify" exactly what happened in the field of Christology over a series of seven councils from Nicaea (325) to Nicaea II (787), as understanding was purified and improved?

56. In the terms used by the Second Vatican Council, may we argue for *ressourcement*, a going back to earlier sources, and for *aggiornamento*, a bringing up to date in the light of further study of the scriptures? May we argue for "discontinuity for the sake of a greater continuity"? Must we argue for a better balance between cephality and synodality? Without these ideas, does the concept of "development of doctrine" become impossible?

57. In the previous question are we arguing for anything more than the Second Vatican Council itself has already done in a number of different fields?

58. Are there any statements in the Nicene Creed that could be considered for change?

59. Are there any statements that one might consider adding to the Creed, for example a statement of faith in the dignity of all people and in the goodness of the world God created and redeemed?

60. Is the Creed too much a list of propositions to which intellectual assent is required? Would it be improved by the addition of the *Shema*?

61. Where do you agree and where do you disagree with the statements in poetic form that end this chapter?

62. Within the Church should binding statements be limited to those truths that are essential to the identity of the Church?

63. Should a later universal Church council have the power to adapt the teachings of an earlier universal Church council?

Questions Chapter 15

1. As well as all-important changes in heart and mind, is there a need for structural change in the Church?
2. Did the Second Vatican Council see hierarchy in terms of service to mystery and community? In any talk of hierarchy, are these the supreme values?
3. Is it difficult to maintain the idea of two bodies holding the same supreme

---

[1] Ormond Rush, *Still Interpreting Vatican II, Some Hermeneutical Principles*, Paulist Press, New York, 2004.

power within a community? In the time since the council, has it been evident that, in fact and in practice, the pope has possessed supreme power, while the college of bishops has not?
4. Is there a solution to this dilemma by maintaining that the college of bishops is the one holder of supreme power, with this one power then being exercised collectively by the whole college or individually by the head of the college?
5. Would it be even better to say that authority belongs to the Church – the entire community – with this authority then being exercised universally by the whole Church, collectively by the twelve and their successors, and individually by Peter and his successors? Should there be wise laws passed by the entire Church regulating the use of this authority, so that the three levels work in harmony?
6. Should we look again at the very ancient idea that the diocese of Rome had a primacy in the whole Church, not because the pope lived there, but because it was the supreme place of apostolic witness to Jesus Christ through the martyrdom of the two great apostles, Peter and Paul?
7. Should the bishop of Rome do everything possible to make present in the Church the witness of Paul as well as Peter?
8. Is it true that the only difference between the pope and any other bishop is the diocese to which the pope is elected, for since the time of the martyrdom of both Peter and Paul in Rome the bishop of that city has had the task and accompanying authority to be the rock of unity?
9. Should a retired pope wear the white cassock and skullcap of a pope?
10. In the light of history, is it better for the Church of today to use the title "pope" or the title "bishop of Rome"?

Questions Chapter 16

1. Do you agree with the idea of God I have suggested, the idea of a god who, like a good parent or teacher, loves deeply and unconditionally but, precisely because of this love, wants people to grow to become all they are capable of being and so is not afraid to challenge them?
2. What are the most important things a priest should say and do to spread a healthy idea of God?
3. Do the four pillars of priesthood seem adequate? Are there others that should be added?
4. Is it an essential part of the role of the priest to recognise the apostles, prophets, evangelists, pastors and teachers in the community, to encourage them and help them receive training?
5. It will never be a matter of a succession of small steps, but what can the priest do to create that moment when the only two people in the church are the individual parishioner and Jesus Christ?
6. What do you think it means to say that a priest must first be a good human being and a good Christian?
7. What do you have to say of the paradigm of simplicity, fidelity and service?
8. Do you agree that it is difficult today for a parish to be a social as well as a spiritual centre? Should a parish simply accept this and seek to be the best

spiritual centre possible? Or should it fight to continue to be the social centre it once was?

9. Should a priest be a ruler or a leader? What practical differences should there be in the way the priest acts? Should all priests do a practical course in the art of leadership? Should a role of leadership be a central focus in seminary training?
10. Should priests see themselves as professionals and humbly submit to all the requirements of being professional? If they don't like all these requirements, who should they blame: bishops or offenders?
11. What do you think of each of the items mentioned under the heading of professionalism? What other items should be added?
12. Is a priest "taken" or "taken up"?
13. Does ordination cause an ontological change in the person ordained?
14. Is there a "mystique" of the priesthood? In what ways does it need to change?
15. Has there been the idea that the priest must at least appear to be perfect? What have been the consequences of this?
16. What other elements of priesthood would you wish to consider further?

Questions Chapter 19

1. Do you accept that the First Testament is the story of a journey, and that this truth applies to marriage as well?
2. Does much of the First Testament reflect a model of marriage based on the idea of the wife as the property of her husband?
3. Was adultery seen primarily in terms of the stealing of the property of a husband?
4. Were there many things in Jewish marriage at the time of Jesus with which he would have disagreed?
5. In his comments on marriage as recorded in the gospels, do you believe that Jesus was commenting on the entire situation concerning marriage or only on the question of divorce?
6. Do you believe that the interpretation of each of the scriptural passages concerning marriage and divorce that I have given in this chapter are:
    - False?
    - Possible?
    - Probable?
    - Certain?
7. If the Church must accept change in its teaching, what should it do to foster a true Christian attitude in approaching marriage and in living marriage?
8. Do you wish to add to, subtract from or vary the three reasons given that would justify leaving a marriage?
9. Do you believe that the Church should base its whole pastoral approach to marriage on distinctions between valid and invalid marriages, or should it accept that marriage is a varied and messy secular reality and put its energy into turning it into a saving mystery, both for individuals and for whole communities? Should the Church allow its life in this field to become

"wonderfully complicated"?

10. What can the Church do to bring about a greater equality in marriage?
11. What can the Church do to bring about a greater equality between men and women in the whole life and work of the Church itself?
12. What can the Church do to bring about a greater equality between men and women in the whole of the community?
13. Titius has been married to Bertha for ten years and they have three children. Then he meets Semphronia, a young, vibrant and marvellously attractive woman, and is captivated by her. He abandons Bertha and his children, obtains a divorce and approaches a Catholic priest, Father Abbondio, to celebrate a new marriage with Semphronia. Since he left Bertha, Titius has given no financial or emotional support to Bertha and the children. Should Father Abbondio:
    - Celebrate the marriage without further question on the basis of Titius' right to his conscience?
    - Tell Titius that his actions are too far away from the mind of Jesus Christ and that, if he wishes to marry, he would have to approach a civil celebrant?
    - Adopt some in-between strategy? If so, what?
14. If Titius is entitled to have a conscience that others must respect, is Father Abbondio also entitled to have a conscience in deciding whether to celebrate the wedding?
15. In resolving all of the above questions should we seek to balance four distinct perspectives:
    - the interpretation of the meaning of the words of Jesus in three gospels and the First Letter to the Corinthians;
    - our understanding of the person, character and values of Jesus as revealed to us in the totality of the New Testament;
    - the teachings of the Council of Trent;
    - the wonderful complexity of life, and especially of marriage, in which we must consider not only the situation of Titius, but also that of Bertha, now abandoned and with three children to care for?
16. Should any one of these four elements be put above the other three?

Questions Chapter 20

1. What is your response to the quotations from the three authors cited at the beginning of this chapter?
2. In your view what are the major ways in which women should have a greater role in the life of the Church?
3. Do you see ordination to the priesthood as in practice essential, or at least very important, to women having a more significant role in the Church?

Questions Chapter 21

1. In relation to abortion, do you agree that the crucial question is: When does a new person begin to exist?

2. Do the arguments given for saying that a new human person exists from the moment of conception add up to the certainty that one hopes for in this field?
3. Are both the pro-life and the pro-choice lobbies claiming a certainty that is simply not possible?
4. Do you agree that a woman has complete charge of her own body, so she alone has the right to decide all questions of abortion? Or must she first answer the question whether there is another person with equal rights present?
5. Do you agree that respect for life is the single most important criterion of civilisation?
6. In all societies do you believe that respect for life is always at risk, and so needs to be carefully defended?
7. Must our concern to protect human life extend from its beginning to its end? Must it include questions concerning the quality of life?
8. Can questions concerning the quality of life ever come before questions of protecting life itself?
9. In a crisis situation such as a train wreck, do you accept the principle of saving as much life as possible?
10. What is your opinion on case 1? Can a holiday be a sufficient reason for an abortion?
11. What is your opinion on case 2?
12. Granted the difficulties of determining whether a foetus is a human being or not, what position should civil law take? Should a woman be able to sue for the loss of what she is carrying, when this loss is caused by the malice or negligence of another person?
13. What are your comments on the mother in case 4 whose eight-year-old daughter was made pregnant by her de facto spouse?
14. What are your comments on the woman in case 5?
15. What do you say to the danger that even the smallest breach in the dyke can lead to the destruction of all barriers, and hence to abortion on demand?
16. Do you agree with the statement that, "When we cannot find a neat solution to a moral problem, we have no choice except to turn to conscience? If I cannot agree with a pregnant woman who simply asserts that there is nothing more than her own body there, I can agree that in the final analysis she alone must determine what she will actually do about her situation, for this is exactly the role of conscience."
17. Do you agree with the statement that, "We have a long way to go in this debate, and the very first step must be a profound change in basic attitudes? As long as the two sides keep hurling accusations at each other, no progress will be made. Physical or moral violence used to prevent a woman from accessing a clinic is always wrong, and unwarranted pressure is counterproductive. On the other hand, conscience is a serious concept and it must not be cheapened by turning it into nothing more than *what I want to do*."